France in the Making
843-1180

JEAN DUNBABIN

OXFORD UNIVERSITY PRESS

1985

Oxford University Press, Walton Street, Oxford OX2 6DP

London New York Toronto
Delhi Bombay Calcutta Madras Karachi
Kuala Lumpur Singapore Hong Kong Tokyo
Nairobi Dar es Salaam Cape Town
Melbourne Auckland

and associated companies in
Beirut Berlin Ibadan Mexico City Nicosia

Oxford is a trade mark of Oxford University Press

Published in the United States
by Oxford University Press, New York

British Library Cataloguing in Publication Data
Dunbabin, Jean
France in the making 843–1180.
1. France—History—Capetians, 987–1328
I. Title
944'.021   DC82
ISBN 0-19-873030-6
ISBN 0-19-873031-4 Pbk

Library of Congress Cataloging in Publication Data
Dunbabin, Jean.
France in the making, 843–1180.
Bibliography: p.
Includes index.
1. France—History—To 987.   2. France—History—
Capetians, 987–1328.
I. Title.
DC70.D86 1985   944'.02   84–16663
ISBN 0-19-873030-6
ISBN 0-19-873031-4 (pbk.)

Typeset by Joshua Associates, Oxford
Printed in Great Britain
at the University Press, Oxford
by David Stanford
Printer to the University

FRANCE IN THE MAKING
843–1180

In memory of my father

Preface

I SUPPOSE this book might be subtitled 'A Nominalist's Approach'. The two classic treatments of the origins of France, those of Flach and Lot, agreed on one point at least: irrespective of whether tenth- and eleventh- century people were conscious of it, France existed, as did political obligation to the French king. More recent scholars have frequently rejected this 'realist' assumption. But because their work has usually been concerned either with a particular region or with a single concept, the implications of this rejection have not always been spelt out. My attempt to synthesize, clarify, reconcile, or modify their insights has led me to a perspective on French history that is less uncontroversial than I aimed at when I began. But I believe it to reflect a wider opinion than just my own.

Acknowledging all debts to other authors is clearly impossible within a textbook format; and I hope that those whose work I have mentioned in the notes and Further Reading will not feel that my brief and crude summaries seriously garble the originals. For the rest, much derives from articles or reviews read long ago in places now forgotten, from conversations in Oxford, or—to put the clock back many years—from my tutorials with Beryl Smalley, who first aroused my interest in the subject. But I must thank R. C. Watson, Patricia Morison, and Jane Martindale for allowing me to read their as yet unpublished theses; Jane's in particular was invaluable in providing an overall view of the history of Aquitaine in this period. Then Elaine Hyams typed the manuscript with exemplary efficiency; Alison Tetley drew the maps on pp. 3 and 45, Mrs Angela Newman that on p. 380; and Leofranc Holford-Strevens eliminated a host of irritating slips (those that remain are, of course, wholly my responsibility). Linda Paterson, Giles Constable, John Prestwich, Elspeth Kennedy, and John Gillingham all replied helpfully to my queries. My chief debts are to Patricia

Morison, who made all sorts of valuable suggestions at every stage of the book's gestation; to Tom Bisson, who read it all in draft and most generously put me right on a number of important points; and above all to John Cowdrey, without whose painstaking and thoughtful criticism this would have been a far worse piece of work.

While producing this, I have benefited from the agreeable environment of St Anne's College, from its excellent library, and from the advice of my colleagues in other disciplines as to the books to consult when I met with legal or literary problems. Most of the actual writing was done at home, where my daughters Bridget and Penny have offered interest, practical help of various kinds, and the occasional bracing criticism of my literary style. But it has been my husband John who has been my chief pillar of support throughout this enterprise; without his encouragement, sound advice, and willingness always to discuss my difficulties, this book would never have been completed.

JEAN DUNBABIN

Acknowledgements

I am grateful to the Executor of the Estate of the late Helen Waddell and to W. W. Norton & Company, Inc. for permission to quote the extracts from *More Latin Lyrics from Vergil to Milton*, translated by Helen Waddell, edited by Dame Felicitas Corrigan (copyright 1976 by Stanbrook Abbey), on pp. 159–60 and 286.

Contents

Maps and Figures

Maps

Figures

Abbreviations

AASS	*Acta Sanctorum*
Annales	*Annales, Économies, Sociétés, Civilisations*
BAR	*British Archaeological Reports*
Cahiers de civ. méd.	*Cahiers de civilisation médiévale*
DA	*Deutsches Archiv für die Erforschung des Mittelalters*
EHR	*English Historical Review*
Études Yver	*Droit privé et institutions régionales: Études historiques offerts à Jean Yver* (Paris, 1976)
Institutions	F. Lot and R. Fawtier, *Histoire des institutions françaises au Moyen Âge*, 3 vols. (Paris, 1957–62)
Medieval Nobility	T. Reuter (ed.), *The Medieval Nobility* (Oxford, 1979)
MGH	*Monumenta Germaniae Historica*
MGH SS	*MGH Scriptores*
MIÖG	*Mitteilungen des Instituts für österreichische Geschichtsforschung*
Order and Innovation	W. C. Jordan, B. McNab, and T. F. Ruiz (eds.), *Order and Innovation in the Middle Ages: Essays in Honor of Joseph R. Strayer* (Princeton, 1976)
PL	J. P. Migne (ed.), *Patrologiae cursus completus, series Latina* (Paris, 1844–55)
RBPH	*Revue belge de philologie et d'histoire*
Recueil Brunel	*Recueil de travaux offert à M. Clovis Brunel* (Paris, 1955)
RHF	Bouquet, *Recueil des historiens des Gaules et de la France* (Paris, 1738–1833)
Settimane Spoleto	*Settimane di Studio del Centro Italiano di Studi sull'alto Medioevo* (Spoleto)

CHAPTER I

843–888

IN the time of Charles the Great of good memory, who died almost thirty years ago, peace and concord ruled everywhere because our people were treading the one proper way, the way of the common welfare and thus the way of God. But now since each goes his separate way, dissension and struggle abound. Once there was abundance and happiness everywhere, now everywhere there is want and sadness. Once even the elements smiled on everything and now they threaten, as Scripture, which was left to us as the gift of God, testifies: *and the world will wage war against the mad.*[1]

So Nithard, Charlemagne's grandson, ended his description of the negotiations leading up to the Treaty of Verdun in 843, by which Charlemagne's empire was partitioned between his three legitimate grandsons, the emperor Lothaire, Louis the German, and Charles the Bald. Later generations were to see in Charles the Bald's share of the inheritance the origin of the kingdom of France. But Verdun was not an auspicious beginning. Because for Nithard and his contemporaries the new land-block had emerged out of a sinful and violent family quarrel, there remained the hope that it might prove ephemeral, that one rule might once again prevail across the whole empire of the Franks. In the deeply pious and conservative atmosphere of the ninth and tenth centuries, this hope was a long time a-dying.

In any case, Charles the Bald and his successors showed little inclination to operate within the terms of the treaty, because it excluded them from the Rhineland area, the Carolingian homeland, where the family's resources were still concentrated. Originally assigned to Lothaire, after whom it was named Lotharingia, the area became a prey for the rest of the ninth century and the whole of the tenth to the conflicting ambitions of its eastern and western neighbours. Though the East Franks were usually more successful and ultimately triumphed, the West Frankish kings did not totally abandon hope until the early eleventh century (when some

West Frankish princes continued the challenge). In the circumstances, they could not with honesty have extolled the Treaty of Verdun as a turning-point in the history of their lands, had the possibility so much as occurred to them. In practice they, like their advisers, were more concerned with models from the glorious past than with capitalizing on their present resources.

Even so, the prolonged lack of commitment to the 843 settlement may seem surprising, in that the kingdom assigned to Charles the Bald had reasonable geographical coherence, good internal lines of communication, and well-defined frontiers to the west, the south-west, and the north. The physical character of the landscape might thus support any aspiration towards unity that the lands from the Rhine mouth to Barcelona felt. The trouble was, however, that the old political and social subdivisions of the Carolingian empire had survived the 843 carve-up to prove formative and centrifugal forces in the new world. Of these, the sharpest was racial. Neither Charles nor any of his ninth- and early tenth-century successors could assert authority among the Gascons —the Basque-speaking inhabitants of the eastern Pyrenean region—who dominated a surviving Germanic and Gallo-Roman population; nor among the Celtic-speaking peoples of the Breton peninsula—originally refugees from Britain— who, under their renowned leaders Nominoë, Erispoë, and Salamon, terrorized the inhabitants of Loire region. But both these peoples were small and relatively unimportant.

It was a matter of far greater concern that, within the lands where their rule was recognized, the kings had to cope with deep-rooted ethnic groupings (in the American sense), the product of fifth-century barbarian settlement within Gaul. The Visigoths of Septimania (Gothia) and the Spanish March, the Burgundians of Burgundy, the Franks of Austrasia and Neustria, all differentiated from the Gallo-Romans of Aquitaine, had by the ninth century lost any claim they ever possessed to racial distinctiveness. But their group identity was maintained, not only by tradition but also by their adherence to the ancient customary laws of their peoples. So strong was the appeal of these laws that individuals claimed them as their personal birthrights. (As late as 985,

Map 1. The Partition of Verdun, 843

Count Bernard of Substantion-Melgueil was still appealing to
Salic law, on account of his Frankish descent, though his
family had long been resident in an area where most men
were proud to be judged by Roman law).[2] When the
Merovingian kings had divided Gaul to provide inheritances
for their sons, they had taken account of these ethnic groups;
the result was that Burgundy and Aquitaine (usually including Gothia) were accustomed to being ruled separately, as
were Austrasia and Neustria, the two Frankish provinces
north of the Loire. 843 changed the pattern in that only
a small portion of Austrasia and about a third of Burgundy
were included within West Francia—the rest of each being

assigned to Lothaire's Middle Kingdom. But internally the treaty had no effect.

So in terms of its human geography, Charles the Bald's kingdom was a ragbag of old sub-kingdoms and peoples, distinguished from their neighbours by race or language or tradition or law or long political separation. Though they had been loosely held together, along with much else, in the confederation which was the Carolingian empire, when that empire disintegrated there were no links, other than geographical proximity or subjection to one ruler, to bring about coherence within West Francia. Had Charles the Bald devoted himself to obtaining unity as soon as he took charge, it is possible that he might have achieved something; but he did not see his task in that light. Besides, both he and his successors were faced with many urgent challenges to their power; by the 860s Viking raids and wars in Lotharingia prevented internal consolidation. So the opportunity which the Treaty of Verdun had provided was allowed to slip.

The result was that the inhabitants of West Francia hardly saw their common allegiance to one king as creating any sort of bond between them. Sometimes, indeed, they described him as ruler over several unrelated ethnic groups, as in a charter of Raoul in which he was called king of the Franks, the Burgundians, and the Aquitanians.[3] In 987, when Richer attempted to explain the effect of Hugh Capet's coronation, what mattered to him was Hugh's recognition as king of the Gauls, the Bretons, the Normans, the Aquitanians, the Goths, the Spanish and the Gascons[4]—obviously he forgot the Burgundians. For him there was no single West Frankish people, let alone one country to which all these different peoples belonged. Richer's words might be dismissed as literary contrivance. But they do highlight a real lack: the absence of a name in common use to describe the realm of Charles the Bald's successors. For 'West Francia' is a historian's term (although Charles the Simple was once called 'king of the West Franks' in a document, in order to distinguish him from his eastern counterpart). In the tenth century, 'Francia' meant *either* the land between the Seine and the Lotharingian border, as in the phrase 'Francia et Neustria', *or*, more commonly, the land-mass from the Loire to the Lotharingian border. What it did not usually mean was the whole West Frankish realm. Earlier in his *History*, Richer had been reduced to 'Gaul' to denominate this, although he was well aware that classical Gaul had had very different frontiers.

This absence of names is worrying. Perhaps it should be blamed on old-fashioned Latin vocabulary, unsuitable for expressing the new political realities. But it does seem likely that, in failing to find a name either for themselves or for the country in which they lived, the men of West Francia were unconsciously betraying their self-image: they still saw their past as shaped by the invasions of the fifth century, they still envisaged their future in the reunited empire of Charlemagne. The development by which they found their roots in the newly-evolved *pays* of France, and their identity in their common obedience to the French king, is the theme of this book; the process was one that spanned three centuries. To follow it, it is necessary first to recount the political history of West Francia's diverse units, and then to examine the qualities that inspired respect and deference in a people traditionally portrayed by historians as craggy individualists prone to create and exploit anarchy to their own self-advancement.

In order to understand the late ninth-century political scene, one must begin first with the system described in the great capitularies of Charlemagne and his successors, in which the principles and structures set down appear to offer a pattern for government across the whole realm. What follows is a brief and bald résumé of recent scholarship, based above all on the work of the Belgian historian Ganshof.[5]

The soul of the Carolingian political universe was the king. As defender of his people, he led the Franks to battle against their external enemies; as judge, he laid down the norms of justice, created peace between disputants, punished the wicked, and avenged the weak; as Christian leader, he cared for the widows and orphans, he gave alms to the poor; as shield of the church, he purged it from error, upheld its authority, protected its means of subsistence. At least according to the portraits presented by his courtiers, Charlemagne fulfilled all these expectations; hardly surprisingly, future generations of the literate were to see the history of the Frankish monarchy as one of sad decline.

Royal authority, however righteous, had to be channelled through local agents in order to come into contact with its subjects. It was a substantial achievement of Charlemagne and his successors to have forged, however tenuously, the links between centre and localities which are the essential constituent of any viable state. The crucial link in their system was provided by the count, an official whose authority stretched over a defined geographical area, the county or the *pagus*. There had been counts in the Merovingian period and, indeed, in the late Roman empire. But the Carolingian count was bound more closely than such earlier officials to his king. During the eighth century his position had become more clearly defined as a *honor*, an office held of the king in return for an oath of fidelity (the word 'fealty' is best avoided as too suggestive of vassalage), for as long as he performed his duties satisfactorily. To support the expenses he incurred, the count was usually given a *beneficium* of land, held only for the duration of his office. In return for his *honor* and his *beneficium*, he had an infinite burden of duties piled on his shoulders.

The count's chief obligations were military and legal. To take the legal first, it was his function to preside over the county court, usually called the *mallus*. What distinguished the *mallus* from the large number of lesser courts in each county was that the leading men of the county were required to attend it, and that it was omnicompetent (though efforts to keep serious crime as its monopoly gradually failed). It was the count's duty to call the *mallus*, to preside over it, and to see that its sentences were executed. But the declaration of what was or was not justice was in the hands of officials called *scabini*; and the law followed was either the customary law of the area or the law personal to the individuals involved, except in so far as that law was modified or supplemented by royal capitularies. Then the count also had the duty of sending judges, whether viscounts or *vicarii* (lesser officials), to preside over the less important public courts, the *placita generalia*, at which the bulk of ordinary legal business was transacted. So the whole royal responsibility of guaranteeing 'to each man his particular law' was exercised through the count in the county. In practice royal righteousness could be deeply dyed with comital prejudice before it reached its proper recipients.

In the military sphere the count's task was just as important. It was his job, in the name of the king, to defend his own county against external attack, relying on the support of his own men, the local lords, representatives from church lands, and on the obligation of all free men to assist him. He was also required to render military service in person to the king when the *ban* was called, and to bring with him the comital levy. Through such levies all the Carolingian dominions could be mobilized for aggressive campaigns; and the calling of the *ban* provided an occasion for direct contact between the crown and its most important subjects, a matter of some moment. But from the middle of the ninth century, as the needs of local defence grew more urgent, the *ban* was called less and less often.

The count, however, could not perform these tasks without also becoming a collector of royal dues—taxes from free men whose military service the king did not require, or fines from the courts. Then, as the local substitute for royal majesty, he was empowered to collect tolls on rivers, bridges, or highways, and on markets enjoying privileges. In return for his efforts, he could often benefit in person from royal rights of hospitality, due to the king from his estates, from some towns, and from the abbeys and churches under royal protection. And in time of urgent necessity, the count could exact from all free men an irregular and undefined tax for the protection he afforded them. All these dues were in essence regalian—that is to say the count took them as the crown's representative; but his own share of them grew steadily. Even in the reign of Charlemagne, he must often have been seen by those he governed as primarily a tax-collector; in the tenth century, that often was his chief preoccupation.

The count's tasks were, then, formidable. In carrying them out, he might, if his county was large, appoint viscounts: delegated officials empowered to perform his tasks in his absence; and he would have to help him local officials usually known as *vicarii* or *centenarii* (but with local variations of nomenclature). Everywhere, however, the ultimate responsibility was his.

Obviously there was a risk to the monarchy in delegating so much effective power in the localities. Kings were well aware of this. They therefore sought both to supervise counts and to create other links between themselves and the counties that could counteract the comital authority. Direct supervision was more difficult, more costly, and only possible in periods of internal peace; but while it lasted, it did secure the end for which it was designed. Creating links with others was a two-edged weapon; it was as likely to weaken royal authority as to strengthen it; but it could be resorted to in a wider range of circumstances.

So far as direct supervision is concerned, the most obvious means was careful appointment to begin with. Strictly speaking, the king could appoint as count any man whom he knew and trusted. In Charlemagne's reign, many counts were chosen from the Austrasian aristocracy, the closed circle of those among whom he had grown up. Others were men who, though their roots lay in the area in which they were to assume office, nevertheless had some special reason to feel gratitude to the emperor. Loyalty was a prerequisite for the job. Once installed in his county, the count attended royal councils, fought with the royal army when summoned, received the king should he visit the county, and noted all royal messages or capitularies sent ot him. But lest any misdemeanour escape the royal eye, counts—at least within Francia, Neustria and Burgundy—were, after 802, regularly visited by special royal envoys, the *missi dominici*, whose function it was to check up on them. And if supervision failed, and the count became seriously delinquent, he might be dismissed from office.

Admirable though these methods of supervision might seem, by 888 they had almost ceased to function. The royal right of appointment had come up against the comital families' natural desire for hereditary succession, a practice which was often expedient in any case, and which Charles the Bald had sanctioned in a limited way in 877. Once installed, the count received no more capitularies—the last known is from 884; the royal *ban* was called so rarely that few counts any longer experienced the thrill of fighting shoulder to shoulder with their sovereign, or even attending his councils. After 864, the system of regular inspection seems to have ended. And as the king's travels were more and more narrowly confined, his chances of knowing what the count was up to declined. Charles the Bald's attempt to dismiss the count of Berry in 867 had resulted in a five-year war; and though he was eventually successful in depriving Bernard Plantevelue of Autun, he had to buy him off with huge concessions elsewhere. It was apparent that, although the king's right in theory to dismiss a count remained, he could do so only with difficulty and danger. As a result of these changes, counts were now free to move down the path towards independence, to assert hereditary right as a principle in all cases, to enjoy for themselves the dues and benefits which it had once been their duty to collect for the crown, to gather free men around them as a private army. It speaks volumes for their conservatism and their sense of responsibility that relatively few of them rushed to take advantage of this new freedom.

Since direct supervision was failing, kings had to rely on indirect means of limiting comital power. One such expedient was essentially negative: the king exempted certain areas or people from comital jurisdiction. The immunities granted to bishoprics, abbeys, and churches usually gave their rulers the right to absent their members and the inhabitants of their lands from the comital *mallus*, and to hold a court of their own to transact the equivalent business. Similar exemptions for laymen were not unknown. More positive in its effects was the taking of oaths of loyalty to the king from the whole free population, to impress on ordinary people that the count was only the king's representative, not his substitute; or the establishment of *vassi dominici* (royal vassals beneficed with land from the royal fisc) in areas far from the centre of government; or, and probably most effectively, the demand that the local bishop, in theory a royal nominee, keep a watching brief on the affairs of the county, and even (on occasion) sit in the *mallus*. Bishops, abbots, and *vassi dominici* were all men of sufficient status and independence to risk reporting the count's misdeeds; and if ordinary men could not, in their own right, afford the luxury of criticism, then they might be able to obtain the support of one of the magnates in making their complaint.

Unfortunately, all these expedients had disadvantages. Grants of benefices to *vassi dominici* impoverished the fisc, while producing an asset that diminished each year, as the link between vassal and king grew looser. Immunities created real and lasting independence; but it was not always an independence sought or desired by churchmen, who might find in comital authority their only shield against other aristocratic depredations. And the oath of loyalty could be taken only if the count organized the occasion. Institutional means of checking comital power were therefore rather feeble in effect. Ironically, immunities, episcopal intervention, and popular oaths continued to have local importance for far longer than they kept any significance as counterweights, in the king's interests, to comital pretension. So, despite the energy and thought devoted to strengthening links between the king and the inhabitants of the counties, by 888 the methods devised had all proved less than effective. On the other hand, the count's role in government had expanded steadily, as each new king added more duties to his list. In this fact alone lies much of the explanation for the marked disintegration of political authority in the last two decades of the ninth century. Within the ship, the count was the undisputed captain over all the crew, but command of the fleet grew ever laxer.

This appraisal of the comital office depends upon documents emanating from the royal court, and therefore expresses both the aspirations and the problems of the central government. But underlying it there are two assumptions that do not seem wholly to accord with other kinds of evidence. The first is that the Carolingian county was a jurisdictional and administrative unit, coextensive with a clearly-defined geographical area, and responsible for all the free inhabitants of that area except those in immunities. If this assumption were true of all Carolingian counties, then it would follow that there would be no counts without counties

or counties without counts; there would be no private jurisdictions other than those of ecclesiastical immunities; and the
freedom of free men could be defined as subordination to no
other authority than the public. But it appears that some
counties were more fluid units than might be expected; that
some private jurisdictions existed; and that freedom was
often compatible with service to lords.[6]

The second assumption is that a count was by definition an
official appointed by the king to exercise public and impersonal powers within the county. That this was normally true
was undeniable; yet the word was sometimes still used in
its original meaning, 'companion'; the king's closest friends
and relations were *comites* in virtue of their regular presence
at court, rather than in virtue of any administrative position
they might hold. Both because the word retained its older,
more general meaning, and because in fact all counts were
drawn from the landed aristocracy, *comes* might come to
mind as a means of expressing high social rank. So Odo of
Cluny, in referring to Geoffrey of Turenne as *comes*,[7] when
we know him to have been a viscount, was simply drawing
attention to his nobility.

The intimate connection between comital office and
aristocratic rank has implications for public and impersonal
powers. The *beneficium* a count received as his reward for
office was simply an addition to his substantial inherited
allodial holdings (effective freeholds), into which it often
rapidly merged. From these holdings, the count derived
jurisdictional rights over his *familia* of unfree servants and
labourers, and dues from his serfs—resources from which to
care for his clients and dependents. These rights were tech-
nically private, and quite distinct from the revenues and
jurisdiction accruing to him from his comital office. The legal
difference between private and public rights was of course
familiar to the Carolingians through their reading of the
classics: Richer put into the mouth of Adalbéron of Rheims
the argument that the Franks would find in Hugh Capet
a capable defender both of the public and of their private
interests.[8] Yet whether in practice either the count or his
contemporaries sharply divided his two spheres of action
is surely open to doubt.

The point has significance in the context of long arguments over the nature of feudalism. The legal definition, given classical expression by Maitland, is 'a state of society in which all or a great part of public rights are inextricably interwoven with the tenure of land, in which the whole governmental system—financial, military, judicial—is part of the law of private property'.[9] On this definition—which prevailed among most French historians until Marc Bloch's work—a sharp distinction can be drawn between public government, in which all administrative and judicial powers are exercised by officials, and feudal government, in which those same powers are exercised by men who owe their position, not to appointment by the ruler, but to their landed wealth, their aristocratic birth, or perhaps to their position inside the church. The models on which this distinction is based are clearly caricatures; they necessitate a complete divorce between private and public attributes which is never in practice obtainable. Yet, because it provides shades and gradations of authority, the old definition remains useful. It might be difficult to revoke the appointment of a Carolingian count, but the fact that it was possible made him more 'official' and less 'feudal' than his successors of the tenth century.

Thus far, the description of Carolingian government has been derived from largely prescriptive sources. It is time now to turn to the scraps of information available elsewhere which cast some light on how West Francia was actually governed in the second half of the ninth century. The most striking departure from the system thus far described was the appearance of groups of counties under the leadership of one powerful figure, a prince (*dux, marchio,* or *comes*) whose *regnum* sometimes bore a marked relationship with the older ethnic units of pre-Carolingian Gaul. This phenomenon, called by the Belgian historian Dhondt 'the evolution of the territorial principality'.[10] has attracted much explanation— perhaps too much. It can be seen either as a response to the decay of Carolingian institutions under the double assault of civil war and alien raiders, or as proof that the Carolingian governmental reform never really succeeded in altering old ways. The latter explanation is perhaps preferable, provided we concede that, even if the Carolingian reformers could not totally change local government, they had gone deep enough to ensure that the late ninth-century conservative revival would provide an adminstrative map which showed differences from, as well as similarities with, the seventh-century past.

To be specific: for the reign of Charles the Bald (843-77), there is sufficient information to trace the growing regionalism of West Francia. The clearest division was that along the Loire, cutting off the more Frankish Neustria and Austrasia from the more Romanized Aquitaine. This division had already been recognized in Charlemagne's day, for he had established Aquitaine as a sub-kingdom for his son Louis the Pious; when Charles the Bald obtained West Francia, Aquitaine was in the hands of his nephew Pippin II, whose reluctance to recognize his uncle lent new sharpness to the old ethnic division. In fact Charles spent much of his reign striving for mastery south of the Loire; and though he was ultimately successful in 855, he still found it expedient to recognize the area's distinctiveness by maintaining a sub-kingdom for his sons. Thus far he had only perpetuated old divisions. But in the latter years of his reign, troubled by Saracen and Viking assaults as well as by campaigns in Brittany and Lotharingia, he innovated. Aware that his teen-age sons could not be expected to protect the whole southern part of his kingdom on their own, Charles entered into arrangements with important southern aristocrats, delegating to them royal dues and powers in return for the defence of vital borders. In 866 the lordship of much of western Aquitaine was given to Vulgrin, count of Angoulême. Most of the rest of the south was then left to two men of high nobility, Bernard of Gothia and Bernard Plantevelue, whose exact spheres of influence were imprecisely defined, and who rapidly became rivals. As a consequence the whole of the country south of the Loire became a region dominated by great families, leaving little room for direct royal initiative. As Hincmar of Rheims told Charles: 'You have so many partners and rivals in that part of the kingdom that you rule more in name than in fact.'[11]

North of the Loire, the process by which power passed to

the great lords was rather slower; but here too the latter part of Charles the Bald's reign was crucial. In the east, it was rebellion rather than fear of invasion which led to reconstruction. In 863, Charles's power in Burgundy was severely shaken by the revolt of Humphrey of Gothia. In response, the count of Autun received authority to supervise neighbouring counts, so that he might constitute a focal point of loyalty to the crown. In the west, the aggressive expansion of Brittany forced the creation of a defensive lordship, based on Angers, which in 862 was conferred on Robert the Strong, a man of Lotharingian birth, the ancestor of the Capetian family. Finally, and in all probability the most serious solvent of royal power, in the last years of his reign Charles ceded control over West Frankish Austrasia to Hugh, lay abbot of St Denis, whom he recognized as duke of the Franks. Hugh the Abbot's authority had its centre in Paris and covered an area of the kingdom in which loyalty to the king was traditionally deep-rooted; it was therefore unwise that it should have been allowed to escape the royal grasp.

If the last years of Charles the Bald's reign saw West Francia divided among great men, the years afterwards were even more disastrous for unity. Charles's pursuit of Lotharingia and then of the imperial crown had met with little support among his magnates. His death in Italy provoked a crisis. His son Louis the Stammerer was forced to make extensive gifts to obtain recognition as king; his coronation ceremony has been seen by some historians of political thought as an attempt to create contractual kingship.[12] Any chance he might have had of overcoming a weak start was lost with his death in 879. The succession dispute that then broke out was only settled by sharing the realm between his two sons, Louis III and Carloman. But they could not carry all their magnates with them. Bernard of Gothia revolted and proclaimed himself king, at the same time as, across the frontier in Provence, Boso of Vienne had himself elected king of Burgundy, so breaking with Carolingian rule in that area. The combination of Bernard's revolt, which it strained all Louis's resources to suppress—and from which the chief gainer was his rival Bernard Plantevelue—with Boso's elevation (which increased the prestige of his brother Richard the Justiciar, new count of Autun) almost annihilated royal authority in the south and east. Louis's great victory against the Vikings at Saucourt in 881 could have offered an opportunity for revival, but his death followed too soon afterwards. His brother Carloman made honest efforts to revive Carolingian government, but to no effect. In 885, after Carloman's death, the West Frankish nobles in despair offered the throne to Charles the Fat, king of East Francia. But the full onslaught of Viking attack, which would have taxed an experienced leader, was a total disaster for the untrained and unskilled scion of the Carolingian house. In December 887 Charles the Fat abdicated, leaving chaos in his wake.

In contrast with the brilliant intellectual achievements of the period—the culmination of the Carolingian renaissance —the years 843-87 were, in political terms, severely disappointing. The kingdom of West Francia carved out at Verdun was neither so large nor so heterogeneous as to be unrulable as a unit in ninth-century conditions. But the combination of severe external pressure, in the form of Viking and Saracen raids, with royal interests in Lotharingia and in the imperial title put West Frankish unity under severe strain. Charles the Bald's response to the challenge, that of creating what amounted to a commonwealth of princes, was no doubt a thoroughly statesmanlike policy. But it contributed to the process whereby the Frankish aristocracy lost interest in the survival of the whole of Charles's kingdom. For aristocratic families began to consolidate their landed holdings within the area in which one of their members had political power; consequently, the federation was subject to strain, in that the interests of the whole could no longer be reconciled with those of its parts. Charles's magnates have been much blamed for their selfishness; and certainly the conduct of Bernard Plantevelue or Bernard of Gothia suggests little concern for the common weal. But it was unrealistic to imagine that heavy burdens and responsibilities could be laid on the new 'princes' without granting them security from dismissal in their own lifetime and some rights for their families after their deaths.

In 882 the aged Hincmar of Rheims, the leading luminary

of Carolingian legal studies, wrote a work of advice for the young king Carloman, the *De Ordine Palatii*.[13] The climax of this work consisted in a description of Charlemagne's great councils: to these the *fideles* of the whole empire were summoned; they came bearing news of their localities and difficult legal cases to be heard by the emperor's ministers; they remained to hear the emperor's future plans; they then returned home to explain the emperor's will. Hincmar deplored the decay of such councils, and urged Carloman to revive them. Had it been possible for later kings to follow this advice *in toto*, the Carolingian inheritance in West Francia might yet have remained intact. But it was not to be.

CHAPTER 2

Sources 888–987

THE tenth century is very ill-served. Whether through civil war, alien aggression, or simple loss of self-confidence, the habit of recording events wore sadly thin. In fact, the period 888–987 in West Frankish history is almost as much a dark age as the seventh century. The historian's task therefore consists of piecing together tiny snippets of information, often ambiguous in import, to create a picture which makes sense when put against the much fuller view derived from the ampler sources of the late tenth and eleventh century. The pitfalls in his path are substantial, the challenge great.

Chronicle evidence provides a framework which no other kind of source can equal in coherence. Where it exists, it is therefore of great value, though obviously it raises questions of interpretation (e.g. how accurate is the chronicler's source of information? how biased is his own view?) Many of the chronicles on which historians have to rely for tenth-century West Francia were compiled in the eleventh century; because of the lateness of their testimony, their use involves more complex value-judgements. But there are two tenth-century chronicles which provide a starting-point for the construction of political history, those of Flodoard of Rheims and Richer.

Flodoard has been compared with Bede as a dark-age historian. The comparison does justice to his reliability, but credits him with too much subtlety and sophistication of purpose. The canon of Rheims who set out to describe in terse prose the events of the years 919 to 966 (the year of his death) was an honest and straightforward man. In Rheims, he could draw on the library which Hincmar had fostered for monastic annals; he could also make use of the charters which the canons had found it useful to preserve —mostly relating to their own interests. He moved among men who could still remember Hincmar himself, his great erudition, and his commitment to recording contemporary events for the moral enlightenment of future generations. Hincmar's shadow must often have fallen on Flodoard's work. But even more important, in Rheims, Flodoard found himself right in the centre of events well worth recording. The archiepiscopal city was on the king's regular circuit; Flodoard met or knew well by reputation the great men of Francia north of the Loire; indeed he was personally involved in national politics. In 940, after the capture of the city by Hugh the Great and Herbert of Vermandois, he was held prisoner for a while by Herbert, who suspected him of disapproving of the substitution of Herbert's five-year-old son for the properly elected archbishop. But Flodoard's discretion, so evident in his historical writing, helped him to escape.

Flodoard's chronicle,[1] then, is a clear and precise description of events from 919 to 966, in which the focus is on the royal court and its relations with the other great men of the north. Aquitaine, Burgundy, and Gothia take a very small part in the narrative; Neustria, Vermandois, Flanders, and Normandy play prominent roles. What is striking about Flodoard's handling of this very complex period is the objectivity of his tone. He offers no judgement on the deposition of Charles the Simple, or on the election of Robert or of Raoul. In this, he is almost unique. Nor does he explicitly criticize the characters he discusses, even Herbert of Vermandois, whom he had reason to dislike. Obviously such objectivity has its drawbacks: it would have been fascinating to know what a contemporary thought were the motives of princes in their networks of intrigue; this is hidden from us. On the other hand, Flodoard's detachment creates trust in his precision. This matters particularly in relation to the titles he gives the great men. When he calls William II *dux Aquitanorum* in 923 or Hugh the Great *princeps* at the time of his marriage, it is reasonable to assume that these were proper and conventional means of referring to them, not a chronicler's flattery. One general fact which emerges from Flodoard's story is the closeness of ties between West Francia and Germany in this period, and the personal interest which Otto the Great took in West Frankish affairs. Frontiers of kingdoms and of kingship were still very fluid within an empire which remembered its one-time unity under Charlemagne.

If Flodoard is properly praised for his objectivity, his successor at Rheims, Richer,[2] though far more amusing to read, makes no claim to it. His literary ambitions and personal prejudices stand out to the most casual reader; his modern editor is scathing about his veracity. Superficially, Richer's aim was the modest one of providing a continuation of the Annals of St Bertin from 882, the year in which Hincmar set down his pen, till 995. Before 966, he relied very extensively on Flodoard himself, but often made careless use of his source. After that, he had the same advantage as his predecessor in being a canon of Rheims, at the centre of royal affairs, and in particular, of being present at the election of Hugh Capet in 987, an election preceded by debate and intrigue which his description has made famous. In his case, however, the advantage of Rheims's distinction as a literary centre has arguably been turned to a disadvantage. The classical historians, in particular Sallust but also Caesar, and the later writers Sulpicius Severus and Isidore of Seville, seem to be more in his mind than the events he is actually describing. So he embroiders, he exaggerates, and he distorts the truth for literary effect. It has been said of him that 'he adjusted the actions of the king to his ideas of what a ruler ought to do'.[3] All his statements of opinion, and many of fact, have therefore to be weighed critically to see if they can be used. Yet for the years 966 to 995 he does provide information not found elsewhere, some at least of which seems to be the simple truth. And though parts of his work may be dismissed as evidence for the late tenth-century literary revival rather than for tenth-century politics, there is still a core of the useful; and if many of his judgements on men are clearly biased, they have value as a contemporary view.

Of the eleventh-century chronicles, Raoul Glaber's chronicle and those of Nantes and St Maixent will be discussed in the introduction to the next part since, though they contain information of importance on events and society before 987, their real significance lies in the later period. But the chronicle of Ademar of Chabannes,[4] although it goes on till 1028, deserves attention here. Ademar was a monk of noble Aquitanian family, who spent his life at St Cybard at Angoulême and St Martial in Limoges. His chronicle seeks to provide a full history of the Frankish people from their origin till 1028—in itself an interesting project for a southerner to engage on—but it is all derived from other sources until he reaches the tenth and eleventh centuries in the second half of book III (from Chapter 16), after which it is original. Ademar has his weaknesses: he knows or chooses to know rather little of West Francia north of the Loire, and his chronology is often difficult to follow. But his account brings alive the politics of the south and lets us catch a glimpse of a changing world of fluid alliances, uncertain lordship, and the slow consolidation of power by the counts of Poitou. In so doing, it complements Flodoard's chronicle admirably. There are some signs of literary convention in Ademar's handling of material, but in general he tells his story clearly and credibly. The different manuscript recensions of the chronicle are now generally accepted as having been Ademar's own work: he revised, added to, and glossed his text over the years. This in itself is testimony to his interest in truth.

Chronicles provide a framework; monastic annals often provide only scraps. Kept by monks of monasteries across the whole country to record events that would seem significant *sub specie aeternitatis*, they are sometimes no more than catalogues of kings' accessions and deaths, interspersed with purely local information. But their local viewpoint can be helpful. The *Annales Blandinienses*, compiled at St Peter's, Ghent, around 1060, but drawing on an earlier compilation, throw light on Arnoul I's capture of Arras, and on the arrangements made for the minority of Arnoul II.[5] The *Annals of St Bénigne* at Dijon tell of Richard the Justiciar's fight against the Vikings in 899, and insert his death in 921 into that text, as though he were a king.[6] Perhaps more useful is the *Cartulary of St Bertin*—ostensibly a catalogue of early charters, but in fact containing a chronicle, written by the monk Folcuin at the end of Arnoul II's reign.[7]

Then there are saints' lives, a large and motley collection. By far the most interesting of these is the life of St Gerald of Aurillac, written by St Odo of Cluny.[8] Odo's purpose was to describe how a noble layman could live out his life in a fashion entirely pleasing to Christ. It has twofold political interest: first, it shows how a lord ought to dispense justice and protect the church; and secondly it gives precise information about Gerald, son of the count of Limoges and *vassus dominicus*, his contemporary and friend Duke William the Pious, and several other southern aristocrats of the early tenth-century, not all of whom have yet been identified with certainty.

Of the same kind are miracle collections. Ermentarius' narrative of the *Miracles of St Philibert*[9] tells the colourful story of a monastic community forced to wander from Noirmoutier to Burgundy, under pressure from Viking forces. Of broader interest are books ii and iii of the *Miracles of St Benedict*,[10] written by Aimon of Fleury, almost in chronicle form, containing information about Gascony, Aquitaine, and Burgundy, as well as Fleury itself, to which St Benedict's bones had allegedly been translated in the eighth century. Of equally broad interest are the first two books of the *Miracles of St Foy*,[11] written by Bernard of Angers around 1020; they provide a rare glimpse into the society of the Rouergue, an otherwise little-chronicled part of the country. Obviously the information contained in miracle stories needs critical handling, since the telling of a good tale was uppermost in these author's minds; but the background they take for granted makes a vivid portrait of late tenth-century life.

Annals, saints' lives, and miracle stories provide very random, though sometimes very illuminating, glimpses of political events. But the hard core of the historian's information has to be derived from documents issued by those in authority. Because there has been a long French historical tradition of charter analysis, all the known diplomas of tenth-century West Frankish kings have been edited.[12] Royal charters were formal documents of a juridical nature, usually a privilege, a grant, a judgement, or a contract, issued by the king in his capacity as ruler, and bearing his sign and seal at the bottom. The act of issuing a charter in itself created the grant or contract—it was therefore dispositive—as well as bearing testimony to future generations of what had been done. To issue a charter was thus an act of power. Both the wording and the form of the document were designed to drive that home, as can be seen in the following example, issued by Louis IV in 939 or 940:

> In the name of the holy and indivisible Trinity. Louis, by the grace of God, king. If we lend our ear to the appropriate petitions of our *fideles*, we preserve the customs of our royal predecessors, and we bring the *fideles* into closer contact with our highness. Therefore let it be known to all our faithful men, both present and future, that the distinguished count Hugh came into our presence and prayed that we would give certain abbeys situated in the *pagus* of Port (?) to his *fidelis* by name Alard and to his wife Adela and their heirs. One of these abbeys, dedicated to St Mary, is called Faverney, and the other, dedicated to St Leger, is called Enfonville. Favouring therefore most willingly the prayers of the aforesaid glorious count Hugh, we concede to the same Alard and his wife Adela, in their integrity, the aforesaid abbeys . . . [13]

There followed a list of the abbeys' appurtenances, and an arrangement whereby they should return to their former owners if the heirs of Alard failed. Beneath this came the royal monogram, the subscription of a notary in the chancellor's stead, the date and place of issue, *In Dei nomine Amen*, and the royal seal.

This charter follows the diplomatic forms that had evolved in the court of Charlemagne and his successors. It projects an image of orthodox kingship, sanctified by God, open to the subject's intercession, generous where appropriate, and above all, in control of events. It was of great importance to tenth-century kings that this image should be maintained. Yet there was a substantial gap between it and Louis IV's actual position in 939–40, when he faced a combined attack from Hugh the Great, Herbert II of Vermandois, and Otto I of East Francia. If the 'distinguished count Hugh' who petitioned was Hugh the Black of Burgundy, then Louis was ensuring his loyalty in the forthcoming crisis; but if it was Hugh the Great—and the difficulty over identifying the places involved makes either Hugh possible—then Louis was desperately trying to overturn his enemies' alliance. Either way, the petition could hardly have been refused, though it forced Louis to treat the church's temporalities as if they were crown lands.

In the above charter, Louis was simply *rex*, king, without

description. Later in the century, it became more usual for charters to call his successors *rex Francorum*.[14] This title has evoked controversy. It has been interpreted either as an admission that the king was now only ruler north of the Loire, in the part of the kingdom traditionally thought of as Francia; or as an assertion of his particular rulership over the Franks, the people of Charlemagne, a title perhaps designed to appeal to Lotharingian sentiment. This difference of opinion is just one illustration of the problems inherent in interpreting the phrases used in charters. It may surely be presumed that care was taken in the choice of words, but linking diplomatic fashion to changing political circumstances has proved a more controversial task than some of its earlier proponents realized.

Nevertheless, the decline in the number of royal charters during the tenth century does seem a clear indicator of the decline of royal power. Whereas about five charters a year survive for the reign of Charles the Simple (898-922), there are only about three a year for Louis IV (936-54), and under two for Lothaire (954-85).[15] The logical explanation is that as time went on fewer people regarded a royal charter as an essential authority for their acquisitions or grants. And there were other changes that pointed in the same direction: charters were increasingly likely to have been written, not in the royal chancery, but by their recipients; in Robert I's (922-3) and Raoul's reigns (923-36), 43 per cent of charters were produced outside the court.[16] Then the dispositive tone of royal charters became muted; often the king simply added his confirmation to a charter already drawn up between two other parties, or, worse still, he only sealed it. This was to reduce the royal initiative to a mere rubber-stamp. The whole impression of a powerful executive was undermined.

Whether royal charters were written at court or by the recipient, they were not filed in the royal archive. Recipients were responsible for their preservation and production in the law-courts if they deemed it helpful. But the troubled political circumstances of the time, coupled with the fact that, if the bulk of the laity could read, it chose not to do so, militated against the survival of lay archives. Religious houses and bishoprics did preserve, albeit carelessly—Charles the

Simple had to reissue a privilege for Corbie when it was discovered that half of it was missing and the other half damaged by fire.[17] But even religious houses rarely made collections of their documents. So, for the most part, the royal charters known to historians are those that the twelfth- or thirteenth-century scribes found when they began to compile cartularies in a more settled and legalistic age. The result is that, outside Catalonia and Narbonne, almost all material relates to the church; laymen's actions can only be traced in charters if they affected a church's title.

Only a small proportion of grants were sufficiently important to warrant royal authorization; yet lesser transactions were often still worthy of record. Religious houses across West Francia encouraged pious donors everywhere to cooperate with the monks in producing written testimony of their generosity, as a safeguard against changes of heart. So 'private' charters were far commoner than royal ones. But because commoner, they were even less likely to be carefully preserved; and those that have survived present a sample even more random (though no less church-biased) than their royal proto-types. Yet, despite their defects as sources, they remain a vital ingredient in all modern histories of the period.

For the history of local government, the most useful charters are those which were issued by princes, bishops or counts. Princely charters, though few and far between, are interesting in that they often follow the royal form, using the first rather than the third person, and therefore sounding dispositive. It appears that, as early as the tenth century, the counts of Anjou sometimes called on the monks of St Aubin's in Angers to produce their charters, as did the counts of Poitou on the canons of St Hilaire in Poitiers. So, though no prince yet had a chancellor or a chancery, some could draw on a tradition that permitted a certain pretentiousness. And it was not just a question of form; content, too, could be royal. Princes began to infringe on the royal rights by issuing grants of immunity to monastic houses on their own initiative; they began to refer to *their* fiscs (a royal term), *their* rights of hospitality, *their* rights to military service, *their* obligation to protect the church and the poor.

On the basis of these charters, Werner[18] has concluded that the princes were representatives of the royal authority, exercising royal rights within a sub-kingdom. Charters certainly prove that princes were exercising once public, delegated rights in their own names; but whether imitation of a king makes a man a royal representative is a rather more thorny question (see p. 90–92).

In one way, though, princely charters differed from almost (though not quite) all royal charters of the tenth century: they were witnessed by men regarded as of character suitable to bear testimony in a law-court. Princes, then, acknowledged that they, like all other men except the king, needed to share the responsibility (for granting or confirming) with others held in public esteem. Their personal action was not enough. The witness-lists can prove a valuable source of historical information, since they afford a glimpse of a prince's entourage, of the important men he could attract to his court, most of whom may well have been his *fideles*. The more historians emphasize the personal element in princely rule, the more significant the witness lists can be. They offer, for example, our only insight before c.1020 into the Count of Barcelona's extremely successful family and client network.

Charters can also give important, though inevitably rather random, indications of the area in which a prince's power was recognized; for if two parties sought princely confirmation of their transaction, they did so because they thought the agreement would gain force thereby. Occasionally, a charter makes recognition quite explicit; some from Aquitaine, for example, give the date by the royal regnal year, and then add the year of the duke of Aquitaine's rule. Other charters indicate local attitudes to royal government. Catalan charters continued to date by the regnal years of Charles the Simple, ignoring King Raoul, until Charles's death in 929; and some refused recognition to the Burgundian king even after that. Similarly there are Catalan charters dated by the reign of Charles of Lorraine after 987, ignoring the election of Hugh Capet. Though the strength of pro-Carolingian sentiment in the south is mentioned by Flodoard and Richer, the charters provide much more striking evidence of its depth.[19]

Despite their obvious uses, diplomatic sources have one

major drawback, more conspicuously for the historian of northern than of southern France: they are in some sense artificial legal documents, based on a form ultimately derived from Roman law. The conventions which guided them, the notion of public power they so solidly proclaimed, were supplied from outside the framework of tenth-century political relations. It may therefore be hazardous to look, as one school of historians has done,[20] for a close relationship between diplomatic change and political change. The royal chancery and the monastic scribes were working within a tradition that had a life of its own.

This section must end as it began, with a reminder that we know very little indeed about the tenth century; its history can only be written in terms of hypothesis and deduction.

CHAPTER 3

Formative trends in tenth-century political life

(a) Disintegration of royal authority

IN December 887, Charles the Fat renounced his throne; he died the following month, leaving no direct heir. The only (probably) legitimate Carolingian left in the empire was the posthumous son of Louis the Stammerer, later known as Charles the Simple, who was only ten years old in 888, and whose claim to the throne had already been passed over twice since his father's death in 881. East Francia saw its salvation in an energetic, adult Carolingian bastard, Arnulf, duke of Bavaria, who was crowned at once. In the West, the decision was more difficult. Pro-Carolingian sentiment was still strong —Charles's cause was eloquently pleaded; but north-west Francia was in imminent danger of Viking assault, a danger made yet more threatening by Alfred of Wessex's victories against the Danes in England, which narrowed future Viking options. In the circumstances, a king who could command armies seemed the first necessity. So, at Compiègne on 29 February 888, an assembly of bishops, counts, and lords elected Eudes, count of Paris and lay abbot of St Denis, to the throne of West Francia.

That the event was momentous was recognized by contemporaries. Regino of Prüm, meditating on the consequences of choosing a king from within the aristocracy, concluded that it

was the cause of long wars; not that there were lacking Frankish princes worthy of dominion by their noble birth, their courage and their wisdom, but because their equality in origin and dignity . . . was a fresh cause for discord. None of them was sufficiently raised above the rest to make them willing to submit to his authority.[1]

This succinct analysis explains much about the political history of West Francia from 888 to 987. To those historians whose interests have concentrated on the development of

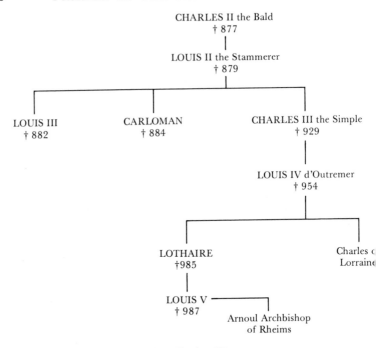

Fig. 1. Carolingian Kings

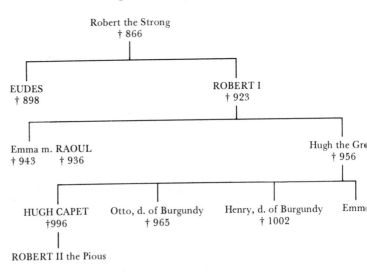

Fig. 2. Capetian Kings

central institutions of government, the period is a depressing morass of failures and rebellions, lit only by occasional flashes of royal initiative. But, as Regino's comment suggests, West Francia's problems sprang from a plethora of organizational talent, not an absence. For the historian of provincial government, this is a period of experiment and modification, in which a real, though very patchy, consolidation of the Carolingian inheritance was achieved.

Eudes's election was owed immediately to his military reputation. His brilliant defence of Paris against Viking attack in 885 had contrasted sharply with Charles the Fat's failures. As defender of his people, Eudes had already established himself. More importantly, he came from a family which was among the greatest in West Francia, and the most conspicuous for its loyalty to the Carolingian house. The Robertians, later to be called the Capetians, were of Lotharingian origin and imperial service, who had migrated to the West in the reign of Charles the Bald, were unswerving in their support of Charles in 858 when his brother Louis the German attacked West Francia, and were rewarded with the powerful position of the Breton March. Eudes, in addition to inheriting his father's march based on Tours and Angers, had been given the honours of Hugh the Abbot, duke of the Franks; so he was count of Paris, lay abbot of St Denis, and overlord of Neustria. If West Francia was to have an aristocratic king, none could be more suitable than he. And the early years of his reign proved his striking ability.

But kingship was not a simple matter of human convenience in this era. The king was God's anointed. If God wanted Eudes, he would make him victorious in battle; if not, not. West Frankish princes were disposed to wait and see before committing themselves irrevocably. Royal diplomas for the early years of the reign came mostly from Neustria, Eudes's own area. And even here, where his military role was most useful, there was a new forwardness in the Frankish magnates' suggestion that the king might pass the winter of 892 in Aquitaine, since Francia was exhausted by the hospitality which he and his train demanded. By 893, a series of reverses against the Vikings, along with a troubled succession to the country of Poitou, led those magnates most closely

related to the Carolingian family, the dukes of Burgundy and
Aquitaine, to judge that God was displeased with Eudes; they
therefore failed to resist the coronation of Charles the
Simple by Fulk of Rheims in 893. Four years of civil war
followed, which bewildered royal vassals and loosened ties
of loyalty yet further. In 897, peace was made. Eudes
remained king; in all probability, he nominated Charles his
successor; Charles was given extensive territories, probably
those round Laon and Rheims which were to be closely
identified with the Carolingian family for most of the rest
of the century. In the following year, Eudes died, and Charles
succeeded him.

Eudes's reign might seem therefore to have been a brief
and insignificant interlude, chiefly notable for the demonstration it provided of widespread adherence to the Carolingian
line. This, however, is an inadequate view. It ushered in a century in which the old loyalties could not but be weakened,
simply because now there was an alternative ruling house to
that of Charlemagne. It was not that the Capetians struggled
to obtain the throne—indeed, their limited aims in this
respect were remarkable. Eudes's brother Robert did nothing
to contest Charles the Simple's succession in 898; Hugh
the Great called Louis d'Outremer back from the English
court to take the crown in 936. Nevertheless, when Charles
the Simple's policies in Lorraine infuriated a sufficient
number of Franks, it was natural for them to crown Robert
in 922, and on his death in battle in 923, his son-in-law
Raoul of Burgundy (a courtesy Robertian); when expansion
into Lorraine had a similar effect in 987, the magnates
elected as their king Hugh Capet, Robert I's grandson, rather
than the last Carolingian, Charles of Lorraine. The mere
existence of an alternative gave new strength to the magnates
who chose the king (usually only the Franks from north of
the Loire), made loyalties everywhere more hesitant, bribery
more necessary.

Examination of the decline of the West Frankish monarchy
entails its subdivision into different aspects, in the discussion
of which no attempt will be made to do justice to the energy
and devotion with which tenth-century kings struggled
against formidable odds. So, by way of introduction, it

should be said that contemporaries at least were aware that their kings were far from *fainéants*. Indeed, Raoul Glaber credited Lothaire with the intention of reintegrating the whole Frankish realm.[2] And the kings did achieve something. The low point of monarchy was probably 936, on Louis d'Outremer's accession; by Lothaire's death in 985, the line of the graph had risen considerably. Yet, for reasons beyond their control, the hard-won upturn in fortune could not be sustained. Too much had been lost for recovery to be anything but temporary.

The first pillar on which royal power rested was the demesne, that bundle of rights and lands which provided income, devoted followers, and patronage for its royal owner. The problem with discussing the secular demesne in the tenth century lies in the fact that there was not yet a clear doctrine of royal inheritance, nor a distinction between royal and family lands. Therefore the demesne of the Robertians was quite distinct from that of the Carolingians. Nevertheless, Louis d'Outremer and Lothaire both struggled to clarify the position, to claim for themselves the lands and rights which Charles the Simple had enjoyed, and to pass them on to the next generation. In pursuit of this policy, Louis IV was prepared to breach Carolingian tradition by denying his younger son any part of the family inheritance; as the *Miracles of St Benedict* put it, Charles 'grew old in private houses'.[3] Primogeniture was born in the royal demesne. But only those lands and rights that Charles the Simple had held around Laon and Rheims, which had in all probability been granted to him by Eudes as the price of peace in 897, proved easy to secure. It was not much on which to sustain majesty. Remnants of fiscal lands and revenues far from this kernel became increasingly hard to maintain. By 950, there was no more fiscal land in the duchy of Burgundy; it had probably disappeared earlier in Aquitaine. This left the last Carolingians as poor men among their princes.

To eke out their slender resources, Louis and Lothaire were forced to rely extensively on hospitality from abbeys and bishoprics. But the royal ecclesiastical demesne also proved a diminishing entity.[4] Exactly which abbeys should still be counted royal at the death of Louis V is not easy to ascertain—the reform movement's effect in changing the nature of lay protection (see Chapter 5c) goes some way to explaining the difficulty—but Fleury, a house in Laon, and one in Compiègne are certain; Lothaire's two visits to Brioude would suggest a link there too; and the abbeys in Soissons and Autun may also have preserved their royal connection. This represented only a small fraction of what earlier kings had claimed. In respect of bishoprics, the kings were rather more successful in maintaining or reestablishing their authority. Although all bishoprics south of the Loire, with the exception of Le Puy, depended by 987 on other men, to the north the position was better. Le Mans remained royal, Rheims and Langres were forcibly recovered for the crown, and most of the bishoprics within the archdioceses of Rheims and Sens (with the exception of Sens itself, Troyes, and Meaux) still acknowledged the king as their protector. Together, these bishoprics made an outstanding contribution to royal authority, to royal revenues, armies, and patronage. Furthermore, they permitted the king to resume, on occasion, the traditional role of defender of the church, when he summoned the royal bishops to councils to discuss important matters of ecclesiastical policy.

In the past, the decline of the Carolingian fisc was usually seen as the chief reason for the decline of royal power;[5] and the connection is undeniable. When Louis d'Outremer granted away the last piece of fiscal land in the Mâconnais at the request of the count in 950, he also deprived the crown of its last assured hospitality there; so no king could visit the area for the next three hundred years. When Baldwin II and Arnoul I wrested away St Bertin and St Vaast from Eudes and Charles the Simple, the Flemish principality grew, the royal demesne shrank. That the later Carolingians attributed their weakness to the decline of their demesne is evidenced both by their anxiety to prevent further attrition —Louis IV, as has been said, denied his second son Charles of Lorraine any part in the family inheritance—and in their concern with conquest in Lotharingia, where the ancestral Carolingian family lands might contribute effectively to the dynasty's wealth and resources.

Yet more recent interpretations have concentrated less

on the fisc than on the opportunities for the exercise of specifically royal power. This change in emphasis has the merit of according with tenth-century opinion in treating kings as rulers, rather than as failed businessmen; and it also explains why the substantial increase in demesne which came with the first Capetian failed to boost royal power by the corresponding amount. The new approach demands definition of specifically royal powers in the tenth century. To differentiate between royal powers and those public powers delegated to counts was never easy in the Carolingian system; it came to be even less easy when the king no longer stood at the apex of the pyramid. As early as the end of Charles the Bald's reign, the right to nominate to countships was largely though not completely inoperative; election to bishoprics began to pass into the hands of others. Some of the most significant royal prerogatives—the sending out of *missi*, the issuing of capitularies—were casualties of the period immediately before Eudes's accession; and Eudes himself called the *ban* for the whole of the realm for the last time in 888, when he set out in pursuit of the Vikings. At roughly the same time, the cessation of minting throughout West Francia meant the end to the royal monopoly; when coins reappeared in the tenth century, they were as likely to be in the control of the bishops or great magnates as of the king. And Eudes's great assemblies of 889 were the last to which southerners, both ecclesiastics and laymen, from Catalonia and Toulouse, troubled to make their way. Again, Eudes's successful intervention in the Poitevin comital succession was in marked contrast with the failures of Louis d'Outremer and Lothaire. Only the proclamation of the *ban* for the whole of Francia north of the Loire in 925 and the last collection of Danegeld in 926 reminded the men of the early tenth century what royal power had once been.

Thus the most striking royal powers were inoperative throughout the tenth century—indeed most of these were to remain inoperative (at least in their Carolingian form) throughout the whole period covered by this book. Still, there were other regalian rights which did survive, though no longer as monopolies. One was the right to issue charters of immunity to monastic houses, and to confirm the grants of others. While the great princes imitated the king in this respect, a disproportionate share of the business remained royal, at least north of the Loire. Although the bulk of royal charters were issued within Francia, both Carolingians and Robertians issued them for Aquitaine and Burgundy on their occasional visits to these areas. (Here it is again worth noting that royal progresses to Burgundy ceased for three centuries after Louis d'Outremer's of 950, the only exceptions being a brief visit of Hugh Capet and the period in which Robert the Pious was both duke and king; and that the failure of Lothaire's plans for a sub-kingdom in Aquitaine meant the end of royal visits, except in a purely private capacity, until the marriage of Louis VII with Eleanor of Aquitaine). More surprisingly, throughout the tenth century, messengers from Catalonia and Narbonne regularly sought out the kings to obtain royal confirmations for grants of land, by their action keeping alive the memory of royal authority within an area where the king had long lost all power of compulsion. It was not until after the change of dynasty in 987 that the far south lost its sentimental attachment to royal confirmations. But if the area within which royal charters were sought remained extensive, the character of those charters changed. Eudes's command to the count of Nîmes to enquire into a complaint made before the royal court was the last firm directive among the *acta* of the kings.[6] Royal charters were increasingly likely to have been written by their recipients rather than by the chancery; they were more likely simply to confirm the actions of others, or even just to seal them: and in any case they dwindled in number.

Another regalian right which survived, though hardly unchallenged, was that of receiving oaths of fidelity from the great men of the realm. Here Louis IV's and Lothaire's determined battle to recover their authority over the bishoprics paid off. The royal bishops were the staunchest of the king's *fideles*, the most regular visitors of the court. As for secular magnates, though some counts of the far south took homage to Louis d'Outremer, they failed to observe the ceremony for his successors. But the dukes of Francia, Aquitaine, and Burgundy, the great counts of the north,

Flanders and Normandy, the counts of the royal demesne, continued the tradition. And if they now interpreted their homage as little more than a gesture of friendship, the king was still grateful for that. Otherwise, the shrinking band of non-princely *fideles* was confined to the areas where the king was territorially powerful.

An important consequence of swearing fidelity to the king was the acceptance of his justice, the duty of resort to his court for arbitration in case of dispute with another *fidelis*. Tenth-century kings were able to maintain this tradition, but no longer to conclude cases in accordance with their own notions of what was right. It is noticeable that the only criticism Richer made of Eudes's energetic kingship was that he was too occupied with military affairs to spend time on settling disputes.[7] Nevertheless it seems unlikely that Eudes would have tolerated, as Charles the Simple was forced to tolerate, the murder of the archbishop of Rheims by a chamberlain of Baldwin II of Flanders in 900. Though the chamberlain was excommunicated, the king had no alternative but to receive Baldwin back into his peace. And later, Louis IV was no more effective in punishing Baldwin's son Arnoul for his murder of William, count of Rouen, in 942. For where royal justice conflicted with expediency, retribution had become a luxury kings could no longer afford.

Therefore the whole nature of kingship changed as the right to command across all West Francia disappeared. Admittedly tenth-century kings preserved more, quantitatively, of the surviving regalian rights than any of their princes enjoyed. Yet quantity was small consolation for the qualitative decay; for confirming charters, taking fidelity, and imposing justice upon the great were all losing their traditional import. So despite the great energy of Lothaire and even of Louis V, their dependence on their princes' goodwill necessarily rendered them incapable of ·ruling as their predecessors had ruled. Contemporaries, appreciating this, were automatically reminded of the last years of Merovingian rule in Gaul. In 985 Gerbert of Rheims declared Lothaire to be king only in name, while Hugh Capet was king in fact.[8] The way was being prepared for history to repeat itself.

But because those who revere and obey seldom pause to analyse the grounds for their obedience, royal resources and powers were not the only pillars of kingship. The scriptural foundation and long tradition that set kings apart from ordinary mortals could, in some circumstances, give force to their authority when more pragmatic considerations would deny it. It is true that the dwindling demesne had its effects here too, since it deprived most of the country's inhabitants of their chance to see the king; and those who could not see his majesty rarely bothered to imagine it. Equally the contraction of *fideles*, the decline of assemblies, and the absence of resources to support ostentatious display limited the opportunities for evoking devotion. The times were out of joint in West Francia for doctrines of sacral kingship such as those that emerged in contemporary Ottonian Germany or, less splendidly, in Wessex. Charles the Simple was the last king to call for a special ceremonial commemoration of a day in his honour in the northern abbeys; the Carolingian *laudes* were seldom sung. During Lothaire's reign, when Ottonian influence was strong, imperial touches did creep in from the east: some diplomas had markedly imperial characteristics, a certain assertiveness crept into royal claims of pre-eminence. But at best it was a pale imitation of an alien form.

Nevertheless one bulwark of royal charisma remained: the coronation ceremony, based on the rituals devised in the reign of Charles the Bald. The large crowds that flocked to these splendid occasions could scarcely fail to observe that, as a result of the unction, the king, however low he might have sunk in the secular power-stakes, transcended all other men in possessing a majesty which was the earthly and impoverished reflection of God in glory. The indelibility of the charisma was attested by the fact that Charles the Simple remained a king between 922 and his death in 929, although he was imprisoned and incapable of rule. And if, excited by the pursuit of their own political advantage, the Frankish magnates sometimes forgot the religious quality of their king's position, there were others prepared to recall it forcefully to their minds. The pope, the king of England, and (most effectively) Otto the Great all intervened to safeguard Louis IV from rebellion at some stage in his troubled reign, a proof that the Lord's anointed had solider backing than either the royal demesne or his royal powers could provide.

But from the Carolingian point of view, the drawback to reliance on unction was that it could be bestowed on others than members of their own family. So in 987, when Lothaire's and Louis V's attacks on Lotharingia had shocked the pro-Ottonian bishops, Adalbéron of Rheims first persuaded the Frankish magnates to elect Hugh Capet king, and then conferred on him the full sacral authority of his new position, by pouring on his head the chrism held to be from the phial brought by a dove from heaven for Clovis's baptism.[9] Once crowned, Hugh's personal authority, in the eyes of the church at least, obliterated for-ever the faint glow of Carolingian rights in Charles of Lorraine.[10]

(b) The raids

The Viking, Saracen, and Magyar raids had deep effects on West Frankish society—so deep as to be rather puzzling. For terrible though they were, they were usually spasmodic; they had at least some beneficial effects on the economy as well as many harmful ones; and since only one—Normandy—of the several attempts at settlement on West Frankish territory succeeded, it would seem that the attackers were far from invincible. Recent historians have therefore expressed some scepticism as to whether monastic chroniclers' claims of damage should always be taken seriously.[11] Certainly the monk Ermentarius, introducing his famous tale of the monks of St Philibert's flight from Noirmoutier to Tournus in Burgundy, felt required to produce a good excuse for depriving the island of its patron saint, whose relics the monks took with them on their departure. Scepticism is therefore fair in the face of his claim that there was no protection against the Viking onslaught:

All take flight; few are those who cry stop! resist! fight for your country, your children and your nation! So, besotted and divided amongst themselves, these buy by ransom what they ought to defend by arms.[12]

But it is a long leap from taking monastic chroniclers' accounts with a pinch of salt to treating the raids as relatively minor affairs. For they turned West Francia's geographical asset of long, navigable rivers and good communications into a means of destruction. And they showed up Carolingian military arrangements at their weakest point. Charlemagne's system had been geared to mobilizing large armies for offensive campaigns; it proved both unwieldy and slow in adjusting to the challenge of local defence. Charles the Bald's concentrated efforts in the 850s and 860s failed to prevent smaller troops of Vikings from wintering on West Frankish soil, and his weaker successors, facing the lager armies of the 880s, had much less chance of success. By 890 the Saracens had established a permanent base at Fraxinetum, across the frontier in Provence, from which they attacked Gothia and the Auvergne from time to time. The Magyar raids of 919 on Laon and 937 on Berry completed the process of making the whole country vulnerable.

A combination of better defence and rather different aspirations on the part of the raiders led to a considerable easing of danger down the west coast in the second and third decades of the tenth century. It may be that the new Viking settlement in Normandy proved effective after 911 in repelling other invaders. But there were grounds for fear long after this. As late as 1000, Ademar tells us, the wife of the viscount of Limoges was captured by Viking pirates, and not restored to her own people until the duke of Normandy had intervened on her behalf.[13] Though the Saracens were less troublesome in Gothia than in Provence, it was not until the destruction of their base in 972-3 that the southerners could breathe completely freely. Only the Hungarians proved a totally ephemeral danger.

From about 920 onwards, the inhabitants of West Francia faced the task of clearing up the confusion that had been created. A story in the *Miracles of St Benedict* sheds some light on the kind of task that faced them. It tells of a certain Viking leader Rainald, who, before turning up at Fleury to suffer the saint's avenging blow, had devastated both Aquitaine and Neustria, capturing large numbers of men and horses, and driving many inhabitants away from their homes.[14] He no doubt expected to enjoy a profitable trading-session; but he left behind him a countryside in which agriculture had necessarily been badly disrupted, and in which labour would be lacking to repair the damage. And the area around Fleury had been comparatively fortunate. The Gâtine of Poitou would seem to have been totally depopulated; the cathedrals of Angoulême and Narbonne had suffered badly; much of Normandy was so devastated that it took nearly a century to recover; in Brittany many of the ruling class had fled before the onslaughts to take refuge at the court of Athelstan in Wessex, leaving behind them the wreckage of a province that had once been formidable.

The long-term consequences of the raids have been much debated. From the historian's point of view, the most clearly attested was the dramatic decline in written sources. The great Carolingian centres of learning, Tours, Corbie, St Denis, St Bertin, St Vaast, Ferrières, lay within very vulnerable regions. Though St Vaast and St Bertin struggled to maintain at least a thread of their literate tradition, elsewhere it sank. Flodoard tells that Archbishop Fulk of Rheims gave a gracious reception to scholars fleeing from other parts;[15] and the relative peace enjoyed by both Rheims and Auxerre in the early tenth century explains their importance as centres of learning. But it was a feeble glow in comparison with past illumination. Besides, the raids had inflicted a psychological as well as a physical blow on the Carolingian church. Accustomed as they were to interpreting disaster as a judgement from heaven, tenth-century ecclesiastics regarded the intellectual self-confidence of their predecessors in the time of Charles the Bald as smacking of arrogance. Diffidence accounted for the declining participation of ecclesiastics in secular affairs which, though it is hard to demonstrate in detail, seems to characterize the period. Leading churchmen no longer acted as *missi*; bishops became rare figures at the *mallus*. In part, this was a result of their absorption in more urgent matters; but equally the fact that they were now dependent on laymen for defence against external enemies sapped their moral authority. There were no Hincmars in the aftermath of the raids. So laymen were once again free, as they had not been since the seventh century, to mould the destiny of their society, untrammelled by high-minded advice from those they had been taught to regard as their betters.

As contemporaries saw it, the sharpest change came with the switch to defence and fortification as the chief priority. In the face of Viking and Saracen attackers who relied on their mobility to plunder helpless communities, the obvious need was for refuges into which men, animals, and precious goods could be rushed as soon as a potential marauder was sighted. Archbishop Fulk, writing to Pope Stephen V in 885 or 886, bewailed 'the incursions which, for eight years now have so infested this kingdom that only those are fortunate who can protect themselves in fortified places'.[16] A real effort was made to extend that protection as far as possible. But there were difficulties, both physical and legal. The Roman defences in many northern towns had been dismantled to provide stone for the building of churches during the Carolingian peace. As late as the reign of Charles the Bald, permission had been given to Hincmar to take down part of the city wall of Rheims for the building of the church of St Denis. His successor was forced to reverse the policy, to knock down the church and rebuild the walls. Then defence on this scale needed labour; the peasantry had to be organized under the *ban* to erect and maintain fortifications, a heavy obligation. According to Charles the Bald's Edict of Pîtres in 864, the task was the responsibility of the counts and viscounts, acting on royal authorization. Many of these responded energetically to the call. Wifred the Hairy established the fortress of Cardona for the security of all who cared to dwell in it, on the condition that they should pay all their dues to him, submit their disputes to his court, work one day each week on the fortifications, and undertake to garrison the place as they thought fit in times of danger. Kings, counts, viscounts, and bishops hastened to do likewise. Of the twenty-odd castles in the Chartres area in the tenth century, three were founded by the king, eight by the count of Chartres or the viscount of Châteaudun, and the remainder by vassals of the king, the count, or the bishop.[17]

Nevertheless, the restriction of fortification to those in the official class created problems. Given the danger of the incursions, neither clerics nor laymen could be expected to wait until others solved their defence problems for them. King Eudes, in a charter of immunity for the abbey of Vézelay, referred to the castle the monks had erected 'on account of pagan persecution'[18]: in fact, the monastic community's response to insecurity was to move the whole abbey from the plain to the crest of the hill, where it stands today, in order to exploit natural geographical defences. If monks were taking the initiative in this way, it is highly likely that other communities were also defying the royal prohibition on self-help. A charter of Philip I referred to the erection and subsequent destruction of a castle in Compiègne that had been built without authorization.[19]

Because the mere existence of adulterine castles was seen as a threat to Carolingian adminstration, the question of how many there were has long been a matter of interest to historians. The problem is complicated by the need to define what was meant by a castle. When Gerald of Aurillac handed over his chief residence to his new monastery, he took to living in a fortified place; all over the south, aristocrats did likewise, as archaeologists have made clear. But whether the large number of simple defended towers in which individual families lived ought to be considered castles at all, and whether they posed any threat to public administration, must be doubted. Then there were the quite contrasting large refuges, the old Roman walled towns, or new ones like Cardona, intended to provide shelter for large numbers in time of invasion, and regular homes for ordinary people. These great urban fortifications could scarcely yet be expected to escape from the domination of a count, a viscount, or even more probably a bishop. Thus it is only the third category of castle, the fortified administrative centre, which is at issue. Castles of this type were, by the end of the tenth century, characterized by a sizeable external wall, a large space left empty for security, and a group of buildings within a second wall in the middle. From the central tower the count, viscount, bishop, or *vicarius* to whom the castle belonged might survey the neighbourhood; and around the tower there might be dwellings for those of his vassals who performed castle-guard. In origin, these castles perhaps replaced the palace rather than the ordinary aristocratic dwelling.

By the late tenth century, when mentions of this type of castle become abundant in the charters, it is clear that they have lost any connection they ever had with the defence of the people who lived around them. Their evolution can therefore only be seen as a secondary, even remote, consequence of the raids. Their function was now to shelter a powerful figure, to intimidate the neighbourhood, and occasionally to provide a base for aggressive expansion in the area. As a consequence, adulterine castles of this type could constitute a very serious threat to the operation of public authority in their neighbourhood. With this in mind, recent historians have devoted much attention to the question of who controlled castles in the West Frankish provinces; and very varying answers have emerged.

From Duby's study of the Mâconnais,[20] Fossier's of Picardy,[21] and Chédeville's of Chartres,[22] it seems clear that, in these areas, as also in Normandy, Catalonia, and Flanders, bishops, counts, viscounts, and their vassals contrived in the tenth century to keep all the great castles within their hands. Duby, using the legal definition of feudalism quoted on p. 12, has therefore concluded that, since the public power continued to assert authority, feudalism had not yet dawned. For him, the independent castellan, the *dominus*, is the characteristic figure of a truly feudal society. Here, he differs from the followers of Bloch, who see feudalism as a social form, a militarization of social convention; for them, the appearance of castles and knights makes for a feudal society, whether or not the castle is independent.

On the other hand, Devailly's study of Berry[23] has shown that here independent castles were well entrenched in the latter half of the tenth century, by which time there was no longer a count in the province. The same was true for the Auvergne, where comital power was confined within a small area. In Anjou and the Touraine, as in much of Neustria, the random distribution of early castles is suggestive of local initiative in their construction; if, by the late tenth century, they were regarded as under comital control, this may mean simply that the counts had authorized the existence of structures they were in no position to suppress. The survival of Carolingian public right may therefore be more apparent than real. Besides, there is the wider problem that charters, on which most local surveys are based, probably underestimate the number of independent castles everywhere, because those who owned them deliberately avoided attracting comital attention. So, even in Duby's restricted sense of the term, 'feudalism' was in all probability common in tenth-century West Francia.

Fortifications alone were inadequate; there had to be warriors to man them. And whereas Wifred the Hairy had expected the dwellers of Cardona to defend themselves, others felt a growing need for more professional forces. Here the church offered a lead: for the armed retainers whom most large abbeys and bishoprics maintained in order to fulfil their military obligation to the king were also available to them for defence against raiders. In imitation, great secular magnates added armed warriors to their entourages and established permanent garrisons in their major castles. Fighting became a full-time career for a small number of dedicated men. Long after the danger of the raids was past, the full extent of the transformation they had started came to be appreciated: in acquiring castles as permanent bases from which to sortie and in which to seek refuge, mounted troops had achieved new military effectiveness, albeit in a limited area; and their commanders, the castellans, had become the true lords of the woods, fields, and valleys they could survey from their fortified towers.

Therefore the impact of the raids transcended their immediate and shocking effects, by triggering the militarization of society as a whole; this continued and intensified long after the real danger had abated, and in the end infiltrated into every aspect of aristocratic life. Marc Bloch was correct in seeing here the dawning of a new age.[24]

CHAPTER 4

The Principalities 888–987

(a) The Princes

'PRINCES' is largely a historian's term. To be sure, it was used in the tenth century: royal charters occasionally describe Arnoul of Flanders or Hugh the Great as *princeps*; more rarely there are references to a general body of *principes*; *et comites.* In charters from Berry, the Loire area, and Provence, the word is often used for counts. But the term was only one among several alternatives. And in general parlance, *princeps* could be attributed to any important man from a king to the leader of a robber band.[1] So, in categorizing as princes those dukes and counts whose power extended over several counties, historians are being more rigid than were contemporaries. The value of the category is not in doubt. Since the Belgian historian Dhondt popularized it, the beam of research has highlighted the creative role the princes played in the formation of France. But the drawback lies in the sharp breach it creates between them and the other counts and lords of West Francia, in the implicit suggestion that the princes formed a stable ruling caste, whose authority was founded on clear-cut principles. For in point of fact, no amount of blue blood, royal recognition, or delegated jurisdictional right could, by itself, maintain the position of a failing princely house—the disintegration of William the Pious's principality of Aquitaine (see below, p. 60) bears this out—while on the other hand, the militarily successful, like Baldwin I of Flanders, acquired blue blood by marriage, forced royal recognition, and created their own form of jurisdictional right. The princes were therefore by definition the successful.

Writing in the first half of the twelfth century, Bishop Gerard of Angoulême produced a portrait of Vulgrin II, count of Angoulême:

Map 2. West Francia c.970

a man of great height and very handsome, prudent, skilled in martial arts, patient in endeavour, the terror of his enemies and the strong tower of his own men, vigorous in body and almost always successful in military conflict and the common struggle. Generous in giving alms, in his veneration for and obligation to the church, outstanding for the chastity and cleanliness of his body, careful and provident in casting down his enemies, praiseworth in everything.[2]

Despite its lateness, Gerard's portrait carries conviction as that of an ideal prince of the later ninth and early tenth century; for what the men of that age sought was a lesser Charlemagne in their neighbourhood. The kings concurred in the desire for strong military leaders in the vulnerable areas of their kingdom; as Eudes declared in a charter: 'It is the custom of royal excellence and sublimity to honour the *fideles* of the kingdom with large gifts and to make them powerful'.[3] What is less clear is whether the authority acquired by the princes was a product of royal planning, the response to crisis situations, or a deliberate usurpation of royal rights. The brief history of each principality that follows later is intended to cast some light on the matter, since generalizations are of little assistance.

But before tackling particulars, it is worth commenting on princely titles, which have been the object of much recent research.[4] For the clearest lesson to emerge from these studies is that there was a marked difference between titles recognized by the royal chancery and those in use within the principalities. In so far as a chancery charter may be assumed to express the king's will (remembering that the decline in the number of royal charters, along with their growing tendency to have been written by recipients, necessarily makes it harder to discern the king's will in the second half of the century), it is important that by far the commonest chancery title for princes was simply *comites*. In the king's eyes, then, a prince was essentially the recipient of public powers like any other count; his accumulation of counties made no difference to his function. When the king chose to confer another and more prestigious title on individuals, invariably in the ninth and early tenth century he coupled it with *comes*. So Arnoul I of Flanders was *comes et marchio*; William the Pious *comes et dux*.

In the king's eyes, *marchio* had by the tenth century lost any connection it ever may have had with lordship over a marcher or border region; instead it had become an uninheritable sign of royal favour, to be bestowed only on individuals of the stature of Arnoul I of Flanders, Hugh the Black of Burgundy, or Raymond III of Toulouse. When Lothaire described Arnoul I as *regni nostri marchio nobilissimus,*[5] 'most noble marquis of our kingdom', he was suggesting both that the title was connected with his own kingship and that the marquisate was non-territorial. But whether others put the same interpretation on it is open to question. Baldwin II was referred to in the *Cartulary of St Bertin* as *inclitus marchisus*[6] well before his son obtained chancery recognition of the title in the reign of Raoul; for Folcuin, who so described him, it was probably Baldwin's great achievement in bringing the whole Flemish seaboard under his domination that entitled him to a more splendid title than simply that of count.

Dux, too, demonstrates the gap between the king's conception and those more widely held outside the court. The only *dux* raised to that rank through deliberate royal action was Hugh the Great (properly the Elder) of Neustria, who prevailed on the young and defenceless Louis d'Outremer to elevate him shortly after he had engineered Louis's return to West Francia for his coronation. In effect then, the 943 gift of the title *dux Francorum* was an act of gratitude. Fortunately for historians, Louis felt it necessary to explain what the title meant; Hugh was second to the king in all his kingdoms.[7] In the king's eyes, then, Hugh's dukedom was a recognition of his viceregal status. Yet Flodoard, commenting on the matter, declared Louis to have bestowed on Hugh the *ducatus Franciae*[8]—the duchy of Francia, a territorially-based office. Even in a place as close to the court as Rheims, the king's view of what he had done did not prevail.

In all other cases—the dukes of the Bretons, the Aquitanians, the Burgundians, the Gascons, the Goths, and the Normans—the title is known to have been in use within the province to which it belonged, well before it was recognized by the chancery. The king only put a seal on long practice. It is true that in the cases of the Aquitanian and

Burgundian dukedoms, the king's approval did also assist in transforming a fluid and personal title into an inherited and therefore permanent family dignity. But if the king's approval was at the least desirable, it was not essential. The rich associations of the word 'duke' ensured that it would be used to describe the great, whether or not the chancery condoned the practice. For *dux* evoked many images: a prince only one step below a king on an Old Testament model; a great and victorious military leader, on the classical model; or the leading representative of an ethnic group within the empire, on the Merovingian model. Dukes of the prestige and personal authority of a Richard the Justiciar could bring all these images together to create around their own heads a formidable aura of authority. Others like the dukes of Brittany could tap only one of them in support of their dignity. Nevertheless, because (in all eyes other than the king's) there were possible ethnic or territorial connotations to the title *dux*, its holders were able, over the course of the tenth century, gradually to exploit it as a means of binding their people to them. The duke of Aquitaine became for his subjects the heir of the Carolingian sub-kings of Aquitaine, and also of their predecessors, the Gallo-Roman dukes of the province; these associations created loyalties beyond the area in which he was actually powerful, making his duchy a reality, albeit a tenuous reality, from the Atlantic Ocean to the eastern fringes of the Auvergne.

So titles were important pillars of princely power, to which royal theories and the royal will made only modest contribution. Indeed, the king could be dispensed with altogether, as he was in the case of the dukedoms of Brittany and Gascony; and even where his role was rather more creative, the princes might prefer to forget it. In 941, Arnoul I of Flanders declared himself *amminiculante superni regis clementia markysus*[9] (Marquis by the aid of God's mercy); and Hugh Capet issued coins bearing the legend *Hugo dux Dei gratia*.[10] As early as the mid-ninth century, some counts had claimed to hold their counties from God; now their successors followed suit with much newer titles.

The value of this discussion lies less in its subject-matter than in the glimpse it provides of the king's relations with his princes, on the pressures and counter-pressures within the West Frankish ruling class. Charter evidence on titles supplements the odd hints found in the scanty literary sources, to offer a picture of a society in which most of the initiative lay with the princes and their followers, and where the king struggled in vain to impose his own interpretation of the constitution. Richer commented bitterly: 'No one cared about the king's profit or about the defence of the realm. Each had only one aim: to take the goods of others.'[11] This denunciation of aristocratic acquisitiveness poses problems of interpretation, because it derived from Richer's model, Sallust, and therefore may have been intended more for literary effect than as a statement of fact. It cannot, however, be denied that there is at least an element of truth in Richer's view; but equally, it does no justice to the princes' side of the case. The traditional honours, property, dues, and judicial rights enjoyed by the Carolingian kings had been balanced by their obligation to defend the people and to enforce justice. If, as a consequence of civil war, external threat, and bad luck, the kings had foisted their task on the shoulders of others, these men were surely entitled to some reward. The history of titles suggests that the king clung to the notion that honours were in his gift and purely personal matters, while the princes, though paying occasional lip-service to this belief, were more inclined to see them as part of the traditional fabric of society, properly exploitable by those who bore the heat and burden of defending the common weal.

(b) Aristocratic resources

(i) Wealth

Around 930 Arnoul I of Flanders fell ill. In his weakness and misery, he sought healing from the great monastic reformer, Gerard of Brogne, whose ideals were to influence him for the rest of his life. When Gerard arrived, Arnoul, still fearing imminent death, drew up a document listing all his disposable wealth for distribution among churches, monasteries, and the poor and defenceless of his realm. The list consisted of gold, silver, splendid clothing, his horses, his beasts of burden, flocks, food, cereals, and cheeses.[12] It offers an insight into the function of riches as the great aristocrats saw them: to enhance prestige; to create charisma; to provide for an entensive entourage needing both food and transport; to permit lavish charitable expenditure. Arnoul was marked out from other men, not just in possessing more than they, but also in putting riches to conspicuous use. How he acquired his goods will concern us below; but of his gold and silver, there is perhaps a hint in a charter he drew up for the lavish endowment of St Peter's, Ghent,[13] in which he compared himself with Judas Maccabaeus rebuilding the temple in Jerusalem and decorating it with precious metal taken from the spoils of his enemies. Whether this implies that Arnoul simply recaptured Viking plunder-hoards or whether it means that his treasury was stocked with the possessions of his defeated neighbours, is unclear. But it is a safe assumption that he regarded fighting as a profitable activity.

The foundation of aristocracy was inevitably land. Remarkably little can be known about the extent of each prince's landed wealth in the early tenth century, because individual estates are usually only mentioned in charters at the point at which they passed into the hands of the church; what was not given away remains largely obscure. But by inference from a later period, the counts of Flanders and Rouen enjoyed huge stretches of their county as private possessions, the duke of Gascony not much less. Elsewhere princes had to share with a well-entrenched local aristocracy, some of whom if Gerald of Aurillac's testament offers a picture in any way typical,[14] could vie with them; and also with the church, which, though it might lack the means of protecting its estates, compensated by receiving regular death-bed donations from the penitent. Even so, the share of the dukes and counts dwarfed their neighbours'.

Then there were ways of increasing what was inherited. Of these, the most profitable was to obtain a grant from, or simply to take over, the lands of the fisc within the principality. Although by 888, the lands of the fisc had already dwindled very sharply, those that remained were probably rather better cultivated and exploited than other lands; in addition, they might include a royal palace or abbey of special prestige or venerable association. That they could be of great value to a prince is evident from the risks Baldwin II of Flanders was willing to run—including open conflict with Eudes and the murder of the archbishop of Rheims—to keep within his grasp the fiscal lands once granted by Charles the Bald to Raoul, count-abbot of Ternois, St Vaast and St Bertin. A decade of war was a small price to pay for the addition to his county of rich fields, along with two of the most famous royal abbeys in the realm. It is unusual for the historian to be able to trace an annexation of this kind. But the fact that Charles the Bald's two great Aquitanian palaces of Poitiers and Chasseneuil had passed into the hands of the count of Poitou, at least by the middle of the tenth century, is suggestive of a similar move. On occasion, as with Louis IV's grant of the last piece of fiscal land in the Mâconnais to the count of Mâcon in 950, royal initiative is clear. And it may be that in other cases where no document survives, a grant was in fact made. Some historians believe that the treaty of St Clair-sur-Epte in 911 (see p. 79) included a gift by Charles the Simple of the fiscal lands which later counts of Rouen are known to have controlled; but this is controversial. In general, a mixture of princely pressure, expediency, and the royal determination to set some limits operated on fiscal land in the same way as it did on princely titles.

Important though land was for patronage, for prestige, and for ordinary household needs, it may not have been as productive of wealth as the exercise of public authority within the county or counties directly controlled by the princes. There they could exploit the traditional public financial rights, the profits of which they were now free to keep exclusively for themselves. So they taxed goods being moved around their territories; commercial transactions;[15] specified goods; free men whose military service was not needed; the inhabitants of the county in time of danger. In addition the counts of Rouen joined the dukes of Francia, Aquitaine, and Burgundy in infringing the royal monopoly by minting coins inscribed with their own names; the count of Blois's coins were impressed with a human portrait, perhaps intended to be his own.[16] But the financial rewards of minting may well have been small, so that here prestige was as much in the princes' minds as profit. The overall value of public rights lay in their elasticity; competent princes could press them to the limits. Arnoul I's extortion of hospitality from St Vaast (p. 73) demonstrated that the exchange of a distant king for a present prince could impose a serious financial burden on a great royal abbey. And it is unlikely that St Vaast was alone in its sufferings.

All in all, the tenth century was one in which wealth, in each great principality and in each lesser unit of rule, tended to concentrate in a few hands at the top of the social scale. The only factors which worked against this concentration were the need to patronize the church, to maintain a household of great splendour, and to arrange a succession within each comital family which kept intact the accumulation of the previous holders. Some families coped very badly with these challenges; the viscounts of Limoges, for example, are thought to have allowed their lands to shrink to a seventh of their original size by the end of the century.[17] But the greatest aristocrats not only preserved, they also prospered.

(ii) Military resources

To win battles was clear proof of divine favour; to protect the weak and helpless from their enemies was the Christian duty from which political power derived. The contemporaries of St Odo of Cluny accepted without thinking the picture of the great aristocratic saint, Gerald of Aurillac, surrounded by his *milites*. They exalted Richard the Justiciar and Arnoul of Flanders in language taken from Maccabees. They received the Viking counts of Rouen into West Frankish society because their values caused no strain to the social fabric. Theirs was a martial world.

The chief task which faced the counts and princes, in a kingdom battered by raids and torn by internal dissension, was to reorientate the Carolingian armies, intended for aggressive campaigns, to the much more demanding task of facing mobile marauders who might strike at virtually any corner of the land. To do this, they exploited to the full long-established Carolingian military obligations under the *ban*, which permitted counts to call upon the rich to serve, the free men to provide taxes, and the unfree to labour, and to assist with cartage or provisioning. In the counties south of the Loire, the *ban* continued as the standard method of raising an army; in the more endangered north, it was exploited rather for its financial than for its military uses. Impressive though it was in theory, an army mustered under the *ban* was slow to assemble and its service limited—for some people and some places to as little as a fortnight's duration. The counts of Barcelona and Toulouse were able to employ it effectively, partly because the old administrative divisions on which the summons were based were still clear in the conservative south, partly because those who had received grants of land from the fisc recognized a clear-cut military obligation when the *ban* was called. Elsewhere, though the *ban* retained its usefulness in that it affected everyone, it had to be supplemented by newer obligations which would impose longer service on a more professional small minority.

In one sense this was no innovation. The system of vassalage had always been used to support the army of the *ban*. Royal vassals, scattered all over Charlemagne's empire, had held benefices of the king in return for personal military service when summoned. Though *vassi dominici* largely lost their distinct status in the second half of the ninth century, some survived, as the Life of St Gerald of Aurillac bears witness.[18] And counts too had had their vassals in Carolingian times. But the crisis years of the wars and raids led officials to increase their followings, to rely more on their entourages. At the same time, they began to recruit men of lesser social status, ordinary free men or even, in Flanders and Champagne, men of serf status, as heavy mounted warriors for the regular defence of the fortified places springing up across the land. In this, they copied the great bishops and abbots of the immunities, who, in order to fulfil their military service to the king, had early recruited a class of men later referred to as *milites casati*, paid by stipend, always available for military duty.[19] As was argued above (p. 43), the link between castles and troops of semi-professional mounted warriors was crucial in the evolution of what Marc Bloch called feudal society. The new group of lesser knights, like those who surrounded Ebbon de Chateau-Larcher in 969, might already own or be given small allods; alternatively, they might be recipients of a money fief or a simple stipend.

The appearance of castles changed military strategy, in that small but effective defence forces now concentrated their activities within a confined radius. But while these arrangements were excellent for defence, they did not contribute easily to the mustering of larger armies for operation outside the locality of the castle. Here, competent princes supplemented the *ban* and the military service of their officials and vassals with troops provided by allies, and even with mercenaries. Often it is not possible to discover in what capacity some part of an army fought. The Auvergnat troops who aided Duke William III of Aquitaine against Hugh the Great's invasion of Poitou may have come because obliged under the *ban*, or as vassals or allies or merenaries.[20] It is probable that they would have considered the nature of their service an unreal question. Given a successful commander and something worth defending, fighting was a natural occupation. It hardly required the ground in obligation which historians have been at much pains to reconstruct.

(iii) Justice

To scourge the wicked, to settle disputes, to bring about peace were the agreed objectives of all medieval rulers, from which the great aristocrats of the tenth century in no way dissented. Yet it appears that in the course of the century, the means available to them for realizing their ends slowly slid from their grasp, except in the far south of the kingdom. The contrast between their ability to profit from new financial and military circumstances, and their failure to adapt on the judicial plane, perhaps accounts, more than any other single factor, for the later history of the relation between the French king and his great feudatories. It is therefore worth attempting an explanation in an area in which the surviving evidence hardly justifies conclusions.

Charlemagne's intention had been that the county *mallus* should be held at regular intervals in the chief town of the county, that the count should decide cases according to the advice of professional *scabini*, that the decisions should be recorded by notaries, and that the competence of the court should be unlimited. Whether all these conditions ever obtained outside Catalonia and the far south, where surviving Roman and Visigothic law prepared the ground for them, is a matter of dispute. But whereas in 908 Viscount Thibaud held a plea at the comital tribunal in the same place in the city of Tours that had been used by imperial and royal officials since the first century,[21] eighty years later the count of Blois, like all his neighbours, held pleas as he moved around his estates: his courts did not meet at fixed times, and the membership was fluid. Equally notaries were unheard-of except in the deep south, and *scabini* died out everywhere except in Flanders (probably in part at least a revival), Catalonia, and the Narbonne area (in which they were last mentioned in 955). By 1000, and possibly as early as 900, the count's court had become a place in which the cases of the most important men were decided, rather than the most important cases of all men. And there were signs that resort to it was becoming voluntary.

That contemporaries were aware of the degree to which legal institutions were changing is evidenced by the declining use of the word *mallus* in West Francia. Though it survived throughout the century in Flanders, Picardy, Catalonia, and the Mâconnais, and appeared (or reappeared) in Normandy by the end of the century, it only lasted in Aquitaine and Angoulême till about the middle of the century; elsewhere tenth-century evidence of the *mallus* is lacking. And even when it is found, it may in any case point rather to verbal conservatism in those who drew up charters than to unchanging institutions.

The obstacles to effective operation of the Carolingian system in the tenth century were manifold. Notaries and *scabini* were likely to be in short supply during a period of turmoil; transport to the chief town was expensive and journeys might be disrupted. On a less pragmatic level, the methods of proof enjoined by Charlemagne—the use of inquest, the dependence on documents—never really accorded with Frankish and much northern practice. If the system did operate north of the Loire in the first half of the ninth century—and this is not certain—it was largely because there was confidence in the authority which commanded it.

Whereas under Charlemagne it was possible to entrust the count with near-absolute judicial authority in his county, because the *missi* from the royal court checked up on him from time to time, and because royal ordinances laid down norms of justice to be respected, as central control weakened the absence of redress against comital judicial sentences began to irk. Men who had almost as much land as the count, who had old claims to office, increasingly made their own views heard; in order to preserve his jurisdiction, the count was forced to take note. In 944, for example, the notice drawn up by Hugh the Black of Burgundy, recounting a judgement in favour of the monks of Cluny, who had disputed a piece of land with the viscount of Lyons, ends 'This notice is confirmed [in the name of the count and] of his *fideles* who have heard the case of the monks'.[22] Clearly Hugh's court was in the process of changing from an old-style public court to one in which decisions were the shared responsibility of the duke and his great magnates. At different stages in the tenth and early eleventh centuries, this change affected all West Frankish comital courts.

The consultation of *fideles* rather than *scabini* meant the abandonment of any attempt to hear cases according to the very complex system of racial, personal, and customary law. With punishable offences, courts faced the problems of trying to decide what method of proof would be acceptable, and on whom the burden of proof should be imposed. Often these decisions could not be arrived at, through differences of opinion; and if they could be, they were very hard to enforce. So though a crime which deeply outraged public sentiment might still on occasion meet with punishment, even if its perpetrator were an aristocrat—the count of Mâcon punished one of his viscounts as late as the early eleventh century—most aristocratic crime came to be treated as an incident in a dispute between two parties. The aim of the court was to reconcile, to make peace, in the way in which Hugh the Great made peace between Louis IV and Arnoul of Flanders after the murder of William Longsword in 942. In ordinary disputes, not involving crime, the aim was to arrive at a permanent settlement which would satisfy both parties for the long term. The consequence was that arbitration took over from justice. In a case held before Geoffrey Grisegonelle of Anjou, an abbey proved its title to a disputed plot of land, but agreed to pay the defendant in the suit a sum of money to propitiate him.[23] Agreements of this kind were drawn up in documents called *concordiae*, intended to have perpetual effect.

So the end-result of changes in procedure at the counts' courts was to make his judgement little more than a reflection of consensus among his own *fideles*, and to deprive him of the capacity to enforce unpopular measures. The decline of comital justice exactly mirrored that of royal justice. Indeed, if anything, the impotence of comital justice was more apparent, because the count had more competitors in his judicial sphere than the king. Throughout his county, viscounts and *vicarii* were continuing with their traditional role in hearing the cases of ordinary free men, by imposing their own legal solutions on their inferiors with considerably greater decisiveness than counts dared to show among their aristocrats; and everywhere large landowners were enforcing their justice on their *familia*—their household and unfree serfs—with a brutality which rarely provoked criticism. Gerald of Aurillac, indeed, was berated by his *fideles* for coddling his peasants; yet, from the peasants' point of view, he can hardly have been an ideal landlord, since many of them tried to escape from his lordship.[24]

The Life of Gerald of Aurillac is instructive at another level of judicial enquiry: in addition to disciplining his serfs and hearing disputes between his vassals and their own clients, Gerald also exercised the kind of justice that ought to have fallen beneath the *ban*; for it is recounted that he heard cases which could have been punished by death or mutilation.[25] Here he was acting like a count; yet he was apparently not an official at all. His private jurisdiction may be explained in three possible ways: that it was normal for *vassi dominici* to enjoy a royal privilege of this kind—but there is no evidence for this; that special privileges were granted by the Carolingian conquerors of the south to noble families to win their loyalty; or that many tenth-century lay lords already exercised rights at the expense of comital jurisdiction, well before the phenomenon is usually recognized to have occurred.

The third hypothesis gains force from a charter of King Eudes, exempting from comital jurisdiction a family in the Spanish March, and from a case in Flanders, where an aristocratic lady, making a grant of Froidmont to St Amand in the middle of the tenth century, included in it 'the whole power of discipline according to legal process which once belonged to royal majesty'.[26] If, in addition to sharing judicial competence with his officials and with the great churchmen who enjoyed immunities, the count already shared it with at least some other great lay aristocrats, there was not much left of the jurisdictional integrity of the county, even in parts of West Francia like Flanders, Catalonia, and southern Aquitaine, where it is normally reckoned to have survived well.

Granted the decline of public law and the fragmentation of the count's jurisdictional role, it was hardly surprising that the most effective way of combating crime and disorder seemed to tenth-century men to be by ecclesiastical sanction, by excommunication. Clearly this did not always work, because St Odo of Cluny, in defending Gerald's punitive role, declared that it was justifiable for laymen to bear the sword to constrain by act of war those who could not be forced to submit to the church's censure.[27] Even the church therefore licensed private war in some circumstances; laymen burning with indignation at their unavenged wrongs were naturally less than scrupulous in availing themselves of this resort.

(c) Duchies and counties

The order in which the duchies and counties are discussed in the following pages is dictated by a desire to assist the reader in moving from the more- to the less- clear-cut forms of lordship.

(i) Aquitaine

887 had seen the end of the Carolingian sub-kingdom of Aquitaine; in spite of continued royal ambition in the area, it had no future after Louis the Stammerer's accession to the French throne. Yet the strong sense that Aquitaine was different from the lands north of the Loire lingered on, to be exploited in turn by three different aristocratic houses.

Eudes's coronation in 888 saw William the Pious, son of Bernard Plantevelue, securely in charge of an enormous inheritance in the south. Through his mother, he was count of Auvergne; from his father he obtained overlordship over Berry, the Mâconnais, the Lyonnais, the March of Gothia, and the Limousin; and although he was forced to cede his father's county of Toulouse to Eudes, son of Bernard of Toulouse, he maintained some form of superiority there. His position was bolstered by his close friendship with Ranulf II, count of Poitou, described by the Annals of St Vaast as *dux maximae partis Aquitaniae*.[28] Between them they controlled virtually all of the country south of the Loire, with the exception of Gascony and Catalonia. It was unfortunate for King Eudes that, out of deep respect for the Carolingians to whom they were related, neither William nor Ranulf was inclined to support the new ruler. In fact, a successful royal campaign in the south forced William to yield in 889 and, despite some tension, he remained loyal to Eudes even after Fulk of Rheims had crowned Charles the Simple in 893. On Ranulf's death, Eudes succeeded in nominating one of his own men to Poitou (though by 902 Ranulf's illegitimate son had returned to power). The iron fist of the first Capetian meant that William greeted with profound relief Charles the Simple's uncontested accession in 898.

William's power was solidly based in the Auvergne. Elsewhere, it depended on his skill in managing counts, viscounts, and other lords. Since he was a close friend of Èble of Déols, Èble's successful intrusion in Berry enlarged William's hegemony. Though Gerald of Aurillac refused to pay homage to him,[29] perhaps because he thought it unfitting in one of his Roman ancestry, the two men remained on excellent terms. On such links were principalities built. By 909 William had brought so many lords into his *mouvance* (the useful French word for denoting networks of *fideles*) that he referred to himself as 'count, marquis, and duke' in a charter that survived in the Brioude cartulary.[30] St Odo of Cluny and Ademar of Chabannes both stressed his two great advantages in dealing with the men of his time: his very noble birth and his piety. His foundation of Cluny in 910 redounded to his glory—his monks kept his fame alive. Even in his own lifetime, he was revered as a man of outstanding holiness. In one respect, he was too holy for his principality's good: he embraced the life of celibacy and left no heir.

William's highly personal federation was bound to be difficult to hold together. His successor, his nephew William II, kept the ducal title and gave it new concreteness by minting coins inscribed with his own name at the mint of Brioude —the first 'feudal' coins of West Francia.[31] This one great gesture of independence, however, belied the rest of William's career. He lost the March of Gothia to Raymond III Pons of Toulouse, the Lyonnais to Hugh of Arles, the Mâconnais to Richard the Justiciar or Hugh the Black of Burgundy, and faced a revolt in Berry which put an end to his lordship there. William's refusal to recognize King Raoul may have accounted for some at least of his losses. In any case, he presided over the disintegration of his uncle's duchy. The last of his line, his son Acfred, who ruled from 926 to 927, was left only with the Auvergne and a form of superiority over the Limousin, which soon passed to other hands.

927 marked the end of the attempt to consolidate the duchy around the Auvergne. The ducal title went to Toulouse, where Raymond Pons briefly bore it. But the political advantage brought about by the collapse of William the Pious's dynasty was mainly reaped by the counts of Poitou. In many ways, Poitou was a better centre for political power than the Auvergne, which had always been cut off by the Massif Central. Although the area around Poitiers had suffered badly from Viking attacks, after 930 recovery was on the way; it was expanding again as the fields around it returned to their former fertility, and within the county the silver-mines of Melles were still producing. The count was well placed to take advantage of Louis IV's accession, because he was of Carolingian descent; nevertheless William III drove a hard bargain for his support in 942. In addition he benefited by an alliance with the new Norman rulers— Èble Manzer, count from 902 to 932, had married William to the daughter of Rollo, first count of Rouen—so he had friends in the north who might be expected to help contain future Viking attack.

The first task Èble, William III Tête d'Étoupe (932-63)

and William IV Fier-à-bras (963–95) faced was that of bringing the neighbouring counts and viscounts into their *mouvance*, into a recognition of their overlordship, however
loosely this might be understood. The counts of Angoulême
and Périgueux, the count of La Marche—who was in the
process of creating his county in the middle of the tenth
century—the viscounts of Limoges, and the newly-established
viscounts of Turenne in the south and Thouars in the north,
all came to the court at Poitiers from time to time, and
expressed their deference by taking fidelity. In the case of
the count of Angoulême, a man of very noble status and
long-entrenched position, the relationship was purely one of
friendship; with the others, there was perhaps an element
of condescension on the count of Poitou's part. But it is
unlikely that he acquired much in the way of financial gain
from any of them: even the viscounts already had established territorial rights in their own areas, and would have
endeavoured to keep their public dues for themselves. In the
circumstances, his overlordship was based on alliance more
than obligation; yet the alliance grew, over the years, into
something solid.

Perhaps the extent of the external opposition they faced
explained the acquiescence in the count of Poitou's leadership within Aquitaine. There were firstly the attacks of
Raymond III Pons of Toulouse, anxious to obtain mastery
over the county; his death, probably around 950, brought
an end to the threat, along with a chance of Poitevin domination in the Auvergne and Velay, and finally the opportunity
to take the ducal title, as William IV did in 965. Then there
were the ambitions of Hugh the Great in Aquitaine, which
received the backing of Louis d'Outremer. Neither Louis's
brief appearance south of the Loire, nor Hugh the Great's
campaign of 955, during which he beseiged Poitiers, did the
counts of Poitou much harm. Indeed they may simply have
rallied local support; for men from the Auvergne are known
to have helped in the relief of the siege of Poitiers. Lothaire's
later attempt to re-establish Aquitaine as a sub-kingdom for
his son was equally fruitless; it simply provided the count
with an excuse for abandoning the Carolingian cause in 987,
in contrast with his predecessors' behaviour in 888 and

923-7. Of far greater long-term importance was the Angevin pressure on the north of the county, which began in the 960s and 970s. But at least according to Ademar, this was easily contained in its early stages; he records that William IV defeated Count Geoffrey Grisegonelle of Anjou, and made him take homage for the honour of Loudun, which he had annexed.[32] (In fact this may have been a compromise rather than a victory.)

Within Poitou the counts were wealthy. The lands of the fisc appear to have passed into their hands early; they used the royal palaces at Poitiers and Chasseneuil and held the royal monasteries in their *garde.* They also preserved most comital rights, including control of the coinage. Furthermore, their position as lay abbots of St Hilaire in Poitiers (see p. 118) gave them influence within the church, which was strengthened during the time that William III's brother was bishop of Limoges. Again, indications that the peasants owed labour service for the erection of fortifications directly to the counts, and that Poitevin castles were built at the centre of each vicariate, are suggestive of unusually forceful comital supervision in the early stages of castle-building within the county. These assets, in conjunction with the regular oaths of fidelity received from their officials, conferred formidable local power on William III and William IV. Only in the sphere of justice did their authority decline, as the *mallus* slowly changed into a court of arbitration for the great men of the area. With this one exception, they proved highly effective preservers of the Carolingian tradition of government, in circumstances that were not particularly favourable to their enterprise; for the *Life* of St Gerald of Aurillac bears witness to the weakness of officials and the fluidity of structures and titles in Southern Poitou and the Limousin in the early tenth century.[33] Given this background, the achievements of Èble, William III, and William IV were more than simple conservation; they involved at least some degree of reconstruction.

When trouble struck, the counts were able to handle it. So William IV defeated an attack by the count of Périgueux and held down the rebellious viscount of Limoges. But in general the mid tenth century was a peaceful breathing-space in Aquitaine. When William IV assumed the title 'duke of the Aquitanians' in 965, he was merely doing justice to his own, his father's, and his grandfather's striking successes south of the Loire. Hugh Capet's reluctant acquiescence in the family's self-promotion in 988 was proof that even outsiders could not deny them their pre-eminence.[34]

(ii) Burgundy

Though most of ancient Burgundy had been assigned to Lothaire by the Treaty of Verdun, five cities, eight incomplete dioceses, and twenty-two *pagi* stretching along the west of the country had fallen to the share of Charles the Bald. This somewhat arbitrary division—churches and families held lands on both sides of the new border—proved surprisingly durable; hence the medieval kingdom of Burgundy, established by Boso of Vienne's coronation in 878, and located within Lothaire's original share of the empire (containing within it the county of Burgundy, the later Franche-Comté) must always be distinguished from West Frankish Burgundy, the cradle of the Burgundian duchy, and our concern here.

After the revolt of Humphrey of Gothia in 863, Charles the Bald determined that the count of Autun should be appointed a permanent royal *missus*, with powers of supervision over all the counts of West Frankish Burgundy. It is not known just how Boso of Vienne's brother Richard the Justiciar became count of Autun in 880; but after his initial promotion or self-promotion, he was exemplary in his loyalty to the Carolingian kings. So it was with their permission that he exploited the authority now inherent in his position and extended his rights until he appeared to his contemporaries as the near-equal of the king himself. By Eudes's accession in 888 Richard was well entrenched as one of the leading princes of West Francia, and within Burgundy itself he had attracted the respect and affection to which his later title 'duke of the Burgundians' attested.

Richard's power depended on three factors, all short-term: firstly on his personal distinction, above all as a warrior. He defeated the Viking raiders who penetrated into Burgundy in 895, and the Magyars who did likewise in 911; but these were small affairs in comparison with the glory he gained by his participation in the great victory over the Vikings at Chartres in 905. Burgundians had reason to see in him their sole protector. Secondly, there were his personal relations; through his wife, he inherited claims in Auxerre that he was able to make good; and through his personal friendship with Manasses, count of Chalon—he and his brother the viscount of Auxerre were described as the chief men at Richard's court[35]—he could extend his sway into areas of Burgundy where he had no rights. And thirdly, he could capitalize on King Eudes's fear of driving him into vigorous support of Charles the Simple: this prevented royal interference in Burgundy in the early years of his rise to power; for Richard's use of force, particularly against the archbishop of Sens, and the bishop of Langres (whose eyes he allowed Manasses to tear out), would have met with royal resistance at any other period than 894–5. As it was, he gained control of all the bishoprics within Burgundy, to the extent that he could secure the election of his own nominees. Given these three assets, Richard was able to extend his domination to the north, where Troyes and Meaux came into his orbit, to the east over Besançon, and to the south over Mâcon. By 916, he was being referred to within his lands as duke; in 918 he so described himself. The chronicle of Bèze declared he owed his sobriquet 'the Justiciar' to the excellence of his justice;[36] Flodoard testified to the splendour of his dress and bearing;[37] and the *Annals of Dijon* recorded his death as if he were the equal of kings.[38]

Richard's Burgundy proved ephemeral, like William the Pious's Aquitaine: both depended excessively on personal factors. The death of Manasses in 918, three years before Richard's own death, heralded its break-up. Shortly after Richard's son Raoul inherited, he abandoned Charles the Simple in 921 to fight with his father-in-law Robert against the Lotharingian favourites. Robert's death only a year after his coronation put the anti-Carolingian party in a difficult position, from which they could only extricate themselves by electing Raoul as their king. From 923 until his death in 936, Raoul kept his father's lands in Autun, Avallon, and Lassois along with his royal position. Virtually nothing is known of the rest of Burgundy, left in the hands of his brother Hugh the Black. On Raoul's death in 936, Hugh was unwilling to recognize as king the young Louis IV, who suspected him of aspiring to the throne himself. So Louis and his champion Hugh the Great campaigned in Burgundy, inflicting heavy losses on Hugh. Flodoard says that the duchy was divided between the two Hughs;[39] in fact Hugh the Great's acquisitions were mainly confined to the area around Auxerre and Sens.

Much of Richard's duchy, then, survived—though divided—until Hugh's death without male heirs in 952. His successor, in Autun at least, was his son-in-law Gilbert, son of Manasses; but his position was weaker than Hugh's in that he recognized the lordship of Hugh the Great. So on Gilbert's death in 956, Hugh swiftly proclaimed himself guardian of Gilbert's orphan daughters, and married the elder to his second son Otto, thus paving the way for the Capetian duchy of Burgundy. There are, however, signs that this move was not entirely popular within Burgundy; and Hugh's own death in the same year, with a consequent four-year minority for Otto, permitted the dissatisfied to make other arrangements. Meaux and Troyes passed into the hands of a son of Herbert of Vermandois; King Lothaire nominated a man of his own choice to Chalon; the bishopric of Langres regained independence; and the count of Mâcon lost all ties with Burgundy. So when Otto, the first Capetian duke, began his rule in 960, his control was confined to Autun, Avallon, part of Nevers and of Auxerre, and lands within Beaune. All that was left of Richard's lands was the central core.

But the rump of Burgundy, the new, shrunken duchy, was a good power-base. For the land was rich and sheltered from attack; and the dukes appear to have annexed much of the royal fisc—certainly the king had none in the area after the reign of Louis IV. Fortified by the memory of past greatness and by the title *dux Burgundionum* bestowed on him in 960 by Lothaire, Otto maintained his control over all the fortifications within his principality, in addition to his right to tolls and hospitality. It is likely that he also received the homage of the counts of Chalon, Tonnerre, and Nevers, even if this homage meant less and less as time went on.

Otto's successor, Duke Henry, who ruled from 965 to 1002, though in every way a less significant man than Richard the Justiciar, was still a prince of standing within West Francia; and his position was more firmly rooted in the soil of his duchy than that of his eminent predecessor had been.[40]

(iii) Neustria

Like Burgundy and Aquitaine, Neustria was both a geographical expression for the territory between the Loire and the Seine, and a reminder of past history in that it had been the centre of a Frankish kingdom since the sixth century. Despite its absorption, by the middle of the tenth century, of territory to the north of the Seine, it was still smaller than either Aquitaine or Burgundy; but arguably it had greater homogeneity than theirs. Its ruler, described at different times as duke of Maine, count of the Breton March, count of Paris, duke of the Franks, and even on occasion king, was always one of the most powerful men in the kingdom.

In the mid ninth century, the formative factor in the history of Neustria had been the threat from Brittany, the Celtic principality whose rulers showed formidable ability in exploiting the weakness of their Frankish neighbours. Charles the Bald had created a lordship based on Maine and Angers to cope with Breton aggression, which he put into the hands first of Robert the Strong, and then of Hugh the Abbot as two of his most trusted lieutenants. Robert's son Eudes inherited the lordship, along with Hugh the Abbot's other Frankish lands; and in defence of these he earned the reputation as a warrior that carried him to the throne in 888.

But towards the end of the ninth century, the military function of Neustria changed: it became a bulwark against Viking aggression and, after 911, a means of containing Normandy's new rulers.[41] Eudes's brother Robert attempted to bring the Normans under his overlordship in 921; when this failed he established a network of semi-independent seigneuries, the most notable of which was Bellême, to act as buffers. In conjunction with the natural decline in Norman aggression, these buffers worked, at least in the short term.

But towards the end of the century, they drifted under Norman influence.

The need to concentrate on Normandy led to a loosening of the reins in the southern part of Neustria. Robert was forced to nominate viscounts for Angers, Tours, and Blois, to perform his functions in his place while he was fighting. His son Hugh the Great, rather less menaced by Normans, nevertheless had to fight for his inheritance against Raoul in the early years of his majority, and then engaged in a complicated three-way struggle with the king—now Louis d'Outremer—and Herbert of Vermandois, to extend his authority north of the Seine. At the same time, he had real interests in Burgundy and nominal ones in Aquitaine. Hardly surprisingly, he had no time to limit the growing power of his viscounts in the south of the duchy. It was in this period that Blois was brought together with Tours to create one of the great new houses of France; while at the same time Angers turned imperceptibly into the new county of Anjou. Hugh the Great's death in 956 considerably accelerated the independence of these house. During the four years' minority of his son, Hugh Capet, Blois acquired Chartres and Châteaudun, then began to push into Brittany, by forced alliance with the count of Rennes; while, at the same time, Anjou penetrated into the Massif Central, in an interesting, though ephemeral, attempt to build up a power block in the south.[42] By 960, when Hugh Capet took control, he was faced with what were virtually two new principalities on his territory, whose rulers could only be controlled by demanding homage and service. His direct lordship was restricted to the Paris basin, an area of land stretching south to Orléans, and an increasingly important bundle of lands north of the Seine. The outlines of Neustria were therefore fading fast.

Still, as was the case with the duke of Aquitaine's Poitou and the duke of Burgundy's Autun, in Paris the duke of the Franks had a strong centre. It is true that Viking raids and political instability had wiped out much of the old Carolingian administrative network. Viscounties had become territorialized, vicariates had disappeared. And whereas in Poitou it was possible to revive the old, in the Paris area new divisions and new entities had already emerged. In a way, though, that strengthened the duke's hand; because castellans sought his endorsement of their new positions, he had a creative role to play in the process of reorganization. And as Viking attacks dwindled away, so his power-base returned to its natural fertility, its excellent river communications became again a source of pride, its large forests offered ample space for further extension of arable cultivation. The two Hughs could call on sizeable resources to defend their interests.

The title 'duke of the Franks' was conferred on Hugh the Great in 943 (or 937) by the young Louis d'Outremer, in gratitude for Hugh's assistance in his elevation to the throne.[43] Hugh kept it for the whole of his life, and was able to pass it on to his eldest con, despite a four-year minority. As has already been said, contemporaries entertained differing views of the title's significance (see p. 47). But it may have assisted Capetian lordship within Neustria, by linking its holder with the great heroes of the Frankish past. (Kienast's contention that it did cannot be refuted simply either by stressing the ephemerality of the title or by arguing that there was no historical justification for ethnic consciousnes of this kind; for in the world of the imagination, myth is as potent as history.)[44]

Despite the title, the close relationship between the king and the duke of the Franks proved not to be in the duke's best interests; for Hugh the Great's and Hugh Capet's involvement in the affairs of the kingdom took them away from their own lands very frequently. And their court suffered by their proximity to the king—for why have a charter confirmed by a duke if the king were as easily accessible? Besides, when their territorial claims clashed with those of Louis or Lothaire, there was a danger of divided loyalties among their vassals. In this respect, then, Hugh Capet's coronation in 987 brought a measure of relief to the area.

(iv) Flanders

The early history of the county of Flanders was unpropitious. Nature was illiberal to this land between the Scheldt and the Canche, except for navigable and interconnecting rivers, and a seashore which, in the ninth century, was still receding.

The land itself was marshy, rather salty, and heather-clad along the shore; while inland the Carbonnière Forest still sprawled across miles of the countryside, limiting population growth even in the more fertile south. Once the Viking raids had begun, Flanders' position laid it open to looting and plundering, and turned its river network into a source of real danger for its inhabitants. Then the county's remoteness from the centres of power accounted for the unresponsiveness of West Frankish kings to its plight. Yet this very unresponsiveness goaded a small local aristocracy into displaying the determination, aggression, and sheer dogged courage needed to transform Flanders into the richest and the most successful of the principalities of West Francia. The story of their achievement is the stuff of a blood-and-thunder epic.

It was against a background of poverty and the misery induced by endless Viking depredations that Baldwin I 'Iron Arm' made a dramatic bid for publicity in 863. Exactly who he was is still open to question. But his character was plain for all to see: he was an opportunist of the first water. Hearing that Charles the Bald's daughter Judith, widow of two West Saxon kings, was being kept at Senlis, he dashed across, abducted her from her guards, and married her. Charles, who had been contemplating an advantageous match for Judith, was furious; he informed the pope and demanded Baldwin's excommunication. But the brazenness that had inspired Baldwin did not desert him now. He bore his wife swiftly to Rome, to intercede in person with Nicholas I. The dash and verve with which the manœuvre was executed excited admiration, however reluctant. The pope rescinded the excommunication, and the king accepted the situation. Then, not wishing his daughter to be demeaned, Charles made her husband count of Ghent, to which after 866 he added the counties of the Ternois and Flanders. Dramatic though these successes were, they might well have proved ephemeral, had it not been that the character of his great-great-grandfather Charlemagne showed itself in Judith's and Baldwin's son Baldwin II, the true founder of the Flemish principality.

The death of Baldwin I in 879 coincided with four years of non-stop aggression by the Vikings; Thérouanne and St Bertin were burnt in 879, Tournai was sacked in 880. Then the invaders seized Ghent, fortified it, and made it their base, devastating the whole country between the Scheldt and the Somme; Arras, Cambrai, and Amiens all went up in flames. Although the great victory of Louis III at Saucourt in August 881 brought some respite, his successor Carloman believed himself faced with an impossible task in the north. So, in order to defend the rich plains of southern Artois, he abandoned Flanders. Here lay Baldwin II's opportunity. By a mixture of conquest, negotiation and moving in on territory which other lords had deserted, he brought under his domination all the land from the Scheldt to the coast, and controlled all comital powers within the territory later to be known as Flanders. The circumstances of his seizure explain the lasting quality of his success; for there was abandoned land in abundance to enrich him or to give to those prepared to fight on his side; men joined his army because it was worth their while to do so. Besides, he had an innate sense of strategy and the ability to get things done. He repaired the Roman walls of Oudenburg and Aardenburg, and the Merovingian walls of Bruges: he built new forts; he defended the vulnerable river banks. Admittedly these fortifications were of an elementary sort and tiny compared with the burghs Alfred the Great was erecting in England; nevertheless they served their purpose. Flanders was no longer the easiest place for the Vikings to plunder.

Despite his huge success, Baldwin's ambitions were unquenchable. To the south of his territory lay Boulonnais, the Ternois, and Artois, rich, fertile lands that had been commended by Carloman in 883 to Raoul, count of the Ternois and abbot of St Vaast and St Bertin. In 892 Raoul's death offered Baldwin the prospect of further expansion. Here, however, he ran into tough resistance from King Eudes, which came close to crushing him, and from which he was only saved by Fulk of Rheims's proclamation of Charles the Simple in 893. Clever though unscrupulous exploitation of Eudes's and Charles the Simple's difficulties eventually brought the Ternois and Boulonnais, along with the abbey of St Bertin, into Baldwin's hands. He had not obtained all he wanted, but he had acquired lands that dwarfed his father's possessions.

By Baldwin II's death in 918, Flanders was a solid block running down the West coast. His son Arnoul I (918-65) pressed on into Artois, Ponthieu, Amiens, and Ostrevant, aided by the quarrels between Charles the Simple and Robert and Raoul, and later by those of Louis d'Outremer and the count of Vermandois. In each case Arnoul's contribution was to weaken the crown. But while pursuing his Picard expansion, he had also to secure his seafront from an aggression similar to his own, because the new Norman duchy's interests in securing the Canche as a frontier led William Longsword to attack the fortress of Montreuil. In reply, Arnoul launched a counter-attack, backed up, in 942, by the assassination of William. In a violent age, Arnoul was an unusually violent man.

So the rise of Flanders was the product of military strength. Thus far, the only complement to naked force had been brilliant marriages—if Baldwin I's had laid the family's fortune, Baldwin II's to a daughter of Alfred the Great had created an anti-Viking alliance. Arnoul I, however, came to appreciate that his position could no longer be upheld solely by these means, now that the Viking danger had receded. So, combining originality and audacity, he established a model for princely authority based on Charlemagne himself. Without denying his theoretical obedience to the West Frankish king, and without allowing any whisper of claimed innovation, he started to behave in his territory in an imperial fashion. He began by reconstructing the Flemish church, relying particularly on the old monasteries of the area. With the partnership between Louis the Pious and Benedict of Aniane in mind, he invited the distinguished monastic reformer Gerard of Brogne to restore St Peter's, Ghent, as a strict Benedictine foundation. To shed lustre on the reformed church, Arnoul obtained for it the relics of St Wandrille. Then Gerard was given authority to reform all the other monasteries within the domain, under Arnoul's special protection. So secular and ecclesiastical power were harmonized, along lines similar to those being pursued in East Francia by Otto I; soon the Flemish example was to bear fruit in England.

In 944 Arnoul and Gerard restored St Bertin, the famous

abbey in St Omer which had made a rich contribution to the Carolingian renaissance, and where the Frankish Royal Annals had for a time been kept up. It was here that the first genealogy of the counts of Flanders was produced between 952 and 955 by the monk Witger. His work offers a precious glimpse of how Arnoul wished to be remembered. It began by citing the generations of the Frankish kings down to Charles the Bald; then came Judith and her marriage to Baldwin I; then a list of their descendants, including Arnoul's son Baldwin III. So the counts of Flanders, placed in Carolingian, royal context, were presented as the heirs of Charlemagne. When Witger came to Arnoul himself, he added an idealized portrait of his character, in the hagiographical tradition:

The lord Arnoul, the most venerable count, fervent lover of the Lord Jesus Christ, outstanding in prudence, powerful in counsel, shining forth in all goodness, the most perfect restorer of God's churches, the most pious consolation of widows, orphans, and wards, a most merciful giver to all those who seek his help in their necessity.[45]

There followed a list of his benefactions to churches, and then an invocation to all those who read or heard to pray, both for Arnoul and for Baldwin. The point of the genealogy, then, was primarily liturgical. It was written to bring men to their knees in prayer for their prince, to establish him in their hearts as an object for reverence, and to bring on him God's mercy. Thus Arnoul I made a clear bid to transform his image from that of a warrior to a defender of the church. It was an imaginative move, particularly on the part of one whose ruthlessness and violence were bywords. And if the monastic chroniclers in their enthusiasm overplayed his success, he nevertheless founded a tradition which Baldwin IV and Baldwin V were later glad to perpetuate.

There are other signs that Arnoul's revival of Carolingian forms was on a broader front that has thus far been suggested. The church of St Donatian at Bruges, built either by Baldwin II or Arnoul, had a chapel modelled on Charlemagne's royal chapel at Aachen; it was probably copied from Charles the Bald's imitation of Compiègne, with which the counts of Flanders were almost certainly familiar.[46] This deliberate imitation of Charlemagne may lend credibility to Pirenne's belief (not accepted by most scholars) that Arnoul also instituted a council for his principality, and that he possessed a seal (though the one Pirenne attributed to him is now known to be a forgery).[47] It is moreover certain that Arnoul insisted on receiving lavish hospitality at St Vaast, after his final seizure of Arras in 932. The *Liber de Possessionibus Sancti Vedasti* of the monk Guimann records the intolerable burden imposed on the house when the Carolingian kings, distant figures rarely in Arras, gave way to the count of Flanders, who was regularly on its doorstep.[48] And no doubt Arnoul chose to revive for his own benefit other half-forgotten regalian rights; for in financial matters his model was plainly imperial.

The one weak point in Armoul's impressive plan of action proved to be the succession. In 962 his heir, Baldwin III, died leaving only an infant son. Arnoul's solution was to confer the first fief within Flemish territory, the county of Boulogne, on his nephew, to appoint his kinsman Baldwin Balso regent, and to buy the support and goodwill of King Lothaire by surrendering Montreuil and some of his Picard conquests, including St Amand.[49] On Arnoul's death in 965, Lothaire annexed Ponthieu and granted it to Hugh Capet; but otherwise, he respected Arnoul II's inheritance. Nevertheless the regency government was weak in comparison with that of Arnoul, and Balso's death in 973 weakened it further. The county began to fragment at the edges, as the advocate of St Bertin assumed the title 'count of Guînes', and other lesser lords grew restless.

However, when Arnoul II attained his majority in 976, the situation was far from desperate. If the boundaries of the county were somewhat fluid, the enormous northern comital domain had survived intact; so the count continued to derive a very substantial income from his great flocks of sheep in the northern plains. Arnoul II sensibly accepted his changes that had taken place, confirmed the counts of Boulogne and Guînes in their titles, but insisted that their fiefs were held conditionally on the performance of service and homage to the count of Flanders. In the same way, he recognized as advocates those lords who had begun to play this role for the big monastic houses of the south during the uncertain years of his minority; but he maintained some lordship over all the monasteries within his territory, which gave him the right to control the advocates, and probably also to extract some revenues. So the nature of princely power changed a little; but most of the substance was preserved intact.

The second minority on Arnoul II's death in 988 was rather more serious as a threat to the integrity of the Flemish principality. It saw further Capetian intrusion and a notable restless assertiveness among lords, particularly custodians of comital castles, who began to claim hereditary right in their office, to exercise authority more in their own name than in the count's, and to enforce their own discipline on the men subject to them. But though Baldwin IV and his mother had to struggle hard to obtain his inheritance, it was a winning struggle. The structure built by Baldwin II and Arnoul I was proof even against two minorities.[50]

(v) Catalonia

If the marshes of Flanders were, at first sight, an improbable base for a successful principality, the Pyrenees were, if anything, even less likely. Yet here too a line of very able counts profited by the opportunities open to them to create a unit of long-term historical importance. Success was almost the only thing Catalonia and Flanders had in common; in other respects, in the dangers faced and the solutions adopted, there were few parallels. The aggressive creativity and growing wealth of Flanders contrasted sharply with the cool conservatism practised in conditions of great poverty among the mountains of Catalonia. Yet the citizens of each would have had an instinctive understanding of the political life of the other that they might not have found in any other part of the West Frankish realm.

To the historian's eye, the Pyrenean counties formed a block throughout this period; but that sense of solidarity was created out of a shared danger, rather than from any unified power-structure. Because neither 'Catalonia' nor 'Spanish March' was a term current in the tenth century, there was no word to describe the counties (fluctuating in number, but between nine and six, depending on how inheritance customs affected them), mostly in the sway of one great family, the descendants of Wifred the Hairy. (The use of 'Catalonia' here is a conscious but convenient anachronism.) After the extrusion of the last Austrasian counts in 878 in the wake of Bernard of Gothia's rebellion, Wifred the Hairy gained his dominant position among his fellow countrymen in the south by leading their armies against the Moorish troops of Tudela and Saragossa, who made repeated raids on the weak and poor Christian communities of the Pyrenean region. Wifred's was therefore a personal ascendancy based on military victory, rather like that of Richard the Justiciar. Though he did in fact gather several counties into his grasp——he was first heard of as count of Urgell-Cerdanya, to which he added the county of Besalú in 870, Barcelona-Girona in 878, and Ausona in 885——he had no intention of maintaining the integrity of his possessions; on his death in 897 they were shared out among his sons. It was not to be until between 1060 and 1070 that the whole of Catalonia came under the direct control of the counts of Barcelona. In the meantime, the Spanish March, with the exception of Pallars and Ribagorça on the border with Aragon, and of Empúries and Rosselló in the north-east, remained a family condominium——though none the less of a unity for that.

Wifred was probably descended from Bellon, count of Carcassonne in the time of Charlemagne;[51] the ties with Languedoc remained close among Wifred's descendants for the whole period covered by this book. He and his family were therefore of Visigothic blood and steeped in the customs of Visigothic law, as laid down in the *Liber Judiciorum*. This background may go some way to explaining their ability to share out in each generation the counties, abbacies, and bishoprics they inherited, apparently without conflict. It was nevertheless a substantial achievement, particularly when set against the failures of the Merovingian and Carolingian families in this respect. The result was that, from Wifred's time onwards, all the central eastern seaboard counties of Catalonia gave the impression of being bound to a single state, while actually remaining independent, equal counties, with no ties to bind them other than those of fidelity to the count of Barcelona and of family relationship.

The sense of pristine innocence that pervades Catalan his-

tory in the tenth centry is presumably an illusion, created by
the nature of the surviving evidence. This, though remarkable
in quantity—there are at least 5,000 documents, mainly
notices of sale, with some wills and some accounts of pleas
—is very impersonal. The chronicle evidence is all late—not
before the twelfth century; there are no saints' lives or
noble genealogies; and Catalonia impinged so little on the
affairs of other places that external sources have little to add.
So despite the wealth of legal documents, much may have
been going on that has left no trace at all. What there is
suggests that Catalan administration continued to operate in
the tenth century on lines of which Charlemagne would have
approved. This is paradoxical in that the Spanish March was
an area where the Frankish political hold had been at best
insecure; the Carolingian reforms might not therefore be
expected to have taken root. That they flourished must
surely indicate their easy absorption into the local traditions
and ways of thought.

In the field of law, this seems clear. For Visigothic law
knew professional judges, here called *iudices*, not Frankish
scabini; and its reliance on written documents was accepted
as an alternative to the Frankish sworn inquest and testi-
monial proof. Since the basic aim of Charlemagne's legal
reforms was to render to each man his own law, the probable
effect of Frankish rule in the Spanish March was simply to
revive and clarify Visigothic practices, including the regular
use of the *Liber Iudiciorum*, which a century of chaos in the
Pyrenees had tended to obliterate. But in administration, it is
not likely that the effect of Frankish conquest was conservative. Though the county boundaries seem to follow natural
geographical lines, there is no proof that they antedated
Louis the Pious's organization of 802. The offices of viscount
and provost, the division of each county into provostships,
the organization for collecting military service from freemen:
these features of Catalan administration in the tenth century
were probably Frankish in origin, not Visigothic or Roman.
But they were approved of and therefore proved durable.[52]

Catalan history in the tenth century is the history of one
family, of its divisions of inheritance, its marriages, its grip
on the local church.[53] It is also the history of an effective

authority wielded by the count of Barcelona-Girona over his fellow counts, not so much in virtue of public powers nor in virtue of homage (though the counts did owe him an oath of fidelity); but primarily on account of his authority as *pater familias*, trusted and respected by his relations. Within his own county (or, when inheritance laws favoured it, counties) he enjoyed all the obligations and privileges of a Carolingian count who had absorbed the land of the fisc and exacted regalian dues for his own benefit. Over the other counts, his authority depended as much on regular public meetings, often brought about by family occasions such as weddings, as on his position as marquis. Because his family links were tight and the nature of his administration conservative, he had less need to bolster his authority than, say, the self-made count of Flanders. The paucity of sources other than legal may perhaps be explained by the absence of need to image-build. His charters, though, regularly call him 'count and marquis by the grace of God', echoing the sonorous tones of royal charters; and towards the end of the tenth century he sometimes referred to himself as *princeps.* His grants were liberal, in that he drew on very extensive fiscal land; he protected the church in Carolingian style, issuing immunities, controlling episcopal elections in the three sees within his county, referring to monasteries as 'his'.[54] He exacted hospitality; he took counsel; he saw justice done in his own court; he led forth the army to battle. He was as much prince as his northern counterparts.

No count of Barcelona met or paid homage to the Frankish king in the tenth century—distance and pressing domestic problems on both sides prevented it. This might make the counts' unswerving loyalty to the Carolingian house seem incongruous: for they were not just loyal, but loyalist.[55] They regularly sent messengers to the court to obtain confirmation of diplomas, at a time when resort to the royal chancery was becoming rarer in the north; and they showed extreme reluctance to recognize any king of the Robertian house. In 995, one charter was dated *regnante Ugone duce vel rege*[56]—in the reign of Hugh, duke or king—indicating real doubt about the matter; and there are signs that the Capetian accession was still unaccepted in parts of the south as late as 1035.[57] However, the very fact of Carolingian impotence in the south helped to preserve Catalan loyalty, since the counts had nothing to lose by it, and much to gain in the authentication of their charters. But the situation changed abruptly in 985, when the great vizier Al-Mansur led the first of his raids on Catalan soil; King Lothaire failed to respond to Count Borell's urgent appeal for help, and the danger of loyalty to a distant king became plain. It was no doubt unrealistic of Borell to have imagined that either Lothaire or Hugh Capet, to whom he also appealed, could have summoned a great army under the *ban* and rushed to his assistance. But things had changed more slowly in the mountains than on the northern plain; Borell's disappointment was deep. After 987, no further diplomas went north for confirmation.

To choose a date at which Catalonia ceased to be part of West Francia is necessarily contentious. There are grounds for opting for 1180,[58] when Catalan charters were no longer dated by the regnal years of the king of France. But since the accession of the Capetians marked the end of regular despatches between the counts of Barcelona and the kings of West Francia, it did constitute a real break; though sentiment remained long after this, allegiance was gone. Catalonia will not therefore feature in the rest of this book, except in so far as the politics of her rulers impinged on the life of Toulouse and the far south. But in conclusion, it is fair to reckon the long delay in recognizing political realities, in coalescing with their southern neighbours, in becoming part of Spain, as proof that the counts of Barcelona were aware of their debt, in terms of administrative framework and political conception, to the relatively brief period of their incorporation within the Frankish empire.

(vi) Normandy

The Norman peninsula, with its flat, well-watered, fertile countryside, its excellent river system and good coastal communications, shared with Flanders its total vulnerability to Viking attack, and then its potential for rapid recovery. But whereas in Flanders this process can be pieced together fairly satisfactorily from (for the tenth century) abundant written sources, for Normandy it is far more obscure. Because the Norman leaders were illiterate Vikings, their outlook and mentalities framed by their pagan past, they at first gave little encouragement to others to record their deeds. And when, by the last years of the tenth century, they had completely changed their attitude, and sought to present themselves in exactly the same mould as their Flemish counterparts, they and their scribes happily reinterpreted their recent past to this end, creating a Norman myth which confronts the historian with almost as many problems as the total silence that preceded it.[59]

Both myth and history are agreed in seeing the origin of the Norman state in the treaty made by Charles the Simple and the Viking leader Rollo at Saint-Clair-sur-Epte in 911. But whereas myth represented this as the grant of the fully-fledged duchy, with all regalian powers, held allodially, history sees it rather as the grant of a permanent base around Rouen, in return for conversion to Christianity and assistance in repelling similar raiders. The Rollo of myth was already the outstanding Viking leader of his day; the Rollo of history was probably simply one successful war leader among many. But under him and his successor, William Longsword (murdered in 942), reality slowly approximated to myth, in that they enforced their leadership on all other Vikings in the area, prevented further settlement in their territory, and steadily expanded the area of their domination by force of arms and agreement with kings who needed their support, till by 942 the Norman dominion covered virtually the same area as the old ecclesiastical diocese of Rouen.

To judge by the brief references in Flodoard's chronicle,[60] Norman consolidation and expansion were owed, firstly to successful military leadership over a group of restless warriors who inspired fear everywhere; and secondly, to the political situation in West Francia north of the Loire, to the weakness of kings, whether Carolingian or Robertian, to the conflicting family property interests of the Carolingians, the Robertians, and the house of Vermandois, to the blatant Flemish exploitation of that tension. Rollo and William Longsword found allies avid for their support, willing to make concessions, willing to accommodate to Norman aggression.

Once Rollo and William had secured their rear against further incursion from Scandinavia, they were in an excellent position to push against their neighbours, against Flanders on the Canche, against Brittany, against Maine, usually with the connivance of the Robertians, often with specific royal approval. In such circumstances, success bred success.

Nevertheless a lordship like this inevitably had very shallow roots. Arnoul I's assassination of William Longsword in 942 came close to ending it. The late eleventh-century chronicler Hugh of Flavigny may be recording authentic tradition when he says that the event brought about a threatened reversal to paganism by the Vikings.[61] Exactly how William's son Richard, evidently only a child on his father's death, overcame the opposition and secured his inheritance is hidden from us. But in his long rule—he died in 996—Normandy was turned into a principality. Aggressive policies were not wholly abandoned in Maine—as late as the year of Richard's death, Richer described him as *dux pyratarum* (pirate leader)[62]—but now they were complemented by peaceful coexistence elsewhere.

As a ruler, Richard had the advantage of great wealth. His grandfather and father had appropriated the lands of the fisc, those of aristocrats who had fled before the Viking advance, and those of the church, which had been almost completely extinguished in Normandy. In addition, there was much booty, some of which attracted traders from elsewhere to the markets at Rouen in the second half of the century. The visible remains of this wealth are to be found in the extensive coinage of Normandy, to which the Fécamp treasure bears witness.[63] Both William Longsword and Richard I had coins with their own names minted in the duchy; a money economy seems to have been further developed in Normandy than in any other West Frankish principality of the period. And Richard was quick to discover ways of channelling the lion's share back to his court. Like Arnoul I of Flanders, he set about reconstructing as much as he could of the old Carolingian framework of government, as the only appropriate and universally-accepted means of bolstering his own power. In some parts of the duchy the old administrative divisions, the *pagi*, survived;

in others, they were probably reimposed. Then Richard appointed viscounts—though the first indisputable evidence comes in 1014—as delegated representatives of his authority in each *pagus*, to carry out the tasks of enforcing justice, collecting tolls, claiming public rights. It is a paradox that the corner of West Francia which suffered more than any other from Viking depredations should, under the rule of a man of Viking blood, become more closely modelled on Charlemagne's original plans for government than anywhere else except Flanders. Richard dispensed law at his court, he issued charters, he claimed the right to military service from all free men of the county, he collected ancient tolls.

But behind the West Frankish statesman lay the Viking war-leader. If Richard did not choose to fight for most of his reign, nevertheless his reputation in the surrounding area was based on the fear he inspired. He attracted warriors to his court, whom he could afford to reward liberally. The question of how the Norman aristocracy was constituted in the reign of Richard has been a controversial one. Norman authors of the eleventh and twelfth centuries were unable to trace aristocratic families back before about 1000, and the same difficulty has faced modern researchers. Probably Rollo found few or no great Frankish nobles within Normandy when Rouen was ceded to him; and Richard's charters provide only one or two names, usually Scandinavian in origin, whose descendants cannot be traced. It has therefore been deduced that ducal favour was crucial in the promotion of men to aristocratic rank, and that Richard refused to concede claims to hereditary succession. A possible objection to this view is that it imposes too sharp a contrast between the Norman and the other West Frankish aristocracies of the period.[64] But it does have the merit of explaining Richard's monopoly of political power in the duchy.

Having revived Carolingian-style administration and built up his aristocratic following, Richard turned to the restoration of the church, devastated by the long period of raids and by heathen intrusions. Under his protection the old bishoprics of the Rouen archdiocese, which had faded into total obscurity around the end of the ninth century, re-emerged as the pillars of the edifice; then the structure was strengthened by new monastic communities, Mont St Michel, St Wandrille, Fécamp. It is true that the pace of restoration was slow, and that by Richard's death in 996 there was still much left for his successors to achieve. But his reign saw the first real push upwards in the climb that was to make the Norman church, by the middle of the eleventh century, the most admired in West Francia.

Though there were still occasional reminders of its pagan, Scandinavian past, by 996 Normandy was once again a Christian country in the Carolingian mould, in which men from other parts of West Francia could feel themselves at home. The speed of the transformation wrought by Richard remains astonishing. And it does not detract much from his achievement that in his reconstruction and reorganization he had an impressive exemplar, his neighbour, Arnoul I of Franders.[65]

(vii) Brittany

Brittany suffered Viking depredations in the last two decades of the ninth century, as did all the rest of West Francia. But Flemish resistance under Baldwin II and the establishment of Normandy in 911 brought horrors of a new dimension, as the full pagan onslaught now fell on Brittany. None of her neighbours were disposed to help her. The Bretons were unpopular in West Francia; the kingdom put together by Nominoë, Erispoë, and Saloman had inflicted too many defeats on West Frankish forces for co-operation to be possible. Indeed in 921 Robert the Strong, count of the Breton March, ceded Brittany and Nantes to a Viking force which was devastating the area; and, if Flodoard's account of William Longsword's homage to king Raoul in 933 is correct, the king then gave the Norman the land of the Bretons.[66] So Brittany twice came close to passing into Viking hands with West Frankish authorization.

That this did not occur was the achievement of Alan Barbetorte, a scion of the ancient ruling house. Alan, along with large numbers of other Breton aristocrats, had fled to England to the shelter of Athelstan's court, thus earning a reputation for cowardice. In the 930s, he set sail to reconquer his homeland, a feat which he achieved in three mighty victories. Then a massive task of reconstruction faced him.

The *Chronicle of Nantes*, a twelfth-century compilation, described it thus:

Once the Normans had been conquered and put to flight throughout Brittany, Alan penetrated as far as the town of Nantes, which had been deserted for several years. To get to the church of the apostles SS Peter and Paul, he had to hack out a path with his sword across thick walls of bushes, both pines and brambles. On his arrival at the church, he found it without a roof, its walls crumbling. Alan and his other Breton companions, deploring the state of their church, called on the apostles for aid. Having considered all the advantages of the site, both internal and external, Alan decided to make his principal residence there. He ordered all Bretons to come to Nantes laden with provisions, and to build a great earth rampart around the church like the wall of an ancient castle. When this was done, he had built a donjon for his own residence.[67]

On exactly what grounds Alan was able to order the assistance of 'all Bretons', and their dues of provisions, is not known; it may have been in accordance with earlier Breton custom, or by imitation of West Frankish regalian right, or a simple response to circumstance. In any case, the Bretons rallied round, and Alan's overlordship came to be recognized in some way over an area which was roughly conterminous with the old kingdom.

But unlike the counts of Flanders and Normandy, the counts of Nantes were simply overlords of other established comital houses—according to tradition, six of them, of whom the counts of Rennes were by far the most important. So when Alan Barbetorte died in 952, leaving only a minor who died young, and bastard sons, whose title to succeed was disputed, war for supremacy began inside the duchy. It was quickly exacerbated when the count of Blois intervened to assist Rennes, while the Angevins pressed the claim of Alan's bastards. As both Blois and Anjou made large profits from their intrusion there must have been corresponding losses for Brittany. The Burgundian chronicler, Raoul Glaber, declared that Breton wealth consisted only in freedom from public dues and in the abundance of milk:[68] though Raoul's Burgundian bias should be suspected, he was correct in thinking that the later part of the tenth century was a time of poverty for the duchy. So by the 980s, the exhilaration engendered by Alan's victories had passed into oblivion.

The distintegration of Alan's achievement suggests that Nantes proved a poor base for a principality. The city, sited at the Loire mouth, was clearly well-placed for taking tolls on river traffic; but it was as far as possible from the Celtic-speaking lands of the west, which had been the bastion of the ninth-century kingdom and which had resented the West-Frankish orientation of Alan's policies. And although Nantes had the advantage of being remote from Normandy and the aggression of William Longsword, it proved an easy prey to the counts of Anjou. So, despite Alan's valiant effort, Brittany failed to regain her ancient splendour. Indeed, for the whole of the eleventh and most of the twelfth century, it remained a weak principality, forced to acknowledge the overlordship of one or other of its powerful neighbours. Nevertheless, it kept its ancient sense of identity; it preserved its memories of past greatness for a time when circumstances would favour it once more.

(viii) Toulouse

The sources for Toulousan history in the tenth century are exiguous. There are no chronicles or annals, and the surviving body of charters provides only scattered and random information about political life. As a consequence, two recent studies—those of A. R. Lewis and E. Magnou-Nortier[69]—have offered fundamentally different judgements on the effectiveness of the count of Toulouse's overlordship; and this section can make no claim to resolve the matter.

The principality—if it was one—of Toulouse was made up of two historically distinct areas, Gothia and Toulouse proper. Gothia, the old Visigothic Septimania, ran along the Mediterranean coast from the Rhône to the Pyrenean foot-hills, a position which drew it naturally into intercourse with its coastal neighbours, Barcelona and Provence. In normal conditions, this was an asset; but in the last years of the ninth century and in the early tenth, it had exposed Gothia to Saracen raids. The damage was extensive: King Eudes had to make large grants of dues and lands to the archbishop of Narbonne, so that he might rebuild his church from ruins. But by about 920 the worst was over, and all was set fair for recovery. The early Carolingian administrators had established

in Gothia the important county of Carcassone (held originally
by a family of Visigothic extraction, but escheating in the
mid tenth century to Arnaud, the scion of a Pyrenean
aristocratic house); and also the viscounties of Béziers, Narbonne, the Rouergue, and Lodève, the last three of which
were held by men believed to have been related to the counts
of Toulouse. At the end of the ninth century another, much
less well-endowed, comital family emerged in the house
of Substantion, whose chief claim to fame lay in its control of the mint at Melgueil, secured by around 950.
Within Gothia as a whole, Visigothic and Roman legal traditions remained powerful, their impact reinforced by the
splendid monuments of the Roman past which bedecked the
landscape.

There was little in common between Gothia and the great
county of Toulouse, originally created as a bulwark against
possible Gascon invasion, and therefore necessarily orientated
to the south-west. Landlocked, but with river communication
to the Atlantic, Toulouse had been an important administrative centre in the Carolingian period. In 877 it had been
absorbed into the impressive but ephemeral principality of
Bernard Plantevelue; but Bernard's son William the Pious had
regranted it in 886 to Eudes of Rouergue, whose descendants
continued to hold it until the Capetian conquest in 1226-9.

In 924 Raymond III Pons of Toulouse acquired control
over Gothia. In acknowledgement of this splendid achievement, Flodoard referred to him as *princeps Gothorum*.[70]
This title lent distinction to a fairly patchy authority. Within
Toulouse, Raymond had extensive family lands; he was lord
of the bishop of Toulouse and of the viscounts of Toulouse,
Albi and Nîmes—again probably all related to his family; and
his ancestors had carefully maintained all the comital prerogatives. In Gothia by contrast, his relations with the count
of Carcassonne were those of near equals—sometimes rivals,
sometimes friends; and although the viscounts of Gothia certainly recognized Raymond's overlordship, they had already
annexed for their own use at least half the revenues they
collected, they regarded their offices as hereditary, and
their lands were clearly allodial. Then the archbishop of Narbonne controlled half of his city; and during the course of

the tenth century, the bishops of Lodève, Uzès, and Cahors built what were in essence simple immunities into independent comital lordships. In general, the lords of Gothia saw their obligations towards the count of Toulouse as pliable, a matter of deference and courtesy rather than of rigid obedience.

Raymond III Pons was the outstanding figure in southern politics. On the death of William II of Aquitaine in 927, he contrived to assert some kind of overlordship over the Auvergne; and he obtained at least a formal supremacy over the Rouergue, whose counts were a cadet branch of his family. He clearly hoped to press further, to bring the counts of Poitou under his sway; it was this ambition that caused him to take the title 'duke of Aquitaine'. But here he was biting off more than he could chew; his over-ambition led to the loss of the Auvergne before his death. His successor William Taillefer confined himself to Toulouse and Gothia, abandoning the ducal title. Even so, contemporaries were impressed by the extent of his power: 'the illustrious count William, according to the disposition of divine clemency, is placed in charge of great kingdoms'.[71]

The second half of the century saw returning prosperity. Nîmes, Narbonne, and Carcassone all increased in size, with new suburbs appearing; the countryside enjoyed stability; wine-growing spread, settlements expanded down from the hilltops. If the count was able to preserve his rights, then his revenues from justice, requisitions, hospitality, tolls, moneying, and particular taxes on pasturage, forests, and saltings, should have been substantial. But it does seem probable that in Gothia the vicecomital families and the bishops were in the process of excluding him from much that he had earlier enjoyed; and although within Toulouse the situation was better, even here there was serious loss in the sphere of justice. For during the course of the century, the old public courts disintegrated: justice at local level became a private matter, a private source of revenue. While the count of Toulouse's court maintained control over important criminal cases in the town of Toulouse, elsewhere it degenerated into a forum for arbitration in the disputes of the local aristocracy. The decline in profits from justice was no doubt considerable.

Surviving charters attest the sprouting of castles all over the principality in this period. Its results, however, are debatable. In all probability the count of Toulouse obtained oaths of fidelity from many (though not necessarily most) castellans, as indeed he was to do later; but the import of these oaths was essentially negative; and it is not even certain that the castellans owed him military service. On the other hand, the mere existence of castles was no proof of declining comital authority—they were features of strong principalities as well as weak. A recent study of castle distribution within the principality[72] has emphasized that the castles of the central region at least were usually peripheral to the main centres of population; so their importance must have been strategic or commercial, rather than administrative. If this conclusion were to be proved true for the whole principality, then castellans could fairly be relegated to the background of the Toulousan scene. But the matter is not yet settled.

Both Raymond III and William counted among West Francia's leading figures. Yet they played almost no role in politics beyond the Loire: William is not known ever to have made contact with the kings. And within the south, Raymond's attempts at hegemony proved ephemeral. Judgement on whether they were effective princes depends largely on whether effectiveness is defined as the ability to bully, in which they were restricted to the area around Toulouse; or as the ability to preserve Carolingian institutions, at which they were probably more competent than most. Of their skill in inspiring friendship, on which so much in practice depended, nothing is known.

(ix) Gascony

Gascony is by far the most obscure of the principalities. The shreds of evidence that do survive suggest that, while the Viking raids were disastrous in the north, they had only superficial effect further south, where society was unusually stable and prosperous. But since the only sources for the period are a handful of charters, it is hard to be sure. One piece of political information can be gleaned from them: in the early years of the tenth century, Duke García Sancho is said to have divided his duchy into counties for his sons, bestowing Fézensac on William, Asterac on Arnaud, and keeping the county of Gascony in the west for his eldest son Sancho García.[73] This statement may be a later attempt to rationalize the position; but even if anachronistic, it is valuable because it draws attention to the real division that emerged between the north-western duchy of Gascony, including the Bordelais, and the rest of the Pyrenean country, whose history lies mainly outside that of the kingdom of West Francia.

The Gascons were feared by their neighbours as an aggressive and barbarous people; yet they did little in the tenth century to justify that fear (though Abbo of Fleury was murdered in 1004 by the Gascon monks he went to reform).[74] The heirs of Sancho García within the duchy appear to have been effective rulers and distinguished warriors. The crucial event in the duchy's history was the duke's assertion of overlordship over the non-Gascon counties of Bordeaux, Agen and the Bazadais, which was converted, in the case of Bordeaux, into direct ownership at some time between 977 and 988.[75] From this time on, Bordeaux became the duchy's chief city; its political centre of gravity therefore moved to the Romance-speaking part of the country. In 982 Duke William Sancho inflicted a grave, and apparently final, defeat on the Viking raiders. The economic revival that had already begun in the area could now flourish unhindered. To secure his southern frontier, he made an alliance with his neighbours in Navarre; and to please God, he instituted a programme of restoration for churches and monasteries throughout his domains. The famous old ecclesiastical centre of Bordeaux revived, while its archbishop worked hand in hand with the duke in reform. So William Sancho's policies had much in common with those of Arnoul I of Flanders and Richard I of Normandy.

Yet there were two drawbacks to concentration on the Bordelais: as William Sancho emphasized the Gallo-Roman part of his inheritance, so he weakened yet further his purely personal authority over the counties of central and southern Gascony, which increasingly went their own way. And in the long term, the Bordelais was to make the duchy vulnerable to external pressure. Here, there was a parallel in policy between William Sancho and Alan Barbetorte of Brittany, who by developing Nantes drew Brittany into West Frankish society, thus opening it to ambitious neighbours. But if there were dangers in William Sancho's choice, there were also solid rewards. The late tenth century was a period of strength and prosperity within the duchy; when the duke died in 996 he left his heir an inheritance in which he could take pride.

(d) Tenth-century Principalities: Conclusions

The main lines of tenth-century West Frankish history are clear: a kingdom, put together in 843 as a solution to a family crisis, possessing a degree of physical coherence but little more, slowly slid apart over the century 888-987. Although ethnic consciousness played its part in the process of disintegration, in the sense that the units into which the kingdom split preserved traditional names and tradition bolstered the claims of their princes, the actual shape of those units was clearly determined by political rather than ethnic factors. Indeed, the rulers of those states that had the strongest sense of racial identity, Brittany, Gascony, and Normandy, all hastened the process of assimilation of their peoples into West Frankish society. So truly ethnic divisions grew less marked as political ones entrenched themselves.

Politically, West Francia was like a deep lake as it freezes; its edges solidified, though there were odd thin patches, while its centre remained liquid. It was clearly easier to impose some kind of government in areas where the sea or mountains offered at least one well-defined frontier— Brittany, Normandy, and Catalonia benefited conspicuously from geographical features; on the other hand, the largely landlocked duchies of Aquitaine, Burgundy, and Neustria were fluid at the edges, and places like Berry and Picardy did not solidify at all. Physical geography therefore had some relevance to the formation of principalities.

Yet it did not lie at its heart. What really counted was that a prince should be seen to fulfil a vital role in the well-being of the peoples over whom he exercised sway. Because the factors that made him valuable were usually short-term and personal, the art of governing a tenth-century princi-pality was largely the art of adapting to circumstances. Of this the counts of Flanders showed themselves the consum-mate practitioners; the Gascon dukes and the counts of Rouen, Barcelona, and Poitou were not far behind. All princes of the last two decades of the ninth century and the first two of the tenth enjoyed the advantage that accrued from being the obvious protectors at a time of danger. But after that, although there were spasmodic raids throughout the rest of the century, princes had to supplement their reputation as defenders by other inducements to loyalty.

In the north of the kingdom, the commonest reaction to returning security was to substitute aggression for defence as a means of attracting counts and lords to a prince's court. The armies that followed Arnoul I into Picardy or William Longsword into Maine and Brittany were made up of those lured by hopes of rich rewards. Further south, Hugh the Great's campaigns in Burgundy and Aquitaine, and those of Raymond III Pons to the north of Toulouse, may also have been inspired in part by a desire to gratify their followers. But the areas ripe for expansion were increasingly limited by the success of other princes; and as the century wore on, the more blatant forms of aggression came in for criticism.

War-leaders were therefore obliged to reinforce their appeal by playing on the prevalent nostalgia, by attracting to themselves the shadow of Charlemagne's charisma, at least some aspect of his reputation as defender of the church and the poor, as dispenser of justice, as fount of righteousness. While for some princes—the counts of Flanders and Rouen —the change of emphasis represented a sharp break with previous tradition, for others—Richard the Justiciar, William the Pious, Wifred the Hairy's successors—the two *personae* were blended from the beginning, as they had been in Charle-magne himself. But whichever path they took, by the second half of the tenth century all princes exacted respect by presenting their authority in what their subjects took to be traditional form. A prince was in person a symbol of the Carolingian past, of stability in an unstable world. In the splendour of his dress, the gravity of his demeanour, the solemnity of the ritual that surrounded him, his subjects could find reassurance, a sense that God had not abandoned them. In the absence of effective kingship, there was comfort to be derived from praising its substitute. Nevertheless, it was not a comfort that could be enjoyed in minorities or in succession disputes. The survival of principalities was thus at the mercy of luck in family life-patterns.

There is, however, another way of looking at principalities: that of Dhondt, as refined by Lemarignier and Werner.[76] For them, what they term the 'territorial principality' was a stage on the path between Carolingian kingship and the disintegration of the old administrative system, to be brought about in the eleventh century by the rise of the castellans. For them, a principality was a subdivison of the old kingdom, in which the royal right to command was now vested in the prince; and it was territorial in the sense that the prince's authority stretched over the whole. On this interpretation, the Carolingian empire fractured before it was ground to dust. While the convenience of this framework for the understanding of West Frankish history cannot be doubted, its truth is open to question. At the least it imposes too rigid a definition on political units notorious for their fluidity.

In fact, principalities either consisted of a number of counties cobbled together by the authority of a royal *fidelis* or, alternatively, were in themselves units controlled by the prince, assisted only by such counts or viscounts as he chose to nominate. In the first case, which covers almost all the West Frankish principalities, the prince's power was not in any meaningful sense territorial outside his own county or counties; for then it depended on the fidelity of other counts or bishops, an essentially personal bond. The second alternative related to Normandy by 942, as to a large area of northern Flanders; but it did not apply elsewhere until the closing stages of the tenth century, when Blois or Anjou might possibly be held to fit its terms. From these four it appears that, instead of marking a characteristic stage in the decay of centralized government, true territorial principalities were a rare and precocious manifestation of new, constructive skills. And even in them, it was the personal, rather than the territorial, character of rule that remained its striking feature.

In an effort to bolster Dhondt's definition, Werner has stressed the essentially royal character of a principality: it 'was not the result of a mere accumulation of counties or comital rights; it represented the king in a sub-kingdom, stood above the counts, and incorporated royal, not comital, powers'.[77] For him, then, the determining feature was that it was a kingdom-substitute in the legal, not the psychological, sense. The prince was the wielder of royal powers. But this surely overstates the significance of those relatively few specifically royal powers that princes did exploit. For the bulk of regalian rights escaped them as they had escaped the king. And while princes did mint and confirm charters, including those of immunity (hitherto royal monopolies), these were icing on the cake of princely government, not its eggs and flour. Justice, the *ban*, and financial rights had always been exercised through counts; these continued to be the mainstay of princely authority. It is true that those who drew up princes' charters never missed an opportunity to describe their masters in royal terms; but propaganda and constitutional reality were not identical.

So principalities were neither notably territorial nor notably viceregal. The *regna* ascribed to princes in charters should not be translated 'sub-kingdoms'; they were rather 'rulerships', personal ascendancies. Admittedly all had a territorial base in at least one Carolingian county; and all were less fluid by 987 than they had been earlier. In that sense they were starting to become territorialized. In essence, though, they were the creation of individuals, subject to all the hazards and variations in fortune that such an origin entails. A *regnum* was a series of brilliant improvisations, not the carefully balanced slow movement in a symphony of Carolingian decline.

(e) The rest of West Francia

It. will not have escaped attention that large areas of the country have not yet entered our narrative. What did not happen in these parts—government did not solidify sufficiently to resist external pressure—is every bit as instructive for political history as what has thus far been discussed;

and in terms of *later* developments, it is of vital importance, since these fluid areas proved to be the natural victims of princely, then royal, expansion. But the ill-defined is by definition resistant to description. What this section therefore aims to do is to illustrate by reference to types. It will cover (i) an episcopal principality; (ii) an independent county; (iii) an ephemeral principality; (iv) an area deprived of strong government by pressure from powerful neighbours; and (v) two areas in which political disintegration was in some sense self-inflicted.

(i) The bishopric of Langres

The history of Langres as the most extensive and the most independent of France's episcopal states begins in the tenth century. In Louis the Pious's time, the bishop had obtained an immunity for his lands, the right to appoint an advocate, and some powers of jurisdiction in the city; he relied on royal protection for the enforcement of these privileges. But King Eudes's resources were overstretched after 893; he was therefore in no position to resist Richard the Justiciar's aggressive move against Thibaud, bishop of Langres, in 895. For the rest of Richard's life, Langres remained firmly under ducal control, an important element in the vast Burgundian duchy; a son of Richard's closest ally, Manasses of Chalon, was appointed its count. Then under Raoul, Richard's son, Langres fell within the part of Burgundy that the king kept in his own control. As a consequence, it was claimed on Raoul's death both by his brother Hugh the Black and by the new king Louis d'Outremer; with the backing of Hugh the Great, Louis was successful in his siege of the city in 937, and Langres returned to royal protection.

Thus far, the bishops had been passive participants in the quarrels. But the proximity of the see to Lotharingia and the kingdom of Burgundy ensured for its holders familiarity with Ottonian policies towards the church; accordingly they aspired to possess comital powers over Langres. King Lothaire, who had been under Otto I's tutelage during his minority, and whose wife was Otto's step-daughter, was alert to the potential advantage of such a grant. In 967, at the request of his wife Emma, he issued a charter fashioned on Ottonian principles, granting the bishop rights over the ramparts, markets, and coinage of Langres, along with comital powers and all tolls taken at the city gates.[78] And in 980 he appointed as bishop a man capable of exploiting these new acquisitions to the full: Bruno de Roucy, his kinsman, grand-nephew of Archbishop Bruno of Cologne.

Under Bruno, Langres became an unstable principality; the bishop's sway extended beyond the frontiers of the extensive county of Langres, to cover Tonnerre, Dijon, Barois, Atuyer, and Ocheret.[79] Langres was therefore distinguished from those southern bishoprics that enjoyed comital powers—Cahors, Uzès, Lodève—by the sheer size of its jurisdiction; and from the northern episcopal principalities—Rheims, Châlons, Laon, Noyon, and Beauvais—not only by size but also by the degree of independence it enjoyed from the king. It was probably during Bruno's time that Langres acquired a well-disciplined force of *milites casati* (see p. 53) for its defence; and that the first member of the de Saulx family was appointed *vidame* (the equivalent of advocate) of the bishopric—the office later became hereditary in that family. But at least some of what had been achieved by Bruno's constructive energies and his aristocratic connections was put at risk in 1002, when he used Langres as a power-base from which to launch an attack on Robert II's claims to the Burgundian duchy. What followed showed that episcopal principalities, like their secular counterparts, were still fluid associations centring on clear territorial kernels; to survive intact, they needed careful tending.

(ii) The county of the Rouergue

In this remote corner of the south, shielded from external intrusion by the Massif Central, it was almost as if the winds of change of the late ninth century had never blown. The count of the Rouergue belonged to a cadet branch of the ruling family of Toulouse, whose overlordship he probably continued to acknowledge, though fidelity seems to have had no practical consequences. Raymond II exercised justice in the traditional way, maintained fortifications, protected the church, and dealt summarily with challenges to his authority. His personal wealth was vast; in his will of 961 he disposed of 127 allods and castles.[80] But it is clear from the evidence of the Miracles of St Foy that there was an established aristocracy in the Rouergue, well-endowed with allodial lands and powerful family connections. The time was not far distant when the count's authority would be challenged.

(iii) Vermandois

The early history of Vermandois falls into a pattern which might suggest the evolution of a successful political unit. Herbert I, count of Vermandois, obtained the county of Soissons before 889, probably in order to ensure the defence of the Oise against the Vikings. He thus secured a good landed base for expansion. He had the advantage over Baldwin I of Flanders, whose career started in much the same way, in that Herbert was a Carolingian in his own right, the grandson of Pippin, king of Italy. It was probably this which led King Robert I, who needed all the royal connections he could muster, to propose a double marriage alliance, whereby he should marry Herbert's daughter, and Herbert's son, Herbert II, should marry Robert's daughter (by his first wife) Adela, with the county of Meaux, and possibly also Mézérais, as her dowry. Herbert II, as a consequence, controlled a stretch of territory in the surroundings of Paris, in the heart of what had once been Hugh the Abbot's power base; now he constituted a threat, both to the Carolingians around Laon, and to the Capetians in Paris. Herbert's initial strategy was to favour the Capetian alliance; he imprisoned Charles the Simple and held him secure till his death in 929, thus earning from the eleventh-century author of the *Historia Regum Francorum* the description 'worst of all Frankish princes.'[81] He followed this up with an attack on Laon, the annexation of Amiens, and the election of his relations as counts of Senlis and Beauvais. More surprising, and an apt illustration of his opportunism, was his coup in having his five-year-old son Hugh elected to the archbishop of Rheims.

King Raoul, appreciating that the monarchy needed a toehold beyond the Seine, by 929 felt threatened by Herbert's manœuvres. In the war between king and count that followed, Herbert sought the moral, if not financial, support of Henry I, king of Germany. At this stage, German help proved inadequate: Herbert's son was chased out of Rheims, he himself lost Soissons. But the death of Raoul in 936 changed the picture; up till that point, Hugh the Great had supported his royal relative, but with Louis IV's accession, he was happy to renew his house's traditional friendship with Vermandois. So Hugh supported the 940 campaign of Herbert (with Otto I's backing), in which Rheims was retaken and Herbert's son reimposed as archbishop; and he did not oppose Herbert's seizure of the Melunais and perhaps also of Provins, or of Sens in 941. The Vermandois cause was in the ascendant when it was jeopardized by Herbert's unexpected death on 23 February 943.

Thus far, the history of Vermandois had proceeded on the same lines as that of Flanders. Herbert's mixture of Carolingian lineage, conquest, clever marriage, and exploitation of opportunity had also characterized the careers of Baldwin II and Arnoul I. But while Flanders survived the minorities of 965 and 988 (though only just), Herbert II's death destroyed his largely Austrasian principality. His eldest son Eudes was for some reason unable to claim his father's inheritance,[82] and his next two sons were minors, for whom Hugh the Great exercised guardianship. In the breathing space after 943, Louis IV was able to reassert his authority not only over Rheims but also over much of the eastern part of Herbert II's domains. All that was left for Herbert's sons was the county of Meaux, from which his elder son Robert later expanded to create the germ of the future Champagne, and the county of Omois, from which Herbert the Old, Herbert II's other son, attempted without success to follow his father's example. On Herbert the Old's death without heirs, his lands were divided between his two nephews, the count of Troyes and the count of Blois. In that form, the rump of the Vermandois principality was an important constituent of the eleventh-century lands of Blois and Troyes.

But Vermandois as Herbert II had conceived it—the Seine-based principality—had disappeared. The lesson would seem to be that in the area north of the Loire, there was only room for two great families. Vermandois had owed its existence to Herbert II's capacity for playing off the Robertians against the Carolingians, to his infinite opportunism, and to Otto I's support. In his lifetime, the fluidity of his alliances so confused the other participants in the drama that they could not clearly perceive their own interests. But his sudden death convinced Hugh the Great that, even though he was guardian of Herbert's sons, it was in long-term Capetian interests not to oppose Louis IV's consolidation north of the Seine, because it secured his own dominance between the Seine and the Loire. So, despite Herbert the Old's swashbuckling career and his formidable degree of temporary success, he could not follow in his father's footsteps. The only course open to him was whole-hearted alliance with King Lothaire, which brought him many advantages, but was counterproductive to securing a power base on the Seine.

(iv) Picardy

The history of Picardy in the tenth century is a copybook example of the destructive effects of external pressure on Carolingian administrative arrangements. For the six counties that comprised Picardy were broken up into twelve separate units during the quarrels between the counts of Flanders and Vermandois, the dukes of the Franks, and the last Carolingian kings that made up the political history of the area. It was a classic example of what Lemarignier termed 'the dislocation of the *pagus*':[83] the old administrative map was obliterated; what took its place was the product of compromise, response to challenge, or new self-assertion rather than administrative principle.

Baldwin II's thrust into Picardy, following the death of Raoul of the Ternois (see p. 70) in 892, began the process by which Artois and the Ternois were in the end annexed to Flanders, despite stubborn royal resistance. But Arnoul I's death in 965 meant the loosening of Flemish control in the area. The county of Boulogne, held by the descendants of Arnoul's younger brother, became a permanent feature of the map. Then on Arnoul II's death, the advocates of Guînes and Ponthieu both arrogated to themselves the comital title and treated their lands as forming a county. While Guînes remained with the Flemish *mouvance*, it was indicative of Hugh Capet's gains within the area that the count of Ponthieu became Hugh's vassal. Meanwhile, further east, Herbert II of Vermandois's annexation of the neighbouring county of Amiénois had led, on his death in 943, to its fragmentation among several local lords, of whom the bishop was one.

So by 987, three of the original Carolingian counties in Picardy—Artois, Vermandois, and the Cambrésis—remained intact (though the grant of comital powers to the bishop of Cambrai had created a very weak political entity, into which imperial influences steadily percolated); a fourth Carolingian county, Ponthieu, had been totally reshaped; and the other two, the Ternois and Amiénois, had fragmented beyond hope of repair. More worryingly, the area was divided between the Flemish counts' sphere of influence—only temporarily weakened by the minority of Baldwin IV—and that of the Capetian kings, which was more extensive, but far less forceful. Picardy was a potential battlefield.[84] From the point of view of its inhabitants, it was frustrating that royal power, though sufficient to keep the counts of Flanders at bay, was quite unequal to the task of supervising the local lords and counts in whose hands lay the day-to-day administration of the area. Picardy benefited neither from incorporation within a principality nor from the total independence of the Rouergue.

(v) The Auvergne and Upper Berry

These areas shared with Picardy the proliferation of weak local lordships; but in neither case was this due to the power struggles of greater houses over their territories. In Berry, the root cause was the sheer size of the Carolingian county, conterminous with the diocese of Bourges—probably a reflection of very light settlement in this central area of the country. It is unlikely that the Carolingian counts of Berry were ever effective rulers there; which perhaps explains why after 925 no more were appointed. By this time, lower Berry had already achieved another nucleus, in the house of Déols, whose lord Èble was a *fidelis* of William the Pious, duke of Aquitaine, and of his son William II. But Upper Berry remained without lay leadership: for the viscount of Bourges, who might have exploited the political vacuum to assert himself, chose not to do so; and the archbishops of

Bourges, though the largest landholders in the area, unlike the bishops of Langres entertained no ambitions to build up a principality. So in the absence of comital direction, relatively obscure families began to exercise local jurisdiction, to build castles for all their dwellings, and to exercise such comital rights as they could. 'The age of the castellans' dawned early in Berry. Hardly surprisingly, outsiders were attracted by the weakness of the political framework; by 987 both the count of Blois and the count of Anjou had begun to build up *mouvances* in Berry; and the threat of outside competition finally stirred the archbishop of Bourges to greater assertiveness. There were, however, still many quite independent castellans. Perhaps Berry's central position, with its vulnerability to invasion from all sides, discouraged assertive lordship.[85]

Both geography and history distinguished the Auvergne from Berry. Remote, protected by the Massif Central, hugging to itself a long tradition of distinctiveness, it had been the heart of William the Pious's principality in the early years of the tenth century. But when, on the death of William's last heir and grand-nephew Acfred in 927, the family lands were dispersed, the principality left no mark on the institutions or way of life of the province. The local lords were free to run things as they would, under the distant overlordship first of Toulouse and then of Poitou. In 963 one of the Auvergnat viscounts began to refer to himself as count and prince of the Auvergne; by 980 William IV of Poitou had recognized the title. Though the new count came of a noble and wealthy family, his claim to authority was far from unimpeachable, and he had no means of imposing his fidelity on his aristocratic neighbours. In Basse-Auvergne, where his lands were, he was strong; elsewhere he relied on goodwill. No sooner had he proclaimed himself count than other families took the vicecomital title without authorization, and established independent lordships, based on castles.[86] These sprouted everywhere in the Auvergne, with no regard for earlier administrative frontiers. So, though it had a count, the Auvergne's development was very much like that of Berry.

Except for Berry, the areas of West Francia we have

discussed all belonged at some stage in the century to a principality; but for all of them that experience was brief. The variety of explanations put forward for the isolation or weakness of government within them cannot but increase our admiration for those who overcame such difficulties to create principalities. On the other hand, the fact that so much of the country lay outside governmental networks should guard against a simple picture of West Francia as composed of Carolingian sub-kingdoms ruled by the heirs of Charles the Bald's princes. There was more to it than that.

The absence of pattern in the mosaic suggests that 'West Francia' was a meaningless concept in this period. For the only link that had held the kingdom together, the 'fealty' of the royal *fideles*, was dissolved when some princes escaped the king's *mouvance*, and much land escaped the princes' rule. By now kingship meant little more than a loose suzerainty over most of the area north of the Loire and the duchy of Aquitaine. And even this loose suzerainty faced a threat of a different kind: in the second half of the tenth century, Louis IV's and then Lothaire's dependence on the East Frankish kings came close to reducing their realm to a mere appendage of its eastern neighbour. Yet when Lothaire reacted against this subordination by launching an attack on Lotharingia, he chose the path that brought about the ruin of his house. As it happened, Otto II and Otto III had too many other preoccupations to exploit the situation, and by the eleventh century Lotharingia melted into the background of German royal policy. West Francia was therefore left in peace to develop as she would. But it had been a narrow squeak.

CHAPTER 5

Aristocratic life 888–987

(a) Ruling families

The lineages of nobles descend from the blood of kings.
(Adalbéron of Laon)[1]

In a sense, all tenth-century political history is family history.
The important men—counts, dukes, and marquises—of the
Carolingian empire were bound together by blood-ties which,
though they did not confer a simple right to rule, were a
necessary constituent of any claim to pre-eminence. As a consequence, the families themselves have been the subject of
much recent research. The standard theory, developed by
Gerd Tellenbach and his pupils, on the basis of such evidence
as the *Libri Memoriales*,[2] is that aristocratic families of the
Carolingian period were loose kinship-groups, in which
cousins, uncles, aunts, distant connections, had real significance, and in which rules of inheritance were fluid, while
personal property mattered less than the family holding.
During the course of the tenth and eleventh centuries, these
large kinship groups slowly gave way to more clearly defined
nuclear families, the paternal element was stressed in the
family genealogy, and primogeniture tended to emerge as the
usual custom of inheritance. The Tellenbach approach is
characteristic of much modern research, in that it substitutes
for the old-fashioned juridical models a model from social
anthropology. While the picture it provides of the Carolingian
family is perhaps not totally rooted in the evidence, the
changes it outlines for the tenth and eleventh centuries
are well substantiated.

To turn from a twentieth- to a twelfth-century view of
what happened, the author of the *Gesta Consulum Andegavorum*, echoing Sallust, saw the reign of Charles the
Bald as the time in which the West Frankish nobility was
infiltrated by new men, who took over military leadership

and hereditary lands at the command of the king.[3] Belief in the 'newness' of the late Carolingian aristocracy has, however, been severely shaken by closer studies of particular families, which tend to show (though perhaps less wholly convincingly than has sometimes been claimed) that the leading families of tenth-century society were already noble by birth. But it is also clear that nobility was a commodity which could be increased by discreet matrimonial alliance; so, though it might be impossible to start from scratch, it was nevertheless easy to mount the noble ladder. The author of the *Gesta* was not wholly wrong in emphasizing change in the top ranks of society.

As would be expected, the acquisition of royal blood at once transformed the status of an ordinary noble family; therefore royal ladies had to be carefully guarded against abduction. The first genealogy of the counts of Flanders reveals that Baldwin I took the crucial step in elevating his family when he broke through the guard and seized Charles the Bald's daughter Judith; as late as the reign of Lothaire, both king and count were still referring to the blood-relationship between them. Their social ascent once under-way, Baldwin's descendants discovered that Carolingian blood was not the only royal blood worth having. Baldwin II married a daughter of Alfred the Great, so forging a politically significant link with England, and Arnoul II married the daughter of Berengar II, king of Italy. In this way a relatively obscure family, distinguished by martial skill rather than blue blood, won recognition as near-equals of the crowned heads of Europe.

A similar, though ultimately less successful, story lay behind the fortunes of the house of Vermandois. Herbert II, count of Vermandois and Soissons, gained by his marriage with Adela, daughter of King Robert I, both increased social status and the county of Meaux. From this kernel he expanded rapidly in all directions, creating a principality which bade fair to reunite the Austrasian part of West Francia under one lordship. Although his death brought the division of the inheritance, his example was not lost on his eldest surviving son, Herbert the Old. In a bold bid to force his claims on Louis d'Outremer, he ran off with the queen-mother Eadgifu, daughter of King Edward the Elder of Wessex. In the short term, the abduction brought him a bride far older than himself, her dowry which he only obtained after some struggle, and Louis's wrath. In the longer term, his marriage succeeded in appeasing the Carolingians, his father's enemies, and in commending him to Louis's son Lothaire, who conferred on him the prestigious title 'count of the Franks'. But in the even longer term, after the Capetian dynasty had established itself, it became clear that Herbert had thrown in his lot with the losing side in Neustrian politics. So even the most advantageous of marriages might prove to have unpredictable drawbacks.

As it turned out, the best political investments in the tenth century were not Carolingian but Ottonian brides. But they were also, as a matter of family policy, the least attainable. As a consequence, Hugh the Great's marriage to Havide, daughter of Henry the Fowler, proved of deep significance to his family: it made Hugh, in effect, the equal of Louis IV, who also had a Saxon royal bride, and permitted Otto the Great to hold the balance between his brothers-in-law. Because royal blood coursed in their veins, Hugh's sons were natural candidates as dukes; and the fact that Hugh Capet's mother was Otto II's aunt had some bearing on his election to the throne in 987 because, for this reason as well as for others, he was an attractive candidate for the pro-Ottonian party.

Since royal families traditionally married within their own ranks, for an aristocrat to obtain a royal marriage was remarkable. A bride from the greater princely families could do much to enhance the standing of an ordinary count, as is evident from the marriage of Raymond, count of the Rouergue, to Bertha, daughter of the marquis of Tuscany and niece of King Hugh of Italy; this illustrious connection temporarily brought the Rouergue out of the obscurity which usually shrouded it. But at this level in social relations, marriages in which one party was clearly more noble than the other usually had detectable political interests behind them. For example, the marriage of Duke William IV of Aquitaine with Emma, daughter of Thibaud le Tricheur, count of Blois, was presumably aimed at containing Angevin expansion in

Aquitaine and Blois. The marriage of Hugh the Black's daughter to Gilbert, count of Chalon, was designed to preserve as much as possible of the Burgundian duchy in the hands of an old friend. In fact, Gilbert's early death, leaving only an infant heiress, put paid to this. For, as is the case with all long-term forward planning, a good match needed a measure of luck before it could yield solid political advantage.

Because aristocratic marriages were pacts directed towards mutual advantage, they tended to be between neighbours. It was rare for southern brides to go northwards, or vice versa. Hugh Capet's marriage to Adelaide of Poitou was intended to smooth over the rupture caused by his father's ambitions in Aquitaine; but usually there was no motive for such marriages, and differences of custom and language may have made them unattractive in themselves, as is suggested by the hostile reaction in the north to Robert the Pious's third wife, Constance of Arles. Marriage in the south was more likely to involve Italian, trans-Pyrenean, or Provençal families than northerners. But one striking exception to the rule demonstrates just what political potential such an alliance could have. The Gévaudan, part of William the Pious's Aquitaine, escaped all superior authority after 927, and was ruled—in so far as it was ruled at all—by a local family which called itself either comital or vicecomital, according to circumstance. Why Geoffrey Grisegonelle of Anjou sought Stephen of the Gévaudan as a husband for his sister Adelaide is not known, but the marriage was followed by a considerable implantation of Angevins into the Massif Central, and the election of an Angevin bishop of Le Puy. So much interest did this network of northerners in the south excite that King Lothaire, seeking to reconstitute the old subkingdom of Aquitaine for his son, thought it worthwhile to marry Louis, the heir to the throne, to the now widowed Adelaide of Anjou, in hopes that this would commend him to southerners. The plan proved abortive; but it demonstrates both the Angevin propensity for colonization and the crown's interest in reviving links with the south.

Among the southerners themselves, marriage-links were just as businesslike as in the north, indeed, where they were accompanied by formal legal marriage agreements, as was common in Catalonia, they appeared even more as matters of family policy. The counts of Barcelona married leading ladies from the Midi as a matter of course in the second half of the tenth century, so emphasizing their West Frankish connections, distinguishing themselves from the lesser members of their own family, and perhaps also giving themselves a possible ground for expansion. Marriage-bonds here, where Visigothic and Roman law survived, were tight, tighter than in the north; so the contracts which accompanied them aimed to protect both partners in all contingencies. Opportunities for self-advancement through marriage were every bit as rich as in the north, but the accompanying responsibilities were more clearly spelt out.

The benefits of marriage, however great, could not be stabilized unless heirs were born. At this, tenth-century West Frankish aristocrats were not notably successful. The Flemish counts managed to keep the succession going by the skin of their teeth; and Richard the Justiciar was the only Burgundian duke of the century to produce a male heir. It was much the same in the south. One of the first miracles attributed to St Foy of Conques was that she helped the wife of count William III of Toulouse to conceive, in return for the gift of golden bracelets.[4] In this case, the saint made doubly sure by allowing Arsinde two sons. But where no saint listened, barren marriages were common. There was also the problem that some aristocrats—William the Pious and Gerald of Aurillac among them—regarded continence as a major virtue; on being urged to marry for the sake of inheritance, Gerald replied that it was better to die without sons than to leave evil heirs.[5] The shades of the cloister closed in on some great nobles.

Granted this situation, problems over divided inheritance were less common than might be expected. For some princely houses, primogenital succession became the norm at a time when the birthrate was very low. Though their succession custom was later to be a matter of pride to the Flemish counts, Baldwin II had intended a shared inheritance for his sons; it was only a matter of chance that kept the whole county intact for Arnoul II. But the Capetian house seems to have decided on primogeniture as a matter of policy, at least by the middle of the tenth century. Hugh the Great's machinations in Aquitaine and Burgundy were largely directed towards making suitable arrangements for his younger sons, so that Hugh Capet could inherit the duchy of Neustria undivided; he was determined to avoid the problem later faced by king Louis IV, who had to disinherit his younger son in order to preserve his kingdom.

But though primogeniture was taking root in some families in the north, it was not the exclusive custom. The house of Vermandois clung to old ways in dividing the inheritance, perhaps out of deference to its Carolingian ancestry. What is remarkable here is the absence of trouble division caused. Despite their aggressive opportunism towards others, the Vermandois brothers and cousins proved exemplary in their behaviour to each other. And in the south, particularly in Catalonia and Gothia, where Visigothic law governed succession arrangements, division of inheritance was undertaken peaceably in each generation. It cannot be maintained that tenth-century princes and kings turned to primogeniture because bitter experience suggested the unworkability of any other system. Nevertheless it was a growing trend, often accompanied by the use of what has been termed 'anticipatory association',[6] the elevation of the heir to his office before his father's death—presumably with the intention of acclimatizing other claimants to the agreed arrangement before the crisis of full accession.

Family policy was not just a question of marriage and succession; it also involved contributing to a continuing family tradition, projecting a myth of family excellence. That noble blood was the source of virtue was almost unquestioned in the period; therefore to acclaim one's ancestry was to demonstrate one's moral superiority. St Odo of Cluny noted of Gerald of Aurillac that he came from one of the most noble families of Gaul, which could count among its forebears St Caesarius of Arles (502-43).[7] Hence senatorial rank vied with sanctity in Gerald's blood. The truth of his claim is beside the point. What mattered was that, out of all the innumerable individuals in the family tree since the sixth century, Gerald's contemporaries chose to light on one alleged ancestor who they thought best illustrated Gerald's qualities. To trace descent back to the sixth century was unusual. But other families were well aware of their roots, and displayed this awareness by the names which they chose for their sons. So Baldwin II of Flanders, arrogant in the confidence inspired by his mother's royal blood, called his son Arnoul, in memory of the Carolingian family saint, Arnulf of Metz. Less ambitiously, Capetian eldest sons were Robert or Hugh in memory of King Robert I and Hugh the Great; the counts of Anjou were Fulk and Geoffrey in memory of Fulk the Good and Geoffrey Grisegonelle, the founders of the house's fortunes.

So common is this pattern that some historians, led by Karl Werner,[8] believe that continuity of Christian names can be used to indicate continuity of descent. On this hypothesis, there would be a prima-facie case for holding that the Ranulf who was count of Poitou at the end of the ninth century was descended, though not necessarily directly, from the Ranulf who held the same position in the reign of Louis the Pious. This technique of tracing names down generations has proved a fruitful one; many thought-provoking genealogies have been constructed using it. For example, the counts of Anjou have been traced back to Louis the Pious's seneschal Adelard, whose descendants intermarried with the family of Lambert of Spoleto.[9] If this genealogy can be accepted, then the later prominence of the house seems unsurprising. But there are problems of evidence; and with some families, the reliance on a common Christian name, Bernard or William for example, makes the technique highly speculative. It seems safer to regard information derived this way as hypothesis rather than fact.

For a family's heroes, and therefore its names, might change. Although Arnoul I's grandson bore his name, the later members of the Flemish comital house, born after the accession of Hugh Capet, reverted to the older family name, Baldwin. The house of Poitou dropped the traditional names Ranulf and Èble when Èble Manzer christened his son and heir William, presumably intending to emphasize the blood-relationship with the family of William the Pious, and perhaps also to make a claim by hereditary right to the duchy of Aquitaine.[10] The name survived till the end of the dynasty;

and, untypically, those younger brothers who succeeded to the duchy through the death of the heirs assumed the name William on their accessions. So family names were a matter of decision. There was nothing predetermined about the way in which a great aristocratic family presented itself and its history to the outside world.

Thus far, attention has been focused exclusively on princely lines, because for them politics and family were inextricably intertwined. But the problem for the princes lay in the fact that all the means of social advancement they employed could be exploited equally by those in the ranks below. A glance at the Roucy family will demonstrate this. The first member of the family who can be traced was Renaud (a name which may suggest Norman origins), the builder of the castle in Roucy in 948. The castle was erected on allodial land, once part of the royal fisc, which may have come into the family's hands through the beneficence of Charles the Bald. Renaud, though he was called count, had no county. The outstanding event in his life was his marriage with Aubrée, daughter of Otto I's sister Gerberga by her marriage to the duke of Lorraine. How a relatively obscure man achieved so dazzling a match escapes our knowledge; but as a consequence the sons of Renaud and Aubrée were worthy of social elevation. The elder, Èble, became viscount of Rheims, which office he combined with his father's title count of Roucy. The younger son must have been intended for the church from birth, for he was given the names of his famous great-uncle, Archbishop Bruno of Cologne. In 980 he fulfilled his destiny by becoming bishop of Langres through the goodwill of his relation, King Lothaire. By now, the Roucy family was well launched on the course which was to make it one of the most distinguished in eleventh-century West Francia, and to lead it to marriages with Spanish royalty. The rapidity of its ascent was both an example and a threat to its princely neighbours.[11]

(b) Ties of Fidelty and Vassalage

The aim of fidelity and vassalage was to create artificial links between men to bind them as surely as if they were blood-relations. But exactly what fidelity and vassalage were has proved a thorny question. Because in the past they were judged to form the crucial social cement of tenth-century society, precision in definition was deemed essential. Now that the relationships to which they gave rise no longer dominate the political historian's horizon to the exclusion of other factors, a rather more plastic approach, taking account of both regional and social variations, becomes possible. Possible, but difficult; for plasticity slides easily into vagueness, and vagueness provokes the (to my mind unfounded) suspicion that neither fidelity nor vassalage meant much in the tenth century.

The problem arises from lack of evidence. Fidelity and vassalage were mainly the concern of laymen; and our sources were written by ecclesiastics. Besides, when Flodoard, Richer, or Ademar mentioned the ceremonies, they saw no need to explain what to all their contemporaries were familiar matters. And the charters, concerned with lands and privileges, offer only a few enigmatic glimpses of personal relations; their greatest value may lie in the witness-lists, *if* it is reasonable to assume that the men who regularly signed a prince's or a bishop's charters were his vassals; but this assumption might be questioned. And in the central body of the charters, such descriptions of personal status as occur are hard to interpret. It may be that tenth-century scribes used language imprecisely; Marc Bloch ascribed their terminological elusiveness to the entirely understandable difficulty they faced, when translating out of the vernacular in which homage and fealty were performed, into Latin, which had no adequate vocabulary.[12] Some more recent historians believe that there was precision; the obstacle to our understanding lies in our unperceptive handling of evidence. The very extensive investigations into feudal vocabulary now being conducted in France may yield rich harvests; or they may produce a picture so complicated and inflected as to be of use only to specialists. The problem is substantial. To take an example from the famous work of Georges Duby on the Mâconnais, why does the word *vassus* disappear from Cluny charters after 930, except for a brief reappearance between 981 and 986? Does the substitution of *fidelis* for *vassus* mark a change in the legal nature of the relationship? If so, why the reversion between 981 and 986?[13]

The oath taken by a *fidelis* to his superior was modelled on that which Charlemagne had demanded of all free men. Its import was negative: the *fidelis* swore not to harm the life, rights, or interests of his lord. How an oath sworn to the emperor in the presence of his official representative was transmuted into an oath taken simply to that official is obscure: in practice, the difference must have been quite small. In the tenth century, all dukes, marquises, counts, viscounts, bishops, and abbots had their *fideles*, and most were themselves *fideles* of others. The relationship as thus far defined existed simply to bolster the authority of the king's officials, introducing no new element. In Catalonia, where the counts were still able to extract the oath from the whole free population, and in parts of Languedoc at some times, fidelity meant simply that.

There could, however, be another element in fidelity, which brought it closer to vassalage. In return for the oath of loyalty, the lord might bestow on his *fidelis* a grant of revenue or land from the comital fisc, a fortification, or an office, on strictly limited terms. Ademar of Chabannes tells how Vulgrin, count of Angoulême, built a new castle at Marcillac, and installed there a new viscount, Ranulf by name. A century later, a family quarrel led to the murder of the viscount's successor. William Taillefer, then count of Angoulême, intervened to bestow the castle on a brother of the dead man: 'And he became his viscount as Ranulf had been the viscount of Vulgrin.'[14] So the viscount was in some sense almost the count's property. The tie was clearly a much tighter one than a mere oath not to harm the count might imply.

Then there is a further complication. The oath of fidelity came to be used in another context in tenth-century Languedoc: it became a normal part of the process of patching up quarrels. Two lords who had been reconciled in a law court would take an oath of fidelity to each other to ensure that the terms would be kept. If one party had accepted defeat, the oath might have the character of submission—this is how Ademar of Chabannes portrayed Geoffrey Grisegonelle's oath to William IV (though the more concrete aspect of the treaty, Geoffrey's gain of Loudun, might suggest that the humiliation was rather William's).[15] If one party was a count or viscount, the oath would be indistinguishable from the older oath to a public official. But at any stage, it could set its seal on a friendly treaty, a marriage alliance, or a mutual defence pact. It was above all an attempt to stabilize a relationship, to give it lasting force.

In origin, vassalage was different. Probably derived from ancient German custom, its roots lay in the commendation of unfree men to their lord. It was therefore by definition an act of submission, symbolized in the vassal kneeling before his lord, placing his hands within his lord's, taking an oath of loyalty and becoming his 'man'. During the Carolingian period, vassalage rose in the social scale, becoming at first a ceremony undertaken by freemen as well as serfs, then exclusively one by the free. As the social status of the vassal rose, the inducement for submission, the *beneficium* received, became more important. Though *beneficia*, as rewards for service, could be of almost any kind, a gift of land grew commoner. Here, then, is the origin of the fief, an institution once thought to be so typical of tenth- and eleventh-century society as to have given its name to the whole age.

Charlemagne and his successors encouraged the mingling of vassalage with fidelity. Their *vassi dominici* were richly endowed nobles established to give support to the crown in lands far from the Austrasian centre of Carolingian power. Their *fideles* became the masters of counties, the recipients of fiscal *beneficia* for which they took homage. In many ways, vassalage and fidelity became indistinguishable. Yet their assimilation was easier north of the Loire: the idea of tenancy in land was well developed, so royal overlordship both of the vassal's land and of his office could easily be conceived. In the south, where memories of Roman law and social convention guarded allodial land and respected contract as the normal way of reaching agreements, vassalage was not well understood. Besides some churchmen, even in the north, regarded it as contrary to the interests of Christianity that bishops should be vassals as well as *fideles* of their king. Given such views, it was natural that when royal pressure slackened, the magnates interpreted their relationship with the king in their own way.

The endlessly debated question of whether the princes
were vassals of the king in the tenth century demands a clear-
cut notion of vassalic status that was conspicuously lacking
in a non-juridically-minded age. Richer described Raymond
Pons's homage to Raoul in 936 as involving placing his
hands between the king's and promising military service and
fidelity; in 944, Louis IV told the Aquitanian princes that
they held their lands and their authority purely by his
delegation.[16] Too much concern with actual truths should
not be imputed in Richer. Nevertheless his stories are valuable in that they show Charlemagne's view of homage was
remembered, at least in some circles. But it apparently found
little favour among the princes of the south. After 944, no
count of Toulouse paid homage to a king of France until the
twelfth century; the counts of Barcelona, whose adherence
to the Carolingian dynasty was well attested, never swore
fidelity or paid homage, largely because the opportunity
never arose; and the same was probably true of the dukes of
Gascony and the counts of the Rouergue. So after 944 the
whole of the far south had escaped the royal *mouvance*.

On the other hand, the dukes of Aquitaine and Burgundy,
along with the northern princes, viewed homage as a courtesy,
to be performed at coronations or at some convenient
moment in the early years of a reign. Normally the act did
not trouble them; though Hugh the Great found it humiliating to have to repeat it both in 946 and 950, after he had
rebelled against Louis IV. On the other hand, homage meant
no precise obligations. The northern princes sent troops to the
king's army as and when it suited them; after the last Frankish call to the *ban* by Raoul in 925,[17] the king's demands
for help were treated like those of any other important men.
If an alliance was profitable, they would fight on his behalf,
but they were equally prepared to fight against him, as
Louis IV found in the dangerous year of 944. And though
they might seek royal approval for their titles, they maintained they held their offices by grace of God and by
hereditary right. So whatever the king believed homage to
imply, for the princes it was little more than a conventional
gesture of friendship and goodwill.

Thus far the argument has stressed that what was important

about homage or fidelity was less the words spoken than what the two parties concerned thought they meant. Yet the whole question cannot simply be relegated to the realm of psychology. For in recent years, an important school of French historians, led by Élisabeth Magnou-Nortier and Pierre Bonnassie,[18] have produced an interpretation of southern history in which the juridical distinction between fidelity and vassalage plays a crucial part in explaining the differences between the tenth and the eleventh centuries. For them, what matters is less the personal relationship involved, or even the question of service, but the *beneficium*. Where a count or other official made a grant from fiscal land as a salary for those who served the public utility and expected an oath of fidelity in return, he was using the resources of public authority to uphold that authority. His action was completely conservative. It had nothing in common with the grant of a piece of allodial land by a magnate to a lesser man in return for homage and service—a purely private trans-action, and one which should be regarded as feudal because it intertwined political authority with private law. On this defini-tion feudal contracts were almost unknown in the south before the last two decades of the tenth century, and of no political importance until well into the eleventh. The tenth-century southerners who might appear to the northern eye to be feuda-tories were in fact officials or servants of officials, fulfilling a public office, and rewarded by public lands or revenues.

There is much about this distinction that is satisfying, for it has proved useful in pinpointing the conservatism of the south. Its drawback is perhaps that it leads to too much over-refinement of small differences. For it cannot have mattered profoundly to ordinary people whether the land they held had once belonged to the royal fisc or not, or whether the service that had earned it had been owed to a count or a viscount, or simply to another aristocrat. The lordship of Montpellier, based on what appears to have been allodial land, had a history very similar to the southern viscounties based on fiscal land. Besides, an interpretation which sees fidelity as above all a bolster to public power tends to exaggerate the unchanging nature of southern society, as the case of the lord of Melgueil makes clear.

For when Bernard of Substantion assumed the title of count of Melgueil, what authenticated his right to it was the fact that William Taillefer, count of Toulouse, accepted his oath. In this case, then, fidelity *made* public authority rather than preserving it. Melgueil became a county.

Still, despite its occasional difficulties, the approach which distinguishes sharply between fidelity and vassalage, and regards fidelity as the social cement of the tenth-century south, vassalage as nothing more than marginal, has justified itself as fruitful. It can, however, hardly be applied to West Francia north of the Loire. For where fiscal land merged into private holdings, where vicariates disappeared from view along with old viscounties and many *pagi*, where new boundaries and new administrative divisions were created across many parts of the north, the old forms of authority became unrecognizable. The counts of Rouen and Flanders, faced with devastated country and a ruined administration, revived what they could, created new *beneficia* where they could not revive, and treated old and new on the same footing. Viscounts and castellans became interchangeable representatives of the count. Neither they nor anyone else knew whether they held their offices primarily as delegated public duties or as private fiefs from their overlord; neither they nor anyone else knew if they were chiefly *fideles* or vassals of their lords. For the counts of Flanders and Rouen enjoyed an advantage in this respect which the kings of West Francia lacked in dealing with the princes: geographical proximity. As a consequence, they could enforce the subordinate character of their officials' authority, the conditional nature of their tenure. Elsewhere in northern West Francia, the counts of Blois and Anjou moved in the same direction in the second half of the century. Fidelity and vassalage were almost intertwined.

The discussion thus far has been limited to links between princes and their officials. There were, however, everywhere important aristocratic families who were not officials. What of their relation with the princes? This is a very difficult question. Where the old public courts survived, in Catalonia, the Mâconnais, and Gothia—though probably not always where they were revived, as in Flanders or Normandy—the local aristocracy was—in theory at least—bound to attend the count's court, and swear fidelity to him. But as the public courts decayed, this link dissolved. When the count's court lost its pre-eminent status and became more localized in its jurisdiction, the lesser lords who remained the count's *fideles* were those resident in the areas where lay the count's chief centres of power. Other lords were drawn into the spheres of viscounts, castellans, bishops, or abbots; some maintained their independence. So the count lost touch with the aristocracy as a whole, though he may have tightened his hold over those who remained members of his court.

The quality of lordship symbolized by fidelity or vassalage varied markedly. Princes, counts, and also kings, could always afford to make heavy demands on their own armed warriors; they could sometimes impose the characteristics of vassalage on their relations with their subordinate aristocrats, whether officers or not, but often had to be content simply with fidelity; and many lesser aristocrats had either escaped from or never enjoyed ties with the prince or count of their area. Where fidelity existed, the bond created was infinitely elastic; it could mean as little as that the *fidelis* would not harm his lord; but, bolstered by marriage alliances, mutual defence pacts, or good neighbourly relations, it could symbolize a real and lasting friendship. Where vassalage obtained, it meant more clearly defined services, a greater emphasis on deference. Under a strong lord, one relationship slid easily into the other. The *fideles* of William IV in Poitou looked on their lord in much the same way as the vassals of Arnoul I of Flanders. To abandon the search for precision on fidelity and vassalage is not to assert their relative unimportance. Successful princes found in them a powerful social adhesive.

In illustration of this, three snapshots of very different relationships are offered. The first, from the *Cartulary of St Bertin*,[19] relates to Winemaros, called *miles* of Baldwin II, who in response to his master's orders murdered archbishop Fulk of Rheims in 900. When accused he claimed that, because he acted in accordance with his oath of fidelity to Baldwin, he was guiltless of crime; and he remained impenitent even in the face of excommunication from Rome. Here was a man prepared to risk his immortal soul rather than cast doubt on his personal duty towards his lord, or reflect on the limits of his obligation. Winemaros was a servant of Baldwin; his social standing was far lower than that of Raoul I de Tosny (whose career has been pieced together by Musset);[20] yet the two men shared a common sense that their destiny was not in their own hands. Raoul I's brother Hugh, archbishop of Rouen, was responsible for bringing him to the attention of Count Richard I of Rouen, from whose son he obtained the castle of Tillières on the frontier. Unlike earlier castellan families in Normandy, Raoul and his successors contrived to hold on to their position; but they did so purely through ducal favour. Their lands were all held in virtue of service, and their dispersal across Normandy indicated the duke's unwillingness to tolerate blocks within the duchy. As a consequence, the Tosny family could only sate their relentless appetite for acquisition outside Normandy, in Italy, Spain, the Rouergue, or (after 1066) in England. So Raoul's oath of fidelity to Richard was indispensable to the family's rise to power; yet though it conferred substantial benefit, it also imposed an unwelcome discipline. It was quite different in its implication from the oath of the castellan of Uxelles to the count of Mâcon, as Duby[21] has traced it. For Josseran d'Uxelles belonged to one of the seven great aristocratic families that stood head and shoulders above the others in the Mâconnais: thus he came close to rivalling the count in wealth and allodial landholdings. The only boon he received from his lord was guardianship over his castle, in return for which he acknowledged himself a comital *fidelis*. His oath involved him in attending the comital court and in some form of military obligation; but its true significance lay in the bond of friendship to which it bore witness. In effect he belonged to the comital *mouvance* voluntarily, out of a desire that the old order should be perpetuated. Should that desire cease, the count would find himself without coercive power to force the castellan's obedience. Fidelity here was a tie of sentiment between near-equals.

These three very different oaths all bound their holders to great men. Yet in this as in most other things, the great set examples for others to follow. In the ninth century, counts, viscounts, abbots, bishops and advocates had all attracted their own *fideles*; the habit continued. But whereas in some parts of the country—Normandy, Champagne, Catalonia for example—it appears that those who held official posts had a monopoly of *mouvances*; elsewhere others also had their dependants. Gerald of Aurillac was always surrounded by a large entourage; he even settled disputes between lesser lords and their own men.[22] Some lords in Poitou did likewise. And it is probable that already custodians of castles in places throughout the country had begun to take oaths from the warriors on whom their security depended. For clientage was an age-old phenomenon in Germanic as well as in Roman society; if those at the top of the social scale could dictate the conventions on which it was conducted, they could hardly hope to deter others from practising it.

(c) The aristocracy and the church

Because of the nature of our sources, evidence on this topic is relatively abundant. The picture which emerges (largely from charters) is complex, and full of regional and personal variations; but everywhere it bears tribute to the aristocracy's ingenuity in turning the church's needs to its own advantage. The princes' activities have aroused in historians just that mixture of admiration and revulsion they often excited among contemporary ecclesiastics.

From the beginning of monasticism in Gaul, the links between religious houses and local lords had always been close. Grants of land, protection against enemies, commendation of noble children as oblates, and death-bed generosities had placed all monasteries in the debt of their neighbouring great men; appropriation of monastic land for the endowment of soldiers, intimidation of monks to obtain forced gifts, and even occasional plundering raids, had constituted the aristocratic pay-off. In the early tenth century, the era of monastic revival and reform, the old pattern remained largely unchanged: West Frankish abbots could not enjoy the benefits of lay protection without the accompanying risks of lay encroachment. But there were a number of different ways of formalizing the relationship, some of which were less disadvantageous to the monks than others.

The most burdensome form of protection was provided by lay abbots, who enjoyed full rights over all the temporalities and estates of their religious houses and therefore left no secular power in the hands of monks. The office had been sanctioned by Charles the Bald, who assumed the lay abbacy of St Denis himself, and conferred similar privileges on a few of his most important friends. Although Charles's intention was that it should be an exclusive honour, after his death it was widely imitated in non-royal houses; indeed, it might have become general, had it not fallen under the disapproval of the new generation of monastic reformers, anxious to secure conformity, on this point at least, with the Rule of St Benedict. They were led in Normandy and Flanders by the followers of Gerard of Brogne, in Burgundy by the Cluniacs. By the second half of the tenth century, the reformers had prevailed. Lay abbacies had disappeared; even where the title continued in use—the counts of Poitou were described as abbots of St Hilaire in Poitiers till the mid-eleventh century—the office in practice was that of an advocate. While lay abbacies lasted, they substantially bene-fited their holders; the abbacy of St Aubin at Angers has been regarded as crucial in the rise of the viscounts of Angers to princely status,[23] in that it provided them with the revenue, patronage, and prestige necessary to pave their way. Sometimes the exploitation involved may have been offset by the safety it guaranteed; in the Fleury Annals Hugh the Great was remembered as a holy warrior for Christ.[24] But in general, the reformers' cause was warmly supported.

An alternative to lay abbots was found in advocates, common in Champagne, Flanders, Picardy, and the royal demesne, or in the *vidames* of Burgundy. The function of these officials was to lead into battle the troops of a monastery enjoying immunity, or to fulfil such of the abbot's judicial functions as were thought unfitting for a monk. In return, the advocate received a *beneficium*, which often turned him into a landed magnate; Hariulf of St Riquier declared that the title conferred domanial revenues along with peasant labour services.[25] As a consequence, the advocate's and the monastery's interests might no longer coincide. The *Miracles of St Benedict* told of the advocate of St Benedict of Fleury who defended the abbey's lands from external threats, but devastated them himself to a greater degree than any stranger could have done.[26] And the transformation of the advocate of St Riquier into the count of Ponthieu suggests that he acquired the landed wealth necessary for his self-promotion by squeezing the monks whom he was intended to defend.[27]

Where there were no advocates, monasteries had guardians. In the south, a written agreement might govern the relations between a religious house and its guardian; elsewhere long custom defined it. But there was always an element of plasticity. For most of the tenth century the count of Mâcon acted as guardian over the monastic houses in his county, whether or not they enjoyed an immunity; but when reforming influences led the great house of Cluny to wish to interpret its immunity more literally, the count withdrew without dispute. The choice of guardian depended on circumstance. A house which feared encroachment from a neighbouring lord would seek protection from a more distant one; on the other hand, if the neighbour were also a friend, his protection would be more easily obtained in a critical situation.

Monasteries were especially vulnerable to pressure from the lords of their localities; but they were not exempt from more distant and powerful depredators. The need for defence pushed even the pious Hugh Capet into annexing three estates from St Riquier in Ponthieu for the establishment of castles.[28] Much commoner was the seizure of lands for fiefs. The estate of Winsterhoven (near Tongres), belonging to the abbey of St Bavon in Ghent, was distributed by a count of Flanders among his soldiers.[29] Were it not for the fact that the relics of a seventh-century saint, St Landoald, were found on one of the fiefs before 980, no record would have remained of the seizure. Actions of this sort were probably taken for granted in the troubled first half of the tenth century, and could be squared with canon law by the imposition of an extra rent, the *nona et decima*, upon the annexed land, as a symbol of their continuing ownership by the church. In these cases it may be argued that St Riquier and St Bavon presumably benefited by the better defence provided. But Hugh the Great's depredations, which came close to dismembering the huge estates of St Germain-des Prés after the middle of the century, apparently brought no reciprocal advantage.[30] They merely illustrate the oft-found phenomenon of a prince who plundered one monastery, while reforming and defending another—Fleury.

An attempt to draw up a balance-sheet of monastic profits and losses in land would probably suggest that losses through provision for fiefs or self-enrichment were greater in the early part of the tenth century, restorations or new gifts more significant later. But the situation was always fluid; great patrons like Arnoul I of Flanders might take away as well as give. And the improvement later in the century was owed, not only to princely gifts, but also to the more active role the monks themselves began to play in reclaiming their property. For Carolingian *polyptycha*, or estate records, were dusted out from their hiding-places and used as proof that land now under lay proprietorship belonged rightfully to the monastery.

Useful though this balance sheet might be, it would have its limitations. It assumes a cleavage of interest between monks and princes which was only sometimes apparent. It is perhaps too easy to dismiss the great lords as exploiters and cheaters of innocent monks, occasionally moved to repentance at the prospect of imminent death. Reality was not quite so simple. The whole movement for monastic reform, which eclipsed lay abbacies, defined the rights of advocates, gave the monks the confidence to challenge annexations of their property, and encouraged yet more lay donations, was powered and directed by princes: by William the Pious of Aquitaine, who founded Cluny; by Arnoul I of Flanders, who brought Gerard of Brogne to his county; by Hugh the Great at Fleury; and by Richard I and Hugh Capet towards the end of the century. Geoffrey Grisegonelle of Anjou, acting in his capacity as lay abbot, reformed St Aubin, and then abolished his own office to please God. The sincerity of their convictions cannot be doubted, even if not all the actions of Arnoul I or of Hugh Capet were consistent with spiritual motivation. And while it may be conceded that there was temporal as well as spiritual gain to be made by patronizing reform, this seems to have played only a small part in their calculations.

Relations between the great laymen and the secular church are more obscure. It is probable that the great princes, like lesser counts and ordinary landowners, were all engaged in building parish churches across their domains. As the old large parishes of the early ninth century were gradually divided into units roughly the size of a village, and often conterminous with one, new churches were required. The building boom reached its peak around the millenium, when Raoul Glaber described the world reclothing itself in a white mantle of churches.[31] Unfortunately parish churches were usually too small and insignificant to warrant charters, so the extent of princely beneficience remains unknown. But they, like all lesser lay patrons, will have received the tithes from their new parishes, and appointed and paid the priest.

There was obviously more political mileage in choosing and protecting a bishop than a parish priests. In theory a royal prerogative, episcopal election to the southern bishoprics (except Le Puy) had escaped the king's grasp early in the tenth cntury. Comital control over the church in Catalonia was so well established that in 970, Borell, count of Barcelona, endeavoured to obtain papal approval for an archbishopric at Vich, with the aim of excluding from Catalonia the alien influence of the archbishop of Narbonne. The attempt failed; but it illustrates Borell's strong sense of the identity of secular and ecclesiastical institutions. Elsewhere, south of the Loire, princely control was less complete. Where the count was strong, as in Poitiers or Angoulême, the bishopric remained in his control; where his authority dwindled, as in Narbonne or Clermont, vice-comital or other important local families gained control. The results varied from place to place. But perhaps the most extreme interpretation of the rights acquired from protecting a bishop was that of Bernard II, count of Melgueil, who appointed his own son to the bishopric of Maguelonne in 979-80, and then dispersed the lands and goods of the bishopric. Though other lay lords were somewhat more restrained, it became common in the south to distinguish between the spiritual duties and revenues of a bishopric and its temporalities, which could be shared out among a lay family, inherited, or used to provide dowries.

In the north, where royal control over bishoprics fluctuated but remained a dominant factor, only the count of Rouen could begin to rival the king, and then not in terms of number but on account of the solid territorial block formed by his bishoprics. The county of Flanders spanned old diocesan boundaries, which deprived the count of lordship except in Tournai; the counts of Troyes, Meaux, and Anjou moved to dominate the bishoprics in their principal seats, but only there. The dukes of Burgundy lost undisputed control of all their bishoprics, though they were still on occasion able to obtain their choice of bishop. Although it was hard to obtain, and even harder to keep, the advantages of nominating to a bishopric were firstly that it increased patronage, and might even solve a tricky succession problem—this was presumably Herbert II of Vermandois's aim when he intruded his son Hugh into the archbishopric of Rheims; secondly, it brought financial profit, especially from the goods of a dead bishop, and sometimes from the temporalities of a see during a vacancy; it could also give territorial solidity to a principality, like Langres in the time of Richard the Justiciar; besides the bishop could be constrained on occasion to offer hospitality, and sometimes even a ceremony of welcome.

Tenth-century bishops were aristocrats, often members of the great families. Though the Carolingians and Capetians usually only promoted their bastards to the church hierarchy, other princes were happy enough to let members of their own family pursue a safe career within a cathedral close. Èble Manzer of Poitou passed his title to his elder son, and had his younger elected bishop of Limoges. This habit could have unexpected consequences. The *Chronicle of Nantes* records that Guerech, count Hoël's younger brother, had already been designated bishop of Nantes before his brother's death and his own accession to the county.[32] So the church had educated and formed the character of the man who became a prince in Brittany.

To promote a son or a close friend to a bishopric did not automatically ensure loyal service and support. It was, after all, Adalbéron of Rheims who was chiefly instrumental in getting Hugh Capet elected, thus betraying the family which had promoted him from relative obscurity. A bishop regarded himself as being as free as a lay aristocrat to interpret his oath of fidelity to his prince as loosely as it suited him to do so. Nevertheless, there was a closeness, a necessary involvement, between princes and bishops which later generations were to deplore. Nowhere was this plainer than in Catalonia, where, towards the end of the tenth century, Ranulf, count of Besalú, was also bishop of Girona, offices which he passed on in harness to his nephew Mir III. The secular church and the princely power that defended it were seen as two sides of a seamless robe. A theoretical distinction between the interests of the church and those of the state was current in the far south, where Roman and Visigothic law provided some foundation for it; yet this was the area where in practice interests blended easily. In the north, where law was far more confused, the theoretical distinction could not be made; in practice, trouble did occasionally occur when princes bullied. Yet even the chronicler Flodoard, who suffered personally when Herbert of Vermandois intruded his son into the archbishopric of Rheims, described the event in a detached tone.[33] Shock and horror at princely intrusion were far from his mind. It was to take the more logical and legalistic approach of the late eleventh century to burst asunder the simple, unselfconscious alliance between secular and ecclesiastical authorities that characterized all West Francia between 888 and 987.

CHAPTER 6

Sources 987–1108

THE eleventh century is richer in source material than the
tenth. A slow intellectual revival, centred on the Loire valley,
Chartres, and Rheims, spread into Normandy, Burgundy, and
Aquitaine, reinvigorating monastic chroniclers, inspiring
learned bishops, creating among princes a new desire to be
immortalized in the written word. And as more came to be
recorded, slowly the emphasis changed: the hand of the
Almighty began to recede a little from the affairs of men,
liturgical needs ceased to provide the commonest framework for literary endeavour, secular interests intruded more
forcefully into the narrative. The barrier between Dark Age
annalists and hagiographers and their twentieth-century
interpreters begins to dissolve.

The most remarkable fact about the chronicles and histories of the period is that kings no longer played a central
role. When Richer ceased his narrative in 996, he had no
worthy successor to paint the canvas of Capetian politics. The
Historia Francorum Senonensis,[1] written after 1015, filled
the gap for a few years, but its author had nothing like
Flodoard's or Richer's knowledge of political events. Hariulf
of St Riquier's chronicle,[2] compiled in 1088, is informative
for some aspects of Hugh Capet's reign; otherwise there is
little. As men, the early Capetian kings are shadowy figures.
The only one to attract a biographer was Robert the Pious,
and the value of Helgaud of Fleury's *Life*[3] lies less in the
information it provides about the king's doings (though there
is some) or his character (his piety is not attested elsewhere),
than in its picture of what reformed monks thought a good
king should be. Helgaud was powerfully influenced by
hagiographical tradition in presenting Robert as a merciful,
humble, and pious paragon; he aimed to paint an icon, not
a portrait. As a consequence, the *Life*'s historical importance
lies above all in its contribution to Capetian royal imagery

(see p. 135). For the other Capetian kings of the eleventh century, there were no lives at all. Their deeds have to be deduced from their administrative records and from the chronicles of men whose chief concerns lay elsewhere. Whether the impression that they were weak kings is simply a reflection of the absence of source material, or whether that absence was in itself the direct consequence of royal weakness, is one of the chicken-and-egg conundrums.

Perhaps, to inspire chroniclers, a prince had to show he needed them. Those great warriors, the dukes of Normandy, were the best-chronicled of the century's potentates. Their victories in the field made them exciting and afforded their eulogists easy parallels with the heroic deeds of the classical past. But to the chroniclers' joy in recounting triumphs should be added the dukes' desire to shroud their pagan, pirating past in a nobler, more dignified myth. The conjunction of these factors can be seen in one of the most original works of the early eleventh century, Dudo of St Quentin's *De moribus et actis primorum Normanniae ducum*.[4] This narrative of the Norman past as the dukes wished to have it remembered was written for Richard II by a clerk from Vermandois, probably educated at Rheims. Dudo flattered his patron; but, on a deeper level, he attested the glorious outcome of Christianity's battle with paganism. The Norman duke, powerful, peace-keeping, pious, ruled as the culmination of God's purpose for his people. Granted this intention, Dudo's interest in retailing the unvarnished truth was small. Modern historians treat most of what he retails with profound scepticism. Yet a few facts can be gleaned from him, particularly for the events of his own lifetime. And as the first monument to princely culture in West Francia, his book has great significance.

The second scholar of distinction to be attracted to Norman triumphs was William of Poitiers[5] (who drew on the writing of a less distinguished predecessor: William of Jumièges);[6] his theme was the deeds of William the Conqueror. Again there was a splendid tale to tell. William, trained in grammar and rhetoric, had the means to present it as the history of deeds which dwarfed those of Julius Caesar. Yet it would be a mistake to dismiss William's work as nothing but propaganda. He was an intimate of the duke's, and had the advantage unusual for a medieval raconteur of combining a good classical education with a past knightly experience that informed his military accounts. Besides, though he certainly sought to extol heroism, he also appears to have cared about truth, at least in so far as he knew it.

The third major historian of eleventh-century Normandy, Orderic Vitalis,[7] was not directly inspired to pick up his pen by ducal deeds, though consciousness of having lived through very important events shines through his writing. A monk of mixed Anglo-Saxon and Norman parentage sent to the monastery of St. Évroul in Normandy in 1085, Orderic used Bede's *Ecclesiastical History* as a model for his own lengthy work of the same name, which was derivative until the last decades of the eleventh century. From then until it ceased in 1141, it provided a major canvas of Norman society; aristocratic life in all its facets, family concerns, castles, legal proceedings, and endless warfare, were all grist to Orderic's mill. His is by far the richest source for the social history of his time.

No other principality approached the Norman richness in literary sources. But Anjou, the second military power, was also well served. And in one respect, the Angevin material was the more remarkable: the most informative history of the comital family was written by a count of Anjou himself, Fulk le Réchin, around the year 1096.[8] The mere fact that a layman should produce a history is extraordinary; that a count should engage in it seems proof that he, like the dukes of Normandy, regarded such literary production as an essential contribution to the image-making on which comital authority largely depended. Admittedly the history may well have had the purpose of self-justification—Fulk's reign was one of failure; but since the part which related to his own day is lost, we cannot be sure. What remains is a brief account of his family's doings from the early tenth century to his own accession, told in a bald, unvarnished style—a sharp contrast with the semi-legendary history later to be elaborated in the *Gesta Consulum Andegavorum*[9] (see pp. 246–50); yet even in Fulk's unadorned words there can be detected a sense that destiny was guiding the family to glory.

The other sources for Angevin history are more conventional

The most useful is the Annals of St Aubin at Angers, which derived from annals written at St Maurice by Archdeacon Renaud, a pupil of the great Fulbert of Chartres. There is also a history of the church at St Florent at Saumur[10] which, although it was written towards the end of the twelfth century, is based on a late eleventh-century source; its value chiefly lies in what it says of the Angevin conquests in the Touraine— Saumur itself was conquered by Fulk Nerra in 1026.

Image-making of a rather different type continued in Flanders, in the tradition of comital genealogies apparently still produced by monks of St Bertin's. The second genealogy broke with the liturgical interest of the first (see p. 72) in attempting to trace the original Flemish family from which Baldwin I came.[11] Although the genealogy itself is now dismissed as legendary, its author's concern with the ruling family's local roots rather than its Carolingian blood, its 'newness' rather than its inherited position, is witness both to a rather different view (perhaps inspired by Sallust) of what constituted nobility, and to a new and distinctively Flemish orientation of thought. Its continuation, dating from the reign of Robert II (1089-1111) had a more obvious political purpose: to deal with the problem of legitimacy created by Robert the Frisian's usurpation of the comital office in 1070;[12] so it was framed to sway the hearts of its earthly readers, not addressed to God, as the first genealogy had been. Apart from it, the chief source for Flemish history remains the *Annales Blandinienses*, fortified by snippets from the Annals of St Amand.

For Aquitaine, Ademar of Chabannes continued to provide vital information until 1028. But, in tune with a more self-conscious era, his chronicle for the last years centred on the life and works of duke William V, whom he portrayed in the terms which classical authors had employed to gratify Roman emperors. After Ademar this style of writing ceased in Aquitaine. Perhaps surprisingly the great duke Guy Geoffrey had no historian, and his troubadour successor was equally unlucky. The only subsequent chronicle source of much importance for Aquitaine was that of St Maixent,[13] compiled between 1126 and 1141, which offers an interesting mishmash on facts on southern political life.

One of the most difficult, but rewarding, sources for early eleventh century history is the chronicle written by the Cluniac monk Raoul Glaber,[14] dedicated to St Odilo of Cluny, and begun around 1048 at St Bénigne under the aegis of St William of Volpiano. Raoul covered West Frankish history, from about 900 to his own times, from the viewpoint of one who felt himself close to the end of the world. As the millennium of the Lord's passion (1033) approached, his apprehension grew; once safely past that dreaded date, he saw new peace on earth. His purpose in writing was to inspire profound meditation on the ways of God; consequently there was nothing mundane in his selection or interpretation of facts. Yet St Bénigne was no backwater; Abbot Odilo was a frequent visitor; William of Volpiano regularly reported back to his old house on his triumphs in Normandy. Raoul's sources of information were good, even though he dwelt less on his native Burgundy than the historian might have hoped.

For Brittany, as also for Blois and Anjou, the *Chronicle of Nantes*, a history of the counts and bishops of Nantes from the time of Alan Barbetorte to the mid-eleventh century, is useful, though it is not now considered to have been written before the twelfth century.[15]

The sources thus far discussed were consciously written for historical purposes, even though they might have powerful didactic undertones. The increase in their number over the paucity of tenth-century histories and chronicles means that historians are less dependent on purely didactic works than in the earlier period. But there is at least one saint's life, that of St Arnulf,[16] by Hariulf of St Riquier, which casts invaluable light on eleventh-century Flanders. In addition, the fourth book of the *Miracles of St Benedict*, written by André of Fleury some time after 1041, has much to say on the Peace of God movement; and Bernard of Anger's two books of the *Miracles of St Foy*, along with those of his anonymous continuator, still shed light on an area of the far south on which there is little other information.

With the return of greater peace and security, eleventh-century intellectuals revived the habit of letter-writing, fashionable in the ninth century. The letters of the distinguished scholar, intriguer, and future pope, Gerbert of Rheims,[17] shed light on the election of Hugh Capet and the complexities of his early reign. But they are of less general interest than those of Fulbert, bishop of Chartres[18] from 1006 to 1028. The greatest schoolmaster of his day, Fulbert was in regular correspondence with his ex-pupil, King Robert the Pious, with Eudes II of Blois, with Fulk Nerra of Anjou and with William V of Aquitaine. His most famous letter is that on the nature of vassalic obligation, a classic in all textbooks on feudalism (see below, p. 233); but his testimony on the political struggles of his time is just as valuable. Much later in the century, the great canonist Yvo,[19] also bishop of Chartres, wrote letters of interest on the conflicts surrounding Philip I's marriage to Bertrada of Anjou and on the Truce of God.

Yet despite the growing richness of literary sources, the most important source of information on political power and position remains, for the eleventh century as for the tenth, charters. To discuss royal charters first: the decline from Carolingian practices noted for the tenth century continued apace until the last two decades of the eleventh.[20] Royal scribes wrote fewer and fewer of the charters issued in the king's name; they lost the distinctively royal attributes of being dispositive and needing no witnesses. Lemarignier interpreted the presence of witness-lists at the end of many royal charters as an overt sign of royal impotence, a view strengthened by the fact that, from the reign of Hugh Capet onwards, kings were particularly prone to record that they acted with the counsel of their great men in making or confirming a grant. And indeed, the 'joint stock' character of royal lordship was now unmistakeable, though its roots went back to the reign of Charles the Bald. The question then arises whether those who witnessed the charters were identical with those who gave the king advice; if this was the case, then the social status of the witnesses could be an indicator of the court's powers of attraction. Lemarignier drew attention to the fact that, whereas in the reigns of Hugh Capet and Robert II most of the witnesses were bishops or counts, towards the end of the reign of Henry I it was castellans of the royal demesne or household knights who

witnessed. From this he concluded that monarchy in West
Francia had reached its nadir between 1148 and 1177.[21]
This highly ingenious way of measuring royal power deserves
serious consideration. It would, however, be dangerous to
deduce from the fact that important bishops and princes
no longer appeared as witnesses, that they had totally abandoned the royal court; Geoffrey Martel of Anjou is known
to have been a firm ally of Henry I from 1052 to 1060,
and a frequent companion of the king; yet he witnessed only
one charter. It is possible that what has been detected could
be explained by a change in diplomatic fashion. (In the last
two decades of the century, witnesses were limited to the
great officers of the royal household, which is an alteration
not easily explicable in terms of a precise relation between
diplomatic convention and royal power. Chanceries therefore
made changes for reasons other than strictly political ones.)
But if it is correct to regard the middle years of the eleventh
century as the nadir of royal power, then the measurement
is against the yardstick of Carolingian court precedent. Seen
in terms of the effectiveness of rule over a principality, the
charters of Henry I and Philip I indicate a solid degree of
success (see p. 165).

Although royal charters have received the most extended
treatment, much work has also been done on the charters of
Anjou, Flanders, and Normandy. For Anjou,[22] the cartularies
of the great abbeys, of La Trinité of Vendôme, of St Florent
of Saumur, of St Nicholas of Angers, point to early recognition by the monasteries of the value of comital confirmation.
During the reigns of Fulk Nerra and Geoffrey Martel, the area
within which confirmation was sought expanded steadily,
to contract suddenly in the crisis of the late 1060s. Comital
charters were drawn up by the monasteries, except during
Geoffrey Martel's reign, when an embryonic chancery
appeared, and after 1080, from which date the chancery
developed steadily. That ninth-century royal diplomas were
used as models is suggested from Geoffrey Martel's revival
of the outworn royal tax *fodrum*—forage for horses on campaign—long forgotten by the kings.

Flemish charters[23] were also closer in form to Carolingian
than to contemporary royal charters; interestingly, they were

also more varied in content. The counts 'by grace of God' not only granted privileges, they also defined advocates' rights, reached agreements with castellans, and publicized administrative arrangements for their absence from Flanders. Comital notaries, who drew up a few of the charters, were based on St Donatian of Bruges, even before Robert the Frisian appointed its provost chancellor in 1081, a practice which gave continuity in form. The witnesses were most usually the castellans or household officials of the province. It appears that there was rapid development in diplomatic form during the last two decades of the century. This impression holds also for Normandy,[24] where, as in so many other aspects of government, chancery practice was much improved after the conquest of England. Here the most remarkable innovation was the writ, the letter of command, not used by French kings since the reign of Eudes.

There is much work still to be done on eleventh-century princely charters as a whole. Full collections are rare, modern editions few. Nevertheless they are invaluable on two counts: firstly, though the witness-lists should not be taken as evidence that only those who subscribed were present, they can positively identify those important people who frequented a prince's court. The ducal charters for Aquitaine point to warm friendship between the duke and the count of Angoulême, as well as regular visits to the ducal court by the bishop and viscount of Limoges, and the counts of La Marche and Périgueux.[25] Likewise, the Burgundian charters suggest a wide friendship network in operation within the confines of the old duchy of Burgundy, transcending narrower territorial boundaries. Secondly, the way in which princes conceived of their authority comes across more clearly from charter formulae than from other material. When Thibaud III of Blois confirmed a gift by the viscount of Blois to Marmoutier with the words *hoc donum Tetbaldus comes, principalis huius terrae dominus, auctoritate sua firmativ*,[26] 'this gift count Thibaud, chief lord of this land, has confirmed by his authority', he intended to make plain to his readers that he was fulfilling within his county the function of lordship once inherent solely in the crown. It was a self-conscious statement. In the same way, Fulk Nerra, in referring to his sources of income as his *fisc*, a word previously applied only to royal income, and in appending to one of his charters the first surviving princely seal, was by implication conferring semi-regal status on himself. William V of Aquitaine went further in a charter for St Jean d'Angély which runs: *per praeceptum nostrae regalitatis conferre dignemur,*[27] 'by precept of our regality we may deign to bestow'. But enlightening and colourful though these glimpses of princely aspiration are, they should not be taken as having juridical significance. The drawing up of charters created a perfect opportunity for propaganda, for antiquarian posturing, for impudent self-aggrandizement, or, if the charter were drawn up by the beneficiary, for flattery. It is an unwarrantable deduction that contemporaries saw in these phrases the precise expression of legal realities.

CHAPTER 7

Formative trends in
eleventh-century political life

IN the first half of the eleventh century, the impotence of the Capetians was openly acknowledged by their subjects. In the annals of Vendôme, under the year 956, there is the following bitter comment:

Hugh, duke and abbot of St Martin's, died, son of Robert the pseudo-king, father of that other Hugh who was also made pseudo-king, as was his son Robert, whom we saw ruling like a dead man. His son, Henry, the present kinglet, has departed not a whit from his father's laziness.[1]

The strength which kingship had derived from its new royal family—the more extensive demesne, the rather different image—was not sufficient to halt its slide. Yet what was important from the point of view of political history was less the further decline—in any case not extensive—than the prolongation of weakness, the continuation of a situation in which royal intervention outside the demesne was a rarity. The mere fact that this state of affairs could continue for over a century meant that there was no counter-pressure against the pace of change elsewhere. This section first assesses kingship, and then seeks to identify developments which had widespread political repercussions.

(a) Kingship

In his *Carmen* addressed to King Robert, the aged Bishop Adalbéron of Laon mourned: 'Though first among Franks, you are but a serf in the order of kings'.[2] The transfer of the crown to a new dynasty had not halted, still less reversed, the decline in the power and prestige of kingship. Nevertheless, the early Capetians did make some gains which, though not immediately decisive, conferred an aura of prestige and sanctity, later to be developed by their successors.

The first of these gains lay in preventing Charles of Lorraine and his family from claiming as their inheritance the Carolingian royal demesne (the lands around Laon and Rheims); by this, Hugh Capet contrived to keep within his own control an area of great political significance—not only in strategic terms as a buffer against future expansionist policies like those of Herbert of Vermandois, but also for the contribution it made to sustaining the Carolingian myth of kingship, embodied above all in the royal coronation at Rheims. If the last Carolingian obtained less than justice, the first Capetian won a prize vital to the success of his dynasty. For as Hugh Capet and Robert the Pious saw matters, it was essential to prevent any rupture or change of emphasis in the ecclesiastical tradition of extolling kingship. In Abbo of Fleury's *Collectio Canonum*,[3] compiled soon after the change of dynasty and dedicated to the new kings, the section devoted to royal functions was simply transferred *in toto* from a work written by Jonas of Orléans in the reign of Louis the Pious, in which kings were portrayed, in keeping with imperial models, as justice incarnate, the scourges of the impious and the perjurer, the shields of the defenceless. The same conservative rendering was offered in Adalbéron of Laon's *Carmen* to King Robert—though in this case the elderly bishop admitted the failure of contemporary kings adequately to fulfil their obligations, and called on Robert to reverse this trend. Robert was to be the new Charlemagne; and therefore by implication a truer protector of tradition than the last Carolingian kings.

The maintenance of tradition was not by itself enough; in order to convince, the Capets tapped a new source of image-making—the monastic reform movement. Hugh Capet extended his father's role as protector and reformer of monasticism by cementing a friendship with St Odilo of Cluny, the outstanding figure of his generation. If Hugh guarded Cluny's interests, Cluny was lavish in its praises. And it was at Fleury, a house under Cluniac protection, that the new vision of Christian kingship was fully expressed by the monk Helgaud. At first sight, Helgaud's hagiographical rendering of Robert the Pious's life[4] might appear to offer very little in the way of political mileage. Hagiography, after all, is geared to the exaltation of virtues other than those connected with successful rule; the monk-like Robert, renowned for mercy, piety, and humility, might seem as alien to the needs of royal propaganda as he was to truth (at least in so far as we know it from other sources). Yet, despite the criticism which Helgaud admits his stained-glass hero aroused in some quarters, his version of Robert touched a chord in popular emotions. For though, at one level, the life was entirely conventional in fusing a Frankish king with the Old Testament David, Helgaud innovated by making David a saint of the church. From this strange confusion of identities, Robert emerged if not quite as a saint, then at least as a miracle-worker. The water used for washing the royal hands cured a beggar of his blindness; when Robert signed the sick with the cross, their pain abated. Thus in a passage designed to illustrate the king's piety and humility, almost without emphasis, Helgaud laid the foundation of the legend which one day would attribute to the French kings the power of curing scrofula.[5]

So the monastic contribution to Capetian propaganda created a new figure in royal iconography: the holy man. It is notable that, whereas French princes appropriated to themselves without hesitation the traditional job descriptions of the Carolingian kings—defender of the church, protector of the weak, bulwark against enemies—they shrank from allowing portrayal of themselves in the terms that Helgaud thought fit for Robert. There were no princely saints, no princely miracle-works. (Though miracles were said to have been worked at the tomb of Count Richard I of Rouen).[6]

To the minds of the hagiographers, nobility of blood was almost as essential to sanctity as nobility of character; invented genealogies demonstrating close links with the Carolingians were a regular feature of the genre.[7] Until the thirteenth century it did not lie within the Capetians' power to substitute relationship with themselves for relationship with the Carolingians as a yardstick, in the families of their subjects, either of nobility or of sanctity. Indeed, it probably never even entered their heads to do so. The rather undistinguished marriages made by certain cadets of the

Capet family—a daughter of Hugh Capet to the man who became the count of Ponthieu, a son of Philip I to the heiress of Nangis—might suggest that, even to themselves, Capetian blood was not much prized. Nevertheless the early kings of the dynasty were anxious by all available means to raise the status of the eldest ruling line, and to this end impressive marriages were the only possible means. Both canon law and the political instability within the empire created obstacles to unions with the Salians; disputed successions, and then the Norman conquest, ruled out the English royal family; so choice was limited. In 988 Hugh Capet sought a Byzantine bride for Robert. Had the emperor been accommodating, Hugh's initiative would have been liberally rewarded. As it was, Robert had to content himself, initially at least, with the daughter of the Italian king, a marriage which, though satisfactory from the point of view of blood and dowry, failed miserably in human terms. Robert's second attempt, the alliance with Berthe of Burgundy, came up against the insuperable obstacle of ecclesiastical opposition, led by the very section of the reforming church on whose good offices he relied so heavily. The third marriage, with Constance of Arles, was a stormy one; yet the lady, though personally unpopular, was clearly valued as a worthy prize for a king. But Robert's son Henry was the winner of the matrimonial stakes. His marriage with Anna of Kiev provided just that mixture of the undoubtedly royal with the exotic that the home-grown aristocratic line of the Capetians craved in its wives. The Russian connection is thought to have provided the name Philip for the couple's second son,[8] who later became king of France. The name then passed down the ruling line, to be borne by two of the most distinguished kings the Capetian family was to produce.

What Weber called 'charismatic kingship' is difficult to discuss, because charisma—the power to inspire devotion—can neither be exactly located nor measured. There is no proven way of plumbing the medieval imagination to ascertain whether the images learned authors were at pains to paint in fact enjoyed popular appeal, or just which aspects of ceremonial, ritual, or kinship tie commanded an emotional response. But in the subject's perception of kingship lay the ground of his obedience. The early Capetians had only rare opportunities to impress by their moral leadership those who dwelt outside the duchy of Francia; even within it, because their ceremonial was on a relatively small scale, opportunities were limited. Yet the care they lavished both on maintaining the Carolingian tradition of kingship and on marrying well to be worthy of it, suggests appreciation that here lay an effective constituent of royal power: to conform with convention was to elicit reverence. Far more imaginative—though also more speculative in its effects—was their innovation in projecting on the traditional figure of the king the new image of the monastic holy man, with its appeal not only to monks but also to the poor, the unfortunate and the sick of the realm, who had no other shield and defender. In permitting Helgaud to attribute miraculous powers to him, Robert the Pious sanctioned a departure that eventually contributed notably to the deep and enduring affection in which his family was held by the ordinary men and women of France.

For the present, however, the crown was weak. The union of the royal demesne with the Capetian duchy of Francia had provided some enlargement of resources and constituted the area within which the king functioned much as any other prince in his principality (we shall consider the royal demesne below, pp. 162). But in a wider sphere, by 987 specifically royal powers had declined to almost nothing; kings could only claim a pre-eminent exploitation of those powers also enjoyed by their princes and by some bishops. Of these, the most clear-cut and easily analysed was the power to issue and confirm charters. Though eleventh-century royal charters were few and far between, numerically there was no great decrease on late Carolingian totals. Hugh Capet issued on average 1.7 per annum, Robert 3.1, Henry 4.3, and Philip 3.6.[9] Of these a high proportion were written by recipients; and most were evidential rather than dispositive. The geographical area within which men sought a royal charter contracted markedly; here the significant change was the disappearance of Catalan charters in the wake of Hugh Capet's failure to render help to count Borell against Al-Mansur in 987. In addition, there were no charters for Brittany or

Toulouse and very few for Normandy. Indeed, charters which concerned lands outside the heart of the old duchy of Francia were rare; their issue could usually be connected with events of special significance—Robert the Pious's direct rule in Burgundy, Philip I's Aquitaine visit of 1076, or the great council of 1077. So the history of royal diplomatic points to a kingship almost passive outside the royal demesne, and explains convincingly the increased attraction of charters issued by princes.

Royal justice, too, remained unimpressive until almost the end of the century. If Robert the Pious intervened successfully to arbitrate in the quarrel between Richard of Normandy and Eudes II of Blois in 1013-14, less than a decade later he needed Richard as a peacemaker in his own quarrel with Eudes. In arbitration, kings were apparently on the same level as their princes. In inflicting punishment on their *fideles* who committed crimes, they were no more effective. Though Robert the Pious successfully waged war in 1015 against Renaud, count of Sens, accused among other crimes of apostasy, he still deemed it imprudent to disinherit Renaud; it was not until after the count's death that Sens returned to the King. And Robert proved impotent against Fulk Nerra, who in 1008 arranged the murder of Hugh of Beauvais, the Count Palatine, during the course of a royal hunting expedition on which Hugh was accompanying the king. Robert's reaction to this appalling crime, committed in his own presence, was to order Fulbert of Chartres to write to Fulk thus:

Your followers have disgraced the king's presence by committing such a dreadful crime that secular judges say it is a capital offence and that you too are guilty of treason for having afterward given them your protection and a place of refuge. Numerous persons asked us to excommunicate all of you on the feast of Pentecost; but since we were concerned for your salvation, we asked for this to be postponed for three weeks so that we could write and admonish you. We also got the king to agree that if you will stand trial, vengeance will not be taken on the life and limbs of the guilty, but rather on their possessions.[10]

It is clear from this letter that both Robert and Fulbert regarded excommunication as the ultimate sanction against murder. The question of whether Fulk or his hired accomplices should stand trial was to be Fulk's choice; light punishment was held out as an inducement to submission. The reference to the Roman-law doctrine of treason was clearly an effort to frighten. Royal justice emerges from this letter as little more than a reinforcement of princely conscience.

By the last decade of the century, however, coinciding with the more assertive imposition of royal criminal justice on the demesne (see p. 168), Philip I was prepared to exploit royal powers of arbitration more effectively. In 1094 Robert Curthose provided him with an excellent chance, in appealing to the royal court against his brother William Rufus, who was engaged in invading Normandy. In fact, the First Crusade proved more successful in calming things down than royal intervention. But the quarrel did offer Philip the opportunity to gather together large numbers of his *fideles* for a hearing of the case. The royal court was once more convened as a court of justice for the great of the realm.

The composition of that court had, however, changed somewhat with the change of dynasty in 987. The new king had brought with him an influx of officials and vassals from the Capetian duchy of Francia. Therefore Hugh Capet's entirely traditional statement, in a letter to the archbishop of Sens, 'Not wishing to abuse royal power towards anyone, we have submitted all the affairs of state to the deliberation and advice of our *fideles*',[11] may have been rather less traditional in its constitutional implication. For the body habitually consulted on day-to-day matters was now composed rather of local bishops, officials of the duchy of Francia, and local lords, than of the great princes from further afield who had been Charlemagne's *fideles*. Only on rare occasions, such as the councils of 1048 or 1077, did the monarchy surround itself with a substantial assembly of its great men. On the second occasion, King Philip I was so conscious of the assembly's exceptional nature—it was convened to create an alliance against William the Conqueror—that he issued charters to mark it which deliberately imitated ninth-century Carolingian productions.[12]

If the majority of the king's *fideles* were now those who had been the duke of Francia's vassals, that did not mean the bond of fidelity between king and princes had disappeared. It continued as an expression of the princes' friendship and goodwill, occasionally even of their moral obligation. But the circle of those who bound themselves by it had diminished. The great southern counts, already lost to the royal *mouvance* during the later tenth century, remained away (Lemarignier believed that their absence was noted by the royal chancery's reference to them only as *comites nostrae dicionis*, not as *fideles*);[13] the Breton counts were also absent. More seriously, the quarrel between William the Conqueror and Henry I in 1051 put an end to what had been a cordial relationship; the dukes of Normandy were not to return to the royal circle until 1144. In compensation, the ties between the king and the dukes of Burgundy were tightened after Robert II installed his son Henry as duke. And new royal *fideles* were acquired when the archbishopric of Sens, the Burgundian bishoprics of Autun, Auxerre, Mâcon, and Chalon, and much later in the century the bishoprics of Amiens and Thérouanne came under the royal protection. So though the bond of fidelity no longer stretched across the whole extent of what was later to be thought of as the kingdom of France, within the narrower geographical area of the duchy of Francia and its immediate environs, the king's *fideles* constituted a fairly solid group.

As individuals, the princes came to court for business and particularly for coronations—the counts of Blois regularly, those of Anjou frequently, the Norman dukes no less frequently for the first half of the century, but not thereafter, the others occasionally. And there were other times on which they might deal with the king—Robert the Pious's pilgrimage to St Jean d'Angély in 1004 led to meetings with the dukes of Aquitaine and Gascony as well as other southern lords; Philip I's visit to Aquitaine in 1076 improved his relationship with Guy Geoffrey. These personal contacts were crucial to the survival of the monarchy. Though, in his absence, the princes might regard their king as almost one of themselves, to be allied with, to deal with almost on equal terms, all the same when they came into the royal presence, they automatically expressed their sense of reverence.

(b) Economic recovery

On one level, the upswing in economic life evident across the whole of Western Europe in the eleventh century needs no explanation. It is far harder to comprehend the reasons for the depression that hit the European economy in the mid sixth and survived until the mid tenth century than it is to see why the area should return to more normal conditions afterwards. Well before 950, there had been signs of reviving prosperity, attested in the Carolingian *polyptycha* of great abbeys between the Loire and the Rhine. But invasions, whether by foreign raiders or by warriors engaged in civil wars, had disrupted growth. It was not until the second half of the tenth century that the forces of recovery attained sufficient strength to prevail against the tide of petty local reverses. By the mid eleventh century, the outward signs, expanding population, new land settlement, growing towns, the quickening pace of trade, were evident everywhere.

Even so, the particular factors that decisively shaped the incidence and quality of economic growth within the West Frankish kingdom deserve brief discussion. Surprisingly it seems that those areas which suffered most from raids and disruption in the early tenth century—Flanders, Normandy, the Gascon coast—were just the places which, by the end of the tenth century, were prospering. This has suggested the apparent paradox that raids, however deleterious their short-term effects, in the long term fuelled growth, in that they released to the open market treasure hoarded in churches or palaces, and provided more vigorous models for the conduct of trade; further, the buffeting they administered to existing social institutions could be economically beneficial in creating a more adaptable mentality.[14] All three of these consequences can be detected in operation in Flanders as early as the reign of Arnoul I; but it was not until the time of Baldwin IV and Baldwin V that the extent of new wealth, of external trade, of innovation in financial administration, could be appreciated. Much the same might be said of the Norman duchy. In the south, the revival of trade and accumulation of treasure (though with less financial innovation) occurred in rather different circumstances: long after the capture of the Saracen base at Fraxinetum in 972 external stimulus to change was provided, firstly by the chance of plunder in Al-Andalus, and then, after the fall of the Cordovan caliphate in 1025, by regular opportunities for campaigning in Spain. As early as 987, Raymond III of Rouergue had returned to his home after participating in the campaign against Al-Mansur, laden with treasure; much of this he bestowed on the church of Conques,[15] but some, including a fine saddle, he kept for his own use. In the eleventh century, many Frenchmen were to follow his example, bringing home gold and treasures from the immense wealth of Spain, to spend on luxurious living and fine buildings.

In itself, the accumulation of treasure may all too quickly lead simply to renewed hoarding. That it did not do so in West Francia was the consequence of forethought by the princes and bishops under whose aegis Carolingian mints were revived (mainly in the second half of the tenth century) and new mints were created. All over the country, silver was turned into coin at a rate faster than had been seen in Europe at least since the early seventh century. And at the same time as the amount in circulation was dramatically increased, coins of much smaller values than previously known were minted: in Aquitaine, bronze coins were produced. At last, coinage began to reflect the needs of the market-place, rather than those of kings, lords, and tax collectors.[16]

Viking shipping, the quickening of trade across the North Sea, new markets like Rouen that flourished on the sale of booty, the profits of the Christian reconquest in Spain, the availability of suitable coin, all in their various ways made long-distance trade an exciting and rewarding prospect. But had the revival been limited to long-distance trade, its effects would have been small. As it was, the stimulus from the edges of West Francia was rapidly transformed into a general movement. Across the land, bridges were constructed (on the Loire, at Amboise in around 1015, at Angers [in stone] in 1028), new markets were established and protected, rivers were dredged, roads repaired, toll houses set up everywhere. To buy and sell goods in the market-place became again a commonplace of ordinary life.

Where the bulk of the population is engaged in agriculture,

a general increase in trade can only be fuelled by agricultural wealth. The rapid land clearance and new settlements found all over the country in the eleventh century were the signs of arable expansion; the new crops, the vineyards of southern Burgundy and Bordeaux, the pulses encouraged in Flanders, along with better methods of ploughing (though this has been controversial), crop rotation, and the regular use of water-mills, pointed to more intensive cultivation.[17] The growing population was a necessary precondition of both processes; equally, when they were well under way, even more people could be fed. And where the land was unsuitable for arable, as in much of northern Flanders, sheep could earn new wealth for their masters; in the rich pasture lands of Normandy and Brittany, cattle increased in numbers; horse-rearing for the needs of war was widely practised. By 1100, it was clear that the richest area of the country was becoming the once-unfavoured northern plains, the Île de France, Picardy, southern Flanders, Champagne, and Normandy, where at last the richer, heavier soils were beginning to fulfil their potential, to produce the higher yields which should be expected. In these areas, the larger workforce produced the bushels of wheat, barley, and oats, the gallons of wine, beer, and cider needed to sustain fast-expanding old towns like Paris, Arras, Ghent, along with comparatively new or revitalized ones, Rouen, Lille, Ypres, Provins.

These changes did not benefit all equally. Indeed, they may well have increased, at least temporarily, the vulnerability of the poor to famine, since large towns were traps in times of food shortage, and risk-taking was built into establishing new settlements or investing in new crops. But for the self-confident, the tough-minded, or those already shielded from the dangers of starvation, opportunities were ripe. Almost unnoticed, a more entrepreneurial attitude toward assets, whether land, goods, or rights, crept into West Frankish society.

(c) Local consolidation

When Raymond III of the Rouergue explained his determination to build a castle on the rock at Conques in face of the resentment of the monks, he said its purpose was that of forcing his yoke and domination on those who would not freely accept his lordship.[18] By the end of the tenth century, it was an already accepted fact of life that castles had *raisons d'être* other than that of defending the nearby countrymen from raids; in the course of the eleventh century their full potential as aids to authority was revealed. Everywhere, these awe-inspiring outcrops on the landscape—Bernard of Angers declared that Castelpers in the Rouergue soared to the sky[19] —acquired new importance as centres to which the surrounding inhabitants were obliged to gravitate. So castles became the focal points of new districts; they began to reshape the map of the countryside.

The increase in the number of castles is attested by charters, by chroniclers, by aerial photogrpahy, and by physical remains—the use of stone for their erection gradually spread from the Loire valley to neighbouring lands. But who built them and why? In some cases there was clear princely initiative. Hugh Capet ordered the building of three castles on land annexed from St Riquier for the defence of Ponthieu;[20] more impressively, Baldwin IV and Baldwin V brought about the division of their whole comital demesne in northern Flanders into castellanies, with a castle at the centre of each, in order to improve the administration of their lands.[21] In Normandy many castles were established by the dukes as centres for their counts and viscounts. The emergence of more numerous smaller viscounties in Northern Burgundy and Poitou, each based on a castle, may be attributable to the initiative of the dukes of Aquitaine and Burgundy; alternatively, it may only suggest their willingness to adjust the administrative system of their principalities to a framework that they had not created. Then there could be princely initiative of an entirely different nature: Fulk Nerra ordered the building of castles on the fringes of the Touraine to undermine the authority of the count of Blois, as a move in the projected Angevin conquest of Tours. Yet once Montbazon and Montrichard had served that purpose, they changed their function to become pillars of Angevin power in an area of potential disloyalty.

Other castles were built by aristocrats on their own allodial lands, a move which automatically challenged the political claims of the princes. The dukes of Burgundy, Aquitaine, and Gascony were successful in maintaining, at least within the kernels of their principalities, the old doctrine that the public power controlled all fortification: this was sometimes symbolized by the demand that castles be rendered up at intervals to their overlord, whose property they remained.[22] In the north-east the rulers of Flanders and Normandy obtained a similar subordination by different means, the enforcement of homage upon castellans. In Anjou the counts combined the two approaches. But in many other areas, the building of castles signalled the breakdown of old lordship, whether only temporarily, as in the royal demesne, or permanently, as in Berry, much of the Auvergne and the Rouergue. Other princes could have sympathized with King Philip, when he remarked to his son Louis that the castle of Montlhéry had made him old before his time.[23]

The political complexities of castellans' relations with their overlords will concern us later. Here what matters is the fact that, at different dates and with more or less friction, castles everywhere came to be recognized as inheritable by their castellan families. How far this had already been true in places before the beginning of the eleventh century is unclear; but it seems likely, particularly for large areas in the south. The rapid spread of inheritance everywhere in the first half of the century was linked to the new practice among castellans of attaching the name of their castle to their own Christian names, e.g. Hugh de Lusignan. This spread of toponymics has been fitted into a broader change in family structure— a new emphasis on patrilinear connections in the family genealogy, a concentration on the nuclear family, leading to a change in custom regarding inheritance;[24] as security of tenure increased, so primogeniture emerged as a common form of succession; castellans thus began to imitate the princely lines. An effect of inheritable toponymics is that historians can begin to trace the genealogies of the great castellan families of France from the first half of the eleventh cetury. Scarcely surprisingly, this exercise has provoked speculation about the origins of these lineages. Recent research, conducted largely by the technique of matching

Christian names across the generations (see p. 107), has usually concluded that the castellans were simply the long-rooted aristocrats of an area, the viscounts, the *vicarii*, or other great men, who had taken up residence in a castle during the late ninth century, and who, by the beginning of the eleventh, were assuming responsibility for the running of local affairs.[25] This may well be true as a general rule; but the method on which the proof rests is not infallible. And for most of France, the meagreness of the evidence is such as to preserve the possibility that 'new men' like the first lord of Montpellier or Humbaud le Tortu (who left Bellême to become castellan of Vierson)[26] were fairly common.

But whatever the significance of toponymics for castellan families, for the local communities they were the outward symbol that the castellan was there to stay; he and his family had taken such deep root in the soil that the name of their castle had become their chief distinction. This might be an unwelcome realization. For a castellan, even one fairly tightly bound to his lord, could have a decisive effect on the ways of the peasants over whom he towered in new eminence. As Hariulf of St Riquier said of Hugh d'Abbeville, 'defended by his castle, he did what he wanted without fear.'[27] And what castellans in general wanted was a high standard of living, supported by revenues extorted from those who were in no position to refuse their demands. The protection rackets that emerged are well exemplified by Josseran of Uxelles' agreement of 1075 to refrain from pillaging travellers in the area, in return for a regular toll paid by the men of his neighbourhood.[28] But it must be admitted that castellans did also offer defence against enemies other than themselves, against other castellans, or other brigands, even occasionally against foreigners. A famous charter of La Trinité de Vendôme (discussed more fully on p. 230) explains the arrangements whereby the count ensured that the castle of Vendôme would always be guarded as a haven of refuge. The word 'protection' was not altogether abused. This explains why historians of a juridical frame of mind have inclined to dignify the castellans' behaviour by the contention that they had now become sharers in the old public rights of the *ban*, once the exclusive prerogative of kings and their servants.[29] In support of this, they cite frequent annexations by castellans of the old public taxes of *custodia* or *guarda*, sometimes supplemented by *pedagium* for protection of the highway, or tolls for the safe conduct of goods, or the *taille* for occasional assistance in emergency. Because the castellan now guarded his people, he had become the proper recipient of public dues.

The juridical explanation of the 'rise of the castellans' suggests a sharper departure from previous practice than in fact normally occurred. For viscounts and *vicarii* had always acted in the way castellans now did; from the peasants' point of view, it was irrelevant that some of the money extorted by princely officials was then extorted from them by their own superiors. Besides, advocates, some guardians in immunities, even some lay aristocrats, had long claimed to protect the peasants in the same way. So it might be argued that what was new was less the protection-racket itself than the increased ingenuity with which castellans exploited it, and the consequent hostility their activities aroused. The new ingenuity was shown in the fact that between them the new lords not only demanded virtually all ancient public taxes, tolls, market dues, taxes on transhumance—in this sense, the antiquarian researches of tenth-century princes provided material for the next generation of their inferiors —but they began, towards the end of the century, to invent quite new obligations: the duty to use only the lord's ovens and mills; fines for leaving the area; taxes on fishing or on cutting wood. Almost any unexpected occasional bonus could be turned into a customary obligation. Later Lambert of Ardres recounted that the inhabitants of Ardres, fascinated by novelty, had generously volunteered to feed a bear given to their lord by the king of England. Long after their good-will was exhausted, a tax to provide for its food was still being extorted as of right from Ardres.[30] In this way, round each castle in France, a network of new taxes appeared, created by the need or the greed of its castellan.

The damaging results of this extortion were almost universally deplored. In 1076, Aganon, bishop of Autun, gave judgement against his own brother Renaud, who had so oppressed Bligny that 'the village and its inhabitants were heavily burdened and almost ruined by the great weight of bad customs.'[31] But in the short term, redress was usually impossible, since the natural legal authority to whom a wretched community might turn to complain was almost invariably a castellan himself. For all over France in the eleventh century, castellans' courts had appeared, whether as evolutions from old public courts or as new developments; either way they vividly expressed the new power base of society. They differed from the old public courts, which it had been the duty and privilege of free men to attend, in exempting local aristocrats and their knights from appearing, save in special circumstances, while requiring the presence of the unfree (hitherto justiciable only in their lord's court) along with the free peasants. As a consequence of their membership, the chief task of the castellans' courts became the disciplining of the peasantry, which, if the *Miracles of St Foy* can be taken as evidence, they performed with brutality. The lesser men of the Rouergue had no resort but to pray for relief to their local saint when imprisoned wrongfully in terrifying dungeons, blinded, or in imminent danger of execution. There is a sense in the *Miracles* of complete helplessness before the irrational vengefulness of superior might.

The judicial rights of castellans sprang from what were, in principle, two very different sources: their absolute rights, as landowners, over their unfree peasants, and whatever they could claim or assert of the old jurisdiction once exercised by the *mallus* and vicarial courts. Their jurisdiction emerged to fill a gap. But because it had no clear foundation, so it had no properly defined competence. What could or could not be judged in a castellan's court differed from area to area, from court to court. Particularly in France south of the Loire, there remained a widely held view that, though castellans might in practice condemn men to death (as those in the Rouergue often did), nevertheless, serious crime— murder; rape, arson—ought to be dealt with by some higher authority.[32]

In defining those crimes over which they did have competence, castellans referred to them as their *consuetudines*, or customs. The same word began to be applied also to those financial exactions which they took with any regularity from the men of their neighbourhood. No distinction was therefore made between the means for repressing crime and the means of vindicating what castellans regarded as their own rights. In effect, then, the *consuetudines* of a castellany came to express the principles operative in the day-to-day running of a community; and ordinary people came to concur in the use of the term. When they complained, as they regularly did, of a castellan's *malae consuetudines*, they were hoping for the abolition of one or two extortionate taxes or the modification of fines in court, not demanding the restructuring of the system which the castellan had created around him.[33]

It has been said that there was no redress in the short term against the castellan. But in the longer term, he proved vulnerable to the regular complaints made against him; and, because this is surprising, the source of his vulnerability must be sought. In part it lay in the fact that few castellanies were coherent wholes, particularly in the eleventh century. The area which could be dominated from a castle might well cover the territory of another allodial landowner, or of an ecclesiastical immunity; in which case one lord could be played off against another. Perhaps, too, the fact that free men were subjected to the castellan's jurisdiction made criticism of him easier. Besides, bishops and princes might find it in their interests to listen to complaints made against important men whom they found troublesome. And even castellans had consciences on which churchmen could work effectively.

But the chief reason for their vulnerability to criticism lay in the fact that the communities which they dominated grew more important and impressive as the century wore on; and often this was the castellan's own doing. Lambert of Ardres recounts that Arnoul I, seneschal of the count of Boulogne, who built the castle of Ardres in the second half of the eleventh century, gathered round him men from other lordships to lend dignity to the new castle, built a market to supply the castle's needs, attracted inhabitants to the area with privileges, and constructed a church dedicated to the Virgin and St Omer, in which he installed the canons whom he had previously brought together.[34] Arnoul I was therefore more than a fortress-builder or an extorter of taxes; he was the creator of a town. On a larger scale, the castles of the count of Flanders, particularly Lille and Douai, became the kernels of cities whose fame reached across Europe. Given the rapid pace of demographic growth and the economically favourable climate, it was natural that such places prospered. In the west of the country, the communities that sought remedies for *malae consuetudines* were often substantial— Rouen in the reign of William the Conqueror, Poitiers under Duke William IX; even in the less developed east, they were hardly defenceless groups of simple peasants. The inhabitants of Bligny who complained to the bishop of Autun against his brother Renaud could afford to offer Renaud a regular tax in compensation for the abolition of those customs they found intolerable.[35] The complex process of bargaining which characterized the evolution of French customary law was inaugurated in the second half of the eleventh century.

If the castles of the tenth century had militarized the higher ranks, those of the eleventh had deeper and more permanent implications for the whole of French society. The contrast between the still rather primitive defensive structures and their widespread judicial, social, and economic concomitants is striking—so striking as to suggest that castles did not so much cause these bigger changes as draw historians' attention to them. Castellanies as judicial, administrative, and social units could conceivably have evolved without castles at all. In fact they did not. Therefore the history of castles remains integral to the study of the changing map of France, of the evolution of customary law, and of economic revival.

(d) The Peace of God

The peace movement was certainly a result of the *imbecillitas regis* (the weakness of the king); it was also a product of a changing attitude towards private warfare which was not purely confined to churchmen. As the year 1000 approached, and the end of the world seemed very near, St Augustine's teaching that all human associations have at their root passionate search for peace began to have new meaning. Bloodshed, and the destruction of property and crops, both necessary parts of private war, temporarily lost their respectability in the eyes of lords who, in their saner moments, might concede that God was not infinitely bribable, that salvation could not necessarily be assured merely by the donation of a large piece of land to the church in an act of death-bed repentance. In a millenarian atmosphere, they were prepared to listen, at least momentarily, to the voices of ecclesiastical reformers, urging on them their duty of self-restraint. Solemn ceremonies, processions, oath-taking on relics, were evolved to catch the lay imagination, to goad warriors into recognizing their obligations.

In the drive to limit violence, three very different models of peace-making were used: the imperial peace, the private treaty, and the episcopal proclamation. The imperial peace had its roots in Charles the Bald's instruction to his *missi* in 857 that they should protect unarmed churchmen, monks, peasants, widows, and orphans.[36] It was a peace of this kind that the emperor Henry II proclaimed in Germany in 1022, that Bishop Adalbéron of Laon recommended without success to Robert the Pious, and which seems to have been in the mind of Duke William V of Aquitaine in the peace councils which he held for his duchy in the last years of his reign. This model, though, demanded secular courts sufficiently well-developed and independent to operate against breaches of the peace. It was therefore of little practical relevance in most of France; even in Aquitaine, William V's successors thought it unworkable. The other two models both depended on the ecclesiastical courts. The private treaty was simply an agreement between two bishops to prevent their own men from violating the other's territory. Like that in 1023 between the bishops of Beauvais and Soissois,[37] it involved a solemn and public oath from the vassals of both bishops not to break the terms of the peace, which usually included protection for all ecclesiastical property and persons; but it only bound those who had actually sworn, and it depended on excommunication as its sanction. The third model, that of episcopal proclamation, was the commonest and most developed form. A bishop or archbishop simply issued a detailed list of peace obligations binding on all the inhabitants of his diocese, which were sometimes but not always enforced by an oath-taking ceremony; violators were punished in the ecclesiastical courts, by spiritual pains—though fines and even banishment were occasionally invoked to reinforce them. This model lent itself most easily to the Truce of God, first used in the 1020s, which protected neither property nor persons, as did the Peace, but feasts of the Church and Sundays. By the end of the eleventh century, the Truce had been systematically extended to include within the sabbath calm the time from Wednesday evening to Monday morning in every week not already covered by another feast. In Narbonne by 1054, 285 days every year were included in the Truce. Very little of the year therefore remained for legitimate private war.[38]

In some form or other, the Peace or Truce spread everywhere in the first half of the century. But it was sporadic in incidence, far from uniform, and dependent for its impact on an outstanding personality—St Odilo of Cluny, Richard of St Vanne, William V of Aquitaine—and so it easily slipped into oblivion when their influence was removed. It has been variously interpreted: as a reinvigoration of the old Carolingian alliance between bishops and counts; as a radical new alliance of the church with the poor against the warring aristocracy; as a significant impulse to the growth of communes; as an almost fatal blow to royal government. All these positions except the last can be sustained. Yet this very fact suggests that historians may have conferred on the peace movement greater significance than it ever enjoyed, that they have been prone to incorporate it into whichever pattern they happened to be weaving.

The most radical manifestations of the movement were also the shortest-lived. In 1038, the archbishop Aimon of Bourges demanded that the peace imposed on his archdiocese should include a clause binding all men over fifteen years old to combine against violators of the peace. André of Fleury,[39] who told the story, was apparently favourably struck by this move, until the point at which the archbishop's militia, having set out against the powerful Eudes of Déols, was soundly defeated in battle and scattered. In the face of God's judgement, André detected the error of the archbishop. No more was heard of the Bourges militia. But smaller peace militias did survive; Hugh of Flavigny included in his chronicle the story of how the bishop of Autun called out his army of God against Hugh himself in 1098.[40]

In the south, where the movement originated, its apparent effect was conservative, in that bishops and counts joined together to reaffirm and extend the ancient rights of sanctuary, to create special enclaves of protection for all men (*salvamenta*) in addition to the normal job of protecting the weak and keeping holy days sacred. But if counts assisted bishops against offenders, and in some cases even obtained a portion of the fines imposed, nevertheless the bishops' courts maintained their monopoly over cases concerning the peace. As a consequence secular jurisdiction, already suffering a crisis of confidence through the counts' unwillingness or inability to impose punishments on their delinquent aristocrats, was also deprived of the chance to present itself as the upholder of the common good. The net effect was therefore to weaken comital authority in parts of Toulouse, in Narbonne, the Rouergue, the Mâconnais, the Auvergne, and even on the fringes of Aquitaine.[41]

After a flying start with William V's peace councils, the dukes of Aquitaine failed to exploit peace movements to their own advantage later in the century. By contrast the dukes of Burgundy, too weak at first to impose peace, were holding councils in the 1070s, reaffirming the essentially Carolingian alliance between duke and bishops. The counts of Flanders moved earlier and more systematically in the same direction. But the chief gainers turned out to be the dukes of Normandy, who by the end of the century had come close to merging the peace of God into the ducal peace; the secular courts which had begun by assisting the ecclesiastical were on the point of claiming all breaches of the peace as their monopoly. By contrast, the Capetian kings were slow to encourage or foster peace movements; but by the end of the century, it became clear that they had had no incentive to do so, because the essentially royal character of peacekeeping was widely accepted as soon as the kings chose to assert it.

It is perhaps ironical that, though episcopal initiative in the peace movement provided a real challenge to all princely jurisdiction, the princes most fitted to answer this challenge turned out to be those who owed their initial position to conquest. For the older, more established secular powers either failed to innovate sufficiently or, where they did, to sustain the momentum. As a consequence of this, and also of the decline of millenarian sentiment, by the second half of the century the peace movement lost steam in the areas where princes had exploited it little. Nevertheless, the twelfth century was to see an important revival in the far south.

Further down the social scale, the effects of this reaction against violence are more controversial, though arguably as significant. In contributing to a sense of solidarity in the military class, whose members were all treated as equal potential threats to peace, the movement tended in some measure to bridge the gulf between aristocrats of high birth and the mounted soldiers whom they commanded. It therefore facilitated the process whereby the knights, at different times in different areas of West Francia, were accepted into the aristocratic class, albeit on the lowest rung.[42] But here, it was only a minor factor in an assimilation fed more forcefully by proximity and mutual interests. More importantly the beneficiaries of the peace movement, churchmen, merchants, pilgrims, and peasants, hitherto the victims of military aggression, were encouraged to feel the injustice of their plight. As they saw it, if bishops were prepared to punish crimes against them on certain days or in some circumstances, then perhaps all such crimes were morally indefensible. There may well therefore be a connection between their sense of moral justification born of episcopal support and their confidence in bargaining with castellans, noted above.

(e) Ecclesiastical reform

The medieval church was never without its powerful impetus towards change, its sense of guilt and failure rooted in recognition of the falling away from Gospel standards, its urgency in pressing for a better world derived from the fear that time was short. But at no other period in the Middle Ages did this impetus evoke so strong and widespread a response throughout the church and its lay adherents as in the eleventh century. And nowhere was that response richer, more varied, more creative than in West Francia.

The period 980–1020 was the culmination of the monastic reform movement which had begun in the aftermath of the Viking raids. The outstanding figures of the period, St Odilo of Cluny, Richard of St Vanne, William of Volpiano, were concerned in the first instance to place the gains of past decades beyond dispute; monastic estates were stringently guarded against future annexation, privileges of immunity interpreted in a more literal, more legal sense.[43] Next, they aimed to found monasteries where none had existed before, or to reform in accordance with Benedictine ideals those that had slipped from the paths of approved practice. And finally, they aspired to infuse the Benedictine spirit into the wider world, to allow others than monks to experience monastic peace, either through encouraging the establishment of reformed houses for canons, or more directly, by playing leading roles in the Peace of God.

Had the princes been men in the Hobbesian mould, motivated by enlightened material self-interest, they would doubtless have perceived the threat to their powers inherent in what was happening: in the demand that immunity be fully respected, thereby restricting comital intervention; in the insistence that monastic land should not be granted to soldiers, even in return for ninths and tenths; in the enlarged ecclesiastical jurisdiction which resulted from the peace movement. As it was, they threw their zeal and generosity behind the reform movement as forcefully as had their grandfathers in the days when the stimulus to reform had come primarily from the great lay magnates. Baldwin IV of Flanders, Richard II of Normandy, Bernard William of Gascony, with the kings Hugh Capet and Robert the Pious, all earned the praise that Ademar produced for William V of Aquitaine, 'he was always the defender of God's servants.'[44] So it was only in episcopal circles—most notably in Adalbéron of Laon's *Carmen*—that criticism of monastic reform was voiced.

The success which crowned reform by the second and third decades of the eleventh century stimulated efforts on a broader canvas. Sacraments should be properly celebrated, not just in the great abbeys, but in cathedrals, in churches of canons, and in the rapidly-growing number of ordinary parish churches across the land. To this end, more fitting buildings were erected, the necessary books copied, the necessary fonts and chalices produced. There was much to be done, and much was acheived. But inevitably those of more fervent reforming ardour came up against human problems; the provision of material objects was useless if the priest, canon, or even bishop who performed the sacrament was incapable of reading the service, or incompetent in explaining its meaning, or too lazy to bother to do either. Cathedral or monastic schools might supply a deficiency in education—by the end of the century Laon was the most famous of the cathedral schools, Bec of the monastic—but this was not at the root of the problem. The real difficulty lay in appointing men fit for office.

As the eleventh-century reformers saw it, there were two answers to their problem: one was to forbid clerical marriage, both in order to prevent the inheritance of priestly office, and in the expectation that a celibate clergy might imitate the monks in a purer vision of truth. That the church ultimately succeeded in this revolutionary aim was a major tribute to the high-mindedness (though not necessarily to the common sense) of the priesthood as a whole. The second solution, which seemed much simpler, in fact proved far more difficult: to alter in some measure the systems by which priests were chosen and paid. To take the second matter first, a priest who was financially bound to his patron, or in receipt of so small a wage that he had to do other work to stay alive, was hardly likely to prove a wholly effective and committed servant of God. So, following the example set by the monks in reclaiming monastic lands, the second generation of reformers demanded the return to the church of sources of revenue originally intended for the maintenance of the clergy—above all tithes—and an end to, or at least a limitation on, those *consuetudines* with which lay lords had burdened churches in return for their guardianship. Here, too, the long-term success of the reformers was impressive; for many—though not all—tithes were resumed, and there was widespread sympathy among influential laymen for the fight to retain ecclesiastical wealth against inventive lay depredation. Though less than was hoped for was attained, the church grew wealthier than it had been at any time since the sixth century.

But the real problem lay with the selection of priests and bishops. Because patronage of parish churches was in the hands of the lay founder's family, and that of bishoprics in the hands of the king or of the lay aristocracy, open abuse had crept into the system. Hopeful candidates for office might be required to buy their way by the sin of simony. To eradicate this was the first objective of the reforming papacy. Pope Leo IX held a great council at Rheims in 1049, at which simony was denounced in the strongest of terms, and those guilty of it among the French hierarchy—including the bishop of Langres—were deposed. The example was compelling. Straightforward simony gradually disappeared, though other more subtle forms may have survived for longer.

However, the eradication of simony was not sufficient to ensure that office would be reserved for those of spiritual motivation. There was an obvious case for the church to reclaim the right of appointment. But here opinions on how far and in what circumstances this should be done began to diverge. For all could see that, if the church introduced a radical programme denying all lay election, it might well lose as much as it gained, by alienating the support of certain great princes for whom control over bishops was an integral part of authority. The reformers therefore proceeded with caution. They were effective in persuading or pressurizing small landholders to abandon their rights of patronage—by the second quarter of the twelfth century, only Normandy retained a large number of parish churches with lay patrons; and even there, proprietorship had given way to a system in which the local lord nominated strictly in accordance with the demands of canon law. But higher in the social scale, the reformers proved respecters of persons. Where great lords habitually appointed excellent bishops, the only change pressed was the abandonment of lay investiture—

the practice whereby princes invested their bishops with the staff and ring, the symbols of spiritual office. From this move intellectuals, led by Yvo of Chartres, developed a clear distinction between the temporalities and the spiritualities of the church, on which much later canon law was founded. But where the appointments did not please, or where princes for other reasons fell foul of the great ecclesiastics, the demand for an election in accordance with canon law—by the monks of the great abbeys, by the canons of the cathedrals—was interpreted in such a way as to exclude lay interference.

The movement for ecclesiastical reform in West Francia was home-grown. Its roots were in the soil. Therefore its championship by the papacy from 1049 onwards only entailed new pace and fervour, not a change of direction. Even the legates nominated by Gregory VII (Hugh of Die, Amatus) varied their actions to suit local conditions; then the pontificate of Urban II saw a Cluniac monk at the helm of Christendom. There were of course potentially destructive implications in what was attempted, as Gregory VII made plain in a famous letter of Wimund, bishop of Aversa:

If perchance, you offer in opposition the authority of custom, you should consider that the Lord said: 'I am the Truth'. He did not say 'I am custom' but 'truth'. And certainly (to use the expression of the blessed Cyprian) any custom whatever, however old, however popular, is to be altogether less esteemed than truth, and a usage which is contrary to truth should be abolished.[45]

These sentences were later incorporated by Gratian into his Concordance of Discordant Canons (see p. 279), and constituted a cornerstone of the church's self-justification. But the chief concern of the popes was never to implement a programme based on abstract principles taken to their logical extreme; it was simply to secure a competent clergy, fully conscious that their high calling marked them out from laymen. To that end, the reformers chose whatever path seemed expedient, they worked with any whom they thought could further their cause. In some places and among some men, custom survived their onslaught remarkably well; in others, 'truth' rapidly prevailed against it.

This contrast can be illustrated by the progress of reform

in Normandy and in Aquitaine, the only two principalities in West Francia whose princes had succeeded in reviving the Carolingian ideal of lay and ecclesiastical harmony, symbolized in the convocation by the prince of ecclesiastical synods. In Normandy, whose dukes had recreated the church, the second half of the eleventh century witnessed an increase in ducal control. William the Conqueror's regime favoured the implementation of canon law in all spheres except those which might threaten his own dominance over his bishops and abbots, a dominance he considered necessary to the church's security, well-being, and spiritual progress. Because he succeeded in convincing Gregory VII that he was correct, the Carolingian mode of church government survived in Normandy well into the twelfth century, its only serious modification coming with Henry I's abandonment of lay investiture in 1107.[46] But in Aquitaine, where William V's successors had not succeeded in building on his inheritance of ecclesiastical councils for the whole duchy, the path of reform proved stormier. Guy Geoffrey, a noted campaigner for the church in Spain and related by his third marriage to Hugh, abbot of Cluny, generally contrived to work with the reformers while moderating their zeal. But even he could not prevent his old friend Joscelin de Parthenay, archbishop of Bordeaux, from falling foul of the papal legates; and on his death in 1086, the real breach came. In 1089, the legate Amatus held a council in Bordeaux, in which he obtained his own election to the archbishopric of that city, *nolente comite*, i.e. against the will of Duke William IX.[47] From that time, papal pressure steadily diminished princely right over episcopal election and princely guardianship over the church in Aquitaine. William IX's unpopularity with the reforming party was testified in a poem often ascribed to Hildebert of Lavardin, in which the poet extolled the memory of Peter, bishop of Poitiers, who criticized William IX's sexual mores, and was banished for his pains:

> Thou wert Elias to this Jezabel,
> John to Herodias; the selfsame sex,
> The selfsame fury drove thee from thy city
> The holy things were flung to palace dogs,

Law broken, trampled right;
Thy priests constrained and harried
By men that turn to crime from wantonness
And no entreaty can entice to good.[48]

The different fates of Normandy and Aquitaine were
sealed by the sharply contrasting reputations of William the
Conqueror and William IX. Elsewhere too personal factors
were crucial to the progress of reform. While Hugh of Die
showed no concern for Fulk le Réchin's interests or feelings,
he happily worked in close alliance with Thibaud of Blois.
As a consequence, lay patronage disappeared rapidly in
Anjou, and the count's choice of men for the bishopric of
Angers was undermined by the deposition of his bishop;[49]
while in Blois-Champagne, though voluntary renunciation
was encouraged—Stephen of Chartres later granted the
bishop of that city that on his death, his goods and dwelling
house should be inviolate against comital depredations[50] —
Thibaud continued quietly to appoint to the bishopric of
Troyes as he had always done. Because Urban II hoped for
Robert the Frisian's assistance in the war against Henry IV
of Germany, Robert got his own way over the diocese of
Arras, and successfully played off the papal legate against
the pope himself in preserving his rights over Thérouanne.
But this gain was thrown away by his pious successor Robert
II, who could not reconcile his conscience with the traditional ways.[51] And if princes were open to persuasion, the
reformers found it easier to deal with those southern aristocrats of the second rank who had taken control over bishoprics in the late tenth century. In 1085, the count of Melgueil
renounced his rights over Maguelonne; later the viscounts of
Agde and Béziers made similar renunciations.[52]

So by the end of the first decade of the twelfth century,
the only princes who retained control over more than one
bishopric were the king and the duke of Normandy; they
retained what they had with the acquiescence of the
reformers, exercising their patronage in accordance with
canon law. Yet the change in methods of election elsewhere
was not often accompanied by a change in the kind of men
elected. Aristocratic bishops continued as the norm across

West Francia; if anything, it became commoner for cadets of princely families to achieve a mitre. Perhaps only in Brittany was an extensive reform put in hand. Although Leo IX's first intervention in Breton affairs (the deposition of the bishop of Nantes in 1049, and the later condemnation of the bishop of Dol) achieved little, by the end of the century the bishops of Upper Brittany were no longer drawn from the top social ranks of the province. Some indeed were foreign scholars of distinction, like Marbod of Rennes or Baudry of Dol, trained in the schools of Angers, interested in bringing the Breton church at last into line with the rest of Christendom.[53] As a consequence of this influx of new blood, the twelfth century was to witness the slow elimination of specifically Celtic practices from the Breton church.

If Brittany was unique in the degree of change inaugurated, it would be wrong to imagine that elsewhere the reformers' victory had been a hollow one. Though the ruling classes of the church continued for the most part to share blood and upbringing with the lay aristocracy, the old social ease, the old certainty of shared interests, was gone. A career in the church set a man apart. No longer could secular and ecclesiastical authority be combined in the fashion of Hugh, count of Chalon and lord of territory in Beaune, Autun, and southern Auxerre, who had been made bishop of Auxerre in 999.[54] At the same time, princely pretensions to the possession of priestly powers received a harsh blow. In the early twelfth century, Hugh of Fleury dedicated his work *On Royal Power and Sacerdotal Dignity* to Henry I of England, to protest against the error of those who tried to sever the links between church and state.[55] A century earlier, the necessity for such a demonstration could never have arisen.

CHAPTER 8

The Principalities 987–1108

(a) The royal principality

Defining the royal principality in the eleventh century has not proved a simple task. In the narrowest sense it could be thought to consist only of the royal demesne, those lands from which the king drew manorial revenues and over which he was immediate overlord. Or, rather more meaningfully and by analogy with other principalities, it could be defined as the area over which the king either directly retained public powers or held in vassalage the counts and viscounts who did. Or, by analogy with the duchies of Aquitaine and Burgundy, it might be held to include those areas outside the king's power to coerce, whose independent counts nevertheless saw themselves as his allies and frequented his court as a matter of custom. Despite the disappearance of the duchy of Francia on Hugh Capet's election to the throne, it is clear that some sense of the old bonds did remain among the northern counts and princes. The problem here, though, is that it is almost impossible for the historian to distinguish between respect and loyalty paid to the heir of the duke of the Franks from that paid to the sovereign. But the latter was certainly much more meaningful within the boundaries of the old duchy than beyond it.

To start with the royal demesne: by 987 its axis lay between Orléans and Paris. Within that area, the Capetian family owned large estates, mainly in three distinct areas: (a) north of the Loire round Orléans; (b) in the Dreux-Poissy-Argenteuil-St Denis-Paris area; and (c) round Compiègne and Senlis. From these they derived revenue of two kinds, both manorial (rents, dues from mills and ovens, serf-labour, profits from grain sales) and public (profits from local courts, hospitality rights, tithes, and tolls.) These revenues are thought to have increased substantially in the course of the eleventh century, a period when forest clearance went on apace all over the Île de France, and when land was put down to large-scale cultivation or vineyards. The Capetians were efficient landlords; the first mention of a *prévôt* on a demesne is as early as 1006,[1] and by the middle of the century there were eleven *prévôtés* to collect revenue. In the reign of Philip I, the king can be detected buying and selling parcels of land or entering into *pariage* agreements with his neighbours to consolidate the royal estates. A rather down-to-earth business sense was characteristic of the family as a whole.

The kings enjoyed revenues from public rights over wider and much more scattered areas than their demesne. They held comital powers in Paris (though Hugh Capet alienated these, his successors resumed them), Senlis, Orléans, and after 1015 Dreux, which were as crucial to their political power as Poitiers, Saintes, and Bordeaux to the dukes of Aquitaine, or Autun, Avallon, and Dijon to the dukes of Burgundy. They also held (sometimes enfeoffed from bishops) a patchwork of regalian and comital rights—bits of counties, bits of vicariates, rights to justice—scattered all across the Île de France, a legacy of administrative disintegration, of escheats and of their own purchases. At this level royal rights were very fluid; they might be granted out or enfeoffed to others to bring royal service; so they constituted as much a stock for patronage as a source of permanent revenue. It has been calcualted that the gains and losses probably just about cancelled each other for most of the century; only in the last decades can a definite increase be seen—in the acquisition of the Gâtinais from Fulk de Réchin, the French Vexin from Simon de Crépy (though it went briefly into Norman hands), Vermandois for a cadet branch of the family, and finally the purchase of the viscounty of Bourges in 1101. These set the scene for the twelfth-century advance.[2]

To tell the story of the royal demesne like this, however, is to miss the main point: in fact the king's right to receive his revenues and exercise his public powers was sharply challenged by his own castellans. The castles of the Île de France, originally part of the successful Capetian defence system against Viking aggression, were in general public fortifications;

one or two adulterine castles existed—Philip I referred in a charter to God's vengeance on one at Compiègne[3]—but they were unimportant. By the early eleventh century, their function of defending an area against external threat had been commuted into one of holding down and governing the surrounding countryside; their castellans had become not just soldiers but judges, administrators, and revenue collectors. As a consequence they demanded higher social status, hereditary successions, a greater degree of independence. When this was not granted, some of them, particularly those from north of the Seine, in the 1020s allied with Eudes II of Blois against the king.[4] From Eudes they learned the determination and persistence which characterized their opposition to Henry I. In the face of their castellans' intransigence, first Robert the Pious and then Henry played the dangerous game of elevating some castellans to comital rank—the Montmorency, Montfort, Épernon, and Nogent-le-Roi families, who had hitherto only enjoyed vicecomital rank, or even complete outsiders like Beaugency; these new counts they charged with suppressing the castellans in their area, to prevent the extreme localization of power. In the end, the crown won: the battle of Pithiviers in 1044 was a royal victory against the concerted ranks of castellans; but it was won at the expense of completely blotting out the already blurred Carolingian administrative map and of cheapening the office of the count. What had been done once in time of crisis was to be done again in more normal circumstances. By the end of the century, there were so many counts in the Île de France that the title was manifestly less meaningful, both administratively and socially, then it had been at the accession of Hugh Capet. Nor was the crown's victory complete. Some castellan families, most notoriously that of Montlhéry, escaped the stranglehold of new comital power and remained to bother later kings.[5]

The creation of new counts simply added to the number of important men whom the king had either to force into his vassalage or to persuade to attend his court. The old comital families of the Île de France, Vendôme (soon sucked into the Angevin *mouvance*), Melun, Corbeil, Dammartin, Clermont, Beaumont-sur-Oise, Valois, and the new ones of Hugh Capet's reign, Ponthieu and Meulan, already put a substantial strain on royal diplomacy. The count of Dammartin had been attracted to Eudes II's circle of vassals as well as the king's; the count of Valois was a firm opponent of Henry I in 1041. Exactly what combination of bullying, bribery and bargaining was employed to bring most of them to heel, is not known. But the witness lists to royal charters, usually used to prove the weakness of the crown, demonstrate that the castellans, the vassal counts and even the fairly independent counts of the Île de France, were regular visitors to the royal court.[6] Henry I and Philip I could count on their presence in some numbers for as long as diplomatic fashion regarded their signature as an asset—mainly between the years 1025 and 1077. This was perhaps a small triumph— the mere fact of their presence was not enough to ensure their loyal service. But at a time when political relationships were intensely personal, for the two parties to meet each other frequently was a *sine qua non* of the system.

If royal efficiency is to be tested by the same yardsticks as those applied to the other princes—ability to exploit and administer the demesne, to keep alive Carolingian public rights, to enforce vassalage on castellans and lesser men, to attract the greater to court—then the Capetians must be deemed efficient by the standards of their time. Though other important principalities had risen within the old duchy of Francia, though the old administrative framework had dissolved, though the kings met with belligerence from their own castellans, still, they dealt effectively with the challenges, they adapted themselves to changing needs, they kept the kernel of their principality under control, albeit with difficulty, and they continued to attract others to them. Less forceful or innovative than the counts of Flanders or Rouen, denied the chance of expansion that so enhanced the duke of Aquitaine's prestige, they nevertheless avoided lengthy internal squabbles of the sort that nearly ruined Anjou at the end of the century and that opened Brittany to external ambitions. Their record was quite good by the standards of any but nostalgic clerics like Adalbéron of Laon.

In one respect, the kings had the advantage over all their

princes—in the extent of their ecclesiastical demesne, which increased during the century.[7] The degree of benefit the Capetians could derive from their control over royal bishoprics depended both on the closeness of the bishopric to the king's lands and on the strength of reforming sentiment among its clergy. To accept a present for performing investiture was widely condemned as simoniacal, even in the first half of the eleventh century. Royal nomination, on the other hand, was acceptable if handled with tact and courtesy; the drawback was that it could not always be effected. For though Robert the Pious's half-brother became archbishop of Bourges, and royal clients were found in other bishoprics, local aristocratic families might be in a better position to impose their own nominees, as is shown by the Roucy family domination over the archbishopric of Rheims in the first half of the century. Still, even if it was an occasional perquisite, royal nomination did increase the king's patronage. Then there might be solid financial advantage where the king could seize a dead bishop's goods and enjoy the revenues of the diocese during a vacancy; but there were practical problems in achieving this; and churchmen disapproved well before the Gregorian reform movement got underway. Probably the greatest advantage of royal protection, at least for Hugh Capet and Robert the Pious, was that it constituted a reason for royal bishops to visit the court; they were, however, less assiduous visitors by the reign of Henry I.

Royal investiture was not attacked by the reformers before 1078—Gregory VII made no objection to Philip I's investing the bishop of Mâcon in 1073; and even when it was proscribed, it was a side-issue to the attack on simony. Philip's rights might well have survived for longer if he had not fallen under severe ecclesiastical censure as a consequence of the marriage with Bertrada of Montfoit, Fulk le Réchin's wife. The newly-elected bishops of the late 1070s and early 1080s, more self-conscious than their predecessors, shunned the investiture of a king in disgrace. Circumstances therefore contrived to confuse the issue during the dangerous later years of Gregory VII's pontificate. Then, in the calmer atmosphere engendered by Urban II, Yvo of Chartres among others succeeded in dividing the bishop's spiritual rights from his temporal ones. As a consequence, though the king lost the right to confer the ring and staff, he continued to bestow the temporalities, and in return for his sacrifice was usually permitted to enjoy the episcopal revenues during a vacancy. Both king and bishops sought compromise; so while Philip conceded freedom of election, the church safeguarded his right of veto.

The ecclesiastical demesne also included royal monasteries, a number swollen by those—for example St Germain-des-Prés and St Martin of Tours—already in Capetian hands before 987. Here Hugh Capet's and Robert the Pious's support of the monastic reforming party led them to limit their interference to the confirmation of the abbots' elections, in return for which they accepted a heavy burden of responsibility in defending the monasteries. This policy bitterly disgusted Adalbéron of Laon, who chided the kings for their powerlessness and attacked Odilo of Cluny for laying claim to royal authority.[8] The aged bishop's point was reinforced by the fact that the early eleventh century saw a tide of new small monasteries and collegiate houses across the Île de France, founded by castellans and lesser lords, who now challenged the hitherto exclusively princely right of monastic guardianship. The king's monastic pre-eminence stood in danger of being engulfed. Yet the new houses often demanded royal charters of confirmation, or on occasion royal assistance against their founders' families; thus there was benefit of a different kind to be obtained from their existence. And Hugh's and Robert's reputation as devoted adherents of Abbo of Fleury or St Odilo of Cluny stood them in good stead among men less biased than Adalbéron. So neither the reform movement nor the proliferation of houses should be entered on the balance-sheet as unmitigated losses for the crown, even in the short term.

In the long term, it transpired that the absence of confrontation between church and state in eleventh-century France brought solid gain. As the kings emerged around 1100, poorer only by those sources of revenue they had voluntarily sacrificed, the value of the trust they had earned in ecclesiastical circles became clear: they had forged a working relationship with the popes sufficiently resilient to survive the occasional tempestuous outburst; and by emphasizing their role as defenders of bishops and abbots, they had created a network of committed supporters across the country. Much of the aura surrounding their successors had its essence in these two achievements. From them also sprang the rather unexpected ability of France's twelfth-century kings to exploit the essentially Gregorian notion of hierarchy as the means of raising themselves to the apex of French society.

In relation to the peace movement, too, the kings' willingness to follow their churchmen's lead rather than striking out on their own in the end proved fruitful. But at first Robert the Pious's stand looked pathetic. He had before him an example in the German emperor Henry II's peace proclamation of how the heirs of the Carolingians might conduct themselves in protecting the weak and the vulnerable; that he did not capitalize on this brought criticism on him. When the peace movement did penetrate the royal demesne, it was in the form of an episcopal peace, a private treaty between the bishops of Beauvais and Soissons in 1023, which the king only witnessed.[9] Robert was already familiar with this means of defending those who did not bear arms, because he had promoted it in Burgundy in 1016 with his ally, Hugh, count of Chalon and bishop of Auxerre. But it was an essentially episcopal move, offering far less scope for royal participation than the pattern followed by William V in Aquitaine or by Hugh in the duchy of Burgundy in 1078; and it even denied Robert the chance of adding royal sanctions to episcopal, as Baldwin V of Flanders and William the Conqueror were to do. So by the standards of its time, the 1023 peace was a feeble thing. And if Robert lost an opportunity, Henry I ignored the peace movement altogether.

Yet the root cause of this apparent inertia was that the peace movement had less to offer to kings than to princes. For when, towards the end of the eleventh century, the tide turned on the royal demesne, Philip I and his young heir Louis took a more active, direct role in the suppression of crime, sending out knights to capture miscreants, forcing criminals to answer charges in their court, executing sentences by force;[10] it then became clear that kings had no need of the peace movement. They had but to revive the

Carolingian tradition of kingship as the scourge of the wicked, for their competence in the matter to be at once accepted. Whereas princes found it expedient to present themselves as the bishops' auxiliaries in the repression of crime, on the royal demesne the bishops were as anxious as everyone else that the king alone should first condemn wickedness and then punish it.

(b) Duchies and counties

(Discussed in order from south to north of the country)

(i) Toulouse

The eleventh century is little richer in sources for Toulousan history than the tenth; indeed, in one respect, the obscurity is greater: the withdrawal of Raymond III Pons's successors from the northern political scene meant that the counts of Toulouse achieved only the rarest of mentions in northern sources. No royal charters were drawn up for Toulouse, no count or abbot from Toulouse sought royal confirmation for a grant. Toulouse bade fair to follow Catalonia, which, after 987, slipped out of the West Frankish kingdom. Only constant friction with the dukes of Aquitaine over the frontier regions of their principalities drew the counts northwards. For the rest, Toulousan politics were firmly orientated south and east, to the Mediterranean..

The economic revival, gaining strength as time wore on, was spurred by the destruction of the Saracen stronghold at Fraxinetum in 972, and by the quickening of the Catalan economy in the first half of the eleventh century. But it also had local roots. Within the county of Toulouse, land-clearance was carried on apace; the town of Toulouse grew from a small ecclesiastical centre surrounded by forest land into a substantial urban area, which slowly revitalized the Garonne as an artery of trade. In Gothia, where there was rather less space for expansion, the comparative peace of the period permitted the renewed exploitation of old urban centres and good coastal communications; while in the hinterland, land was cleared by groups of peasants operating within new *salvamenta*, sanctuaries created by the peace movement.

Prosperity may well have been the underlying cause of political conservatism in the area. For if the old public courts had disappeared, if charters were declining in number because written proofs were held in less esteem in courts, if castles multiplied, these seemed small changes in comparison with what had survived: the old *pagi*, the viscounties, old public obligations and dues; even, in the comital house, the division of inheritance among sons. William Taillefer's two sons Pons and Bernard split the family lands and titles on their father's death in 1037, as did Pons's two sons on his in 1061. It was not until Pons's younger son, Raymond IV of St Gilles, united Toulouse and Gothia again that a change was effected in the succession custom. In the twelfth century Toulouse joined the other principalities in recognizing primogenital succession.

The county of Toulouse survived division of inheritance; its only rival within the area, the county of Carcassonne, did not. The table below shows how Carcassonne and the comital rights that went with it were fragmented among the heirs of

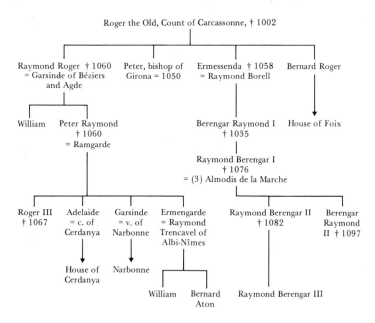

Fig. 3. The Descendants of Roger the Old

Roger the Old. As the table explains, through family deaths between 1060 and 1067 the greater part of the rights over Carcassonne and Razès, along with the viscounties of Béziers and Agde, came into the hands of Ermengarde and her husband, Raymond Trencavel of Albi-Nîmes. But in 1068 Raymond Berengar I, count of Barcelona, grandson of Ermessenda, determined to increase the small number of Carcassonne rights he had inherited by buying their share from Ermengarde and Raymond, as the big step in reconstituting the county of Carcassonne for Raymond Berengar II, a son by his third marriage; the count of Barcelona's motive here was to provide for his younger son while protecting the integrity of Barcelona as the inheritance of his son by his first marriage. In fact, his plans came to nothing; his eldest son murdered his stepmother and then vanished; in 1082 Raymond Berengar II was killed by his brother, Berengar Raymond II, the Fratricide, who was unable to assert his rights over the newly reassembled county of Carcassonne. At this point, Bernard Aton, viscount of Béziers, stepped in, taking control over Carcassonne, perhaps in the name of Raymond Berengar III, then a minor. But when Raymond Berengar III assumed his majority, Bernard Aton held on to Carcassonne, turning to the count of Toulouse in support of his claim.[11]

This complex story is worth dwelling on for several reasons: in the first place, it demonstrates that partible inheritance could transform public rights into saleable commodities. But the house of Barcelona's determination to reconstitute the county of Carcassonne shows the reverse process. Thus the past was not totally forgotten in the scramble for self-enrichment. The old counties of the far south proved more resistant to fragmentation than might at first glance appear. Secondly, the Barcelonese initiative from 1067 to 1082 had created solid Catalan rights within Gothia; if, through the death of Raymond Berengar II, those rights went into cold storage, they were not forgotten; the twelfth-century counts of Barcelona were to reassert them as part of a larger initiative beyond the Pyrenees. Lastly, and perhaps most importantly, in these events the famous Trencaval family can be seen to carve out the beginning of its family dominions, through Raymond Roger's marriage with Garsinde, through Raymond Trencavel's marriage with Ermengarde, and through Bernard Aton's seizure of Carcassonne.

In all this the counts of Toulouse, the nominal over-lords, were passive spectators. Until Bernard Aton sought Bertrand's overlordship in 1107, they had played no part in the drama. Yet it must have been of some interest to them that their viscounts, nominally within their control, were changing the nature of their office by building up solid land-blocks for themselves, and by impudently intruding on the rights of others. Nor was this initiative confined to the viscounts of Béziers and Albi-Nîmes; in the far south, the descendants of Bernard Roger, son of Roger the Old, con-solidated their estates and had, by the middle of the century, arrogated to themselves the title of counts of Foix; the vis-counts of Narbonne had expanded their lordship to cover the whole county of Narbonne, with parts of Roussillon and Girona; the counts of Substantion-Melgueil had taken control over the bishopric of Maguelonne, which they held till 1085; the lords of Montpellier were building up their principality.[12] All these changes were slow, almost frictionless, and may have been governed by agreements;[13] but they did have the effect of excluding the count of Toulouse from much of his territory; and they almost certainly reduced his potential revenue.

In compensation, the counts exploited their Provençal lands, inherited from Raymond of St Gilles's marriage, along with the area around St Gilles, the natural gateway to Provence. St Gilles grew rapidly, as a comital residence, as a pilgrimage centre, and as a trading-post. It was con-veniently sited, too, for visits from the lords of Gothia, on which the count's lordship depended. In 1076 Raymond of St Gilles obtained the guardianship over the young heir of Montpellier; in the course of his rule he heard at least one appeal from the Rouergue. Indeed, there are signs that Raymond was in the process of building up some distinctive competence for his court, by attracting appeals from nobles and ecclesiastics of Gothia. His heirs, however, were unable to maintain this initiative;[14] for there was an alternative to the count's jurisdiction in the many effective but short-term and localized peace arrangements established across Gothia.

By the second half of the eleventh century, lay lords including the count were sometimes asked to assist the bishops by levying fines from those convicted of breaches of peace, but the counts of Toulouse were never able (nor did they exhibit the desire) to imitate their northern counterparts in exploiting their support to annex peace jurisdiction. Nevertheless, they earned popularity by throwing their weight behind ecclesiastical authority, and so they revitalized the alliance between count, bishop, nobles, and ordinary people that the peace movement at its best could constitute.[15]

Within the area around Toulouse itself, the count's power was of a different order from that enjoyed within Gothia. Here his court was an effective and lucrative source of authority; both the bishop and the viscount were under his direct protection; the town was firmly in his grasp.[16] Had he been able to concentrate his efforts here, he could have built up a formidable, if small, principality. In fact, he was often absent, in St Gilles, in Provence, or after 1105 in Tripoli. For Raymond IV's decision to go on the First Crusade in 1095 jeopardized much of what he had achieved in the course of a busy reign of consolidation. His absence permitted a dangerous attack on Toulouse by William IX of Aquitaine, in pursuit of his wife Philippa's claims (she was the daughter of Raymond's brother and predecessor William IV); the Aquitanian campaigns were only abandoned in 1119, probably in return for a solid financial inducement. Worse still, the lure of Raymond's Outremer principality of Tripoli (not finally conquered until after his death) exercised a fatal attraction on the heirs of his body. The early twelfth century was to prove a testing time for the counts of Toulouse.

(ii) Aquitaine

The Poitevin duchy of Aquitaine had been built up by a combination of military skill, diplomatic agility, and inherited claims, to the point where it exercised some sort of hegemony from the borders of Burgundy to Gascony, and from the Loire to the southern fringes of Périgord. So when William V, the Great, became duke in 990, he had only to expand upon the traditions of his predecessors to take the pre-eminent place among the princes of West Francia. In

Ademar of Chabannes, he had the benefit of a lavish eulogizer:

Duke of the Aquitanians, count of Poitou, the aforesaid most glorious and powerful William was amiable to all, great in counsel, outstanding for his prudence, most liberal in bestowing, a defender of the poor, father of monks, builder and lover of churches, devoted to the holy Roman church.[17]

William stood comparison with Louis the Pious, Charlemagne, Theodosius, and even Augustus. After that, it is an anti-climax to be told that he seemed more like a king than a duke. Ademar was not alone in portraying William as an emperor in the classical mould; Fulbert of Chartres, who had less incentive to indulge in blind flattery, called him *piisimus dux, serenissimus princeps*—imperial adjectives— in his letters. And their contemporaries saw no exaggeration when these terms were applied to a man whose daughter married the emperor Henry III and whose son was a contender for the throne of Lombardy.

Yet there was little imperial about William's authority over the other great counts of his duchy. It was a cornerstone of his policy, as Ademar relates,[18] to maintain close friendship with his powerful neighbour, the count of Angoulême; Count William was a regular visitor to the ducal court, held fiefs of the duke, and joined him in military expeditions; but the duke had no right of interference within Angoulême. With Boso II, count of La Marche and Périgueux, Duke William's relations were not quite so smooth: Ademar and Richer tell of fighting over castles in the early years of his reign;[19] this suggests that William had at least some claim to authority in Boso's lands. With the help of Robert the Pious, William defeated Boso, and lived on good terms with him from thenceforth; but it is possible that the division of Périgord and La Marche that occurred on Boso's death was brought about by William's fear of further trouble.[20] With the viscount of Limoges, however, the duke had less need of diplomacy: he disciplined him in 1000, and appointed his successor in 1025. So outside Poitou, William bullied where he could and beguiled where he could not bully. That his lordship had powers of attraction even for the great and independent is evident from Eudes of Déols's willingness to swear fidelity to him; Eudes was described as William's *satelles fidelissimus et familiarissimus*,[21] his most faithful and intimate henchman; this tie established a very loose Aquitanian hegemony over Lower Berry, significant only in so far as it blocked any infiltration there by Blois or Anjou.

Inside Poitou, William's extensive demesne lands and the 'lay abbacy' of St Hilaire in Poitiers produced a solid power base in the south of the county; further north, however, Angevin intervention and the viscount of Thouars's demesnes checked his ambitions. The contrasting poles of the count's authority can be seen in his relations with Hugh IV de Lusignan and Fulk of Anjou. Hugh held allodial lands of moderate size near Poitiers, and was advocate of the monastery of St Maixent; he was therefore a man of some social standing in his neighbourhood. Yet in order to reinstate himself in William's favour after an act of defiance, and to guarantee for himself the possession of one of the castles he had sought, he was forced to acknowledge that he owed William suit of court and military service; that he was obliged to accompany the count on military expeditions even when his own lands were under attack; that he had no right to build a castle on his lands without the count's authorization; and that his marriage might be his lord's affair. In every way, Hugh was subject to William's whim: *Meus tu es ad facere meam voluntatem*, you are mine to carry out my will.[22] Fulk of Anjou, on the other hand, held the trump cards in coming to terms with William, after his steady expansion from the Angevin fief of Loudun into much of the Gâtine of Poitou and into the Saintonge. William was forced to ratify these gains. In exchange, Fulk became his vassal, attended his court, produced propaganda for the duke's Italian enterprises and even, after William's death, restrained—albeit ineffectually—his son's ambitions in Poitou.[23]

So Ademar's claim that William 'subjected the whole of Aquitaine to his rule'[24] suggests a uniformity of control which was absent. Nevertheless the duchy was still an entity; the finely-decorated palace that was William's base in Poitiers had magnetic force; Aquitaine meant something. This was even plainer in ecclesiastical affairs. For the ecclesiastical synods which were held at various times in his reign were remarkable in that they were attended by churchmen from the whole duchy—a breach with tradition, since Aquitaine was divided between the metropolitan jurisdictions of Bourges and Bordeaux. The greatest of these synods was the council William called to Poitiers in 1010. Whereas the earlier peace councils of the duchy, those of Le Puy (975 and 994) and Charroux (989), had been summoned by bishops, their canons enforced by excommunication, now William took the initiative, and lent his coercive power to the canons produced by adding punishment in secular courts to the sanction of excommunication. The peace was as much his as his bishops'. His action here, and in convening the later council of Charroux (1028) for the condemnation of heresy, revived memories of Charlemagne.[25]

The Council of Poitiers was the high point in the early history of Poitevin Aquitaine. William V's death in 1029 was followed by a decline in ducal power during which his creation was threatened with destruction. His son William VI was captured in battle and imprisoned by Geoffrey Martel of Anjou; on his release in 1036, he was a sick man. His death in 1038, and that of his brother Eudes duke of Gascony in the following year, left infant heirs, whose nearest relative was their grandmother Agnes, widow of William V, recently married to Geoffrey Martel of Anjou. So the minority of William VII was a period of opportunity for the Angevins. As regents, Geoffrey and Agnes consolidated Angevin interests in the north to such an extent that they became a permanent feature of the landscape; it was probably during the eleventh century that this part of Poitou embraced the *langue d'oïl.* Further south, Angevin rule was conservative; Poitevin castellans were kept under ducal control; public rights continued to be asserted. Even on his majority, William VII never fully emancipated himself from others. It was not until 1058, with the accession of his younger brother Guy Geoffrey (who took the title William VIII), that the ducal house flourished once more.

It was Guy Geoffrey's great achievement to unite Aquitaine with Gascony. The last years of the tenth century and

the first decades of the eleventh had been times of consolidation and prosperity in Gascony; under Bernard William
(996–1009) and Sancho William (1009–1032), William
Sancho's successors, the church had revived, monasteries
had been restored, sees reestablished, and the whole subjected to the firm rule of the duke. In the course of this
reconstruction, the famous scholar Abbo of Fleury had
visited La Réole in 1004, and made his much-quoted comment that there he was as powerful as the king of France,
since no-one in Gascony feared the king.[26] But apart from his
independence, not much is known of the duke's secular
powers. The Bordelais, enfeoffed to a cadet of his own
family, and much of western Gascony were firmly in his
grip; his control over the south and east was looser. The
attractions of Gascony to the dukes of Aquitaine lay in the
salt, wine, and grain trades, which were lucrative, and in the
ancient archbishopric of Bordeaux, which William V had long
aspired to influence. Eudes, William V's son by his Gascon
wife Prisca, succeeded Sancho William, though not without
controversy; on his death Guy Geoffrey, his half-brother,
fought long and hard against the count of Armagnac to win
control. It was not until 1063 that the duchy of Gascony
was incontrovertibly Guy Geoffrey's.

From 1063 on, the dukes of Aquitaine were also dukes of
Gascony. In acquiring the Atlantic seaboard, they reorientated
their whole regime southwards; Poitiers, Saintes, and Bordeaux
became the three great cities of their duchies, the places
where the dukes were to be found most frequently, the axis
of their new interests. Although Guy Geoffrey and his heirs
held the duchies separately, with different courts, different
legal proceedings, different officials, nevertheless by the
combination they reinforced the imperial pretensions of
William the Great. It was no accident that Guy Geoffrey's
intervention in the Spanish *reconquista* and his great victory
at Barbastro in 1064 came during the time when he was
seeking to consolidate his reputation in the south. And
respect for his military skill was one factor in attracting the
Gascon lords, the counts of Fézensac, the viscounts of
Bigorre and Béarn, to his court in Bordeaux.[27] Two of his
daughters married into the royal houses of Spain, where his

son William IX was to enjoy his greatest triumph in thrusting down to Granada in 1125. The Gascon inheritance therefore conferred a whole new dimension on the duke of Aquitaine's standing within Europe.

There was, however, one drawback to this splendid new asset: it endangered the long friendship between Poitou and Angoulême that had been central to William V's policies; for the counts of Angoulême were irked by the toing and froing of the ducal entourage and its residence in Saintes, close to Angoulême spheres of interest. This coincided with new signs of trouble within Poitou—it was recorded that in 1060 the duke killed Hugh V de Lusignan. After Guy Geoffrey's death in 1086 and during the regency of his son William, control in the kernel of the duchy of Aquitaine, in Poitou itself, grew looser. When William IX began to rule, he was faced with a long war against Hugh VII de Lusignan, trouble with Parthenay, the intervention of Fulk of Anjou, and the hostility of Angoulême. Had William concentrated on the home front, it might have been possible to solve these problems. But he was called away firstly by a brief Norman imbroglio, then by his claims in Toulouse, of which he became effective lord until 1119; by his crusade of 1101 to the Holy Land; by his famous Spanish campaign; and by trouble in Gascony, where his defeat in 1120 permanently excluded him and his successors from Fézensac and all parts south. As a consequence of his absences, the castellans of Poitou began to escape from ducal control, to take ducal tolls for their own benefit, even to build fortifications without authority.[28]

The more censorious of William's contemporaries were inclined to attribute his troubles to his failings of character; and certainly he did little to earn the approval of his bishops. The sensitivity of his love poetry, which has excited the admiration of modern critics, appalled them; its biblical echoes no doubt struck them as blasphemous.[29] Yet after Amatus' elevation to the see of Bordeaux (see p. 159), William may have calculated that, since he could not hope for ecclesiastical support, there were political gains to be made in blatant anti-clericalism; for it attracted sympathy among young laymen exasperated by clerical self-righteousness.

The jibes, the sardonic humour, the sexual imaginings of William's poetry were part and parcel of the chivalric ethos for which his court was famed, and which attracted to his *mouvance* natives of most of southern France. The duke set the style for knighthood as he set it for troubadour poetry. And here perhaps lay the rub. For Spanish expeditions, crusades, or even aggressive action in Normandy and Toulouse, had far more appeal among the adventure-hungry group that William gathered about him than the endless small wars within the duchy. If the duke's 'instability'[30] (the word is William of Malmesbury's) should be blamed for his failures, it was the instability of the crusader, rather than that of the romantic poet, that was culpable.

For most of the eleventh century—excluding a few short years at the end—relations between the dukes of Aquitaine and the kings of France were cordial but infrequent. William V was at the French court in 1027; Richer recounts that Robert the Pious had earlier assisted him against the count of La Marche.[31] Guy Geoffrey's position as first liegeman of the king of France was openly proclaimed at the coronation of Philip I, when the duke headed the parade of *fideles*; he later proved his fidelity against Gregory VII's attempts to lure him into opposition to Philip I in 1074. (But his homage entailed no military obligation; for when Philip I sought help against the Normans in 1076, the king had to hurry to Poitiers to beg for it.)[32] William IX also attempted to prevent an ecclesiastical synod being convened in Poitiers in 1100 to condemn Philip's marriage; his failure merely added to his evil reputation in the church's eyes. So relations were usually governed by goodwill but not, it seems, by any sense of inferiority on the part of the duke of Aquitaine. He did not claim to be royal; in many respects, though, he was at least the equal of his king.

(iii) Burgundy

For the first seven decades of the eleventh century, the loosening of political ties noted in tenth-century Burgundy continued slowly, though without erasing old identities; the result was a situation somewhat similar to that in the county of Toulouse: the sea-change in ducal power is clearer to historians than it can have been to contemporaries.

On Duke Henry's death in 1002 without direct heirs, the duchy was claimed by his step-son Otto William, count of Burgundy and of Mâcon, in virtue of Henry's expressed wish —so the Chronicle of St Bénigne says.[33] Robert the Pious, Henry's closest blood relation, disputed the claim, his chief supporter in Burgundy being Hugh, bishop of Auxerre and count of Chalon.[34] Perhaps Robert sought to reassert royal rights of appointment to duchies; perhaps he thought the opportunity to replenish crown lands should not be allowed to slip; or perhaps he feared that Otto William would absorb the duchy into the kingdom of Burgundy. In any case, the king risked war in support of his claim, which by 1006 he had won. So in the following years he extended his sway by asserting control over Sens, the gateway to Burgundy. In the meantime, he had decided to make the duchy an apanage for his second son Henry, in order to protect the royal inheritance intact for his eldest son Hugh; since Henry was a minor, Robert acted as his guardian. Although it is clear from charters that Robert both as duke and then as guardian for Henry, did have a Burgundian policy and did seek to co-operate with the local lords, nevertheless the absence of a duke resident in the duchy, at a time when personal links were vital, weakened the whole. It was not until 1031, with Duke Henry's accession to the throne, and the accession of his younger brother Robert to the duchy, that stability returned.

By then, the crown had made inroads into the duchy that proved irrecoverable: Sens and its archbishopric were under royal control; the bishops of Chalon, Autun, and Auxerre had learned to look to the king for protection. Perhaps more important, in 1031-2 Renaud, count of Nevers, married to Robert's daughter Hadvise, was given the county of Auxerre; his new, extended principality was to act as a centre for royal influence on the borders of the shrunken duchy.[35] Internally, the chief effect of the long period of loose government was to encourage the growing sense of independence among those counts—Mâcon, Chalon, Troyes—who might regard themselves as the duke's *fideles*. Though they visited the ducal court at intervals throughout the eleventh century, they were no more willing than, say, the count of Angoulême, to brook ducal interference within their counties. The count of Troyes, scrupulous though he was in maintaining the old courtesies, was drawn into a different political world by tight alliance with his cousin, the count of Blois; his concerns therefore became those of the north and west. And Mâcon, which had always been orientated to the south and east, strengthened its ties with the kingdom of Burgundy. Only Chalon retained its essential connection with the duchy. So by 1031, the kernel of the duchy, Autun, Avellon, Beaune, Dijon (the one important addition to the demesne), and perhaps Oscheret, survived; but beyond these lands, the duke's rights depended on his personal skills. He might seem little more than the equal of the counts in his area.

For Burgundy as a whole, the eleventh century saw the old Carolingian administrative pattern erased; and everywhere this posed a threat to the old methods of comital control. The counts of Mâcon, as Duby has shown,[36] saw their authority fragment to the benefit of their castellans. By 1030, castellanies in the Mâconnais had become hereditary, castles were being claimed as allodial property, castellans absented themselves from the comital court and built up their own jurisdictions; some even began to make alliances outside the county, the lords of Uxelles with the duke of Burgundy, those of Beaujeau with the emperor. The count had been reduced to little more than a castellan within his own demesne.

Nowhere else in Burgundy did established comital power suffer similar disintegration. Yet paradoxically, further north the change in administrative pattern was greater. For while Mâcon kept its old divisions—its castellanies grew out of its vicariates—further north such continuity was rare. New vicecomital families appeared, no longer functioning as the count's deputies but as powerful local officials; old counties disappeared—Lassois split into the county of Bar-sur-Seine, soon to be absorbed in Champagne, and the lordship of Châtillon; new counties like Atuyer appeared. Beneath them, new castellanies intruded into vicariates, in some cases swallowing them. The bishops of Autun, Auxerre, and Chalon built up lordships for themselves. These changes had immediate consequences on the way in which armies were gathered and justice dispensed. Castellans, with their regular household knights, had to be persuaded to fight by greater pressures than the old Carolingian obligation; so vassalage assumed new significance. Equally, because they were now crucial to defence, castellans could hardly be disciplined by the old public law. So comital courts became simple courts of arbitration to establish peace.[37]

In the struggle to accommodate themselves to change, the dukes of Burgundy were moderately successful. Within their own lands, they preserved a degree of control over their castellans that their neighbours might envy. Perhaps the military character of the original duchy retained its impress on men's memories for longer than might have been expected; perhaps the dukes simply had to deal with fewer great aristocratic castellans than the counts of Chalon or Mâcon. Whatever the reason, the challenge to ducal authority was contained; the vassalage of almost all the castellans was a reality: they attended the duke's court and acknowledged themselves bound to military service. The fact that they all owned allodial lands exceeding those they held in fief from the duke was not sufficient to outweigh in their minds the benefits derived from their castles, over which they recognized his right. So they came in response to his summons. In a famous assembly in 1078, duke Hugh I was able to gather all his vassals around him to discuss means for keeping the peace. This assembly gained for Hugh the European reputation attested by Orderic Vitalis: 'His outstanding justice pleased meek and honest men, but struck those who were godless with the force of lightning.'[38]

The assembly of 1078 was attended not only by castellans but also by independent counts and bishops, as was that of 1106 where, after consultation, the duke issued instructions for the operation of lawcourts. Throughout the century, ducal charters were occasionally witnessed by the counts of Nevers, Chalon, Mâcon, even Troyes, and the bishops of Langres, Auxerre, Chalon, and Autun. So it appears that the dukes of Burgundy were as successful as the dukes of Aquitaine in making their court a resort for those not in any way bound to be present who would have resented bitterly any show of superior authority in their affairs. Therefore though the old duchy had completely disintegrated, a network of personal relations still kept its outline from oblivion. Marriages, the education of counts' and castellans' sons at the ducal court, arbitration in disputes, all offered regular opportunities for reinforcing old loyalties. But perhaps the most effective way of binding together the Burgundian aristocracy was by the great expeditions into Spain undertaken by Robert I, Hugh I, and Eudes II, expeditions which excited a common fervour, reinforced chivalric conventions and also often brought reward.[39]

Keeping a splendid court and encouraging Spanish expeditions was an expensive business. But the eleventh century was a prosperous period for Burgundy, and probably nowhere more so than in Autun and Auxerre. Here the soil was particularly good for vines, while the Saône, Marne, and Aube made easy routes for shipping away the heavy casks of wine to be sold in distant places. And the higher agricultural output—the result of both improved climate and forest clearance—encouraged farmers to take the risk of putting down land to vines. All landlords in the area made rich profits, the duke among the foremost. He was also able to cash in on the pilgrim routes connecting Cluny with Rome and with Compostela. The old Carolingian tolls and customs he had always enjoyed became more lucrative as a consequence of increased trade in the area. His comparative wealth did not prevent Eudes I from taking to brigandage, perhaps for excitement's sake; but he was careful to ensure that the sufferers from his depredations were churchmen (he planned to attack Anselm of Canterbury) or pilgrims, not his own aristocracy.

Unlike the dukes of Aquitaine, the eleventh-century dukes of Burgundy enjoyed no huge increase in demesne land, no new title. They saw their authority within neighbouring counties dwindle to almost nothing, and had trouble in controlling even the kernel of the duchy. But by the end of the century, they had survived, they held their own lands firmly in check, they had developed relationships of friendship and warmth to replace the old power, and they had built up their economic resources. To dominate their neighbours by military might was quite outside their ability; but they could and did dominate by chivalry, by friendship, and by cooperation.

Relations between the dukes of Burgundy and their cousins in Paris were episodic, though friendly. The dukes only rarely went to the royal court. They dutifully sent troops to the king's assistance in 1059 and 1071—on both occasions the royal army was soundly beaten—and Eudes I also helped Philip I when he was hard pressed by Hugh du Puiset. It is unlikely that this help was sent in strict recognition of feudal obligation; it was more a question of friendship. And the same sentiment seems to have lain behind homage, which the dukes occasionally performed.

A cadet line of the ruling house, holding one of Francia's most honourable titles, the dukes of Burgundy might well have played a great part on the European stage. But neither in their marriage policies nor in their external diplomacy did they show ambitions to match those of the dukes of Aquitaine, or even of much lesser men like the counts of Anjou. Only in Spain did their crusading zeal fire them into prestigious action. And it was in Spain that they were to enjoy their great triumph, when Henry, Eudes I's younger brother, married into the royal house of Castille and went on to found the royal dynasty of Portugal.

(iv) Anjou

The accession of Hugh Capet to the throne of France coincided with that of Fulk Nerra to the county of Anjou. In 987 Anjou consisted of the Carolingian *pagus* of Angers, running down to the Loire; of the honour of Loudun, to the south, held of the duke of Aquitaine, along with a good part of the Gâtine of Poitou; of rights of overlordship in the county of Nantes; and of expanding land rights eastwards in the direction of Tours. It was Fulk's achievement to add substantially to his inheritance, to develop it into a true principality, while still scrupulously discharging his personal obligations, his fidelity to his overlords, Hugh Capet and William V of Aquitaine. Guillot,[40] in an important recent study, has contrasted Fulk's juridical status with that of his father Geoffrey Grisegonelle, arguing that, while Geoffrey recognized the king as having enfeoffed him with the comital office, Fulk merely acknowledged that he held a few small parcels of land as fiefs of the crown. This explanation of Anjou's new importance perhaps imposes greater clarity than the evidence warrants, presupposing on the part of both king and count a more precise implication for homage than either was likely to have conceived. But it nevertheless highlights a significant fact in Angevin history: the greater independence of its eleventh-century counts was unopposed by their Capetian overlords, who may even have seen it as a natural corollary of their own elevation to the kingship.

The driving force behind Fulk's expansion of Angevin territory was his rivalry with the neighbouring counts of Blois. In 988 Guerech, count of Nantes and vassal of Anjou, was assassinated by the count of Rennes, who was in the *mouvance* of Blois. The only surviving heir of Guerech was his young nephew, on whose behalf Fulk launched a savage attack, and won the first great victory of his reign at Conquereuil in 992. Safeguarding Angevin interests in Brittany mattered to Fulk, for the revenue derived for his services, for the blow to Eudes of Blois, and also because it protected access towards Maine. Some Angevin rights in Maine dated back to the tenth century; at some stage in his reign (probably before 1016) Fulk claimed suzerainty over the county of Maine (a claim which was, in the future, to be firmly opposed by the dukes of Normandy).

There was another source of conflict with Blois closer to home than Brittany—the Touraine. In geographical terms, Angevin ambitions on Tours were explicable in that the city commanded one of the best Loire crossings; if securely in Angevin hands, it would safeguard Loudun and the holdings in Poitou won in Geoffrey Grisegonelle's time. In 994-5, Fulk built, on Eudes I's territory,[41] the castle of Langeais, the first known stone donjon in West Francia. In the war which followed, he captured Tours, but was later forced by Robert the Pious to return it. Thwarted, Fulk began to encircle the town with castles (Montbazon, Montrichard, Loches) and to build up a network of vassals in the immediate neighbourhood; his greatest triumph was in establishing a friendship with the lord of Amboise. In 1016, he succeeded in defeating Eudes II at Pontlevoy—a battle which finally put paid to Blézois ambitions in Brittany; in 1026, he captured Saumur. But the ultimate triumph, the final fall of Tours, was delayed till after his death.

Angevin expansion to the south comprised much of the Gâtine of Poitou and Saintes, held as a fief of the duke of Aquitaine. Fulk secured his position here by inducing important Poitevin lords, most notably the viscount of Thouars, to enter his *mouvance*, and probably also by establishing castles, of which Parthenay was the most famous.[42] Diplomacy was clearly a significant factor in his success, as it had been in his conversion of a temporary guardianship over the county of Vendôme into overlordship. So in his reign, Anjou evolved from a Loire-based county to a principality with interests from the Norman frontier to Saintes, from Nantes to Amboise.

This dazzling success was owed in part to the solid foundations on which Fulk built, in part to the fact that the count of Blois, his chief enemy, was distracted by other problems. But Fulk's cleverness, his ability to make very long-term plans for annexing Tours, his courtesy towards his overlords, his demanding treatment of his own vassals, were formidable assets. The historian of St Florent in Saumur, with all the bitterness of the recently conquered, declared of Fulk and his son Geoffrey that they were only just inferior to wild beasts in their strength, ferocity, and cunning.[43] Militarily, Fulk was not invincible; he came close to being routed by Eudes II of Blois at the battle of Pontlevoy in 1016, when only the last-minute arrival of reinforcements turned defeat into victory. But his record in the field was good. Apart from his personal qualities as a leader, the reasons for his initial success are not obvious. He had after all, only the same military resources as his neighbours. Clearly success bred success in that, as he expanded, he was able to impose service on lords new to his vassalage and to grant out new fiefs to loyal servants of his house. The viscount of Thouars promoted his interests at Nantes, the count of Maine fought for him at Pontlevoy. But there was one important and novel feature of Fulk's strategy: more than any commander before him, he integrated the castle into warfare, as a base for aggressive action, as a threat to his enemies. He covered the Angevin marchlands with stone donjons, some of which survive to this day; and by his building campaign he ensured the security of Anjou until 1204-6. As Archdeacon Renaud summed it up, he was *elegantissimus bellicus rebus*, most adroit in military matters.[44]

The dramatic expansion of Anjou was Fulk Nerra's achievement; his son's consisted in strengthening the underpinnings, creating the elements of a state. Interestingly, the years of his reign 1040-60, coincide roughly with those of the two other great state-builders, William the Conqueror and Baldwin V of Flanders. All three ruled by combining feudal elements (vassalage, fiefs, homage) with exploitation of Carolingian public rights. In Geoffrey's case, his effrontery in claiming Carolingian public rights over all Anjou was considerable; for the creation of the new county was a breach with Carolingian administrative tradition, and such rights as the viscount of Angers had once exercised in the *pagus* of Angers derived from delegation by the duke of the Franks. Yet Geoffrey asserted his authority as firmly and as comprehensively as either William the Conqueror or Baldwin V. His court became the central court for the whole of his domains, including the Touraine and Vendôme; all free men had access to it and all might on occasion be required to attend, whether or not they were vassals of the count. As a result, he claimed two jurisdictional rights which escaped other contemporary princes, the right to hear cases when only one party asked for judgement, and the right to reform bad legal customs, at least within the kernel of his domain.[45] Both set precedents for Angevin justice as it was to be more than a century later, under his distinguished successor Henry II of England. Equally, Geoffrey summoned all free men to the army, as Charlemagne had done, and used fine imperial language to defend his right: he referred to *proelium generale pro defensione regni ac principis*, a public war for the defense of the kingdom and the prince. In fact he may have been less concerned to gather a mighty army for the protection of Anjou than to collect fines for failure in attendance. But whatever his motive, he was acting in the manner of a king or an emperor, not of a mere count.

At the same time, Geoffrey built up the feudal base of his principality, particularly in the Touraine, where he banished the count of Blois's men, put in his own castellans, and made heavy demands on their service. William of Poitiers, a hostile witness, accused him of obtaining the loyalty of the castellans of Alençon and Domfront by turning a blind eye to their brigandage,[46] a bargain which, though in keeping with eleventh-century practice, seems at odds with Geoffrey's imperial pretensions. If the famous Vendôme charter, codifying the *consuetudines* of the town and the services due from it to the count, can be dated to Geoffrey's reign,[47] then he was a pioneer among French princes in appreciating the importance for princes of sanctioning by *confirmatio* the new customs emerging in all castellanies. He also claimed military service from the unfree as well as the free in time of war, a considerable extension of comital prerogative. Thus, if Geoffrey's government chose to present itself in traditional robes, it was none the less innovative in several ways.

Though the chief interest of Geoffrey's reign lies in his internal management, his external policies were also notably successful. In 1044 he brought his father's endeavours to fitting climax by capturing Tours (a victory which Raoul Glaber interpreted as the achievement of St Martin, indignant at the count of Blois's depredations on his church).[48] Then Geoffrey pressed on into Maine, which by 1051 was virtually in his hands. During the years 1043-52, those of his marriage with Agnes, widow of duke William V of Aquitaine, he pursued an alliance with the emperor Henry III, who had married Agnes's daughter by her first marriage; with Henry's backing, he attempted to further his own interests in Provence, Lorraine, and even Italy. All these proved abortive, and were abandoned after his divorce from Agnes in 1052; nevertheless they made him a figure on the European scene, and demonstrated vividly Anjou's newly won position of distinction within West Francia.

But what followed on Geoffrey's death in 1060 proved that the establishment of a principality was not quite such a simple affair as it had seemed up till now; luck and the absence of succession quarrels were important ingredients, doubly important in a state without roots in the past and without geographically-defined frontiers. Geoffrey had no direct heir. He was therefore succeeded by the elder of his two nephews, Geoffrey the Bearded, while his younger nephew Fulk's thwarted ambitions were temporarily quenched by an endowment of extensive estates in Aquitaine. But this arrangement was rapidly overturned when Duke Guy Geoffrey of Aquitaine reconquered the Saintonge in 1062. Fulk le Réchin found himself without his largest possessions; in his anger, he turned on his brother when opportunity arose, imprisoned him, and proclaimed himself count in 1067.[49] This immoral action was condoned by his neighbours because it gave them an opportunity to claim what they wanted of Anjou. The count of Blois succeeded in extorting homage for Tours; the duke of Normandy moved in on Maine; the king of France received the Gâtinais by way of a bribe for accepting Fulk as count, and later, in 1106, the specific recognition that the county of Anjou was held as a fief from the crown, a recognition which apparently neither Fulk Nerra nor Geoffrey Martel had conceded. All this, though humiliating, could have been borne. But the castellans of the Angevin lands, clearly unhappy with the *coup*, engaged in private war, using the disputed succession as an excuse for forwarding their own local interests, and could be brought in the end to recognize Fulk only in return for concessions. Thus far most castles on Angevin territory (with the exception of those in the Touraine, already seigneurial before 1044) were comital property, built by the counts, held by comital appointees, without absolute hereditary right. Now castles beyond the comital demesne lands slipped gradually from Fulk's direct control, becoming the hereditary fiefs of their castellans.

The papal legates took advantage of the troubles in Anjou to press on hard with reform. The legate Stephen punished Geoffrey the Bearded for his intrusion on Marmoutier's liberties by recognizing Fulk le Réchin in his stead; then in 1082 Hugh of Die excommunicated Fulk, and later Paschal II deposed the bishop of Angers. The last remnants of the once-tight comital control over the Angevin church were destroyed; Fulk could neither resist, nor in acquiescing derive benefit from a reputation for piety.[50]

In the course of the 1080s, there were signs of recovery,

especially in Maine; but all was still far from plain sailing. In 1103 Fulk's son Geoffrey, supported by William IX of Aquitaine, revolted; in 1106 the lord of Amboise destroyed the count's castle there, thus jeopardizing Fulk's hold on eastern Touraine.[51] Fulk's death in 1109 was greeted with relief; but his successors were faced with three decades of hard work to re-establish comital authority over the area that had recognized Geoffrey Martel's sway.

But in one respect, Fulk le Réchin made a unique contribution to the prestige of his family: his history, which begins 'I, Fulk, . . . have desired to write down how my ancestors came by their honour and held it until my own time, and then how I myself have held it by God's grace,'[52] was an undertaking worthy of the family soon to be recognized as the most learned among the ruling families of Western Europe. Baldly though he told his tale, Fulk's pride in his lineage comes across vividly. A similar pride was evident in the encouragement he is thought to have given to the monks of St Aubin at Angers to draw up comital genealogies, which shed lustre not only on Geoffrey Martel and his predecessors, but also on the collateral branch of the family that now held the county.[53] Fulk's hand has also been detected behind the archdeacon Renaud's contributions to the annals of St Aubin, covering the years 966-1075, with their strong interest in the doings of the counts of Anjou.[54] Compared with the Norman ducal propaganda, the Angevin may seem small beer; but it was all home-grown, and the seed Fulk sowed was to flower luxuriantly in the next century.

(v) Blois-Chartres-Champagne

Thibaud le Tricheur was count of Blois, Tours, Chartres, and Châteaudun; he was lord of the count of Rennes, and had many vassals in northern Berry. On his death c. 974, the stage seemed set for the establishment of a true principality. Yet despite Thibaud's successors' gains, particularly in the northeast, their lands were never fully welded together until the twelfth century, when Champagne became the dominant partner. Whether because of royal or Angevin pressure, a distaste for unmitigated primogenital succession, too many outside interests, or a reliance on gentle persuasion rather than bullying, the house of Blois failed to exploit its geographical and inherited advantages to the full before 1125.

Thibaud's successor Eudes I was marked out as one of the greatest West Frankish aristocrats by his marriage with Berthe, daughter of the king of Burgundy. Raoul Glaber contrasted the lady's royal ancestry with Eudes's obscure origins, but failed to explain why her family had permitted the marriage.[55] From a humbler connection, his maternal uncle Herbert the Old, Eudes made the crucial territorial gain of his reign: on Herbert's death (between 980 and 984), he and his cousin Herbert the Young shared between them the lands to the north-east of Paris which had been the Vermandois power-base.[56] From this sharing was born a family solidarity which characterized the relations between Blois and Vermandois for the whole of the eleventh century; alone in the north, the Blois cousins achieved harmony like that of Wifred the Hairy's descendants in Catalonia. Eudes's inheritance led him to concentrate rather on the northern part of his domain, round Chartres, than on the Loire valley, the traditional kernel of his family's power. To this new orientation, Lothaire and Louis V were indifferent; but Hugh Capet could hardly welcome it, since it meant that his demesne in Paris was almost surrounded by the two cousins' lands. On Hugh's accession to the throne, bad blood stirred. This lay behind the unsuccessful plot to overthrow Hugh, led by Eudes and Adalbéron, bishop of Laon, in 993. When Adalbéron employed his customary cunning in sliding out of trouble, Eudes was left to bear the brunt of royal displeasure. Only his death in 996 saved his lands from being torn apart in Hugh's vengeance.

The minority of his sons Thibaud and Eudes II would have been disastrous for their house, had not Robert the Pious, already his father's partner on the throne, fallen in love with Berthe, Eudes I's widow, and determined, against paternal advice and canon law, to marry her.[57] Though the church ultimately prevailed, Robert proved a generous guardian to his step-sons. He persuaded Fulk of Anjou to return Tours, which he had captured in 996,[58] thus postponing the final Angevin domination of the Touraine for nearly half a century;

and he kept their other lands intact. Therefore when Thibaud died in 1004, Eudes II inherited a substantial patrimony. As far as can be seen, the fact of Robert's divorce from his mother did not weaken the king's affection for Eudes, who was often at court, and thus earned for himself the title 'count of the palace', an honour with a distinguished Carolingian past. It was presumably the fact of their long friendship which made the breach between king and count, when it came, so bitter. The breach itself is somewhat mysterious. Its occasion was Eudes's claim to inherit Meaux and Troyes on the death of his cousin Stephen in 1021. On purely political grounds, it would be easy to understand why the king should object, since Eudes's lands would almost encircle the royal demesne. But in fact Robert did invest Eudes with the northern counties on his cousin's death, and only changed his mind a year later, when he ordered their confiscation. The true quarrel may have been over control of the archbishopric of Rheims.[59]

Whatever the reasons, the consequences of the breach were widespread. Resistance on Eudes's part was met with the threat to deprive him of all his lands, and an appeal to Richard duke of Normandy to assist the king. Eudes retaliated, not only by rallying support among his own *fideles*, including Fulbert, bishop of Chartres, but also by building up a network among castellans on the royal demesne which sapped at the roots of Robert's power.[60] Despite his famous letter declaring his loyalty to the king,[61] Eudes fought so hard that in the end Robert had to give way. At Whitsun 1027, Eudes entered legally into his Champagne inheritance, though shorn of control over the archbishopric of Rheims. The royal demesne was surrounded by the house of Blois, the dangers to the crown of hostility with Blois had been demonstrated, the count had shown his ability to enforce his will on his resisting sovereign.

Dramatic though these events were, and important in their consequences for the future, in the short term they were swiftly submerged in the tide of new happenings. Eudes spent his last years engaged in a battle for the Burgundian kingdom, to which he had good claim. And when he died in 1037, unsuccessful in this his most ambitious project, his inheritance was split again. His elder son Thibaud III got the patrimonial lands of Blois, Tours (which he lost to Anjou in 1044), and Chartres, while his second son took Meaux and Troyes. It has been argued that this arrangement was made as a result of a Machiavellian move by King Henry I;[62] but there is no evidence to support this contention. It recalls rather the divisions of Toulouse (which were regular), and the later succession arrangements of William the Conqueror. Besides, the effects of the division can easily be over-estimated, for unlike the Normans the branches of the House of Blois worked together remarkably well. In any case, when Stephen died at some date between 1045 and 1048, leaving Thibaud as guardian for his son Eudes, the two parts of the dominion were brought together again, on a temporary basis.

The years until 1052, while Geoffrey Martel indulged his aggressive ambitions, brought relative peace at home for Thibaud, since King Henry I needed his help against the Angevin menace. He assisted, with 500 knights, Henry's attack on Anjou in 1049. Then, as Henry's anxieties focused on Normandy rather than Anjou, Thibaud sent troops to the 1054 campaign in the duchy. During this time, he proudly used his title of Count Palatine. But as the crown and Anjou drew closer together, particularly after 1055, Thibaud could not but be alienated. Nevertheless he played his hand very carefully. The only serious threat to peace with his king came when Eudes III of Troyes reached his majority, 1058 X 60, and sought royal aid in rebelling against his uncle; but here Thibaud was saved, first by the death of Henry I and the minority of Philip, and then by the Norman conquest of England, which lured Eudes away, never to return to Champagne. After 1066 Thibaud once again governed all the lands of the house of Blois.

Unlike Fulk le Réchin, Thibaud was able to turn the movement for ecclesiastical reform to his own interest by championing it, so obtaining a reputation for piety without losing anything of substance. His moment of triumph came when, with his consent and in his presence, Hugh of Die convened the great reforming council of 1081 at Meaux, at a time when his rivals, Philip I and Fulk le Réchin, were both in bad odour in reforming circles. Of the great bishoprics on on his lands, Chartres and Bourges had never been in the control of his family; claims to Sens and Rheims had been irretrievably lost in the reign of Eudes II; so, by allying himself with a movement which aimed to reduce lay pressure on bishoprics, he stood only to injure himself in Troyes and Meaux, an injury which in practice he did not sustain since the reformers were understandably more anxious to criticize their enemies than their friends. At the same time, his alliance with Hugh of Die, along with his encouragement of monasticism (especially round Troyes and Meaux), brought him almost universal veneration.

Though Thibaud did not die until 1089, his sons were exercising effective power well before then, Stephen as count in Sancerre, Blois, Châteaudun, Chartres, and Meaux, Eudes IV in the rest of Champagne. Again goodwill prevailed between the two branches, and survived Eudes IV's death and his son Hugh's succession. Stephen's marriage to Adela, the formidable daughter of William the Conqueror, might well have presaged a more aggressive policy towards Philip I; but Stephen's own easy-going nature prevented any open breach before 1095, when the First Crusade claimed his attention.

It is almost inevitable that the eleventh-century history of the house of Blois should be told primarily in terms of its relations with the crown; for unlike the other princes, the counts of Blois and Troyes were regularly at court. Because of their proximity, their domestic affairs had immediate repercussions on crown interests; royal hostility, as in 1022 or 1060, was potentially very dangerous. This has led a recent scholar properly to emphasize the weakness of their principality, to see its history as dictated by their surviving vassalage to the duke of Francia rather than by the independence proper to princes.[63] But though there is value in this viewpoint, it should not be forgotten that the relationship was reciprocal. Robert suffered much from Eudes's network of vassals on the royal demesne, Philip I was affronted by the Council of Meaux.

How Blois-Chartres-Champagne was held together is hard to ascertain, largely because of its fluidity. At the beginning of the century, it was still Loire-based, focused on Blois and Tours, with important interests to the south in Berry

and to the west in Rennes. After 1015 Eudes II withdrew
from Brittany; after the battle of Pontlevoy in 1016 his
grasp on the Touraine slipped. In 1044 Tours fell; despite
the homage Thibaud later obtained for it from Fulk le
Réchin, the old focal-point of the principality was gone. With
the decline of the Loire, Chartres became more important,
though half of the city was in the hands of its bishop, protected by the crown. Even in the north, there were losses:
Dreux went to Robert the Pious in 1015 and La Perche under
its count Geoffrey IV (1079–1100) to Philip I.[64] But these
were compensated for not only by the counties of Troyes
and Meaux, sometimes held directly by the count of Blois,
sometimes by a cadet of the family, but also by gains in
northern Berry, an area which linked Champagne with Blois,
and where the absence of other great lords allowed Thibaud
to build up a network of vassalage covering more than half
of the diocese of Bourges.[65]

In the early years, the counts of Blois were famed for
castle-building. The *Chronicle of Nantes* records that Thibaud
le Tricheur used his Breton profits to build castles at Chinon,
Chartres, and Blois.[66] Eight of the twenty castles built within
the Chartres area were comital.[67] But the links between the
count and the southern castellans on his territory soon
loosened. By the time the Touraine fell to Anjou, its castles
were reckoned to be seigneurial, their castellans far more
independent than their Angevin counterparts. There are
signs of more assertive lordship in Champagne, but even
there some important families escaped comital vassalage
altogether. And in Berry, where the counts were making
alliances with established families, the terms had to be
undemanding. So their lordship was characterized rather by
persuasion than by insistent pressure. It has been said of
them that 'they knew how to appear at the head of their
fideles, they did not care to administer their subjects; in
short, they commanded but did not govern'.[68] This, of
course, may explain their success in Berry, and Eudes II's
attraction for the lords of the royal demesne who entered his
vassalage.

Yet their court was not inert. The monks of Marmoutier,
whose lands lay in disputed ground between Blois and

Anjou, often took cases to the court of Blois for trial; White says in explanation: 'During much of the century, the court of the count of Blois seems to have been particularly prone to employ procedures that led to clear-cut decisions in Marmoutier's favour.'[69] But he also points out that, in general, the monks preferred to conclude cases out of court by arbitration, because legal decisions in their favour could not necessarily be enforced. The Anglo-Norman source which ascribes Eudes III of Troyes's decision to remain in England after 1066 to the fear that he might be severely punished in his uncle's court for the murder of one of his vassals[70] suggests, if true, that on occasion the count might display unusual jurisdictional assertiveness. But this is a unique indication. Most lords entered the count of Blois's court ready to bargain hard for their own interests, even though they could see the value in reaching a permanent settlement.

The fairly relaxed lordship the counts exercised may be related to their wealth. They had no need to insist on collecting old public dues, or to demand heavy services, because their demesne lands, though scattered, were very extensive, and well exploited. In 1063, Thibaud III and Eudes III together issued a charter to assart lands in Brie; and the earliest known mention of a *prévôt* on a lay estate relates to Blois in 1004.[71] Once they abandoned the expansionist policies of Eudes II, the counts could therefore afford to preside at the head of a loose confederation of self-interested parties, on whom their yoke was easy and their burden light. If in the eyes of future generations they seemed somewhat unconstructive, their policies satisfied and therefore proved adequate.

(vi) Brittany

The end of the tenth and the early eleventh centuries were difficult times for Brittany. The fighting between Nantes, backed by Anjou, and Rennes, backed by Blois, which had begun shortly after Alan Barbetorte's death, was sharpened in 988 with the death of Guerech, count of Nantes. Fulk of Anjou's interests in Brittany as a source of revenue and as a gateway to Maine ensured that Angevin efforts would be unsparing; his victory at Conquerueil in 992 protected his position, if not that of his protégé in Nantes. The counts of Rennes, Conan and Geoffrey Berengar, found themselves hard-pressed; so in 996 Geoffrey Berengar, realizing that assistance from Blois was inadequate, entered an alliance with Count Richard I of Normandy, whose daughter he married, while Richard's heir, Richard II, married Geoffrey Berengar's sister Judith. As a consequence, Geoffrey Berengar's death in 1108 was followed by a Norman regency; his son, Alan III seems to have been a vassal of Duke Robert the Magnificent. The extent of external interference in Brittany was dismaying.

Internally, however, there were some hopeful signs. Alan III was engaged in building dikes around Dol as early as 1020,[72] suggesting an awareness of the value of good estate management; and it may have been business sense that inspired him to marry his daughter to Hoël, heir of Nantes and the county of Cornouaille. After both Alan's death in 1040 and that of his son Conan in 1066, Hoël succeeded to the county of Rennes, thereby combining in his own hand all the great landed blocks of Brittany except Penthièvre (created as an apanage for Alan III's brother Éon)[73] and the county of Léon. So in terms of the size of its princely demesne, Rennes in the closing decades of the eleventh century was rivalled only by Flanders. The marriage alliance had the additional advantage of putting an end to the old rivalry between the houses of Rennes and Nantes that had exposed Brittany to avaricious neighbours.

Nevertheless, there were serious internal problems. For Hoël's succession was hotly disputed by Éon of Penthièvre, son of Éon, brother of Alan III, who obtained support from Philip I in 1076; and William the Conqueror was anxious to reimpose on Brittany the Norman overlordship he had lost in the time of his minority. As a consequence, Hoël was beset by opponents, not the least among them his own castellans. In the end his son Alan IV Fergent (1084–1119) secured the succession; but it had been an uphill job. And the quarrels had obstructed Brittany's move towards coherence; it remained a fragile unit, with the inhabitants of Upper Brittany somewhat isolated from their neighbours.[74]

In the long term, it was the ecclesiastical reform movement rather than the counts of Rennes that effected change here. In 1049 Budic, bishop of Nantes, was deposed by Pope Leo IX, and a papal nominee established in his place. Though this dramatic gesture had only short-term effects—the new bishop made little impact—it was nevertheless an important stage in the opening up of Brittany to outside influence in ecclesiastical matters. For Rome disapproved of Celtic monastic customs, and denied the claim of the see of Dol to metropolitan status. In 1081, at the council of Saintes, the bishops of Brittany were condemned for their support of Dol, the views of outsiders at last began to percolate, even in Upper Brittany. The chronicler of Nantes, with his hostility towards Hoël because he did not favour reform, was symptomatic of a new spirit among some at least of the Breton clergy.[75]

If the counts of Brittany could not chalk up many political successes during the eleventh century, they nevertheless continued to exploit those aspects of Breton tradition that favoured princely rule. When Conan I of Rennes asserted his supremacy in Brittany in 988, Raoul Glaber recorded that he placed a diadem on his own head, according to royal custom.[76] The occasion may have been unique; but Conan II's accession in 1048 was marked by some measure of ceremony, for the bishop of Rennes is recorded as having declared: 'We honour today an earthly prince, and also the heavenly one.'[77] In charters and coins the counts occasionally referred to themselves as *reges* or *monarchi*—though usually as *comites, principes*, and *duces*.[78] And along with the old, they mixed the new. The chronicler of Nantes included in his mainly factual account of Alan Barbetorte's reign a splendid, legendary story of a single-handed combat between Alan and one of Otto's Saxons at the siege of Paris in 942.[79] Alan had already become to the Bretons a hero of chivalric romance, performing an exploit later attributed to many other scions of important houses. The chronicler's account is proof that the Bretons were precocious in the race to embroider their princely history with rich tales, that were satisfying to listen to of an evening in the lord's hall, perhaps even inspiring to remember on the battlefield when engaged in fighting on behalf of Alan's descendants.

(vii) Normandy

By 1100 what distinguished Normandy from the other West Frankish principalities—even Flanders, its nearest rival— was its integrity. Raoul Glaber had perceived this in the 1040s, comparing the whole province with one household or one family.[80] By then Normandy had already expanded to reasonably well-defined frontiers, roughly coinciding with those of the old archdiocese of Rouen, which gave it unrivalled ecclesiastical and political coherence. Within these frontiers, in the course of the eleventh century, the duke's direct authority was coming to be recognized everywhere, and the province's disparate legal customs were coalescing to the point at which it became possible to think of only one law for the whole of Normandy. The duchy was evolving into a territorial principality in the full sense of the term. It was perhaps not surprising that medieval intellectuals, following Orderic's example, attempted to locate the cause of this remarkable development in the peculiar genius of a mighty race.[81]

In 1091, William Rufus and Robert Curthose agreed to rule their father's lands jointly. To discover on what principles they should do this, they ordered an inquest into the ducal rights and prerogatives that William the Conqueror had enjoyed in Normandy. The employment of sworn inquest— a Carolingian judicial procedure—for the purpose of establishing how government should be conducted was proof that, in Normandy at least, law was conceived once more as capable of precise definition, and the role of government seen as set within the confines of that law. The *Consuetudines et Justicie*,[82] as the results of the inquest were known, reveal a degree of ducal control over justice unique in contemporary West Francia. Major crimes, such as arson and rape, were the monopoly of the duke's court; and many specific breaches of the peace automatically rendered a man liable to ducal judgement. Clearly, a factor in this development was the influence of English judicial institutions on Normandy after 1066; for in England the concepts of the king's peace and of the public character of law had remained clearer than they were anywhere in West Francia. But equally important was

William the Conqueror's exploitation of the Peace of God in the earlier years of his rule. The earliest Norman peace, perhaps proclaimed after Val-ès-Dunes in 1047,[83] was inspired by Richard of St Vanne, so bore obvious similarities with Flemish peaces: ducal service was exempt from the peace oath; punishments for breach of peace included confiscation of goods and banishment, both of which could only be enforced by the secular arm. This meant that the Peace of God in Normandy was, from its inception, susceptible of transmutation into the peace of the prince.

The inquest of 1091 specifically allowed for other legitimate judicial rights than the duke's within the duchy. Yet there were no advocacies in Normandy, and immunities from comital jurisdiction were not granted to any monastery founded after 1037; so the degree of ecclesiastical independence was small. In the secular sphere, the duke's control over his castellans and viscounts allowed him to exact recognition that their justice was exercised by his delegation, that his court could hear appeals from theirs. As a consequence, the customs (*consuetudines*) enforced across the duchy were moulded to a degree of uniformity not found elsewhere in West Francia. If it was still too early to speak of 'the custom of Normandy' in the sense in which thirteenth-century lawyers would use the phrase, meaning one internally consistent rule applied rigidly throughout a clearly defined territorial entity; nevertheless the full growth of the future could be predicted in the shoots of the late eleventh century.

A rather different aspect of the duchy's integrity attested by the *Consuetudines et Justicie* was the ducal control over all fortifications within the duchy, enforced by a prohibition on the construction of castles over a certain size and by the duke's right to occupy any castle he pleased. The survival of this Carolingian right should be ascribed both to the fact that the ducal demesne of the early eleventh century was so extensive that almost all the pre-1066 castles of the duchy were in origin domanial; and to the success of William the Conqueror in preventing the large number of new castles that sprouted in his reign from attaining the degree of independence their hereditary castellans doubtless desired. The importance of ducal control to the political coherence of the duchy can hardly be over-estimated. The other rights attested in 1091, the monopoly over coinage, the tolls and customs, which also pointed to a determined revival of the Carolingian inheritance, were lesser factors. But, taken together, and extended across the whole area of Normandy, they made for formidable power.

The administration through which the *Consuetudines et Justicie* were exploited was developed from the plan established by Richard I: viscounts appointed by the duke held sway over *pagi*, of which there were twelve, in origin Carolingian. The extremely conservative and imperial mode of government employed by the earliest Norman dukes was maintained as far as possible by Richard I's successors. But in the period following Richard II's death in 1026, the vicecomital position became hereditary in great aristocratic families, following the example already set by the very few comital offices created for Richard II's close relatives. In limiting the duke's rights of choice this development posed a problem of control, which William the Conqueror tried to solve by more frequent travels across the whole extent of his duchy, to keep track of what was happening.[84]

While itineration was a policy followed to a greater or lesser degree by all princes, for most others it proved inadequate. Behind its success in Normandy lay the more fundamental factor of the duke's authority over his aristocracy. This has traditionally been interpreted as feudal; and the word still seems appropriate, in that the Norman lords recognized, their obligation to military service and suit of court, even though that obligation retained for much of the century an ill-defined, personal character; then greater definition did creep in in the decades after the conquest of England. More troublesome is the question of how the dukes secured this tight bond. In the late tenth and early eleventh centuries, there was little problem. The counts established by Richard II were his close relations; the other families that sprang to importance, the Tosnys, the Montgomerys, the Taissons, the Goz, the Bocquencés, whether in origin Scandinavian or immigrants from beyond the Norman frontier,[85] all owed a particular debt of gratitude to the ducal house for their elevation. But as the number of aristocratic families expanded fast in the course of the eleventh century, the intimacy of their tie with the duke was lost. That newer families too should have bowed to the unusually tight discipline needs some explanation. It is perhaps to be found in the fact that many of them had lands on the old ducal demesne, which shrank markedly after the death of Richard II: the ruling house may yet have preserved sufficient strength to bargain hard for compensation. Later, the conquest of England created a bond of mutual self-interest between William the Conqueror and his lords on which the rulers could capitalize to extend and define feudal rights.[86] For by then, the Norman aristocracy plainly saw (though they might on occasion prefer to forget) the connection between self-enrichment and acquiescence in masterful rule.

The effects of aristocratic amenability were to be seen, not only in the extent of ducal rights, but also in the military power of the duchy. Given competent leadership, the Norman host could and did defeat its enemies convincingly; William the Conqueror followed the battle of Val-ès-Dunes with two victories against the king of France (who was supported by armies from Burgundy and Anjou) in 1054 and 1057. William's reputation as a general attracted into his army for the invasion of England the count of Troyes, the viscount of Thouars, and a host of Bretons and Flemings, to support the core of the Norman army, the heavily-armed warriors on horseback who featured vividly on the Bayeaux Tapestry. The assurance of opportunity for deeds of valour, the lure of prospective plunder that attracted outsiders to Norman wars, reinforced the call of duty for the Normans as they followed their duke into battle. But victory was also the fruit of wealth; mercenaries were an essential constituent of William's armies; paid soldiers, both mounted and on foot, provided crucial reinforcement to Norman military endeavours. Their presence was accounted for by the well-developed money-economy, a striking feature of Normandy since the mid-tenth century; and also by the duke's ability to tap the duchy's resources.[87]

Despite its outstanding achievements, in comparison with Flanders or Anjou ducal administration seemed rather behind the times until the last two decades of the century; its success was ascribable to satisfactory personal relationships in the upper classes rather than to administrative innovation. Ducal charters were usually written by their recipients; the ducal chamber was a simple affair; the employment of *prévôts* on ducal lands from the 1030s was not notably early. It was English practice, along with the stimulus to innovation and the self-confidence induced by conquest that subsequently carried Normandy into the van of administrative reform. The use of writs and sworn inquest in the 1080s were a presage of what was to come.

The Carolingian character of early Norman government was even more conspicuous in ecclesiastical than in secular matters. The debt the church owed to Richard I and Richard II, who generously re-endowed it after its almost complete disappearance at the time of the Scandinavian settlement, bore fruit in the remarkable degree of pressure their successors were able to impose on it. Orderic caught the spirit of this with his remark: 'if any monk from his duchy dared to bring a plea against him (William the Conqueror), he would ignore his cloth and hang him by his cowl from the top of the highest oak-tree in the wood near by'.[88] The Norman bishops were the duke's nominees, they attended synods over which the duke presided, they acknowledged their obligation to support him militarily by sending soldiers from their lands. All Norman monastic houses founded before 1037 were founded by the duke; he supported the bishops in their aim of increasing episcopal control over the other monasteries founded later by members of the aristocracy; he employed monastic scribes, he promoted monks to the episcopacy. William the Conqueror's view of the proper relation between church and prince was old-fashioned and, by 1087, open to 'iticism; yet it was compatible with a vigorous, alert 'lesiastical community, which excited the admiration of contemporaries.

the eleventh century, the results of the build-up of 'wer in Normandy are more important than the 'ereby it was achieved. The brief résumé of the 'ts which follows is geared less to shedding light 'c course of that build-up than to clarifying 'ternal relationships. For the long reign of

Richard II (996-1026) was the time in which the duchy emerged as a major force in north French and even in European politics. Richard supported Robert the Pious in Burgundy in his struggle against Otto William, he arbitrated for him with Eudes II in 1023, he arranged the marriage of his own son and heir with Robert's daughter Adela. His own marriage with Judith, sister of the count of Rennes, was the first step in the process whereby the dukes of Normandy asserted overlordship in Brittany. And his sister's marriage in 1001 to Ethelred II of England was the seed from which sprang the Norman claim to the English crown.

The whole orientation of Richard's policy bespeaks a desire to be counted among the other princes of West Francia. In his reign the Scandinavian element, both in the language of the duchy and in the characteristics of ducal rule, was submerged. After his death, his policies were continued, not by his elder son Richard, who ruled for just one year before dying in suspicious circumstances, but by his second Robert the Magnificent, who disposed of his brother's small son in a monastery and held undisputed power from 1027 to 1037. Robert forced the count of Rennes, who had rebelled, back into his vassalage; he so assisted the young king Henry I in the early troubles of his reign that he earned the Vexin français as a reward (a gift Henry later much regretted); and he supported King Ethelred's children against his aunt's new husband, Cnut the Great.

On Robert's death in 1037—which occurred on a Jerusalem pilgrimage to atone for his sins—the recognition of his young bastard son William by most of the Norman lords provided an unexpectedly clear proof of aristocratic loyalty to the ruling house. Nevertheless the ten years' minority that followed saw a considerable relaxation in the government's grip, which William struggled hard to reverse. His determination provoked rebellion. But the great victory of Valès-Dunes in 1047 brought William relief, along with the opportunity to impose stringent terms on the rebels. The long-term result of his early experiences was to convince him that expansion at the expense of his neighbours would pay dividends in securing loyalty at home. In 1054 he began an advance into Maine which, after Geoffrey Martel's death

1060, he put into the hands of his son Robert—though without disputing the overriding suzertainty of Anjou. He secured his northern fringes by alliances with the counts of Ponthieu, Boulogne, and Flanders; then in 1064, he campaigned in Brittany to recover Richard II's dominance. By 1066 the way was cleared for the great conquest of England, which brought rewards beyond their wildest dreams both to the duke and to the Norman lords who followed him.

William's expansionist programme attracted the wrath of King Henry I; in 1051, in a total turnabout of policy, he launched an attack on his erstwhile protégé, which he repeated in the unsuccessful campaigns of 1054 and 1057. Though the royal army made little headway, Henry's death in 1060 was fortunate for William, in that it prevented overt opposition to the conquest for England. Once crowned, William felt no disposition to kowtow to King Philip. Probably none of his predecessors had believed that either their office of count of Rouen or their county of Normandy was held specifically as a fief of the king of France, for the spasmodic employment of the title 'duke' in Norman charters from 1006 onward suggests consciousness of independence. But they had proved firm allies of their king until 1051, performing all that was expected of a *fidelis*. William's breach with this tradition after 1060 was dramatic and long-lasting; it was not to be until 1144 that a reigning Norman duke again did homage to his king.[89]

The break with the Capetians was of little political significance before William ran into trouble with his eldest son Robert Curthose in 1077. Then Robert's warm reception in Paris as a rebel against his father offered an ominous precedent for the future; Philip I had to be bought off with the Vexin français. Opportunities for further royal intervention occurred after William's death, during the disputes of 1089 between Robert and William Rufus, when the Norman baronage also moved to exploit their ruler's temporary weakness. But after Rufus' death and Robert's capture by his younger brother, King Henry I of England, the stage was set for rapid recovery. The victory of Tinchebrai in 1106 inaugurated the revival of the ducal peace in Normandy, the extrusion of royal armies, the return to the past.

Raoul Glaber, writing in distant Burgundy, extolled the Norman dukes as God's warriors fighting for peace.[90] Closer to home, other less disinterested intellectuals applied themselves to the task of enhancing ducal prestige, of abolishing the memory of the pagan past, still alive in Richer's mind when in the 990s he entitled Richard II *dux pyratarum*.[91] Dudo of St Quentin, in his *De moribus et actis primorum Normannie ducum*, employed legend and poetry (if that is what his panegyrical verse should be called) to paint the dukes as heroic soldiers, pious Christians, and admirable men. Less predictably, he imputed to them acts of government befitting an emperor: Rollo, the violent Scandinavian adventurer, was credited with having legislated; William Longsword was said to have preserved the judgements, laws, and statutes of Duke Rollo in all respects.[92] Dudo's Richard brought about peace within Normandy by his righteous rule, and concord beyond its frontiers by his adept arbitration in other men's quarrels. 'In his house there was truth and glory, in his works equity and justice shone forth.'[93] Overall, Dudo's portraits were pen-and-ink sketches of the ideal Carolingian ruler, owing much to the nostalgic dreams of his old master, Adalbéron of Laon.

They form a contrast with the far more historically credible portrait of William the Conqueror offered by William of Poitiers in his *Gesta Guillelmi*. William's hero was also a true Christian, a defender of the church's best interests, an impartial judge, a seeker after peace. But it was in battle that he truly fulfilled his potential; then he was as mighty as Julius Caesar. In other respects, however, the comparison was weighted in William's favour; for while Caesar's invasion was prompted solely by ambition, William's was justified by Harold's tyranny; and while Caesar allowed his victorious troops to pillage the conquered land, William preserved the inhabitants of England and ruled them pacifically. William of Poitier's William the Conqueror was a larger-than-life hero in the classical mode. The contrast between Dudo's and William's ideal points to the dawning of the twelfth-century renaissance in Normandy.

(viii) Flanders

The author of the *Encomium Emmae* declared of Bruges: 'It enjoys great fame for the number of its merchants and for its affluence in all things upon which mankind sets the highest value.'[94] So even in the first half of the eleventh century the prosperity of northern Flanders was notable. In the second half, Arras, St Omer, Ypres, and Ghent began to make their mark on the European economy by importing wool from England and Spain to turn into cloth for sale in the markets of the world. The one important industrial activity of the central Middle Ages, weaving, took root in this small northern province, slowly transforming its whole social life. The Flemish loom, too large to be operated in private houses, brought workshops in its train; the balance between town and country was altered; Flemish towns were set on the path which in the end made Flanders by far the most important urban area of north-west Europe, second only within Christendom to northern Italy.

By 1100 the extent of this development could not have been predicted; the problems it brought in its train were easily postponed for the future. At the moment, what it meant was steadily increasing wealth, especially for the counts of Flanders, who were in a notably good position to exploit the change. After about 1042, when the last major flood subsided, they were leading figures in the reclamation of the polderland in the north-west of the county. They ordered diking, draining, and clearing;[95] they pastured sheep on their expanding demesne lands; they sold their wool. They protected the merchants who brought wool from abroad, as well as those who came to buy Flemish cloth, and obtained tolls and customs for their pains. And they encouraged the growth of towns, which looked to them for arbitration in their internal troubles. This was the backdrop to their solid political achievements.

The eleventh century did not begin well for the counts of Flanders. Indeed, in 988, on the death of Arnoul II, the future had seemed grim. It was a tribute to the political skills of Baldwin IV the Bearded (988–1037) and Baldwin V (1037–67) of Lille that by 1067 Flanders was again the most brilliant success among the principalities of West Francia. William of Poitiers said of Baldwin V: 'kings feared and respected him; dukes, marquises, bishops trembled before him'.[96] The keystones of both their policies were aggression northwards into Lotharingia; the acceptance of new feudatories; and the reorganization of their own demesne lands to reinforce control. They mobilized public opinion behind each of these changes, so that little internal friction resulted. And at the same time, they earned themselves a reputation as defenders of the church which was to stand their successors in good stead during the difficult years of the late eleventh century.

To take external policy first: it is by no means certain that military expansion was still vital to the success of Flanders, now that internal colonization and reorganization were paying rich dividends. On the other hand, the count of Flanders could command around a thousand knights from the military service due to him; in addition, he had the capacity to buy the services of large mercenary armies; indeed, Flanders was one of the chief suppliers of mercenaries for the rest of Europe, as its population increased · with a rapidity which outgrew the sources of employment for the upper classes. So it was probably desirable that the count should use his formidable army: at the end of the century, it campaigned as far away as the Byzantine Empire and Outremer. But the traditional direction of external expansion, Picardy and the Norman border, no longer appealed. Baldwin IV's decision to turn eastwards may have had something to do with gratitude towards Hugh Capet, who had been his guardian during his minority. It may also have been the consequence of reflecting on his predecessors' inability ever to establish firm lordship in the area. Whatever the reason, he contented himself with taking directly into his own hands half of the Ternois, obtaining tight oaths of homage from the counts of Guînes, St Pol, and Hesdin, and leaving the rest of the area alone. Royal influence was allowed to increase in the vacuum created, and Ponthieu was left in Hugh Capet's protection. The result of this limited Flemish withdrawal was a long stretch of good relations between the Capetians and the Flemish counts, cemented by Baldwin IV's homage to Henry I in 1032, by the marriage between Baldwin V and Robert the Pious's daughter Adela, and by the choice of Baldwin V as regent in Philip I's minority (1060).

Throughout the century, Flemish interests in Lotharingia grew at the expense of the emperor. At first self-defence may have been a factor in this, for the march along the Scheldt established by Otto II seemed to threaten Flanders. The troubles on Otto III's death provided the opportunity for Baldwin IV's first aggressive campaign; Valenciennes fell to the Flemings in 1005-6. Then came attacks on Cambrésis and Hainault. But securing Flemish gains was uphill work. To this end, the marriage of Baldwin V's son to the widow of the count of Hainault proved more effective than military campaigning. It was not until the death of the emperor Henry III and the minority of Henry IV that Baldwin V obtained recognition in 1056 from the regent Agnes of his right to the whole Scheldt march as a fief of the empire. At around the same time, he married his younger son Robert to the countess of Holland, in preparation for more northward expansion.

In their internal policies, Baldwin IV and Baldwin V were pragmatic. They made no attempt to eliminate the lordships which had emerged in Baldwin IV's minority. The counts of Boulogne and Guînes were obliged to render homage, to accept the obligations of suit of court and military service, but were otherwise left alone. (The count of Boulogne in fact pursued an independent foreign policy, and also obtained homage from the counts of the newly formed counties of St Pol and Lens. By the beginning of the twelfth century, when the kingship of Jerusalem had brought lustre to their line, the counts of Boulogne were reckoned among the leading families of western Europe.)[97] In the same way, the two Baldwins permitted the lords of Béthune and d'Aubigny in Artois and of Bouchin in Ostrevant to retain the rights of high justice annexed in the minority, but brought them to recognize that they were held in fee. So though feudalism grew apace in the south of Flanders, it remained under tight comital supervision.

By contrast, on the huge comital demesne further north,

the aristocracy played a much less independent role in the new pattern of government. A late version of the twelfth-century chronicle *Flandria Generosa* says of Baldwin IV: 'He first ordained knights and nobles in Flanders, and distributed to them vills and towns.'[98] This has been interpreted as the chronicler's way of decribing the division of most of Flanders into castellanies, administrative districts based on castles, entrusted to the count's *fideles*, usually members of old families. The castles, fairly rudimentary in form, remained the count's property: the knights in their garrisons took oaths of fealty directly to the count to emphasize that fact. The castellans took over the public courts, acted with their garrisons as a police-force, and collected the profits from justice. In each castellany, a receiver was appointed to take charge of the count's revenues and forward them to the comital treasury. The oganization encouraged urban growth: Lille, Mersines, Ypres, Cassel, and Thourot all expanded as centres of castellanies.

To a certain extent the consolidation of comital authority assisted the church. In the years of the minority, advocates and guardians of monasteries had been tempted to exploit their positions to their own advantage, a development on which Baldwin IV looked with disfavour, not only because he thought it his duty to protect the monks, but also because independent advocates could endanger comital authority— after all, the county of Guînes had grown from the advocacy of St Bertin as had Ponthieu, now under royal control, from that of St Riquier. Therefore to control advocates was to shield the county from disintegration. So he and Baldwin V issued charters defining advocates' powers in conservative terms to ensure that they acted as defenders, rather than exploiters, of monasteries; and in so doing, they pleased the monastic reformers, led by Richard of St Vanne, whose efforts were devoted to recovering monastic lands and to building great churches across Flanders.

Richard of St Vanne's influence has also been detected behind the development of the Peace of God movement in the county; Hugh of Flavigny said that his was the spur behind the summoning of the first peace council at Thérouanne in 1042-3.[99] Here the bishop of Thérouanne, in

Baldwin's presence, issued a peace for all the inhabitants of his diocese, backed by the usual ecclesiastical sanctions, but also by exile, a secular punishment. This was the opening move in co-operation between bishop and count, which was to characterize later Flemish peace councils. Important for the future though this was, for most of the eleventh century peace councils had only marginal effects on the violence endemic in Flemish society, because neither Baldwin was as yet prepared to punish criminous lords with severity. The consequent misery could only be appeased by divine aid; saints and relics were much in demand as vehicles for justice in a society otherwise lacking in the means for its enforcement. The life of St Arnulf of Soissons gives clear evidence of this.[100]

Baldwin V's death in 1067 led to the brief reign of his son, Baldwin VI, and then, in 1070, to the usurpation of Baldwin VI's younger brother, Robert the Frisian, at the expense of his two small nephews left in the guardianship of their mother Richilda. The genealogies of the counts of Flanders, with their varying views on whether Robert was justified, hint at the contention his action aroused. King Philip I was sufficiently shocked to launch an attack on Flanders, in which he was helped by the counts of St Pol, Boulogne, and Guînes (he also obtained troops from Aquitaine, Burgundy, and Normandy). Nevertheless, the battle of Cassel in 1070 proved so expensive for the royal army that, though Robert himself was taken prisoner, Philip decided on peace. Robert was officially recognized as count of Flanders.

Robert's marriage to the countess of Holland meant that he was drawn into a combination of defence and attack along the north-eastern frontier of Flanders. He made an alliance with Cnut IV of Denmark to squeeze imperialist interests in the north, as a result of which he found himself embroiled in a Danish attack on England, which was brought to an abortive end by the assassination of Cnut. Nevertheless Robert's interests were served by this; his reputation as an opponent of the emperor endeared him to Pope Urban II, who overlooked his bullying of Flemish bishops, and gave his approval for the removal of the bishopric of Arras from the imperial diocese of Cambrai, in hopes of winning Robert's active support in his war against Henry IV.[101]

Internally, Robert kept to the lines drawn up by the Baldwins. He was renowned for his development of Flanders' economic potential, particularly for his encouragement of draining and ditching, and for his proclamation of 1083-4 covering the county's fairs by a special peace. This pointed to growing comital initiative within the peace movement, culminating in the episcopal synod of 1099, called at Robert II's behest, which stated, among the usual provisions, that because all fortifications in the county were held of the count, those built without his authorization could lawfully be captured by him, even in times of truce.[102] Robert I's entourage became more feudally oriented; it was in his reign that there occurred the first mention of the 'peers of Flanders' (vassal counts with particular responsibility for the defence of the county's frontiers).[103] Moreover, his court had a full complement of household officers: the butler, constable, sensechal, and chamberlains of Flanders. Both were part of the more distinctive social hierarchy that Robert favoured. Administratively, too, the reign saw development: one or two castellanies were added to the demesne; and on his departure for Jerusalem in 1089, the count appointed a chancellor, the prévôt of St Donatian's at Bruges, with an office of notaries under him, to carry out financial and judicial administration.[104] All in all, Robert the Frisian's reign presents a parallel with that of King Henry I in English history, in that both saw the rapid extension and intensification of central authority.

His son Robert II (1092-1116) extended his father's policies, by issuing a peace in his own name, not that of his bishops, at Thérouanne in 1111, and by actively encouraging the wool trade. In 1101, he made a famous treaty with King Henry I, undertaking to provide 1,000 knights for service in England or 500 for service in Normandy, should Henry need them, in return for a money fief of £500 sterling; this was striking proof of his extensive military resources.[105] But by far the most significant event of his reign was his participation in the First Crusade, which brought him a hero's welcome on his return to Flanders, the title Robert of Jerusalem, and European renown.

So Flanders entered the twelfth century as a highly

successful, administratively precocious, rich principality. Though its prince did homage to the king of France (Robert II died fighting for Louis VI against the Normans), and might also, when expediency dictated, proclaim his allegiance to the Emperor, he was to all intents and purposes a sovereign within the county.

(c) The rest of France

It is noticeable that none of the areas discussed in the corresponding section of Part I—those which had not been absorbed into principalities in the tenth century—were to find new strong government in the eleventh. The time for laying the foundations of principalities was apparently past.

(i) The bishopric of Langres fell into obscurity after Bruno de Roucy's death in 1016. Though Bruno had made his peace with the victorious Robert the Pious in 1005, and remained a significant figure for the rest of his life, his action in backing Otto William against the king deprived him and his successors of the certain royal support they had enjoyed under the last Carolingian kings; to earn Robert's goodwill, his successor was obliged to cede the Dijonnais to the duchy in 1016. Later (some time after 1065) the bishop also lost Tonnerre to the count of Nevers. Yet a substantial kernel still survived, from which the episcopal principality expanded, until by 1107 it included twelve castles inside the diocese and five outside.[106] The prospects for Langres looked bright.

But the independence that Bruno had highly prized was jeopardized by two very different threats: firstly, by ducal influence over episcopal elections—as many as four of the eleventh-century bishops of Langres are thought to have been relations of the duke of Burgundy; and ducal charters reveal that other unrelated bishops frequented the court at Dijon. The reason for the revival of ducal control over the bishopric was to be found in the sharp decline of royal influence in the area after 1031, a lasting consequence of the troubles of the early years of Henry I's reign.[107] Secondly, the reform movement imposed new strains on the count-bishop. In 1049 Pope Leo IX condemned the incumbent of the see for simony and deposed him. As a consequence, his successors at Langres were scrupulous in upholding reform; Hugh Renard, for example, played a conspicuous part in the reforming council of Meaux. But the contradiction inherent in a count-bishop's position had been revealed; a new uneasiness reigned. Already by the late eleventh century, the relief with which the bishops of Langres were to greet royal intervention in Burgundy in the mid twelfth was predictable.

On a more local level, the city of Langres grew fast; the bishop had to accommodate his government to new trading interests, to the protection of foreign merchants, to the exploitation of new sources of income. In temporal matters, he may have had to rely more on his *vidame*, a post by now hereditary in the de Saulx family, and therefore no longer in his appointment.[108] It was not perhaps surprising that the bishops were too absorbed in everyday matters to cut fine figures abroad.

(ii)   The Rouergue underwent sharp transformation in the course of the eleventh century. At the beginning, its count was the notable figure Raymond III, famed warrior in Spain, liberal benefactor of Conques, son of the daughter of the marquis of Tuscany, a man whose nobility and achievements set him apart from his predecessors in office. From the extensive lands he inherited in Narbonne came his right to the title 'duke of Gothia', which he occasionally used. The *Miracles of St Foy* offer a glimpse of him exercising justice in the traditional way, protecting the church, maintaining old and building new fortifications; conservatism produced rich rewards. But the old ways could not long be maintained. With the failure of male heirs to Raymond's son Hugh, who died around 1054, the county was drawn into a confederation by the marriage of Hugh's daughter to the heir of Auvergne and the Gévaudan. This marriage augured well for the future, in bringing together counties with a common geographical and cultural background. But it aroused the jealousy of the house of Toulouse, the overlords of the Rouergue. In 1079 Raymond, second son of Count Pons of Toulouse, took the Rouergue and the Gévaudan from the count of Auvergne, as the first step on the ladder to reuniting the ancient county of Toulouse with Gothia. So by the end of the century the Rouergue had become absorbed as a fringe area into the county of Toulouse.

Loss of independence from 1054 meant that the count, whether of Auvergne or Toulouse, was hardly ever present. If the lords of the Rouergue wanted judgement, they had to leave the county to find it, as did the abbot of Conques when he sought a hearing against Bermode of Agde 'in parts of Gothia', where Raymond of Toulouse was to be found.[109] Within the Rouergue itself, comital authority declined rapidly. The third and fourth books of the *Miracles of St Foy*, written in the second half of the century, never mention the count (though the Auvergnat social influence is easily detected).[110] As a consequence, local political life became purely a matter of balancing out rival castellans' interests. For the monks of Conques, the only protection they could devise against the depredations inflicted on them by the neighbouring castellan was to carry the standard of the Cross and the statue of St Foy into the centre of the town, calling publicly for God's vengeance.[111] It worked—the castellan, all his sons, and his three daughters came rapidly to unpleasant ends; even his castle was blown down. But for those without direct divine assistance, the absence of any superior authority was no doubt painful.

(iii) The rather greater stability of the eleventh-century political scene ensured that there were no ephemeral principalities as important as Vermandois had been in the tenth. Indeed, with the exception of the very short-lived Auvergne–Rouergue merger mentioned above, the only one of any significance was that built up by Raoul de Crépy on land which had once been largely within Vermandois. Its history suggests that the old mixture of clever marriages, inheritance, usurpation, and force was no longer sufficiently potent to establish lasting lordship.

Raoul de Crépy, count of Valois, began his career as a violent opponent of King Henry I, by whom he was captured in 1041; the experience led to a complete volte-face; he became a loyal supporter of the king, and then, in Philip I's minority, second only to Baldwin V of Flanders as royal counsellor. By his first marriage, he obtained the county of Bar-sur-Aube (just over the border in imperial territory); in 1063, he inherited Amiens and the Vexin from his cousin in a complicated family share-out, making him lord of a large block of land between the Seine, the Somme, the Marne, and the Meuse, to which he added the lordship of Montdidier by usurpation. It was an ideal area from which to pursue expansion, both in Lotharingia against Verdun, and in Troyes, where he opposed Thibaud's annexation of Eudes III's lands after Eudes had departed for England in 1066. Perhaps his cleverest coup was his third marriage, to Henry I's widow, Anna of Kiev in 1061. This lady brought with her a useful dowry, including the abbey of Notre Dame at Laon, and all the prestige of a royal wife, with an accompanying whiff of the exotic to distinguish her husband's court from those of his neighbours.

But if Raoul showed the relentless acquisitiveness of Baldwin II of Flanders or of Hugh the Great, his younger son Simon, who survived him in 1074, had a completely different temperament. Though initially prepared to defend his inheritance—indeed to extend it, for he projected a marriage with Judith, daughter and heiress of the count of Auvergne —by 1077 he had withdrawn into a monastery, leaving the delighted king to divide his honours as he thought fit. The speed with which the whole was dismembered bore witness to the resentment Raoul's acquisition had aroused in other possible claimants to the land. No sense of cohesion had been generated in the counties during the years they were ruled together; Raoul's attempts at foreign expansion had not been crowned with sufficient success to generate loyalty. And Philip I, his stepson, was a dangerous man in whom to arouse jealousy.[112]

(iv) In Picardy the pattern of politics was much simplified by the disintegration of the Vermandois principality and the amalgamation of Capetian with royal interests in 987. This, along with the cessation of Flemish aggression in the minority of Baldwin IV, soon to be elevated into conscious policy by both Baldwin IV and Baldwin V, gave the Capetians a solid advantage in the area. It says much for the strength of local interests that the kings were only able to use this advantage to negative effect, to prevent the encroachment of other powers on the area. Non-Flemish Picardy remained a mosaic of small counties cheek by jowl with new castellanies.

Though Baldwin IV and his son Baldwin V relaxed the relentless pressure which their ancestors had exerted in Picardy, they kept intact their rights in Artois and much of the Ternois. Here, far from the comital demesne, their lordship took a much looser form than in the north; only over the towns of Aire and St Omer where they established castellanies, did they exercise direct rule. Elsewhere, they operated by feudal ties with the local aristocracy, the counts of Guînes and Boulogne, of St Pol (emerged 1031) and Hesdin (emerged 1065), the lords of Lens, Béthune, or Lillers. Enjoying a considerable degree of independence, these lords paid the count of Flanders the compliment of imitating him to a large extent; they mixed viscounties with castellanies, kept intact what they could of Carolingian jurisdiction alongside their feudal courts, held their areas under tight control. A century later than their Flemish overlord, they had learned the lesson that new men (in the political though not the social sense) ruling new units must clothe themselves as far as possible in time-honoured garb.

Further south, in Ponthieu, the Capetians already had a strong base around Abbeville in the time of Hugh Capet, whom Hariulf of St Riquier describes as annexing three pacels of the monastery's land to build castles in the area; Robert the Pious added to this when he obtained Montreuil as a dowry with Rozala, widow of Arnoul II, in 988. Important though maritime Picardy was to them the Capetians were unable to hold the area directly throughout the century. In the late 1040s or the 1050s, Enguerran, lord of Abbeville and advocate of St Riquier, killed the count of Boulogne, married his widow, and 'he took the title of count because his wife was a countess.'[113] Henry I and later Philip I accepted the *fait accompli*, received homage from the new line of counts, and relied in future on their loyalty. Ponthieu now had the same status in relation to the crown as Boulogne enjoyed to Flanders.

Vermandois changed internally less than the other Picard counties; it kept its frontiers, which were roughly Carolingian, and its counts retained many ancient rights, along with their memory of Carolingian descent. They never had another opportunity to create a principality: their claim to Troyes and Meaux was passed over in 1021 in favour of Eudes II of Blois; but the last Carolingian count, Herbert IV, was the successful claimant of Montdidier and Valois in 1077, when Simon de Crépy retired into a monastery. Herbert left a son, described as *fatuus et indiscretus*, and a female heiress, thus providing a perfect solution to Capetian succession problems: at the instigation of the barons of the county Philip I married her to his younger brother Hugh, Vermandois became the possession of a Capetian cadet branch, its history closely entwined with that of the royal demesne. A lucky marriage was the architect of the crown's only real success in Picardy.

Between Vermandois and Ponthieu, the ancient county of Amiens, disintegrating in 1000, totally lost its identity. A prey to the counts of Ponthieu and St Pol on its western fringes, with a new lordship of Montdidier occupying a southern position, the rest of the old county gravitated around the count of Amiens in the west, the abbot of Corbie in the east. Hardly surprisingly in this fragmented area, because comital authority was weaker, seigneurial enterprise met with greater rewards. The brief hegemony of Raoul de Crépy, by bringing together Amiens and Montdidier, offered a new kernel; its disappearance encouraged further relaxation of old bonds. Of more relevance for the future was Philip I's seizure of Corbie in 1071. But it was to be a long time before the French monarchy was able to exploit its new gain to extend its power.

Picardy was always a wealthy area; its agricultural surplus increased in value with the rise of the demographic curve in eleventh-century France. It could thus afford numerous lordships, each with its own power base. Although the ambition of a weak king in the south combined with a limitation of Flemish interests in the north-east to produce a mosaic of independent counties and castellanies across the whole area, nevertheless most of these lordships were internally well-organized and resilient. Only Vermandois (through the accident of marriage) and Amiénois offered easy pickings for a determinedly expansionist prince.[114]

(v) Upper Berry and the Auvergne were rather different. In both of these, the tenth century had brought a localization of power, a fragmentation into units much smaller than those in Picardy. In the Auvergne, this fragmentation had been partially mitigated by the appearance of the new comital house in 951; but the count's authority outside his own lands and small *mouvance* in Basse-Auvergne was minimal. His clever marriage with the heiress to Velay and the Rouergue might have mended his position, had its effects lasted. As it was, the count found himself surrounded by a powerful local aristocracy which took very little notice of him. The Auvergne became a prey to private wars. One such, which raged for a long time in Planèze, led to the destruction of peasants' homes and the pillaging of land belonging to Conques abbey.[115] The neighbouring bishops of Le Puy and Mende were forced to defend themselves by assuming comital powers; this example moved the bishop of Clermont, who also assumed them, against the wishes of the count. Here lay the source of much future friction. Remote, enjoying a rich but eccentric culture, containing extensive ecclesiastical estates which proved vulnerable to the ambitions of tough castellans and viscounts, the Auvergne was to prove a tempting prey to strong princes in the twelfth century.

Upper Berry, too, was a land of independent castellans, each having authority over very small areas. With no count of its own, and with unambitious vicecomital families, Berry rapidly proved vulnerable to external influences. By the early eleventh century, the counts of Blois had built up a network of client relationships with many castellans, a loose bond of mutual convenience, which they gradually consolidated by purchase and by using the patronage that escheats provided. Anjou, too, had entered the race, though with less than its usual vigour. And in 1101 King Philip I bought the viscounty of Bourges from its holder (who needed money to go on a crusade), to be the kernel of a royal demesne in the county. A new era was about to dawn. But neither Blois nor royal hegemony yet had much bite.

The only local figures who exercised authority were the archbishops of Bourges. In the first decades of the century, they collected vassals around them, to make their court a place of resort for the neighbourhood. So great was their local influence that Archbishop Aimon de Bourbon, a scion of one of Lower Berry's most important families, introduced the Peace of God into the area in a distinctive form, by adding to the normal obligations of not attacking ecclesiastical land, churchmen, merchants, or peasants, a vow to pursue breakers of the peace and apprehend them by force. As a consequence, the man of God led the first and most famous of peace armies against Eudes de Déols in 1038.[116] But Aimon's defeat at the battle of Cher convinced at least André of Fleury (author of this part of the *Miracles of St Benedict*) that his action had been against God's will. Aimon's successors shared this belief; therefore they confined themselves to religious matters.

So in Upper Berry as in the Auvergne, neither secular authority nor the Peace of God offered security. There would always be those who would appeal to external powers for help. Upper Berry had already attracted the king and the counts of Blois and Anjou, but their hold was still loose and localized. The Auvergne only knew the nominal subjection involved in its count's fealty to the duke of Aquitaine. It would not be long before both were to fall under sterner management.

(d) Conclusions

The importance of the eleventh century in the evolution of France is hard to estimate. In one sense, it was a time of setback in that, for most of the century, the frontiers of the West Frankish realm were highly fluid. Flemish expansion across the Scheldt, Norman into England, Champenois into Bar-sur-Aube, Toulousan into Provence, Aquitanian and Burgundian into Spain, and conversely, Catalan empire-building in southern Gascony and Gothia, confused the Carolingian map of the country without substituting new certainties. The once-clear definition of West Francia as the area acknowledging the suzerainty of the West Frankish king lost sharpness as principalities stretched into the domains of other kings, and princes acquired other allegiances, while the West Frankish kings devoted themselves to affairs on their own doorstep. On the other hand, the survival of the kingdom was now assured. The end of the Ottonian dynasty, with its powerful commitment to lordship in Lotharingia, brought release from the threat either of absorption or of subordination. The king and princes could work out their own destinies, free from most external pressures.

This breathing space allowed the principalities to take deeper root in the soil. In the course of the century, these essentially political units, so fluid in their early years, slowly gained cohesion and concrete shape as the *pays* of France. The provinces Flanders, Normandy, Anjou, Champagne, even Burgundy and Aquitaine, took their place on the map along with the surviving old Roman subdivisions—e.g. the counties of Poitou and Bordeaux—as the internal political divisions of the country which was to be known as France. So behind the outward confusion of the political scene, a constructive force can be detected at work.

The principalities led by men of outstanding military capacity—the Normandy of William the Conqueror, Flanders under Baldwin V, and Robert the Frisian, Aquitaine under Guy Geoffrey, Anjou under Fulk Nerra and Geoffrey Martel —coalesced fast and established themselves indelibly on the map, because in them that mixture of public and private rights on which all princely authority was based achieved a marked degree of recognition from their inferiors. It is true that, since this recognition was based on the princes' personal achievements, its survival *in toto* under their successors could not be assumed; indeed in the event of a succession crisis its partial disappearance was almost inevitable. Yet at a time when even relatively passive princes like the dukes of Burgundy and the counts of Blois could chalk up solid achievements in government, those of greater ambition usually overcame temporary setbacks with ease.

Nevertheless the process of consolidation in the principalities was bound to meet a counter-pressure from below; for what the prince could do, so, for the most part, could lesser men. Ademar tells the (legendary?) story of the exchange between Aldebert of Périgueux, an ally of Fulk Nerra at the siege of Tours, and the kings Hugh Capet and

Robert the Pious. Infuriated by Aldebert's aggression, the kings scornfully demanded 'Who made you a count?', only to receive the damaging retort 'Who made you kings?'[117] Few in the future were to challenge the Capetian right to rule, partly because kingship was relatively unimportant, partly because there were no other obvious candidates. But the logic of Aldebert's reply pinpointed the weakness of princely authority, its lack of clear constitutional status. If princes stressed the public character of their powers, they were liable to the charge of tyranny: Geoffrey Martel was accused of it by William of Poitiers,[118] Robert the Frisian justified his usurpation by the allegation that Richilda, as regent for the young Baldwin, had acted tyranically in exacting new taxes.[119] If, on the other hand, princes relied on a magpie-like acquisition of private rights, they put their authority on the same basis as that of any of their lords, so risking their superiority, like the counts of Blois.

Meanwhile each princely innovation inspired imitation. Dependent counts, viscounts, castellans, consolidated their territorial rights, took all comital dues in their neighbourhoods, organized their courts for arbitration among their vassals, built up their *mouvances*, even founded their own monasteries. And in most of West Francia, they acted with the tacit acquiescence, sometimes even the open approval, of their princes, who needed their support to survive. As a consequence, the crucial factor in the political consolidation of principalities came to be the forging of personal links between princes and their lords. The significance of feudal ties could not but increase.

CHAPTER 9

Aristocratic life 987–1108

(a) The ruling class: its resources and means of self-aggrandizement

(i) Wealth

'To him that hath shall be given' was a truism of early medieval society. Because lords owned large tracts of land at a time when the opportunities for its exploitation were particularly favourable, and could add to this profit from tolls and customs on increasing trade, they could hardly avoid a substantial increase in their resources in the course of the eleventh century. But the fly in the ointment, from the princes' point of view, lay in the fact that their advantages were now more widely shared than they had been in the past. And in some cases, most strikingly in Normandy, the landed gains of castellans had been made at the expense of the comital demesne. There was thus a real danger, not of impoverishment, but of the closing of the gap between princes and other lesser lords, just at the time when display and liberality were increasingly important elements in princely political armouries. Renewed effort to enrich themselves was therefore demanded.

Prima facie, it seems likely that princes joined with other laymen and ecclesiastics in encouraging the extensive forest clearance that characterized the French countryside; but proof is lacking. The famous letter from the archbishop of Rheims to Baldwin V of Flanders, praising him for his activities in draining and ditching the coastal areas (presumably after the Dunkirk inundation of 1014–42 had at last subsided) is explicit evidence of an interest in agricultural expansion.[1] And the fact that wine-growing developed markedly on lands much visited by the dukes of Burgundy and Aquitaine is perhaps also suggestive of ducal initiative. On the other hand, it is unlikely that the duke of Normandy,

who granted out the larger part of the demesne in feudal
tenures, or the count of Toulouse, who was slow to consolidate his lands, was a major contributor to agricultural
progress.

Encouragement of trade was more widespread. Again, the
counts of Flanders were in the vanguard, with Robert the
Frisian and Robert II offering protection for merchants
crossing the county and their peace for the duration of fairs.
But at least as important was the provision of coinage suitable for reasonably small deals and sufficiently abundant for
merchants to be able to rely on the supply. Here, Normandy
was outstanding. As early as the beginning of the century,
wealth in the county was reckoned in monetary terms; the
implication that coins circulated freely was borne out when
the Fécamp treasure was discovered in 1954. But by around
1020, the quality of Norman coins declined markedly as
a concomitant to the rapid increase in quantity. Here there
may have been a connection between the temporary weakening of ducal control over minting, in the troubles following
Richard II's death, and the prodution of a currency useful
for traders. In Aquitaine, too, this connection seems likely,
in that silver coins modelled on those of Charles the Bald circulated until the serious financial crisis of 1103, brought on
by William IX's crusading expenses; then the silver coin was
devalued, followed in 1112 by a further devaluation, which
preceded a period of marked economic growth.[2] In Toulouse
also, the steadily falling value of comital coins in the second
half of the century made them relevant at last to the needs of
the merchant classes. There was, of course, nothing disinterested about princely debasement; but in this instance,
princely profit was consistent with mercantile gain.

Deliberate assistance to economic growth went hand in
hand with administrative reform aimed at channelling its
profits firmly into princely treasuries. This policy indicated
that princes were ceasing to regard their demesnes, those
ragbags of rights and scattered pieces of land, chiefly as
means of buying support, whether on earth or in heaven, and
were viewing them instead as permanent assets, to be cultivated in a more business-like fashion. Ironically the church,
which had gained so much from the older cast of mind, was

prominent in propagating the newer outlook. For the monastic reformers Odilo of Cluny and Richard of St Vanne were renowned for their consolidation of monastic demesnes, their determination to ensure that what had once been granted to their houses should remain their inalienable property.[3] Inspired by this objective, other churchmen, both bishops and abbots, appointed officials called *prévôts* for the task of collecting rents and dues from their estates. Their examples were not lost on princes; Eudes II of Blois employed a *prévôt* in 1004 (see p. 196). These officials differed from their predecessors as tax- and rent-collectors, the *vicarii* and viscounts, in that they were rewarded, not with a *beneficium*, but with a cut from the profits. Initially, the office was often sold to the highest bidder, who would recoup his losses by assiduity in collecting. But later it became hereditary. The job always excited unpopularity, sometimes even danger. Ademar of Chabannes told of the murder of the duke of Aquitaine's *prévôt* at St Jean d'Angély in 1026, and the destruction of his house by the angry inhabitants of the town.[4] But despite the risks, for a man of ambition and determination the reward was ample; for a *prévôté* might bridge the gap between the upper peasantry and the lower echelons of the aristocracy.

The introduction of these new officials on princely estates was a piecemeal affair. Only in Flanders, where the comital demesne was in any case a large and solid block, was a complete network of *prévôtés* created before the end of the century. Elsewhere, their appearance depended on favourable opportunity. Some princes did not employ them at all until the second half of the century. And where they were employed, their duties varied from place to place—some fulfilled judicial as well as financial functions, others might even have a military role. But in performing their tasks all both reflected and further promoted the territorialization of power which was so prominent a feature of the eleventh century political scene.

Husbanding the demesne proved more difficult (except in Flanders) than appointing new officials to administer it. Huge grants of land to the church became rarer (but so did the chances of resuming what had once been granted); from the middle of the century, gifts were more likely to be of *consuetudines* from ecclesiastical lands or of other tolls and dues. But the real losses in princely revenues were to secular lords, by a process of slow attrition. For any moment of weakness in the fortunes of a great house—the minority of William the Conqueror, the early years of Fulk le Réchin —provided the perfect opportunity for castellans to establish their hereditary rights, or to exercise for their own benefit prerogatives which had hitherto brought profit to the princes. The very substantial endowments most princes had accumulated in the ninth and tenth centuries could be curtailed without disaster in the favourable economic climate of the eleventh century. And the assiduity with which Carolingian taxes like the *fodrum* or the *pedagium* were revived compensated in some measure. Nevertheless, it must be supposed that there were economic as well as social inducements to the policies of expansion beyond the West Frankish frontiers pursued by the dukes of Normandy, Aquitaine, and even Burgundy, as well as by the counts of Toulouse, Flanders, and for brief periods Blois and Anjou. Plunder proved a useful temporary boost to revenues; the annexation of new lands, with the opportunities for tougher exploitation which conquest brought in its train, could restore to princes their dominant position as by far the richest men within their principalities.

(ii) Justice

In 1010 Raymond III of the Rouergue died, leaving to Conques abbey, among other gifts, an estate called Pallas in Narbonne. The monastery's right to Pallas was challenged by the Lady Garsinde, wife of Bernard le Velu, who declared that the estate had belonged to her first husband Raymond, from whom count Raymond III had taken it by force. The monks' first attempt to obtain a judgement in their favour proved abortive; a second trial was therefore arranged at Pallas itself. The abbot of Conques travelled there with his knights and vassals, to put his case before the chosen arbitrator, a certain Bernard. Then the Lady Garsinde and Bernard le Velu arrived, accompanied by an even larger following. When each side had pleaded its cause very noisily, the arbitrator decided in favour of the monks, though the Lady Garsinde was to receive a monetary recompense for abandoning her claims; a concord was to be drawn up. At this point, one of Garsinde's noble followers, unwilling to accept the verdict, arose and demanded that the decision be made not by arbitration but by battle. In the tumult which ensued, the terrified monks made their escape, only to find their way blocked by the same young lord with fifty knights, who threatened them with death. At this juncture, St Foy sent a storm, the aggressive aristocrat was struck by lightning, his terrified armed men ran away, and when the news of divine intervention reached her, the Lady Garsinde abandoned her case.

So, at least, is the story presented by Bernard of Angers in the *Miracles of St Foy*[5] (it is clear, however, from the subsequent narrative that, whatever the short-term effects of the thunderbolt, Garsinde's claims were pursued again later by her husband.)[6] But what is important in the episode is what the narrator takes for granted: that when men of standing disputed, arbitration was hard to arrange, and often immediately unacceptable to the party which felt itself the loser by the judgement, even where monetary compensation was offered to soften the blow.

This point was a truism for contemporary princes. In a case which occurred some time between 1037 and 1054, the abbot of Marmoutier complained in Geoffrey Martel's court that a certain Bouchard had seized back a mill which his brother, with Bouchard's consent, had earlier bestowed on the abbey. In the course of the hearing, Bouchard was brought finally to admit that the abbot's complaint was true. But out of pity for Bouchard's poverty, Geoffrey prevailed on the abbot to allow him possession of the mill for the rest of his life.[7] The strictly legal weighing of rights and wrongs played only a subordinate role in the outcome of the case, even where the judge was, in other respects, assertive of his judicial strength (see pp. 187-8). and if Geoffrey chose to conciliate in aristocratic disputes over property, he was forced to the same resort on matters of crime; even powerful princes refrained from tough measures against those supporters essential to their own position. So, though Geoffrey expressed his anger after the knight Walter had killed one of his kinsmen, he accepted two mills from him as the price of his peace.[8] Likewise Robert the Frisian chose a mixture of mockery and persuasion, rather than judicial force, to bring to heel one of his knights who had injured another in a brawl. Outright condemnation was as rare as condign punishment where the criminal was a man of high social standing; for if the delinquent vassal chose to submit himself to his lord, he had performed an act of self-abasement which, in itself, merited courteous handling. In so far as the system worked—some disputes were settled, some crimes fully atoned for—it did so because it accommodated to the plastic and multifarious notions of justice obtaining within a small group of men, known to each other from youth up, often related by marriage, who had to reckon on continuing to live as neighbours after the case was over.

Because arbitration called for personal authority, tact, and understanding, some princes—Hugh of Burgundy, Robert II of Flanders—achieved a high reputation which attracted many disputes to their court. On the other hand, with the expansion of feudal ties, there was a growing expectation that any lord ought to resolve the disputes among his own vassals. As a consequence, even feeble princes like Fulk le Réchin met with requests for judgement. There was, however, a technical difficulty in the path of litigants: because princes' courts were peripatetic, they had to be pursued around the countryside, as Geoffrey le Preuil pursued Fulk le Réchin in 1093;[9] and this fact offered a convenient excuse for those summoned by their lords as defendants in a case. In 1100, Geoffrey of Vendôme assured William IX of Aquitaine that he was trying to answer the summons to the ducal court, but that every time his messenger reached the appointed place, he found William had moved on.[10] This may have been the simple truth; it may, alternatively, have been an instance of the use of delay by an intelligent but reluctant pleader. For the great weakness of feudal jurisdiction lay in its lack of muscle to enforce the appearance of both parties in court. And this weakness was almost automatically exacerbated in some instances by the alternative of episcopal jurisdiction for infringements of the Peace of God; this created procedural uncertainties in the minds of plaintiffs and judges, to delay yet further the chance of obtaining justice. Only in Normandy were these problems transcended.

Jurisdiction over the peasantry operated on markedly more authoritarian principles; as a result, it was both arbitrary and capable of producing solid financial rewards. But most of it had already escaped the princes' grasp in the tenth century; in the course of the eleventh, it passed squarely into the hands of local castellans, who exacted fines and imposed penalties on their peasants with remorseless vigour. Princes derived profit solely from the courts on their own manorial lands or from those areas whose castellans were held in sufficient subordination to render dues to their lords. As the number of these dwindled, princely jurisdiction apparently reached its low point.

Yet there were spasmodic and disparate indications of development in the opposite direction. Geoffrey Martel and Raymond of St Gilles both had some—though temporary — success in asserting the superiority of their courts over all others within their principalities. All over the south, men remembered, if they did not yet always act on, the tradition that serious offences, murder, rape, arson, ought to be justiciable in a higher court;[11] by 1091, the *Consuetudines et Justicie* declared this Carolingian survival to represent the practice in Normandy.[12] In Flanders, the count's peace was becoming a meaningful concept, at fair times at least. It was precedents like these which fired Philip I and his young son Louis VI to renewed policing of the royal demesne at the end of the century.[13] Less visibly, but just as significantly, by confirming agreements reached between castellans or advocates and the communities over which they held sway, princes played their part in the evolution of customary law across the whole of West Francia. And that role was not always simply confirmatory. Geoffrey Martel claimed the right to abolish bad customs;[14] William the Conqueror worked towards securing uniformity of custom across the whole duchy.[15] The trail was blazed for more active princely participation in the following century.

(iii) Military resources

The exact date of the Vendôme charter, in which Count
Bouchard gave full details of the military service owed
to him from the area of Vendôme, is still controversial; but
it is now accepted as an authentic document of the time
of Fulk Nerra or Geoffrey Martel.[16] The charter provides
evidence of a surprisingly well-worked-out system to ensure
castle-guard of the town: in April, May, June, July and
August, it was the count's responsibility, though he paid only
for the first two months directly out of his own treasury;
the inhabitants of the town produced a tax for the following
three. Then the rest of the year was covered, a month at
a time, by each of seven vassals, in return for the fiefs they
held of the count. Each night, five men were needed, three
for the gates and two to move between them, so the responsibility was heavy. The mixture of feudal service (the vassals'
obligation) with mercenary forces (the count was reckoning
to pay for his share of the duty) is characteristic of the
eleventh century.

After treating of castle-guard, the charter goes on to
specify all the fiefs in the surrounding area, and their military
obligations, *ost* and *chevauchée* (long and short expeditionary
duty).[17] The document presupposes a direct connection
between the fully mounted warrior and the fief, which is
unusually specific for a period as early as this; it is therefore
indicative of well-developed feudal institutions, at least in
part of the area under Angevin control. The drawback to
feudal service from the count's point of view was its
limited duration. The charter does not mention this, and
the period may still have been imprecise; but it is not likely
to have been above two months at most, which limited its
usefulness considerably. As a consequence, feudal contracts
in the full sense of the term must have been more important
for supplying castle-guard than for campaigning (though it
would be pushing the argument too far to deny them any
significance in the field).

In his *conventum* with William V, Hugh de Lusignan was
entitled *chiliarchus*,[18] the commander of a thousand. Later it
was recorded that the castellan of Amboise's army numbered

200 knights and 1,000 footsoldiers.[19] Though the figures may well be inaccurate, they attest the contemporary impression that even local forces could be very large, at least in time of emergency. How many of the 200 knights should be counted as members of Lisiard of Amboise's household cannot be determined; the number is rather more what one might expect of the household of a great prince. But some of them will have been men who lived permanently within their lord's gates, his closest companions, who, after several years' service, might hope to be rewarded with fiefs. Others may possibly have enjoyed what later came to be described as 'money-fiefs', the regular receipt of some tax or source of revenue in return for service. (Tenure of this sort was once regarded as an exclusively late development; but its roots are now thought to have been very old.)[20] Others again may simply have received pay for appearing to help Lisiard in his emergency, a battle with Thibaud of Blois. The large number of foot-soldiers suggests either that they were mercenaries, or that their presence was accounted for by a surviving obligation under the *ban*. Whichever it was, it argues for a strategy more concerned with battles, with expeditions, with sieges, than with *chevauchées* to dominate the locality. In this, the lord of Amboise's armed forces provided a pattern for the future.

Granted these sizeable forces at local level, the princes' military success on their own territories was dependent on their ability to win active support from their castellans. Supplicius of Amboise's refusal to assist Fulk le Réchin in the field, because Fulk's enemy was Thibaud of Blois to whom Supplicius had also paid homage, proved that the task was not always straightforward.[21] On the other hand, William the Conqueror was well supported against the royal invasions after 1051.

When the campaign planned was one of aggression outside the principality, there were solid grounds for assisting it, in hopes of booty or even territorial gain. And an expedition which combined the prospect of gain with that of notable adventure, such as the forays into Spain or the Norman conquest of England, could rely on widespread support. In these cases, the prince might well be surrounded by vassals who owed him military service; but they would be present not from obligation but from desire, and they would be accompanied by large numbers whose reason for being there had nothing to do with feudal ties or fidelity. William the Conqueror's host for the invasion of England, with its contingents of Bretons and Flemings, is proof that the military resources of princes could, on some occasions at least, far outrun knights' fees.

Troops who fought for pay were little discussed in the sources; but Henry I's insurance policy in the treaty of 1101 —not invoked, as far as we know—cost £500 sterling a year.[22] The treaty shows that money could be a decisive element in warfare. It also provides a glimpse of Flanders as a place where a substantial number of fighters could be expensively equipped and then encouraged to leave the county for long periods. This corner of West Francia, abandoned and defenceless in the late ninth century, had totally changed its character by the beginning of the twelfth.

Henry I was only concerned with hiring knights; hiring foot-soldiers was probably commoner. It has been conjectured that the archers and many of the foot-soldiers who fought at Hastings and feature in the Bayeux Tapestry were fighting in return for pay. The growing population, particularly in the towns of Flanders, provided the manpower for conflicts throughout West Francia; in the future, they were to collect an odious reputation for pillaging as they crossed the countryside. Their great unpopularity may have been the consequence of the heavy financial burden they imposed on their employers; their mere existence is proof that money was circulating fast in western Europe; but that they were not always paid implies an economy too immature to support them readily.[23]

(b) Feudal Ties

A notable innovation in the eleventh-century diplomatic vocabulary of the north was the occasional use of the term *fevum*, a fief. Its late appearance was inexplicable to the older school of historians, which regarded fiefs as characteristic of social organization throughout the ninth to the thirteenth centuries. Nowadays its appearance constitutes a convincing argument for those who believe that fiefs and vassalage were insignificant in aristocratic society before about the second quarter of the eleventh century. But although the use of the new word probably does imply the growing importance of a hitherto minor institution, it may also reflect an intellectual change, a dawning awareness of the need for greater clarity in the realm of feudal relations.

A famous letter written by Fulbert of Chartres to William V of Aquitaine rehearsed the duties of the vassal in terms deliberately chosen to be easily remembered by the warriors to whom it was to be read:

He who swears fidelity to his lord should always keep these six terms in mind: safe and sound, secure, honest, useful, easy, possible. Safe and sound, that is, not to cause his lord any harm as to his body. Secure, that is, not to endanger him by betraying his secrets or the fortresses which make it possible for him to be secure. Honest, that is, not to do anything that would detract from his lord's rights of justice or the other prerogatives which have to do with his honour. Useful, not to cause him any loss as regards his possessions. Easy and possible, not to make it difficult for his lord to do something that would be of value to him and that he could otherwise do with ease, or to render it impossible for him to do what was otherwise possible. That the vassal should avoid injuring his lord in any of these ways is only right, but this does not entitle him to a fief; for it is not enough to abstain from evil, it is also necessary to do good. So it remains for him to give his lord faithful counsel and aid as regards these six points if he wished to be considered worthy of his benefice and secure as to the fidelity that he has sworn.[24]

Fulbert's application of ideas drawn directly from two ancient manuals of rhetoric, the *Ad Herennium* and Cicero's *De Inventione*,[25] to an entirely medieval social institution, is a vivid illustration of the way in which churchmen moulded the ethical perceptions of the military classes.

In the letter, Fulbert used the words *fidelis* and *vassus* interchangeably; a vassal was one who had sworn fidelity and who enjoyed a fief. But there are signs that not all his contemporaries saw the relationship in such simple terms. Indeed, the cause of Duke William's concern on the matter was his clash with Hugh IV de Lusignan; in the course of this Hugh, embittered by William's failure to keep his word, renounced his oath of fidelity, except in so far as the count's physical safety and the safety of Poitiers were concerned.[26] His words implied that there were two grades of fidelity: one which obliged a *fidelis* to promote his lord's interests in all things, and another that simply bound him not to injure him.

There was logic in this distinction; for if the duties of a vassal were such as Fulbert defined them, then in fulfilling them the *fidelis* whose estates were close to those of his lord would have to make many sacrifices, while for one who lived several days' journey away, not making a nuisance of himself would be a relatively painless matter. Differences in perception of feudal obligation were partly a matter of simple distance.

Another variant in perspective was that lordship intensified as the social gap between lord and man increased. Yet even with vassals of the same class, there might be differences. Hubert le Hongre, a knight of the Mâconnais, lent his lord the castellan of Uxelles aid and counsel, witnessed his charters, testified for him in lawsuits, acted as hostage for his family, and entered Cluny's clientage when his lord became a monk. His whole life was bound up in this relationship, despite the fact that the fief he received was not large, and that he also possessed allodial lands.[27] On the other hand, though the knights of the count of Vendôme (see p. 230) were heavily burdened with castle-guard and military service, their obligation was clearly defined, and once fulfilled, they were their own masters.[28] As far as can be seen, they were not involved in their lord's personal life. There were, then, at least two models of knightly service.

On occasion, the vassalage extorted from a noble might, like that of a knight, emphasize his dependence on his lord. When Herbert of Maine renounced his homage to Geoffrey of Anjou and recognized William the Conqueror as his lord, he received back everything from William 'just as a knight received it from his lord'.[29] The point being made here was that William claimed superiority over all Herbert's lands; it was no mere personal bond he was enforcing. The same might be inferred of the relationship between Baldwin IV and Baldwin V and the castellans of the comital demesne. Here the counts rubbed in their superiority by appointing *prévôts* in each castellany to collect comital dues, and by taking direct homage from the knights of the castle; therefore the castellan could scarcely forget the conditional nature of his tenure. But any weakening, however temporary, in the prince's dominance would serve to produce a more normal relationship.

For over West Francia as a whole, the eleventh-century castellans became but loosely subordinated to their princes. If fully independent castellans such as those of Berry and the Mâconnais remained a rarity, nevertheless the princes' claim to control fortifications was at best spasmodically enforced, at worst absent in practice if recognized in theory. For the concession of hereditary tenure, though made piecemeal over a long period of time, was universal by the end of the century. Only rebellion could deny a castellan his inheritance; then, the punishment might be harsh. In 1070, Fulk le Réchin, not content with disinheritance, pulled down the castle of Trèves, and blinded Hardouin, its lord.[30] But for the most part, later eleventh-century castellans had contrived to convert their homage into little more than a symbol of deference and willingness to perform service; the implications that their castle and office were enjoyed purely by delegation, that their duty lay in exercising powers and privileges only for the benefit of their lord, were swiftly transmuted into something much less rigid; exactly what depended on the prince's powers and proximity.

Perhaps ironically, one important factor preventing precision and continuity in princes' demands of their castellans was the intervention of other princes. Royal control over the castellans of the Île de France was relaxed by Eudes II of Blois, who created his own network of vassals among them;[31] in the same way, the dukes of Aquitaine attracted the lords of Parthenay to their court, though they were Angevin vassals.[32] Although, in the short term, these manœuvres attained their political objectives, in the end they simply conferred new independence on the castellans. Double allegiance could be a useful weapon, as Supplicius of Amboise had found (see p. 231). In 1090 the lord of Montpellier exploited it even more successfully when he rose against his lord, the bishop of Maguelonne; worried by William's defection, the bishop bribed him back into the episcopal *mouvance* by extending his fief. In return, William was required to recognize that, since the fief he held of the bishop was now larger than those any other lord had bestowed on him, he ought to be 'a better man' of the bishop than of any of his other lords.[33]

To mount the social scale again, the higher the rank of the underdog, the less his obligation would be defined. When the counts of La Marche and Périgueux paid homage to the duke of Aquitaine, it implied acceptance on their part that to injure the duke's person or property would be a breach of faith, but little more; if they came to his court or assisted him on campaigns, it was because they saw profit or pleasure in so doing. A similar relationship obtained between the count of Flanders and the comital family of Boulogne, between the Capetians and the old-established comital families of the Île de France, between the dukes of Burgundy and the counts of Mâcon, Chalon, and Meaux.

At the apex of the pyramid came the princes' homage to the king—at least where they took it (excluding therefore the counts of the far south and of Brittany, and the duke of Normandy after the breach of 1051). Helgaud reported that Robert the Pious secretly removed the relics from the reliquary on which he obliged his *primates* (magnates) to take oaths, in order to shield them from committing perjury.[34] The tale, if true, showed little confidence in the princes' intention to abide by the exact words of their fidelity. But what was implied by the oath was genuinely in dispute. At the beginning of the century, Dudo of St Quentin produced the argument that, since the homage of Duke Rollo of Normandy in 911 had been purely in gratitude for his baptism, it did not mean, either for himself or for his successors, that Normandy was a fief. Rather Rollo and they had rendered services to none other than to God.[35] A less elevated but similar claim was made by Eudes II in a letter written to King Robert: 'If it is a question of the nature of the benefice you gave me, the fact is that it does not come from your domain, but from the estates which come to me with your consent by hereditary right from my ancestors.'[36] In Eudes's eyes, then, he held Champagne allodially; it was not subject to the king's decision to grant or not to grant. The fact that the king thought differently on both these issues was of little moment. On the other hand, William of Poitiers imputed to Guy Geoffrey, Thibaud, and Geoffrey Martel irritation at being obliged to perform military service when summoned[37]—which suggests acceptance of their duty; Orderic's words imply that Fulk the Young clearly recognized the dependent status of Anjou in 1106 when he did homage to Philip I.[38] The differences of opinion on a point that later lawyers were to regard as fundamental to the monarchy's position must be taken as proof that, for the great at least, the equation between a *fidelis* and a *vassus* could not yet be taken for granted.

Interestingly, there are signs that those who had escaped from the royal *mouvance* were not entirely comfortable in their independence. In the absence of the king, they sought a higher authentication of their rights. So Raymond of St Gilles, after he had claimed the Rouergue in 1079, prepared himself for his attempt to oust his brother as count of Toulouse, in a ceremony at the shrine of St Robert at La Chaise-Dieu:

Raymond took homage to the blessed Robert, received back his sword from the altar, and declared that he would have and hold the county of Toulouse from none other than St Robert, if God would deign to give it to him.[39]

The adoption of an overlord in heaven lent weight to Raymond's doubtful title in Toulouse, while infringing not at all on his earthly independence. So the patron saint had become absorbed into the feudal world. It was an example that, in rather different circumstances, was later to commend itself to the Capetians.

(c) Ruling families

As the count of Roucy journeyed to Rome, he fell into a trap laid by Falco, count of Burgundy, who demanded, as the price of his release, his daughter's hand in marriage.[40] The incident shows that force might still play some part in the creation of marrige alliances in the eleventh century. But the swashbuckling approach grew rarer; and with the disappearance of the Carolingian and Ottonian houses a measure of excitement drained out of the game, for neither Capetian nor Salian brides enjoyed the same cachet as their predecessors. In any case, as a result of the growing emphasis on patrilineal descent in all aristocratic families, even the noblest of wives could do less for an eleventh-century lord than she could have done for his grandfather. The marriage between Robert the Pious's daughter and the count of Nevers brought obvious political gain to the king because it strengthened the royal hold upon Burgundy; the count on the other hand gained only temporary advantage, and subsequent generations in Nevers made little of their royal connection.[41] Behind this change lay a new and more business-like concentration on landed possession.

Symbolic of this was the slow decline in the importance of marriage portions conferred by husbands on their new wives, and a correspondingly avid interest in the bride's dowry. Dowries could prove major blessings; that brought by the heiress of Rennes to Hoël of Nantes transformed the otherwise weak count into a major landholder. But if the wife died before her husband, his right to keep the dowry might well be challenged by her family. The war that broke out between Richard II of Normandy and Eudes II of Blois in 1013–14 was over Eudes's right to retain the dowry of his dead wife, Richard's sister. And Raymond of St Gilles attacked the Rouergue immediately on the death of its countess, married to Robert of the Auvergne, rather than allow his family's claims to her lands to be forgotten. Without military strength to assist in their retention, dowries could prove but short-term gains.

On the other hand, marriage might still create claims to territory which good luck and force could convert into possession. Although in the end William IX of Aquitaine failed to make good his wife's right of succession to her father in Toulouse, a generation earlier his father Guy Geoffrey had succeeded in annexing Gascony, pleading in justification his father's marriage with the heiress Prisca. And marriage beyond the frontiers of the West Frankish kingdom was seen as a preparatory step towards expansion by the counts of Flanders in their dealings with the houses of Hainault and Holland, by the ducal houses of Burgundy and Aquitaine in Aragon, Barcelona, and Navarre, and by the count of Toulouse in Provence. (These alliances had the additional advantage of earning ecclesiastical approval at a time when there was growing pressure from canonists against unions within six degrees of relationship.)[42]

Because the death-rate was high, marriages were usually short-term; and divorce could be obtained where nature did not intervene. On the other hand, greater prosperity and more settled political conditions combined to make barrenness less common than in the tenth century; Geoffrey Martel of Anjou and Duke Hugh of Burgundy were unusual in producing no heirs. Problems were now far more likely to arise in determining the rights of succession among competing members of a princely family. It has been stated that the principle of primogenital succession was increasingly observed in the eleventh century; but there was a substantial difference between accepting the customary right of the eldest son to succeed, if he were of age and competent, and accepting it as an inviolable rule, as was proved by the usurpation of Robert the Frisian, and perhaps also by the succession of Raymond IV of Toulouse (though here the facts are rather uncertain). And the plight of even generously endowed younger sons like William Rufus and Éon of Penthièvre could arouse sympathy among their contemporaries. Besides, where a prince had contracted more than one marriage, there might be disputes among the offspring of his various wives, as occurred after the death of William V of Aquitaine, and in 1032 in the royal family. On that occasion the energetic opposition to Henry I's accession put up by Constance of Arles and her sons created a serious crisis, in the course of which Henry was driven to take refuge at the court of the duke of Normandy. Though in the end his rights prevailed, the dispute had long repercussions on his control over the counts and castellans of the demesne.

So primogeniture was not automatically accepted; and where it was, it could create problems of a rather different sort. Heirs grew over-ambitious: both Baldwin V of Flanders and Geoffrey Martel the Younger rebelled against their fathers in an attempt to establish their own dominion ahead of time; more problematically, princes had the headache of finding adequate endowments for their younger sons without infringing on the patrimony. But despite its drawbacks, primogeniture did offer a rule of thumb that commanded widespread respect. So the real difficulty remained in families where there was no direct heir, as the Angevin succession crisis of the 1060s proved. Perhaps a mature perception of this fact lay behind the rather surprising acquiescence of most Norman lords in William the Conqueror's succession as duke in 1035, though he was but a child and a bastard. The uniqueness of this step was long remembered. As late as the 1180s, St Hugh of Lincoln dared to tease Henry II of England about the tanner's blood in his veins. (William's mother was thought to have been Herleva, daughter of Fulbert, a tanner of Falaise).[43]

William of Poitiers strove to emphasize the nobility of the West Frankish aristocracy, by calling Guy Geoffrey the Emperor Henry III's brother (he was his brother-in-law through the marriage of his sister Agnes), and by ascribing to Baldwin V connections not only with the ruling houses of France and Germany, but also with that of Constantinople[44] (what he had in mind has not yet been established). Nevertheless it seems that the eleventh-century history of princely houses was more mundane, more businesslike, than it had been in the past. Marriage and inheritance were matters for bargaining and negotiation, no longer open to inspired manoeuvres. And it is notable that harmony in succession policy evaded those whose political achievements were otherwise outstanding —Geoffrey Martel, Baldwin V, William the Conqueror. Indeed it might almost be conjectured that those families in which political nous was widely distributed were just those that found the principle of primogeniture unpalatable.

(d) Courts

The life of the high aristocracy was lived on the move and in the open; tranquillity and privacy evaded them. For a lord's status was directly related to the size of following he could support, and the larger his entourage the more frequently he had to move from estate to estate to feed them. The count of Flanders was usually accompanied by between fifty and a hundred armed men; the duke of Aquitaine took a hundred knights with him on a visit to the viscount of Ventadour.[45] Besides, there were the animals. Duke Robert of Burgundy expected Gilly, an estate of St Germain-des-Prés, to provide food for his dogs as well as lodging for his horses and their grooms.[46] It was hardly surprising that few places could afford to entertain their lords for weeks on end.

On the march, there was little room for ceremonial. When Geoffrey de Preuilly caught up with Fulk le Réchin's men to obtain a hearing for his plea, he found the count sitting on a table, his steward standing before him, his huntsman below, mounted and carrying the count's falcon. The scene suggests a lifestyle familiar to the Franks from their first penetration of Gaul.[47] Just as informally, William the Conqueror once confirmed a grant 'while sitting on his carpet between the church and the forester's house.'[48] Dirty, bloodstained, and exhausted lords surrounded by brutal warriors, making their way from primitive wooden castles to austere monastic refuges, must have been common sights on the West Frankish roads. And if, on occasion, they pillaged or, like the following of Eudes of Burgundy, held up caravans of pilgrims and merchants to make a quick profit from their ransoms, few can have been surprised; for it was adventure, self-interest, and companionship that bound knights to their lords. Rarely can St Augustine's dictum that bands of brigands are but petty kingdoms without justice (*City of God*, iv, 4) have been so easily comprehended as in the eleventh century.

There were, however, short breaks from the itinerant routine, when the great festivals of the church provided occasions for large gatherings, rich feasts, fine dress. Princes usually celebrated Easter, Christmas, or Whitsun in cathedral towns or important monastic centres within their territories, giving advance notice of their intention so that other lords might forgather with them. When Robert II of Flanders passed Christmas at St Omer, 'there came to him the dukes, the counts, the lords of many regions, nobles and knights from the whole of Flanders, and many French bishops'.[49] In such company, the ancient rituals of Christian worship shed their warm glow of splendour on the court. There might be some ceremony of welcome; there might be special prayers for the ruling family (the genealogies of the counts of Flanders at St Bertin and the counts of Anjou at St Aubin's suggest this). And occasionally the bishop might call for the *Laudes regiae*, the litany 'addressed solely and triumphantly to the victorious Christ in his divinity as the eternal king of heaven and earth, and as the exemplar and guarantor of power and prosperity to all *potentes* who upheld the fabric of a unitary Christian society—pope, king, royal family, clergy, lay magnates and warriors'.[50] This litany served to keep alive in French Christian memory the true place of the king as Christ's representative on earth, at a time when political realities bade fair to obliterate it; but it also elevated the lower ranks of earthly powers. Only the duke of Normandy presumed to make this explicit, allowing his own name to be introduced into the chant after the prayers for the French king, so that the congregation called on the great warrior saints to guarantee the duke's safety and perpetual peace. His arrogance was soon rewarded by a royal position which legitimated it. But the caution of other princes may not have blinded their followers to the possible propaganda value of the *Laudes*.

Beyond the portals of the church, festival days were active ones. Bishops might seize the opportunity to urge support for peace councils, abbots to press for protection, lay lords to obtain charters while plentiful clerical help was available to draw them up and suitably important men present to act as witnesses. With his friends and allies about him, a prince might discuss future strategy, consider marriage alliances, resolve disputes. Far from being rest days, the festivals of the church were times of heightened activity, in an atmosphere redolent of older, grander, more disciplined ways.

As the century wore on, the returning prosperity of the countryside brought a markedly higher standard of living in its train for those best able to exploit their opportunities; the revival of trade facilitated the acquisition of luxuries. Inevitably, princely trains grew to expect more lavish hospitality from the castles and monasteries that they visited. When Robert II of Flanders called at St Thierry with his sister, widow of Cnut IV of Denmark, the abbot Rudolph cleansed the whole building, hung it with rich hangings and tapestries, filled it with carvings, sculptures, and other precious objects, to turn his simple Benedictine house into a suitable environment for the reception of so magnificent a prince.[51] Though his extravagance was well rewarded, it must have placed a severe strain on the house's finances. Even when living at their own expense, princes had higher expectations. Fécamp, Bruges, Limoges, Chartres, Dijon provided backdrops for displays of occasional grandeur. Because attracting important men to his presence was essential to princely authority, ostentation might offer sound political investment.

A prince's entourage provided his closest friends, his most trusted servants, the knights on whom he relied in time of crisis. Throughout the century, these households retained the military character that was at the core of their lord's authority. The household of William the Conqueror was the nerve-centre from which his military victories were planned, from which his duchy and the kingdom of England were held in subordination;[52] so its members held themselves always ready for battle. The armed following that accompanied Robert the Frisian on his Jerusalem pilgrimage so impressed the Emperor of Byzantium, Alexius Comnenus, with its martial bearing that he requested similar assistance from the west.[53] Although many household knights were men of free rather than noble birth—in Flanders there were even recruits from among the unfree, like the German *ministeriales*—the prince's relatives and the sons of his neighbouring lords also found careers within their ranks. So in the long term, the entourages of the great proved effective as social melting-pots.

Yet as the century wore on, their military character ceased to be the exclusive distinguishing feature of princely households. When the countess Adela of Blois issued an important charter, it was noted that she was surrounded by her *capellanus* and her *clerici, barones, milites et servientes*.[54] her chaplain and her clerks, barons, knights, and servants. The household chaplain, whose role it was to minister to the spiritual needs of princely families, could also produce letters, such as those written for Stephen of Blois to his wife

Adela while he was on the First Crusade; or charters, like those produced for the post-Conquest dukes of Normandy. In Normandy, indeed, their importance grew so great that they began to be promoted to bishoprics after about 1060, a move reminiscent of Ottonian and Salian practice.[55] William of Poitiers, William the Conqueror's most learned and literate biographer, had been his master's chaplain for some years; in the future, household chaplains were regularly to combine the roles of secretary, teacher, and propagandist for princes, as he had done.

The mixture of usefulness and display that explained the growing importance of the chaplains also lay behind the rise of other household officers. With growing princely income and expenditure, the charge of the purse became more responsible; chamberlains appeared everywhere—in Flanders as early as the tenth century—to control it. Then large households required butlers and stewards to satisfy their material needs, marshals for ceremonial. Someone must always have discharged these duties; but the mention of these officials in eleventh-century households pointed to two developments: firstly, a conscious imitation of Carolingian ways (for Charlemagne and his heirs had surrounded themselves with seneschals and stewards), and secondly, a revived interest in administration. It is perhaps characteristic that the best evidence for the appointment of household officers in the first half of the eleventh century should come from Normandy, which combined reverence for the Carolingian past with respect for efficiency to a degree unparalleled elsewhere.[56]

By the second half of the century, the practice was spreading. In Flanders, in Champagne, in Anjou, on the royal demesne, chamberlains, butlers, stewards, marshals made their appearance. Because their duties involved close co-operation with the prince, their holders were usually men of high social status, the prince's more intimate friends among his following. In ceremonial, their role was everywhere prominent; interestingly, some household officials were beginning to discharge governmental functions, as in Normandy. But their commonest duty was to act as witnesses in charters; by the last two decades of the century, the royal household officials were excluding other lords from this task.

Along with the knights, the chaplains, and the officials, there travelled the ladies of the court with their servants, and a sizeable contingent of young boys. Of these, some were present involuntarily, as hostages for their father's good behaviour—Supplicius of Amboise, for example, had to put his son Hugh in Fulk le Réchin's power as one of the terms of a peace treaty;[57] but others were the sons of friends or allies, sent to the prince's court for the sake of education in knightly virtues, and to meet the men on whom their future political happiness could depend. Princely households had common characteristics with the English public schools of past generations. And though they too set social connection and sporting activities—hunting, combat, riding—above literacy, nevertheless it was possible to acquire learning at them; the opportunities exploited by William V of Aquitaine, William the Conqueror, Robert the Frisian, and Fulk le Réchin—all regarded as educated men—must have also been available to some of those who were brought up with them.

So eleventh-century courts were centres for ceremony, business, education; Charlemagne would have sympathized with all of these. He would have understood, too, the presence at Norman and Angevin courts of clerks whose function it was to extol the deeds of their princes. But, despite Einhard's assertion that he loved barbarian poems, he would surely have been disconcerted by the evolution of the Poitevin court under William IX as a centre of troubadour poetry, its prince as the most distinguished poet of all. And he might well have dismissed the Flemish court, with its prince who hedged and ditched, its chancellor who audited accounts, as mercenary. What must have surprised him, as it still surprises us, was the sheer variety of court life, its different rhythms, its stately ceremonial in buildings still primitive both by Carolingian and later standards, and the unique character bestowed on each court by the personality of its prince.

CHAPTER 10

Sources 1108–1180

IN the twelfth century, writing blossomed. Once an élite activity, almost the exclusive prerogative of monks, it now spread to the swelling ranks of secular clerks, to servants in princely households, even to some ordinary townsmen. As it spread, its uses diversified so fast as to make any introduction to twelfth-century sources on the scale attempted in the earlier parts of the book (pp. 17–26, 124–32) impossible. Nor indeed is it necessary; for the men of the twelfth-century renaissance used words and literary forms derived from the main stream of the European cultural inheritance. Their writings speak for themselves. In fact that familiarity can sometimes be deceptive; behind the restored classical vocabulary lurk more of the earlier aristocratic assumptions than would have been conceded by most nineteenth-century historians; so if anthropological interpretations become less useful, there is still danger in pushing narrowly juridical ones. But it must be said that the historian's task is substantially simplified by the transformation. Therefore the point of this section is only to draw attention to some aspects of intellectual and administrative change that can be more easily observed in a discussion on sources than in a more general context.

Few literary sources are more revealing of aristocratic culture than the *Gesta Consulum Andegavorum*[1] and its off shoot the *Gesta Ambaziensium Dominorum*,[2] produced in the Touraine in the first six decades of the twelfth century, for the pleasure and edification of the counts of Anjou and their castellans, the lords of Amboise. The skeleton of the *Gesta Consulum Andegavorum* lay in a set of geanealogies less reliable and less complete than those found at St Aubin's in Angers under Fulk le Réchin.[3] These may originally have been compiled by a Touraine monastic house so that the new rulers of the area could be commemorated in its prayers;

but like the genealogies of the comital house of Flanders, they were soon adapted to a more secular purpose. Around 1109 on the death of Fulk le Réchin, a monk, perhaps the abbot Eudes of the great house of Marmoutier, produced the first version of the *Gesta*, a series of brief biographies of the counts. The literary form he followed derived from the *Liber Pontificalis*, that famous compilation of papal lives produced in Rome at the end of every pontificate by the pope's own clerks; especially in West Francia it had been adopted in the tenth and eleventh centuries as a model for the history of dioceses (e.g. the *Deeds of the Bishops of Auxerre*).[4] And it now provided a convenient framework for the praise of a comital lineage.

The author set the context for his story with a lengthy but fairly conventional genealogy of the kings of France, tracing their origins back to the Trojans as Frankish historians had done since Merovingian times. This blend of Old-Testament-inspired genealogy with legendary classical origins enjoyed a new vogue in the eclectic learned circles of the period. A possible Trojan link was claimed by William of Jumièges for William the Conqueror as soon as he became king;[5] a late eleventh-century genealogy of the counts of Boulogne produced a similar conceit;[6] and Genealogy IV of the Counts of Flanders, written about 1120, made them the most important non-royal family to trace its ancestry back to Priam.[7] So a legend which had originated with the attempts of Dark Age royal servants to give their masters a lineage as old and distinguished as that of the Western Roman emperors they had displaced continued in the twelfth century to satisfy the needs of new royal families and even of some princely houses.

In the *Gesta* this genealogy creates a sharp contrast between the kings and the counts of Anjou, whose origins are said to lie in a 'new man', a forester of the reign of Charles the Bald.[8] At first, the choice of such a humble beginning is puzzling, especially since Werner believes that the Angevin comital family was of the old Carolingian aristocracy, with connections by marriage into an Italian royal family.[9] But it is clear from Fulk le Réchin's history that the counts themselves knew nothing of their ancestry before the time of

Ingelgerus, Fulk the Red's father, an indication of the block that earlier, looser kinship ties created in human memory.[10] Besides, the author of the *Gesta*—like his predecessor who had produced the second genealogy of the counts of Flanders —was heavily imbued with Sallustian learning. If he could not posit an ancient line for his comital family, then he would choose to emphasize its newness, its local roots, its dependence on heroic deeds for its rise. For it was possible, on a reading of Marius' *contio* in Sallust, to associate the old nobility with inertia, the new with virtue. The choice of a forester—also made by the author of a thirteenth-century Flemish genealogy[11]—is interesting: the word itself was a new one, having no classical or late-antique Latin form; perhaps its associations with hunting and riding made it particularly appropriate for a family renowned for its martial skills. From the author's point of view, its humble status highlighted the outstanding achievements of the individual counts in each generation of the family's history. So though modern research has tended to discredit the idea of a medieval aristocracy 'of service', to insist on blue blood for the great lines of the tenth and eleventh centuries, and to see in the later eleventh and the twelfth centuries an ever-sharper patrilineal descent obliterating other considerations in family history, it should not be forgotten that at least one great princely house was encouraged to view its progress in quite other terms. What made them lords were their noble deeds.

The clearest proof of this comes in the *Gesta*'s treatment of Geoffrey Grisegonelle, Fulk Nerra's father. Whereas, in Fulk le Réchin's account which preserved the comital family's own early tradition, Geoffrey was a solid but unremarkable figure, in the *Gesta* he has undergone transmogrification. He is a chivalric hero, a mighty slayer of the Danes, a triumpher in single combat, a victor over the invading German hordes.[12] Halphen, who edited the text, believed that here the author was drawing on a vernacular epic;[13] this may well have been so, for in the late eleventh-century manuscript of the *Song of Roland*, Geoffrey featured as Charlemagne's standard-bearer.[14] He had become a figure of legend. His appearance in his new guise in the *Gesta* pinpoints the process by which the house of Anjou built up its own chivalric myth.

Apart from Fulk le Réchin, the other counts of Anjou are portrayed (albeit less colourfully than Geoffrey Grisegonelle) as pious and valiant defenders of their inheritance. Fulk, however, comes in for stern criticism.[15] Indeed the aim of the work was to demonstrate how far he had fallen from ancestral glories, in order that his successors might rectify his errors. The earliest version of the *Gesta*, finished just after Fulk's death in 1109, was a stern warning to the young Fulk V.

But the story of the *Gesta* did not end in 1109. Just as later monks came back to the Flemish comital genealogies to keep them up to date and to add new material, so the *Gesta* attracted amplification. The first to turn his hand to the task was Thomas de Loches, chaplain and chancellor to Fulk V and Geoffrey le Bel. The significance of his additions lies largely in the proof they provide that a Touraine monastic source was the subject of study within the count's own household by a secular clerk of distinction. His successor Breton d'Amboise's version was more influential in that it provided the base for three other amplifications, one anonymous, the other two by John of Marmoutier. Of the latter, one was dedicated to King Henry II of England in a prologue taken almost word for word from Bede's preface to Ceolwulf at the beginning of the *Ecclesiastical History of the English People*.[16] There could hardly be a more appropriate blending of Henry II's traditional Angevin and new English cultural backgrounds.

Each of the later authors added to the legendary element in the *Gesta*. The figure whose character achieved clearest focus was that of Fulk the Good, Geoffrey Grisegonelle's father. Plagiarizing from the *Miracles of St Martin at Tours*, Breton produced material to turn Fulk into the conventional saintly layman who, assisting a leper, found that he had helped Christ. It was recorded of him that he sang with the monks in the divine offices; when taunted by the king for his clerkly tastes, he responded that an illiterate king was a crowned ass[17] (a cliché much favoured in twelfth-century Angevin circles, for it sprang from a sense of family superiority —the counts of Anjou were, by any standards, learned men). So Fulk joined Geoffrey as an alternative model of the perfect layman.

As well as adding to the old part of the story, the continuators brought it up to date till the death of Geoffrey le Bel, occasionally slipping into detailed narrative of events: there is a long and useful excursus on the politics of 1118. The original epic style was maintained for the description of Fulk V's Jerusalem journey and his coronation as king of Jerusalem in 1131, which was portrayed as the fulfilment of the family destiny, the union of its chivalric and pious traditions. All in all the *Gesta* provided a somewhat daunting set of exemplars for King Henry II. His ancestors were formidable men. And—despite the fact that their portraits were largely drawn by monks—they were men in a distinctively lay tradition: not for them Gerald of Aurillac's yearning for the cloister; though they might put their sword to the service of the church, they wielded it just as often for secular purposes and to gain renown. Their piety was set in a classical mould, a matter of obligations duly performed. Their chief functions were of this world. They were *consules*, men chosen for the protection of the common weal, men of ancient Roman *gravitas* and *auctoritas*.

The original version of the *Gesta* provided a model for the *Gesta Ambaziensium Dominorum*, written about 1155; and it, in its turn, influenced later versions of the *Gesta*. Its author, perhaps a canon of St Florent, wrote after the death of Supplicius II, castellan of Amboise, to warn later generations of the family that a repitition of Supplicius' acts of disloyalty towards his overlords might ruin the family.[18] Yet despite his didactic purpose and his concern with detailed narrative, he produced the first work to immortalize a castellan dynasty in France. From the historian's point of view, it provides valuable evidence about a corner of the Touraine crucial to Angevin domination but very difficult to hold, and about the resources and stratagems open to a second-rank aristocratic family determined to maximize its assets. It is an unusually vivid piece of local history, told with an absence of contrivance or literary device that contrasts with its model. Together, the works bear witness to the originality and liveliness in the learned circles of the Loire valley at the height of the twelfth-century renaissance.

The *Feoda Campanie* of 1172 shows originality of a different order.[19] It was compiled for Count Henry the Liberal of Champagne, by clerks of tidy but innovative mind, alert to the political potential in acquiring, recording and categorizing information. They set out to discover the names and fiefs of all lords and knights resident within the county, their liege lords, and the services each owed to the count. The means employed was the sworn inquest, the ancient Carolingian legal procedure for establishing the facts of a case by procuring statements on oath. Although this procedure had been used for administrative purposes in Normandy (where the English example of Domesday Book was an inspiration) and in Anjou before Geoffrey le Bel's conquest of Normandy, the *Feoda* marked an important step in its use in eastern France. When the sworn statements were collected and sorted, the results were set out in a list preserved in the count's treasury at St Étienne in Troyes. Until 1190, they were kept up-to-date; but in that year, Count Henry II of Champagne took one copy of the list with him when he set out for Outremer, and this may have inhibited his officials from making further changes in the copy left behind at Troyes. Nevertheless, the document was still consulted in the early thirteenth century, which shows that it was regarded as an important statement of custom. In committing the count's rights to written record, Henry's clerks had conferred on them new authority.

The *Feoda* contains the names of around 1,900 lords and knights, ranging from substantial aristocrats to landless warriors, grouped under the headings of the twenty-six castellanies of Champagne. The grouping demonstrates Henry's clerks' clear conception of the administrative geography of the county. On the other hand, the fact that some lords and knights are double-listed suggests doubt as to their rightful position. It seems likely, therefore, that in the process of drawing up the *Feoda*, as clerks and local lords decided under which heading most fief-holders should appear, they helped to crystallize the castellanies. And if the process of inquest clarified internal boundaries, it almost certainly also compelled fief-holders to reflect on the extent of the services they owed to the count. Henry's clerks had perceived the important truth that asking the right questions was the path to consolidating gains. All respondents acknowledged they owed service in times of war; rather less than half were obliged to provide regular castle-guard. The figures were high for a county in which comital lordship had not been noticeably demanding; the count's fortifications should have been adequately defended.

There was a correlation between those who owed castle-guard and those who recognized the count as their liege lord, again rather less than half the total. Thirteenth-century inquests were to see a substantial increase in this percentage. But if comital liegelordship (that superior bond to which all lesser allegiances must, in case of conflict, yield) was less advanced in Champagne than in Normandy or Flanders, it completely outclassed that of any other secular or ecclesiastical lord within the county.

The *Feoda* therefore provides a revealing glimpse of aristocratic society in Champagne; its full potential as a source has recently been exploited by Evergates.[20] Just as significantly, it betrays Henry the Liberal's view of feudalism as a clearly defined contract in which the holder of a specified fief of land performed a set amount of military service for the privilege; and, in cases where he had fiefs of several lords, had the obligation to recognize one homage as overriding. This view—later to be the standard one among feudal lawyers—was not one which earlier counts of Champagne had embraced. (Their own very complicated feudal position had been an inhibiting factor.) It may be that Henry had to dispense largess to make it acceptable to his lords;[21] but the *Feoda* is evidence that he had somehow overcome potential opposition, and could now capitalize on his position at the apex of the feudal pyramid in the county.

The *Feoda*'s apparently innovative character makes the fact that it was produced in the same year as the Norman inquest into knights' fees seem more than simply coincidental. Robert of Torigny described the Norman proceedings thus:

In the year of the Lord 1172, all the barons of Normandy met on the birthday of St Mary the Virgin at Caen, at the precept of King Henry II, and there a return was made from each of the barons before the king's justices of how many knights each baron owed to the service of the king and how many he had for his own service.[22]

The Norman and Champagne processes were not identical. But they were similar enough in method and assumption to suggest possible cross-fertilization. The new bureaucrats may well have been willing to learn lessons from their fellows across the boundaries of principalities. If so, they were preparing the path for the closer integration of French provinces achieved in the thirteenth century.

Finally, a short comment on charters as sources for twelfth-century history. The most notable fact is their proliferation everywhere across the country. Their chances of survival were increased by the creation of new archives—monastic cartularies became common, lay lords, notably the dukes of Burgundy and the lords of Montpellier, began to preserve their letters. But much more importantly, there were new incentives to have grants or judgements enshrined in writing. Confidence in the written word, noticeably low in the eleventh century, increased everywhere. This reflected important social changes. Earlier, in a small, strongly aristo-cratic society, where all those likely to resort to legal process were well known to their fellows, reliance on verbal con-tract before witnesses had proved a sound policy, allowing for future elasticity of interpretation within clearly-defined limits. Now, with rising population, greater social mobility, and wider resort to legal processes, human memory ceased to be an effective guarantee of human contract. As Geoffrey le Bel said in the preamble to one of his charters, 'whatever happens at one point of time will scarcely every reach the next generation in a reliable and true account unless it is committed to writing.'[23] This was particularly true for those small communities, small towns, or groups of peasants, who had won their privileges after long struggles against a higher authority. Without the protection of a properly sealed and attested charter, their struggles might prove vain, since it was in nobody's interest but their own that their moment of victory should be prolonged.

There was, too, an underlying legal change: even though arbitration might still play a crucial part in their actual proceedings, courts gradually inclined to perceive justice as lying in precedent, or principle. As a result the written record of an earlier judgement given in the court, or of a grant, could create a prima-facie case for a favourable verdict. In one dispute at least, that between Vierzon and St Florent of Saumur in 1105, the judges seem to have confined their role to inspecting the documents provided by each house, before delivering their verdict in St Florent's favour.[24]

One factor inhibiting the spread of written documents had been fear of forgery. And the increasing use of charters in lawcourts naturally created an incentive to forge, as those who had lost or never enjoyed documentary proof of their rights strove to make good the deficiency. There was little prospect of containing this. What made it easy was that earlier charters had been produced by so many different monastic scriptoria in so many house styles that spotting the inauthentic was a task for the dedicated scholar—who in any case was more likely to be employed in propagating fraud than in hunting it out. But for new grants or privileges the answer, or at least a partial answer, lay in insistance on proper confirmation by the legitimate authority; by the second half of the twelfth century, all charters produced across the Angevin empire had to be confirmed by the Angevin chancery. And better than mere confirmation was production. As princely chanceries evolved across West Francia, their output was welcomed by the population at large because the set formulae they employed offered some assurance of authenticity. Demand switched, from charters produced locally and confirmed by the attachment of a princely seal, to those written in a princes's name by his own clerks in his writing office. Under the pressure of new business, chancery clerks standardized their output, streamlined by cutting down on lengthy prologues, stated their business as succinctly as possible.

While chanceries were adapting their wares to public needs, they were also evolving new formulae for their princes. Here the Anglo-Norman chancery was in the vanguard with the production of writs—commands addressed to the king-duke's officials, used in eleventh-century Normandy, but developed in the course of the twelfth into the chief instrument for central control over the localities and for legal innovation. With Henry II's accession to the English throne in 1154, the king-duke's chancery operated over Western France from the Pyrenees to the Canche, and set an example to all other princes, not least to the kings of France. Everywhere the new crisp dispositive style began to displace the older random recordings.

From the historian's point of view, twelfth-century diplomatic makes it possible to study the legal, administrative, and political history of the period with a confidence and an ease simply lacking in earlier times. Because writs, charters, and other chancery letters became everyday affairs, their language was now intended to express everyday realities. The scribes had their eyes on the lawcourts, on the current political situation, on tangible concerns capable of exact definition. They were assisting in the birth of government as the modern world has known it. As sources, their work is of crucial importance in understanding their world. Yet its very pragmatism bears with it an inbuilt limitation. There was no room in their streamlined productions for that revealingly individual note—the self-justification, the expression of highly personal piety—which had occasionally flashed through earlier charters. In growing common, twelfth-century charters also became commonplace.

CHAPTER II

Formative trends in twelfth-century political life

(a) The revival of royal power

In naming his son and heir Louis (Louis = Ludovicus = Clovis), King Philip I had consciously aspired towards the glories of the Carolingian and Merovingian past. Had Louis been inclined to forget the destiny his father had mapped out for him, he would have been forcefully reminded of it in the last decade of his reign, when his chief adviser was Suger, abbot of St Denis between 1122 and 1151, a man of humble birth consumed by a passionate devotion to the cause of monarchy in the Carolingian mould. A letter Suger wrote for Louis's son to the bishop, chapter, and people of Beauvais began: 'Heavenly and earthly peace from the king of kings· and the king of the Franks'.[1] Charlemagne himself could hardly have matched this confident assumption of harmony with God's will. In the century inaugurated by the Investiture Conflict, Suger's greeting was doubly remarkable. Only the head of an ancient monastic house, confident of his standing with the Pope, would have dared to pen it.

The appointment of a Benedictine abbot as chief adviser to the king was sufficiently unusual to call to mind Benedict of Aniane's position in the early years of Louis the Pious's reign. Though Benedict's austerity and reforming zeal were missing in Suger, his twelfth-century counterpart, there was perhaps a similar commitment to abstract political principle, to the notion of undivided imperial or royal power. In Suger's case, this power was given sharper focus by its place at the apex of the terrestrial hierarchy; for, as he had learned from the presumed patron of his monastery, Pseudo-Dionysius, this was the proper ordering of earthly political authority. What marked Suger out from other Pseudo-Dionysians was firstly, that he translated his abstractions into concepts directly relevant to French politics in his own time, and secondly that he proclaimed his views in the influential *Life* of Louis VI, written in the early years of Louis VII's reign.[2]

As Suger saw it, the French king was feudal lord of the princes. In his *Life* he made William X of Aquitaine protest against Louis's meddling in the Auvergne, with the words: 'If the count of Auvergne has committed any fault, it is my duty to present him at your court on your order, because he holds the Auvergne of me as I hold it of you.'[3] Behind these words lay the belief that all offices and counties were fiefs held of the king, whether directly or through an intermediary. Here again Suger was reasserting royal supremacy in a world which had long been deaf to such claims. He was also prepared to grapple with the practical consequences of his view. Clearly it was illogical that the king, chief lord of all, should be vassal of any. So Suger persuaded Louis to begin the task—not completed till the reign of Philip Augustus—of extricating himself from the bonds of homage which bound him to various bishops in the realm. Historians have considered this step as an essential preliminary to the later evolution of French royal sovereignty.[4]

But in depriving the king of any earthly lord, Suger risked isolating him. His solution to this problem showed his creative intelligence at work. As abbot of St Denis, Suger was in charge of one of France's oldest and most revered houses, whose connection with the ruling dynasty went back to Merovingian times. It had long been the traditional burial ground of kings; all Louis's royal Capetian ancestors—with the exception of his father Philip—were buried within its confines. Suger devoted many years to rebuilding the great abbey church (in a style which was later to be hailed as the prototype of Gothic architecture)[5] to make it a fit royal mausoleum, as well as a place of worship in which mere men could obtain a brief insight into the grandeur that surrounded the king of kings in heaven. For Suger, in common with the monks of his house since the late ninth century— and challenged only by the foolhardy Abelard[6]—regarded St Denis, the apostle and martyr of the Gauls, as the author of those writings produced in fact by a sixth-century Syrian mystic, now known as Pseudo-Dionysius. The most famous of these writings, that on the *Celestial Hierarchies*, provided the abbot both with his theory of the function of ecclesiastical architecture, and with a means of integrating the earthly power structure into that of heaven.

Under the abbot's influence, Louis recognized St Denis as his patron saint—a traditional enough step. More surprisingly, he also saw in his patron a feudal lord. This second relationship arose from an ingenious cover-up to a less than wholly honest piece of political self-enrichment. Among the lands earlier ceded to the abbey of St Denis was the Vexin français, that natural bulwark between the French royal demesne and the now hostile Norman duchy, which had been held as a Norman fief, had formed part of Simon de Crépy's state (see p. 216), and finally was reclaimed for the French crown by Philip I. The Vexin had had a comital family, in origin probably the advocates for the abbey; but Philip had bypassed their claims, granting the territory to the young prince Louis, who met with such opposition in the area that it was not until 1119 that his possession was secured. When Suger became abbot of St Denis in 1122, he reinterpreted the relationship between the abbey and the new count of the Vexin, to the profit of both. Louis became the liegeman, not of the abbey, but of its saint. In 1124, when the king summoned the great army to meet the threat of the Emperor Henry V's invasion, he bore the standard of St Denis at the head of his troops. As Suger said much later, the king recognized that he held of St Denis and that, if he were not king, he would owe the saint homage.'[7] Here was a new dimension in the essentially Carolingian view of kingship that Suger restored to the centre of the French political stage.[8]

Scepticism as to the historical importance of this highly personal view of monarchy seems in order. Our dependence on Suger's *Life* as the chief source for Louis VI's reign makes his interpretation inescapable for us, as it was not for his contemporaries. It is possible that twelfth-century laymen regarded his outpourings with an indulgent smile. Nevertheless Suger was no cloistered academic. As chief adviser to Louis VI in the last decade of his reign, and as Louis VII's most trusted minister until his death in 1152, he had many opportunities to impress his theories on princes and lords who would not dare to scoff. And for the crown itself, Suger's doctrine was timely. The ecclesiastical reform movement had drawn a new, sharp divide between temporal and spiritual, forcing all temporal authorities to redefine their self-image. The Emperor Frederick Barbarossa, the kings Henry I and Henry II of England, had abandoned theocracy to develop the secular potential inherent in their offices. The French king, with fewer resources, was reluctant to go so far. Suger offered the vision of divinely inspired harmony, a place for the king below the saints and martyrs of the church, with his vassals the princes on the rung below, and other lesser men in their serried ranks below again, all enveloped in St Denis's protection, fulfilling their roles on earth until they took their place in heaven. It offended no one; it preserved at least a whiff of the old tradition. As vassal of St Denis, Louis enjoyed special spiritual favour which marked him out from those whose lord was a mere mortal. Yet there was nothing in this relationship to grate against the susceptibilities of the reformers, for it implied no set position in the ecclesiastical hierarchy.

Naturally the monks of St Denis, who had most to gain by it, were happy to keep Suger's tradition fresh. They imitated him in producing histories of the Capetian kings—the earliest being Suger's successor's work on Louis VII's crusade.[9] Suger and Odo of Deuil between them established the norms for the house's long tradition of royal historiography; of these the chief was that whatever the Capetians did should be presented in the most favourable light possible. The image projected was consistently conservative; to the end of the dynasty, the kings remained the pious and holy defenders of Mother Church, the preservers of the kingdom's integrity, the faithful battlers against local tyrants. The good press they obtained was no doubt deeply irritating to their rivals.[10]

Louis had another method of attracting the devotion of those to whom abstract hierarchies were mere nonsense: he touched for scrofula, as Guibert of Nogent attested in a work written before 1124. Many churchmen may have disapproved of the practice; but to those who flocked for cure, it was a proof of the king's holiness, and a sign that Helgaud's miracle-worker king had not been entirely forgotten.[11]

But if royal charisma continued as a dominant pillar of kingship, it was now well bolstered in more mundane ways. Royal charters bore witness to renewed vigour outside the demesne as in it. Louis's annual average production of charters—12.1—was a notable increase on the 3.6 of Philip's reign.[12] The new charters were likely to have been written in the royal chancery rather than by their recipients, permitting greater uniformity, a more dispositive note, and the regular appearance of only a few royal officials as witnesses. At the same time, the geographical area within which royal charters were sought expanded again, particularly in the south, including the county of Toulouse, where the Capetians had never granted them before. Louis VII's marriage with Eleanor, duchess of Aquitaine, meant more royal charters for Poitou and Gascony; his own political endeavours resulted in an increase for Berry and the Auvergne. And thirdly, among the grants and privileges traditionally produced by the royal chancery, there appeared again regular records of judgements made in the royal courts, and royal letters of command, *mandements*, like the English writs absent since the reign of king Eudes. The chancery had returned to Carolingian practices, but with an energy which outran its model.[13]

If Louis VI's reign was decisive for the revitalization of the chancery, his son's saw the dramatic extension of royal visitations across the realm. Louis VII's pretexts for visiting were many and various, but his aim was always to emphasize the specifically royal nature of his authority, to reclaim the Carolingian right of hospitality. As was said:

When a progress or his own wish caused the lord king or one of his men to arrive at any episcopal dwelling, it pertained to the royal prerogative that he should be honourably received and sufficiently cared for.[14]

He began his reign with a splendid procession into Aquitaine as Eleanor's husband, in the course of which he arranged an inauguration ceremony for himself—either a repeat coronation for the southerners or a service to mark his accession as duke of Aquitaine[15]—in the city of Bordeaux, where no king had penetrated for at least three centuries. He used the opportunity to issue charters for places across the whole duchy, he gave judgements and established lasting friendships with one or two important lords from which he was later to reap benefits. His journey through Toulouse in 1155, on his way to Compostela, was equally unprecedented, and equally fruitful.[16] Louis renewed contact with Raymond V, by now his brother-in-law, and met almost all the bishops of the Narbonne province; their subsequent requests for his assistance strikingly increased his authority. In 1173, for example, he issued a diploma bringing the church of Agde under royal protection. His interventions in Burgundy were more forceful. The royal expeditions of 1166 and 1171 were undertaken in order to protect Cluny and to suppress 'schismatics'—the supporters of the imperial anti-pope Victor IV. They met with little armed resistance (which must have been a relief to Louis, who had little confidence in his own military skill), and gained considerable incidental profit: the king's person was seen in an area unvisited since the reign of Louis IV; the counts of Nevers, Chalon, and Mâcon were brought to heel; Burgundian lords appealed for the king's mediation in their quarrels (he also sought theirs); the count of Forez, hitherto only a vassal of the Emperor, declared his most important castles to be held as fief of the crown of France, the first step in the integration of Forez into the French realm. All these benefits were acquired by a wily diplomacy.[17] Louis was perceptive enough to gauge the degree of royal influence that would be welcomed in the great principalities. He avoided the bullying tactics his son was to employ; yet the results of his modest pursuits were in their own way as remarkable as those of Philip Augustus' domineering interventions.

To expand the circle of their *fideles* was a regular objective of both Louis VI and his son. They recognized that a return to the Carolingian situation, in which, in theory at least, all free men were bound by oaths of loyalty to the crown, was an unrealistic aspiration; and they did not even succeed in asserting their lordship over all French rear-vassals, on the lines suggested by Suger. But they did dramatically increase

the number of persons and groups of persons who recognized a bond with the crown through fidelity. Their most
notable achievement was their insistence that, for the safety
of the church, all bishops not yet under the protection of
a powerful prince should enter the king's *garde*.[18] As the
bishops of Clermont, Le Puy, and Mende fell into this category, the Massif Central was opened to royal influence. Then
Louis VI claimed the bishopric of Arras for his patronage in
1128—the only gain from his inglorious intervention in the
Flemish succession. By 1180, more than half the bishops
of France were again royal *fideles*, with the consequence
that they sought royal justice against their local oppressors.

Closely connected with fidelity was liege homage, which
the kings were equally determined to extend. Louis VI's
reign began inauspiciously, with the refusal of some great
princes to do homage, on the grounds that it was not customary.[19] Though their scruples were overcome, their
objection pointed to their awareness that the ceremony was
changing its meaning. In 1106, after the death of his brother
Geoffrey, Fulk of Anjou was recorded by Orderic as having
received the county of Anjou from King Philip I;[20] his
homage therefore implied feudal subordination. In the course
of the century, Louis VI and Louis VII succeeded in
imposing this interpretation on all their princes' homage.
In 1158, for example, Henry II swore to Louis VII:

I, King Henry, will safeguard the life, limbs, and landed honour of the
king of France as my lord, if he will secure for me as his vassal and
fidelis my life and limbs and lands which he has settled upon me, for
which I am his man.[21]

The Angevin lands were recognized without equivocation as
fiefs of the crown. This new precision allowed the king to
capitalize on his princes' territorial consolidation: when
William X took homage, both Aquitaine and Gascony
were included in the contract; when Raymond V became
Louis VII's man, the Rouergue, Gothia, and part of Provence
joined Toulouse as fiefs of the crown of France. Thus effort-
lessly the kings extended their realm.

One royal prerogative never to be revived in its full Carolingian glory was the holding of assemblies for the whole

military aristocracy of the realm. Ironically, this was a source of strength of the dynasty because, unlike its English counterpart, it did not have to face the potential opposition a corporate body of the great magnates could provide.[22] But both Louis did find useful public gatherings of bishops and great men, largely though not exclusively from within the duchy of Francia, on the model of the assembly Philip I had called to Orléans in 1077. The most famous of these meetings —that held in 1155 and attended by the count of Flanders, the duke of Burgundy, the counts of Troyes and Nevers, in addition to the lords of the royal demesne—provided the occasion for Louis VII to come as close to legislating as any twelfth-century French or English king was to do. Here he proclaimed the Peace of God for the whole *regnum* (realm—an ambiguous term, which may mean simply his demesne, or the old duchy of Francia), in accordance with the twentieth canon of the Second Lateran Council (1139), and established penalties for the violation of that peace. The princes present consented to the extension of the peace to their dominions—though not necessarily in *toto* or without alteration.[23] The action lacked that forceful superiority which had characterized Carolingian capitularies, at least in the time of Charlemagne; but it revived the tradition whereby the crown was seen as the author of society's moral norms.

A commoner function for assemblies was coordinating plans for war. When, in 1124, the Emperor Henry V planned an invasion, Louis summoned his nobles to Rheims to debate tactics and draw up the battle-lines. Along with troops from the royal demesne and from those towns which relied on royal protection, the dukes of Burgundy and Aquitaine, the counts of Blois, Troyes, Nevers, Brittany, and Anjou, came in person with their men. The assembly was so formidable that Henry V decided to abandon his campaign.[24] 1124 found the French princes unusually united; assemblies to discuss wars against Normandy could never command such support. Excuses for failures to attend abounded. Yet though irregular both in incidence and attendance, assemblies provided a golden opportunity for the dissemination of royal propaganda, to insist on the notion of 'public' war (see p. 288), and to depict royal campaigns as undertaken 'for the defence of the realm,'[25] rather than simply for the king's self-interest.

One further return to Carolingian precedent occurred at the very end of Louis VII's reign, when coinage from the king's mints and bearing his image began to circulate outside the royal demesne for the first time since the late ninth century. Admittedly, its circulation in the kingdom was small, its rivals powerful. Nevertheless it marked the first step—though only that—in the restoration of royal coinage inside West Francia.[26]

As judges, Louis VI and Louis VII were far more impressive when operating inside the demesne (see p. 296) than when acting, in their royal capacity, beyond its frontiers. The difficulty was the standard feudal one of failing to get both parties to appear. In 1153, for example, when the bishop of Langres brought a complaint against Duke Eudes II of Burgundy in the royal court, all four royal summonses to the duke met with excuses; in the end, therefore, the royal verdict was given by default to the bishop, but without much expectation that a long-term solution to the conflict had been achieved. Still, the case was important, because Louis had summoned Eudes for a breach of the peace, in accordance with the Second Lateran Council's definition.[27] The crown was thus establishing its right, even before the 1155 assembly, of prosecuting violence beyond the frontiers of the demesne. And with lords of lower rank, the king dared more. As early as 1108–9, Louis VI had led a campaign into Berry to force the lord of Bourbon's submission to the judgement of the royal court.

Where there was no breach of the peace, the kings continued to arbitrate, employing persuasion or pressure according to the standing of those involved. In the 1158 peace between King Henry II and Louis VII, it was agreed that Henry's quarrel with Thibaud of Blois should be ended by arbitration. To increase the chances of success, Louis offered Henry two teams of mediators; if he did not like the methods or conclusions of the first set, he could turn to the second.[28] But Louis was prepared to take a much tougher line with the count of Nevers to resolve his dispute with the abbey of Vézelay: although relatives of the count were allowed to participate in drawing up the terms of settlement, Louis insisted that, if it failed, further aggression against the abbey would be treated as aggression against the king and punished accordingly. The dispute could not be allowed to drag on.[29]

So the reigns of Louis VI and his son proved a decisive turning-point in the history of the French monarchy. After three centuries of decline, the first steps had been taken on the path to restoration. A royal letter to the people of Limoges *c.*1137 ended, 'You know that those who despise our orders lose our favour and incur our displeasure.'[30] This might seem a rather feeble threat. But at least the people of Limoges had been reminded that royal favour and displeasure were worthy of consideration.

It is inevitable that the kingship of the Louis should be discussed in terms of a return to the past, for this was the way they themselves justified it: their innovations were resumptions. Nevertheless behind the traditional concepts there lurked a marked change. For Carolingian royal rights had applied everywhere except where a grant of immunity blocked them; but Capetian royal rights were respecters of strongly entrenched vested interests. On the other hand, whereas Carolingian rights had been static, therefore subject to attrition, Capetian rights were elastic; with skilful manipulation they grew. An example of this can be seen in Louis VII's second Burgundian expedition, already mentioned. The occasion, in 1171, was a complaint by the monastery of Cluny against the count of Mâcon. Louis's duty to respond arose from the fact that in 1119, Cluny, caught between its need of lay protection and fear that the local lords would seek to violate its famous immunity, had turned to the distant but pious Louis VI and placed its whole order in his guardianship. So his son, no doubt unwillingly, was compelled to mount an expedition to discipline the count. The king's appearance in the Mâconnais revived ancient memories of Louis IV's visit in 950, which his successor exploited effectively, stressing the justice of his cause and the royal obligation to suppress evil. Having subdued the count, Louis toured the castles, to remind castellans of the long-forgotten doctrine that fortifications were the monopoly of public authorities. But while reasserting the old, he also broke new ground in the claim that he was rightful lord over all men in the area who had hitherto had no lord. And for good measure, he entered into an important *pariage* agreement with Cluny and the bishop and chapter of Mâcon, that resulted in the creation of a royal enclave within the county. From this nucleus, royal territory was in the future to expand to the point at which, in 1239, the whole county could be annexed to the royal demesne. In an area of weak lordship, Louis was prepared to capitalize on a simple right of protection to claim an old public obligation, a new feudal lordship, and a new territorial stake. The innovative character of Capetian kingship is unmistakable.[31]

The same point can be illustrated from the solid profit which was derived from the expanding royal protection of bishoprics. On the face of it, Louis VI's claim to be lord of all bishops not already under effective protection looks a modest attempt to regain only part of the Carolingian inheritance. And in one sense so it was, for by 1180 almost half the bishoprics in France still escaped crown control. But there was nothing conservative about the way in which Louis and his successor exploited the bishop of Clermont's complaints against the count of the Auvergne to secure a foothold in the county; it was their preparatory work that made possible Philip Augustus' annexation of the Auvergne to the royal demesne. Equally, Louis VII's intervention in the disputed election at Langres in 1138 prepared the way for his charter of 1179, taking the city and the whole episcopal fief under crown protection. As caries sets in at a weak point in the tooth's enamel and spreads to rot the whole tooth, so an appeal to the crown could trigger the decay of local autonomy.

A different view of royal opportunism can be seen in the confirmation of charters for leading monasteries outside the demesne. In 1146 Louis VII was asked to confirm the privileges enjoyed by the great abbey of La Trinité de Vendôme, under the patronage of the counts of Anjou. In return for his good offices, the king inserted into the charter, after a clause designed to deter his own servants from causing depredations, a reservation of the ancient Carolingian rights of hospitality, procuration, *ost*, and *chevauchée* which no

Capetian king had hithertofore enjoyed there.[32] It was a lavish *quid pro quo.* Less dramatic but far commoner was his habit of inserting a prohibition on religious houses trying cases of arson, rape, murder, and theft. The motive behind this may have been the desire to assist monasteries in living according to canon law; for the Second Lateran Council of 1139 had forbidden churchmen to participate in *justice de sang* (the trial of crimes punished by corporal or capital penalties).[33] But if Louis's intention was high-minded, his own profit was well served; for the gap left by disappearing ecclesiastical jurisdiction was to be filled by the crown and its officers.

The extent to which Louis VI and Louis VII had consolidated royal powers was masked from their contemporaries by their policy of pushing hard only where they knew that resistance was weak. Therefore the greater aggression, the more systematic pursuit of self-interest which characterized the reign of Philip Augustus seemed a decisive break with earlier Capetian trends. Yet Philip's methods were those of his father and grandfather; and although he had a clearer notion of feudal lordship and a broader canvas on which to exploit that lordship, even here he drew on his predecessors' achievements. Symbolic of the change that the Louis had effected was the increasing use during the twelfth century of the term *corona,* the crown, to describe the body of royal rights to be kept intact from generation to generation. The impersonal and durable character of these rights was highlighted during the last years of Louis VII's reign, in the use in charters of the phrase *corona regni* (the crown of the kingdom), a phrase which marked out royal rights from princely by asserting their value to the kingdom as a whole. This pretension was to be dear to the heart of Philip Augustus.[34]

Walter Map, reflecting on the changed character of French kingship in the twelfth century, saw the period between Louis the Pious's reign and the accession of his namesake Louis VI as one of deep depression, with 1108 marking a decisive turning-point. Louis VI

when he was young was unable to go outside the gates of Paris to the third milestone without the leave or escort of the neighbouring princes, and not one of them either kept or feared his orders. His high spirits gathered wrath at this, and he would not brook being confined in these narrow limits. The Lord waked him as one out of sleep and gave him a mind to fight and frequently the grace of victory, and fulfilled his labours to the perfect unity and peace of all France.[35]

There were those who might doubt the beneficial character of revived kingship; but no one could quarrel with Map's view that Louis was responsible for a major change of direction in the history of France.

(b) Communities

For one school of distinguished late nineteenth- and early twentieth-century historians, led by Luchaire, the twelfth century was essentially the century of the communes—those sworn associations of burghers who, spurred by economic change, challenged with violence the feudal order-ing of society, and brought about a new world. Few would now concur wholeheartedly in the terminology or the argu-ments of Luchaire and his school.[36] Yet they were surely correct in their fundamental premise, that what distinguished the twelfth century from its predecessors was above all the proliferation of new political communities, juridically defined by their *consuetudines* or *coutumes.* For their appearance broadened the context of French political life, previously confined to the military aristocracy and the higher ranks of churchmen; and in the process of broadening it, changed its nature.

The roots of the new communities must clearly be sought in social and economic change. As the swelling rural popula-tion cleared land and settled new territory, the isolated tillers of the soil acquired new neighbours; as lords, both lay and ecclesiastical, colonized the countryside to maximize their profits, villages replaced hamlets, towns villages. La Rochelle, for example, established by a *pariage* agreement between Duke William X of Aquitaine and Louis VI of France in 1130, grew in the second half of the century into the chief port for the export of Gascon wines to England; the prospect of employment attracted immigrants, the settlement became a substantial town. And old centres expanded as rapidly as new. The great abbey of Vézelay, dedicated to St Mary Magdalen, was so thronged with pilgrims in the early twelfth century that a rebuilding programme was carried out, resulting in some of the finest Romanesque sculpture to be seen in all France. To satisfy the needs of monks and pilgrims, the small settlement beyond the abbey walls expanded into a town, its inhabitants including innkeepers, victuallers of all sorts, mercers, and some prominent money-changers. Similarly the old Roman cities in Languedoc, Burgundy, and the Loire valley regained a truly urban character, after centuries of being pared down to walls, cathedral church, and market place; townsmen outnumbered clerics, new streets were built for their houses, roads inside the walls began to be levelled to prevent rubbish from blocking the entrances to new stone churches or entrance gates, trades diversified, immigrants poured in. In Flanders, where the cloth trade provided an urban-based industry, the transformation of small centres like Ghent, Ypres, and Lille into the greatest cities of northern Europe was startling.[37]

In themselves, congregations of people do not necessarily form political units; social and economic bonds may suffice. But the inhabitants of some twelfth-century towns and villages moved fast to associate for the protection of their interests against those of their overlords—bishops in the case of most ancient towns, abbots or castellans for newer foundations. The most famous, and one of the earliest, associations made its appearance in Laon in the early years of the century, as a consequence of the expanding wine trade in the area. The merchants of Laon, irritated by servile taxes, offered a large sum of money to the 'the clerks, the archdeacons, and the nobles' of the town for the privilege of having a commune—a sworn association for self-protection. In 1112, however, the bishop Gaudry bribed the king to suppress the commune. Guibert of Nogent, a distinguished raconteur, was in the city on 26 April, the day on which the burghers' resentment boiled over into rebellion, and left this account of events:

When the bishop and Archdeacon Gautier were engaged after the noon office in collecting money, suddenly there arose throughout the city

the tumult of men shouting 'Commune!' Then through the nave of the
cathedral of Notre-Dame . . . a great crowd of burghers attacked the
episcopal palace armed with rapiers, double-edged swords, bows, and
axes, and carrying clubs and lances. As soon as this sudden attack was
discovered, the nobles rallied from all sides to the bishop, having sworn
to give him aid against such an assault if it should occur. In this rally,
Guimar the castellan, an older nobleman of handsome presence and
guiltless character, armed only with a shield and a spear, ran through
the church. Just as he entered the bishop's hall, he was the first to fall,
struck on the back of the head with a sword by a man named Rimbert,
who had been his close friend.[38]

In the slaughter which followed, the bishop himself was slain.
From the burghers' point of view, his death was a serious
blow, for it forced Louis VI to punish them. As a consequence, it was not until 1128, and then in return for a very
substantial sum, that they obtained royal recognition for
their association, now called a peace confraternity rather
than a commune. The charter legitimated some degree of self-
government, limited the charges on serfs, guaranteed justice;
it therefore formed the foundation of the town's liberties.[39]

Revolution was only one, and not the commonest, method
pursued by burghers; taking advantage of political disturb-
ance could bring more speedy results. Here the classic case was
that of the Flemish towns' exploitation of the succession crisis
on the death of Count Charles the Good in 1127. We are well
informed about this by Galbert, a notary of Bruges,[40] who
wrote his account of the events as they occurred, betraying
a humanity and reflectiveness rare among men of his generation. The two most influential men in Bruges, the castellan
and the dean of St Donatian's, *ex officio* chancellor of
Flanders, were both members of a powerful new family, the
Erembalds, which had risen from servile origins to prominence by the route of comital administrative service. Their
exploitation of this recently opened path aroused jealousy
among the knights, one of whom refused to answer a charge
levelled against him by the Erembalds in the court of Charles
the Good, on the ground that his accusers' lowly social
origins barred them from comital justice. This allegation
threatened the Erembalds' whole social and political position;
so, when it appeared that Charles the Good was sympathetic
towards it, they murdered him. Chaos followed, for Charles

had no direct heir; and several of his cousins had roughly equal claims to succeed. Louis VI intervened on behalf of one of them, William Clito, son of Robert Curthose, and therefore a claimant also to the duchy of Normandy; for some months it looked as though Clito would establish his right. But his candidacy was naturally unacceptable to Henry I of England, who feared that the wealth and military power of Flanders would give Clito an unassailable advantage in Normandy; and the risk of antagonizing Henry was not one which the cloth towns cared to take, because they feared disruption of the wool supply. So, in 1128, when Clito's violation of the Ypres fair peace provided an excuse, the burghers of Ghent sent to Bruges for support in pressing the claims of Thierry of Alsace. Despite Louis VI's military aid, Clito died of wounds received in battle, and Thierry's claims to the county were upheld.

The outstanding lesson to emerge from this story was that comital succession, hitherto a matter determined within the comital family, could now be affected by interests from outside, even from outside the military aristocracy as a class. The precocity displayed by Ypres and Ghent in securing a candidate favourable to their industrial future was not to be imitated in the rest of France in the twelfth century; still, other rulers, particularly those of Champagne, learned from it of the profit to be derived from allying with the increasingly powerful mercantile or industrial classes. The part the Flemish towns played in the crisis of 1127–8 not only highlighted their importance, it also guaranteed their liberties. For, in his endeavour to secure their support, William Clito began his reign by issuing charters to Bruges, Ghent, Aire-sur-Lys, and St Omer. Of these, only the St Omer charter survives.[41] It included, along with clauses concerned with tolls and mercantile rights, a grant of freedom for the town and all dwellers in it; the abolition of the judicial duel, unpopular with merchants; the use of inquest in its place; and an enlarged competence for the *échevins* or *boni homines*, the successors of the Carolingian *scabini*, re-established in the town at the very beginning of the century. It was the *échevins* who were to represent the towns in all the proceedings of the following year; and once Thierry of Alsace was safely ensconsed as count, he could hardly subvert their position. Until his successor Philip moved to establish greater uniformity in urban law, the *échevins* of Bruges (and probably of other towns as well) were free to fix the customary law of their own community, which implied a remarkable degree of emancipation from external control.[42]

In the south of France, other cities achieved as much independence by slow, steady accumulation. In Toulouse, for example, while episcopal jurisdiction shrank under the Second Lateran Council's prohibition on *justice de sang*, the *boni homines* emerged before 1120 as important judicial figures, their competence enhanced by their control over the *salvamenta* established as a consequence of the peace movement. The count of Toulouse, who had succeeded in uniting all areas of the town under his domination by 1119, was happy to allow the *boni homines* day-to-day management of the town's legal affairs, provided that the profits of justice remained largely his, and his rights to tallage, unlimited military service and forced loans at will were preserved—as they were until 1147. In practice, the count's absence in St Gilles and Provence allowed the *boni homines* gradually to accumulate powers and the town to acquire liberties, to a degree that shocked Raymond V after his return to the city in 1180. His attempts at resumption provoked rebellion in 1189, which facilitated the establishment of the consulate in the city, the final step towards true urban independence.[43]

The Flemish cities, Laon, and Toulouse were all commercial centres of more than local importance before they launched their campaigns for privileges; and if their leaders were not highly educated men at the beginning of the century—it has been suggested that the reason why weaving was concentrated in towns in Flanders was that illiterate merchants could not keep the complicated records necessary for a scattered cottage industry—then they rapidly acquired learning along with their corporate awareness in the course of the century. In 1196, the dowager countess Matilda, confirming Ghent's privileges, ensured that no barriers would obstruct any competent person who wished to open a school in the town.[44] The church's monopoly of formal education was broken. Before this was achieved, where the new town governors' literacy proved too feeble to cope with challenges, it could be supplemented by the skills of notaries like Galbert of Bruges. Thus the complex administration necessary for repairing and extending city walls, channelling water supplies, ejecting waste, hearing legal cases, punishing offenders, policing the streets, could all be supplied. The culminating symbol of so much diverse activity was to be achieved in the thirteenth century, when the independent cities, led by those of Flanders, erected fine belfries so that their bells should rival those of the churches in summoning the flock to meet.

However the movement for some degree of independence, some autonomy, was not confined to substantial towns. It is true that the privilege of smaller towns was generally couched in more negative terms: by defining their *consuetudines* they prevented other powers—usually castellans—from arbitrary exactions. Yet very rapidly a list of prohibitions or limitations on the overlord's power could become a guarantee of the citizens' rights. In a letter to Suger, Robert of Montfalcon declared that a case over whether or not a certain man was his serf should be tried either in the royal court or before the archbishop of Bourges, provided that the proceedings were in accordance with the customs of Bourges;[45] for him, the *consuetudines* of his native town had assumed the status of a law binding on outside authorities. Bourges was a community in a vital sense, bound by rules of the inhabitants' own making.

Both Bourges and Laon were wine-growing areas. A contributory factor in their campaigns to secure charters was that the peasants who grew the vines around the outskirts of the town found arbitrary and unpredictable seigneurial exactions an intolerable burden on a form of agriculture for which long-term planning was essential. Rural pursuits as well as urban required the protection that written and confirmed *consuetudines* could bestow. In 1155, the customs confirmed by Louis VII for Lorris on the royal demesne established that no parishioner should have to pay taxes on food intended for his own consumption or on grain grown by his own labour; he should be exempt from tolls when he took his produce to the neighbouring towns of Étampes, Orléans, Milly, or Melun; if required for a *chevauchée*, he must be allowed to return home at the end of the day; the only labour service he owed his lord was in carrying seigneurial wine to Orléans twice a year; and the burgesses of Lorris as a whole were exempted from seigneurial *tailles*.[46] These concessions, ideally suited to promote the interests of an agricultural community, ensured widespread publicity for the customs of Lorris; they were therefore sought and obtained by a number of other rural communities, particularly within the royal demesne, in the second half of the twelfth century.

The appearance of privileged communities was not quite as haphazard as it may seem. Where lordship was strong, as in Paris, the degree of self-government was strictly limited. The same was true in Normandy, where Henry II's concession to Rouen between 1160 and 1170, soon to be a model for other cities across the Angevin empire, permitted internal self-government by a mayor and town council, but also allowed the duke to choose the mayor from a list of three names submitted to him by the council, and protected the ducal right to military service.[47] Elsewhere, the degree of urban independence varied with the amount of pressure the community could exert, its ability to exploit political crisis, and the condition of its neighbours. The interplay of these factors was complex; the two areas where the most advanced urban institutions were found were Flanders, where comital control was tight, and Gothia, where by contrast the count of Toulouse's authority within the great cities was almost negligible, and where the clashes between vicecomital and episcopal powers facilitated independence.

On the lower rung of legal self-determination the grant of customary franchises might be in a lord's interests, for it could secure his revenues in perpetuity, even as it barred him the chance of arbitrary exaction; besides, an early concession might prevent more explosive demands later. Some castellans and bishops were therefore amenable to bargaining; but others needed forceful persuasion. Again, where local lordship was strong, above all in Normandy, the chances of concessions were small. Those communities which did not receive franchises seem to have suffered a greater degree of extortion, as their lords strove to recover some of the profits they were losing elsewhere. As a consequence, the condition of the peasantry in twelfth-century France varied markedly from community to community, the extremes of contrast coming between those villages on the royal demesne protected by the customs of Lorris, and those in Champagne where serfdom retained its original rigours, where peasants remained the property of their lords, their labour services heavy, their safeguards against exploitative lordship non-existent.[48]

On a pragmatic level, the pressure for self-government or franchise complicated the aristocracy's game of preserving their own lordship while subverting that of their rivals. It could offer opportunities for embarassing independent lords, as Alphonse-Jourdain of Toulouse showed when he assisted the rebellious inhabitants of Montpellier against William VI;[49] but his own financial losses when the right to take tallage or forced loans from Toulouse escaped his grasp in 1147, outweighed any advantage elsewhere.[50] No lords appreciated the possibilities inherent in the movement so clearly as Louis VI and Louis VII. Their consummate skill in limiting demands for independence on the royal demesne, while favouring them elsewhere where a royal confirmation might create allies, has often been remarked. But the clearest example of royal skill was found in Louis VII's cynical suppression of Vézelay's revolt against its abbot in 1152. The rebels, provoked by Ponce of Vézelay's unyielding determination to maintain a monopoly of justice within the town, won much self-interested support in the neighbourhood; from the bishop of Autun, who wished to subject the abbey to episcopal control, from Cluny, which hoped to reabsorb the abbey into its order, and from the count of Nevers, who resented the legalistic and literal interpretation the abbot put upon his charter of immunity. On the other hand Ponce was strengthened in his intransigence by a papal letter forbidding him to make concessions on the immunity. But when his isolation rendered him vulnerable, he turned to Louis for assistance. As a price for his reduction of the rebels, Louis forced from the very reluctant abbot the recognition that in temporal matters he was subject to the decision of the royal court.[51] Louis's behaviour betrayed no interest in abstract justice: he was prepared to force modifications of the immunity in his own favour, but not in those of the count of Nevers or of the rebels; moreover, his opposition to the commune was inconsistent with his behaviour at Rheims or Amiens, and with long-term royal policy (by the end of the century, Vézelay had won its liberties). But in the short term, the king was the only party to the dispute who benefited by it; for it allowed him to display vigorous royal action within the county of Nevers.

For all princes, the communal movement raised a rather different problem: each privileged community, whether fully self-governing or merely franchised, constituted an enclave subject to different rules from its neighbours; it was not therefore easily absorbed into the administrative framework of castellanies which the princes of the north were seeking to clarify and define. Indeed, towns were as anomolous as the independent lordships the count of Champagne was bent on integrating into his castellan network.[52] Since what distinguished communities was their legal customs, anomalies could be reduced by greater legal uniformity within a whole castellany or, better still, a whole province. There was no problem in Normandy, where, by the middle of the twelfth century, one customary law obtained virtually throughout the duchy. Elsewhere in the north strong rulers, the kings, the counts of Flanders and Anjou, increased standardization by modifying customs when they confirmed them, or by persuading new communities to accept wholesale already existing customs. But though the patchwork of random entities slowly yielded in places to more solid blocks, nevertheless between them many separate customs survived. Later in the Middle Ages, the *pays de droit coutumier*, the land of customary law, was reckoned to consist of more than three hundred different customs (though only sixty of these were important and there were considerable similarities across blocks).[53]

In the far south, Gascony, the Saintonge, Toulouse, Gothia, and the southern fringes of the Massif Central, things developed differently. There the eleventh-century proliferation of *consuetudines* and castellanies had been modified by the survival (in places at least) of the old administrative framework, and by the tradition that serious offences were justiciable in a court higher than that of the castellan. The growth of independent towns in the twelfth century lent force to the revival of public courts on the Carolingian model; while Mediterranean contacts ensured a warm welcome for the learning of Bolognese Roman lawyers in the early decades of the century. Although the academic study of Roman law took a long time to have practical effect, by the 1170s and 1180s it was occasionally cited authoritatively in some at least of the courts of the south. The *pays de droit écrit* (land subject to written—Roman—law) was emerging, encompassing castellan and communal courts within its framework. By this means the south was to achieve a rather greater legal homogenity than the north.[54]

(c) The emergence of government

What distinguishes government from personal control is its unremitting character. To be governed is to be subjected to the regular pressure of an authority operating according to fixed rules. In the full sense of the word, it is arguable that nobody was governed before the later nineteenth century; it would certainly be foolish to maintain that either royal or princely government in the twelfth century operated according to fixed rules or without intermission or over all the inhabitants of a defined area. Nevertheless, the perception that this might be desirable was reborn, whether for good or for ill, among the twelfth-century rulers of France.

What provoked it was in part the ecclesiastical reform movement. For the reformers' vision of a fully-developed hierarchy, each man with his own sphere of competence, all subject to canon law and all beneath the discipline of the papal rod, evoked a mixture of admiration and envy in those laymen, accustomed to deference, whose position in the ecclesiastical scheme was lower than they would have wished. They neither cared nor dared explicitly to challenge this picture, as the pro-imperialists among the Germans had done. Rather they contented themselves by pointing out that, if the secular power was now confined to the rather lowly role of protecting the church's interests with the material sword, that sword was in practice essential to the well-being of the church. So Baldwin VII of Flanders, confirming the privileges of Zonnebeke abbey, declared:

Let it be known to all sons of holy church that I Baldwin, by God's grace count of Flanders, according to the power of secular dignity granted to me by God, am required to defend and protect all things within my principality, and especially the churches of God, and to keep intact all gifts justly bestowed on them, not only in my own time, but also in the times of my predecessors; and am required to maintain the shield of my protection faithfully and indefatigably lest they be disturbed by the presumptuous and infuriating attacks of jealous and avaricious persons . . .[55]

It was powerful pragmatic argument. But it did involve the acceptance of a spiritual authority beyond his control, to which his ancestor Arnoul I could never have bowed. And those among the princes who refused to recognize that authority—notably Duke William X of Aquitaine in the Anacletan schism—suffered a weakening of their secular power.

In returning to the old imagery of the prince as the bearer of the sword, the reformers had in fact triggered off an important set of associations. They recalled the Augustinian view of political authority as established not merely for defence against external enemies, but also for internal peace. Thus far, French princes—with the notable exception of the Norman king-duke—had been wary of claiming for themselves the peace-keeping function within their lands. It was no accident that Baldwin VII of Flanders moved to a new repressive interpretation of comital justice at just the same time as he claimed the superior advocacy over all ecclesiastical houses in Flanders. His successor Charles the Good increased his own powers of coercion to protect the weak and the tillers of the soil, while limiting those of others through prohibitions on weapon-carrying in markets or towns, and on the lighting of beacons to signal the start of a private war. For if the princes were to take seriously the one task the church now allowed them, they could not achieve it without also enlarging their criminal jurisdiction. The epitaph on Geoffrey le Bel's tomb:

Ense tuo, princeps, praedonum turba fugatur
Ecclesiisque quies, pace vigente, datur[56]

(By your sword, O prince, the crowd of robbers is put to flight, peace flourishes and churches enjoy tranquillity) demonstrated the new expectation.

As ecclesiastical reform refocused ideas on the prince's function, it also had an effect on the way he fulfilled it. In 1140 the monk Gratian in Bologna produced his *Decretum* or *Concordance of Discordant Cannons*, in which he demonstrated that, given the proper techniques of critical examination, the authoritative statements of church fathers and ecclesiastical councils could be harmonized to yield fundamental principles of church law. This approach, in which lay the seeds of later scholasticism, revived the notion of truth as an objective reality, attainable in the end by human endeavour; its appeal to the optimistic humanism of the twelfth century was therefore strong. And its implication for the conduct of trials in ecclesiastical courts was that the processes of human inquest could yield objective facts which human reason was competent to judge. Law could become once more an intellectual's chess-game.

Canon law was a practice as well as a theory well before 1140. Bishops in every diocese in France could be seen sorting out conflicts in ecclesiastical organization according to its principles; parish priests and laymen were drawn into the processes, whether as parties to disputes or as witnesses. For secular courts, the consequence was a revival of inquest proceedings on a much more extended scale than had been common in the eleventh century, causing a demand for documentary proof that chanceries and monastic scriptoria were hard pressed to satisfy. Slowly it sapped at the roots of the kind of justice which had been dependent on the judgement of God; ordeal—in any case a last resort—grew rare;[57] though trial by battle continued as a privilege of the military classes (in some places till the end of the middle ages), it too became somewhat of a curiosity. Oath-helpers were still employed to swear to the good character of the accused; but everywhere evidence as to the facts of the case grew more significant. Self-governing towns were swift to embrace this new—or rather revived Carolingian—form of trial; for disputes between merchants were hardly susceptible of solution by battle. And the areas of greatest urban expansion— Flanders and Gothia—were also those where Carolingian judicial forms had survived longest. Their example inspired others.

But inquest necessitated a professionalism long absent from castellans' courts. *Boni homines* or *échevins* ousted them in the self-governing towns; and slowly the day-to-day work of running courts in the non-franchised areas was taken over by knights or clerks with special knowledge of the law, leaving castellans to revert to their military role. That this did not happen to princes was a mark of their ability. Thibaud V was held by John of Salisbury to be one of the most learned lawyers of his day;[58] Philip of Alsace was a man of rare competence; other princes gathered around them their band of learned advisers, their counsellors on whose pronouncements they could depend. So all were seen by their subjects in their role as peace-keepers, and also as upholders and definers of customary law. Only where the demands of the Anglo-Norman and then the Angevin empire dictated it was there regular delegation of the prince's judicial rights to an official; even then, this delegation was revoked when the king-duke visited. Elsewhere, though crusading might cause a temporary break, the link between the prince and his court was close. When Geoffrey le Bel was unable to arbitrate in person between the seneschal and the monks of Baugé in a quarrel over tithes in 1146, he insisted that his part in the case be acknowledged. The charter setting forth the terms of the agreement ends:

I Geoffrey, by grace of God duke of the Normans and count of the Angevins, ordered this quarrel to be concluded by judgement, approved the judgement given, ordered a charter to be drawn up, and have confirmed it with my seal.[59]

Princes were happy to exploit those elements in the intellectual ferment of the twelfth-century renaissance, which exalted their position as executors of justice. Geoffrey le Bel would have been flattered by John of Marmoutier's comparison of his judicial aims with those of ancient Rome.[60]

The study of the classics, even when unfortified by specific reference to Roman law, was a potent weapon in strengthening princely jurisdiction at the expense of others. Equally, the theologians' new concentration on the literal meaning of the Bible produced a new view of the judge's obligations which Charles the Good of Flanders exploited for himself:

> Because Justice looks forth from heaven, in order that we should preserve justice we ought, according to the precept of our Lord, to judge with equity between man and man, just and unjust, so that, after the dangers of this life, meeting with mercy and truth, we may rest eternally on Solomon's bier.[61]

So behind and above the person of the prince, there formed again the abstract concept of 'the public person', the punisher of the wrongs and injuries, the bearer of peace, the mighty distributor of justice and equity.

Yet the scholarly energy which reinvigorated abstract concepts of political function was identical with that which satirized them. For to believe in abstract principles of justice was to face a long series of disillusionments in everyday life, as the Goliardic poems, written by scholars trained in the new learning, amply demonstrated:

> Apud nostros judices jura subvertuntur
> Et qui legem faciunt, lege non utuntur
> Sed attendant miseri mala quae sequuntur
> Hi qui damnant alios primo damnabuntur.[62]

(Our judges subvert the law, our legislators ignore it; but let these wretches await the evils to come—those who condemn others will be the first to be condemned.)

Having raised quite unreasonably high expectations, the intellectuals were among the first to invoke God's judgement against those very processes they had so recently emancipated from God's direct intervention. Now, in the absence of ordeal, they could only await the final vindication of their cause in heaven.

The roots of disillusionment—in so far as they were the fruit of twelfth-century conditions and not merely the natural response to too high or too vaguely expressed expectations—lay in the intellectuals' belief, stated by John of Salisbury:

Who . . . in respect of public matters can properly speak of the will of
the prince at all, since therein he may not lawfully have any will of
his own apart from that which law or equity enjoins, or the calculation
of the common interest requires?[63]

But even when princes did strive to fulfil this ideal, there
were considerations which might subvert their intentions.
Thibaud IV of Champagne defended his decision to hang
a criminal by asserting that he was the devil incarnate; yet
the prince could not prevail against St Bernard's cry 'I will
hang this murderer myself!' And though for St Bernard
incarceration at Cîteaux was the equivalent of perpetual
crucifixion, the criminal's reception into the monastic order
may not have satisfied everyone's sense of justice.[64] The
temperance of justice by mercy was therefore random in
incidence when the criminal was not of aristocratic birth;
when he was, political considerations entered into the
verdict. For though princes might now punish delinquent
vassals or officials (see pp. 360, 286), there was solid political
sense in not subjecting them to the same penalties as lesser
men. When Philip of Colombière's nephew killed the niece of
the bishop of Bayeaux, King Henry II's court behaved as it
would have done in the previous century in reconciling the
parties by arranging a settlement between them.[65] On the
other hand, princes felt free to vent their own anger in ways
which they now blocked to others. So Geoffrey le Bel, who
would brook no interference with the privileges he had
granted, tore up one of his own charters when its beneficiary,
Gerald Bellay, had infuriated him.[66] A prince's treatment
of his *fideles* was not susceptible to rules of impersonal and
eternal justice; and no attempt was yet made to make it so (see
p. 349). Yet because a prince could now justify his coercive
authority by reference to his peace-keeping function, those
who failed to obtain what they saw as justice at his court, and
who now stood to suffer punishment if they disturbed the
peace to vindicate their rights, grew embittered. Gerald Bellay's
rebellion against Geoffrey le Bel, with his appeal for support to
Louis VII, were significant presages of future developments.

The intellectuals' contribution to the practice of government was, at least in the short term, less of a mixed blessing
than their political and legal theorizing. It lay in producing

those written documents—charters, writs, letters, accounts —by which hitherto spasmodic personal contacts between princes and their officials and subjects could be regularized, and in inventing new ways of increasing efficiency. The evolution of a rudimentary bureaucracy was, by 1180, the distinguishing feature of royal and princely administrations. Again the example of ecclesiastical organization was forma- tive; but by 1180, lay bureaucracies had acquired a momen- tum and an approach all their own.

Shortly after the middle of the century, John of Salisbury finished his famous *Policraticus*, a discursive and unanalytical work devoted to criticizing the contemporary *mores* in the ruling circles of church and state, and to putting forward a higher code of conduct. Relying on the Bible, Roman law, and the classics to explain what ought to be, John also drew on his own experience to describe the contemporary scene. Though primarily a commentary on Henry II's govern- ment in England, the *Politicraticus* used the terms of Roman law, *princeps* for ruler and *provincia*, province, for the area of his rule; these suggest that John also intended his book to be relevant to France, the land in which he had been educated and to which he was to return as bishop of Chartres.

The most famous chapter in the *Policraticus* is that which sets forth the organic image of the commonwealth, the prince the head, the church the soul, the senate the heart, the soldiers the arms, the peasants the legs—a classical cliché brought up-to-date.[67] The importance of this image in the history of western political thought has long been recognized; indeed it has been hailed as the rebirth of the concept of state in the Middle Ages. Its most striking feature is the importance attributed to princely officials: judges and provincial governors are the eyes, ears and tongue of the body politic; officials are the hands; and financial officers the stomach and intestines. By the middle of the twelfth century, John's French readers would have had no difficulty in making the necessary identifications: castellans and viscounts, *baillis* and *prévôts*, household officers, the clerks, knights, and chamberlains of princely courts abounded. Bureaucracy, long absent from the country, was making a rapid return, both at central and at local levels. And John of Salisbury was not alone in believing that the administrative class was in dire need of instruction, lest it subvert the common good in its own or its master's interests.

The social origins of the new administrators have interested historians. The Erembald family, of which the chancellor of St Donatian's and the castellan of Bruges were members in 1127, was alleged by its opponents to be of servile origin; that its members chose to murder Charles the Good rather than dispute the allegation suggests its truth. If this was so, their social ascent was uncommonly sharp. But a recent study of the Capetian kings' household has traced a growing reliance on knights of lowly birth and clerks whose claim to prominence sprang solely from their usefulness.[68] The Cleer family in Anjou were of knightly status. And in Normandy, both Henry I and Henry II favoured 'new men', some at least of whom were of modest families.[69] How their absence of social distinction affected the performance of their duties can only be guessed. But it may be that, as men of little social consequence, they lacked that sensitivity to personal relationships on which the aristocratic society of the tenth and eleventh centuries had depended; for the newcomers, what was sauce for the goose was likely to be sauce for the gander. Because they saw the world as composed of groups rather than of individuals, they found it easy to articulate rules of general application, to which exceptions required specific dispensation. But of course this viewpoint was liable to emerge in any case at a time in which government was extending its reach down the social scale, to affect towns, privileged communities, and even on occasion serfs.

The schools springing up all over France in the twelfth century probably had a formative influence on the administrators, though this can rarely be proved. At the court of Louis VII, there was Mainier, a lawyer, whose name was prefaced by the title *magister*, meaning that he had received a *licentia docendi*, a licence to teach.[70] Elsewhere, it is uncertain how many of the clerks and knights of princely households obtained from schools the pragmatic literacy on which they called in their day-to-day business. It is rather more likely that clerks had benefit of formal education than knights. But courts themselves were places of education;

'With the king of England it is school every day',[71] as Peter of Blois remarked. And literacy, at least in the vernacular, could certainly be acquired without the aid of schooling. But whether directly or indirectly, the incipient bureaucracies clearly owed much to scholastic methods, to the categorization of information, the use of abstract nouns, and the search for system, that the schools had pioneered.

Because administrators depended on their lord's favour, they devoted themselves with vigour to promoting his interests. Here lay the spur to innovation, as can be seen in the Norman and Flemish accounting systems, which combined the techniques of survey and inquest with the new arithmetic to protect and increase the revenues available to the duke of Normandy and the count of Flanders. The Norman exchequer (probably instituted in the early years of the century, at the same time as its English counterpart) used the tally, the chequered cloth, and the abacus to provide records for the illiterate and to overcome the considerable problems posed by the use of Roman numerals in addition and subtraction. These were not new expedients; but their regular and systematic application to the ends of government effected a solid gain in efficiency. The aim of the Norman exchequer rolls was to provide a complete record of the debts and revenues due from each administrative unit of the duchy.[72] The aim of the 1187 *Grote Bref* in Flanders was a little different: in adding all revenues and expenditures together, it offered a rough estimate of the count's total income (though in fact there were resources not mentioned in the account.)[73] A less exciting but equally innovative characteristic of princely officials was that they now existed in sufficient numbers to be used to check up on one another. Henry II noted threateningly at the end of a letter of command addressed to one of his *prévôts*: 'If you do not do this, William of Vernone or his servants will do it; and if they do not do it, my justice shall do it.'[74] Princes were at last within reach of achieving their ends—or some of them—without having to resort to lengthy persuasion, to bribery or to the use of force.

Hardly surprisingly, officials were unpopular, both with sophisticated men like Walter Map and the Goliardic poets and with ordinary peasants. So, despite the enormous gains they conferred on their masters, they were often cheated of the loyal support they deserved. There were few things more calculated to endear a prince to his subjects than a display of stern retribution on unjust officials. John of Marmoutier tells the legend that Geoffrey le Bel dressed up as a rustic and listened to complaints about his *prévôts'* rapacity; on his return to court, he paid back the sums they had extorted, and threatened them with death if they continued to defraud the peasantry.[75] Though almost certainly untrue, the tale succinctly illustrates the prevailing princely ambivalence: they distanced themselves from the servants on whom they relied.

(d) Warfare and crusades

The poet Marbod of Rennes celebrated (in Latin) the vengeance which would befall a wicked castellan and his troops:

> Though forts of adamant shall ring you round,
> The ninefold thickness of a solid wall,
> And molten metal pour in rushing torrents,
> Though the dragon crouch in your gate with thrashing tail,
> And the foul chimera bellow her flaming wrath,
> It will avail you nothing.
> Think not, you troop of murderers, blackguards, thieves,
> To escape one jot of the judgement of your crime.
>
> Not because giant catapults will hurl
> Their crushing bolts, and breach your palisade,
> Not because death swarms in on every side
> From hook and battering ram and sling
> And blazing bomb and burrowing mole.
> But because Almighty God fights for the women
> Whom you have widowed.[76]

The poem highlights two important twelfth-century developments: the use of force in punishing aristocratic crime (the fruit of princely peace-keeping), and the increasing significance of siege-engines in warfare. Intellectuals claimed a formative influence in the second too: John of Marmoutier declared that monks from his own monastery had read Vegetius' *De Re Militari* to Geoffrey le Bel when he was investing the castle of a rebellious castellan, and ascribed his success to their advice on firebombs.[77] But common sense may have been more important than learning in perceiving the vulnerability of most castles to battering-rams and catapults; for even in 1100 they were, as a rule, primitive structures.

Siege-engines demanded on the one hand skilled operators, and on the other a plentiful supply of unskilled labourers to move the necessary materials. This effectively restricted their use to the wealthy and to those whose claim to assistance under the *ban* was incontrovertible. Equally, the improvements in fortification needed to withstand their effects—thick stone walls, inner as well as outer defences—required incomes greater than those of simple lords. The net effect was that, given dedication, princes—Louis VI, Geoffrey le Bel, Alphonse-Jourdain—could subdue rebellious castellans within their own demesnes, and could build castles of their own which were impregnable to all but lengthy and sustained attack. Henry II's castle at Chinon, where the treasury of Anjou was situated, was the model for its generation, with its halls, upper chambers, tower, and curtain walling, set on a high point above a strategic crossing of the Loire. It could be copied only either by those of nearly equal wealth or by those who could concentrate their resources chiefly on defence—princes, great bishops or, in the south especially, towns. All others became vulnerable. John of Salisbury's comment that not only the towns but also the fortresses of Gaul feared Henry I of England was revealing of the new situation.[78]

Similarly, campaigning in the field imposed an increasing financial burden. The treaty between Robert II of Flanders and Henry I of England, renewed by their successors,[79] stipulated that each knight supplied to the English king should bring three horses with him—this at a time when a horse represented a major investment. Then knightly armour grew more elaborate and costly throughout the century. And though some knights might be supplied free by feudal service, household ones had to be maintained by their lords, mercenary ones needed pay, and those with money-fiefs constituted a regular charge on the treasury. Besides, away from their home base, knights were useless on their own. In open battle and in the plundering expeditions that constituted the normal form of aggressive warfare, they needed the backing of archers, both mounted and on foot, and of numerous infantrymen. The usual source of supply was town militias—Suger mentions those of Rheims, Châlons, Laon, Soissons, Orléans, Étampes, and Paris in the royal army of 1124.[80] But they might have to be supplemented by mercenaries from Flanders and the Low Countries, where the rapidly expanding population forced large numbers of young men into military careers. In the eyes of the faithful, these 'Brabanters', with their freebooting and lack of discipline after the end of campaigns, were as dangerous as heretics; in 1171 Frederick Barbarossa and Louis VII agreed to expel them from their lands. Their value in battle, as shields behind which the knights could shelter before they launched their charge, ensured their continued employment by those who could afford them—notably Henry II of England. But the hatred they aroused meant that they were liable to be brutally slaughtered if captured afterwards.[81]

Inevitably, therefore, war on the grand scale as fought by princes bore little resemblance in practice to the feuds of lesser men. The divergence was sharpened by the application of a theoretical distinction, the fruit of Augustinian theology, amplified as the century went on by canon and Roman law reference; princes pronounced their campaigns just wars (fought against aggressors with the aim of re-establishing peace) or public wars (declared by a competent authority in the public interest), while they condemned the wars of lesser men as infractions of the peace.[82] Geoffrey Martel had perceived the propaganda potential of public war as early as the mid eleventh century; later it enabled Henry the Liberal of Champagne to claim the military service of all lords within his county, a reapplication of the Carolingian *ban*. So it could be a powerful weapon. Yet the logic of the definition suggested that it would benefit especially kings, whose competence to declare war could not be impugned: thus Thibaud of Blois failed to persuade the monks of Marmoutier that they owed him service when he fought against Louis VI; they claimed discretion in the matter;[83]

and in 1184, the mighty Philip of Alsace hesitated to commit to battle the army he had summoned against Philip Augustus, through fear that its ranks might melt away. The contrast with the united front Louis VI and his troops presented to the emperor Henry V in 1124 was marked. A royal banner now bestowed respectability on a cause; kings' wars were assumed to be for the sake of peace, even when cripplingly expensive and increasingly savage. This goes some way to explaining why the complicated campaigns within Toulouse in the second half of the century were largely fought out under the banners of the Angevin, Aragonese, and French kings; and why the revolts of Henry II's sons had widespread ramifications.

The twelfth century was characterized, therefore, by fewer but more protracted wars, which smouldered for long periods between short, sharp bouts of conflict, like the war that covered most of the reigns of Henry I of England and Louis VI of France, the one inaugurated by the great rebellion of 1173, which outlived both Louis VII and Henry II, or that against Catalan claims in the south. Into these large numbers of local conflicts were subsumed.

The pattern caused problems, in that the circumstances which might trigger off renewed fighting were unpredictable; yet the moment an opportunity offered, princes had to be prepared for invading their enemies; there was no time for lengthy preparation. The usual tactic was to march troops across the enemy's territory, plundering and looting; to take fortified places if the task was easy; to obtain allies among the lords of the locality; and to retreat without fighting a battle if at all possible—in effect an application to a wider canvas of the same technique of warfare which had earlier made castellans formidable in the immediate environs of their castles. It necessitated the rapid mobilization of auxiliaries to join a core of highly-trained troops kept constantly at the ready—the princes' military households, which became the linch pin of the system.

John of Marmoutier's life of Geoffrey le Bel offers a glimpse of how strong bonds were created between the prince and his followers within the household, and how a high level of training was maintained at all times. Geoffrey was brought up from infancy with the sons of neighbouring Angevin lords, on whose companionship he relied. When it came time for him to be knighted by Henry I in Rouen, he set off for Normandy with a crowd of these young men about him. In Rouen, the occasion was celebrated with pomp, eleborate dress, and a great feast, and then the youths all demonstrated their military skill at a grand tournament, at which Geoffrey naturally won the highest honours.[84] It was within this kind of environment that chivalry flourished, that young men learned to identify their vassalage towards their lord as a symbol of their honour, that they debated the relative merits of Roland's and Oliver's way of displaying loyalty; and that they learned the finer points of jousting. Tournaments were disapproved of by ecclesiastics, for they could be both bloody and dangerous. Yet they supplied real needs: that of an instruction in the martial arts compatible with the maintenance of a prince's peace; that of an outlet for competitive instincts within the claustrophic confines of a court; and that of display to maintain princely social status. So they flourished everywhere. They offered opportunities for men of skill to acquire great position in the world—Arnoul of Ardres caught the eye of Countess Ida of Boulogne through his exploits;[85] and they also conferred lustre on the great— Geoffrey le Bel and Philip of Alsace were renowed throughout France for their distinguished performances in these show battles.

All this formed a background to the first century of crusading; and it goes some way to explaining the more secular aspects of the magnetism which drew French knights to take up the cross in their thousands. Urban II, launching the First Crusade at Clermont in 1095, presented it as a natural evolution of the peace movement: warriors were to forget their petty feuds and squabbles in a campaign to promote the interests of Holy Church. The war, declared by one whose moral authority was unimpeachable, was to free the Eastern churches, to end Muslim guardianship of the holy places, to restore Jerusalem to its proper state.[86] As princes saw it, it was a just war in the fullest sense of the term; those who were slaughtered in its battles were regarded as among the martyrs of the church. When Raymond of Toulouse,

Robert II of Flanders, Robert Curthose, Stephen of Blois, and Hugh of Vermandois responded to the call, past and present members of their military households fell almost automatically into rank behind them, to test themselves against terrible dangers, but also to enjoy the companionship in arms, the adventure, the deeds of daring which were the stuff of the *chansons de geste*. That they shared, along with all other participants in the crusade, a fervent devotion, a conviction that their sins would be forgiven, is certain. Yet for them crusading necessitated no large leap of the imagination, no millenarian vision; it was simply a challenging and a deserving extension of their everyday activities.

In French eyes, the hero of the First Crusade was Robert II of Flanders. While Raymond of Toulouse remained in Outremer, Stephen and Hugh disgraced themselves in escaping from the siege of Antioch, and Robert Curthose, no matter how gallant, at least in his lifetime failed to impress, Robert II's prestige soared to the skies. He became Robert of Jerusalem to his contemporaries; his deeds were recorded in the *Song of Antioch*; his pious bravery totally expunged the memory of Robert the Frisian's usurpation; and after his death his son Baldwin VII harped on his father's achievement to justify his substantial use of coercion against the enemies of the church.[87] Outside Flanders, Robert's sister's marriage to Roger of Sicily was a mark of his new position in the world; like Louis VI's sister's marriage to Bohemond of Antioch, it stretched French kinship connections into the new Norman colonies, ensuring that travellers from the homeland would find a welcome in those distant parts. Robert's example was a potent one. After the next change in dynasty, Thierry and Philip of Alsace strengthened their shaky claim to the comital position by attaining for themselves the prestige attached to being the outstanding crusaders of their generation. Thierry's remote connection with the family of Godfrey de Bouillon, along with his marriage with Sybilla of Anjou, Fulk V's daughter, gave him some claim to the throne of Jerusalem; as a consequence, the aristocracy of Outremer viewed him and Philip with mixed feelings, expecting much of them, yet fearing their ambitions. In the end, it was not in Outremer but in the newly conquered

Byzantine empire that the Flemish crusading achievement was crowned with the elevation of Count Baldwin IX to the imperial throne in 1204. But in the twelfth century, the house of Alsace could afford the high costs of their expeditions—Thierry went to Jerusalem four times, Philip twice— and the counts' repeated absences in fact promoted administrative reform; the *baillis* and the *Grote Bref* were as much the products of crusading as the English and Norman judicial system and exchequers were the product of the king-duke's divided attentions.

But if, on balance, the Flemish counts benefited materially from crusading,—as, arguably, did the Angevin—they were far from typical. For other French houses a commitment to Outremer often represented a sacrifice of domestic political interest. The achievements of Raymond IV St Gilles in consolidating his authority within Toulouse were threatened by his departure in 1095, especially since it was known that he had no intention of returning home. Then his example lured his elder son Bertrand to Tripoli in 1112, and his younger son Alphonse-Jourdain there in 1147. Had not his grandson Raymond V fulfilled his crusading obligation in his early youth, thereby freeing himself from the necessity of interrupting his career in the county, the principality of Toulouse might have disintegrated altogether. William IX's crusade of 1101 brought about serious financial problems in Aquitaine which caused rapid devaluation in the hitherto stable currency; and Robert Curthose's decision to mortgage Normandy to William Rufus in order to cover his crusading expenses exacerbated a conflict over the duchy which was not settled until the death of his son William Clito in 1128. All in all, it was not surprising that Suger, mulling over the precedents of early crusading, tried to dissuade Louis VII from embarking on his Jerusalem journey in 1145.[88]

Yet the appeal of crusading was, if anything, even stronger to those aristocratic houses just below the level of the princely: it was, after all, the house of Boulogne which produced the first two rulers of Jerusalem. The counts of Nevers, the lords of Montpellier, the lords of Amboise and Lusignan, the Trencavels, were fervent devotees of the ideal; so the problems of absences, shipwrecks, death abroad plagued them as much as their princes. On occasion, their determination to sacrifice for Christ played directly into their overlord's hands, as when the count of La Marche, who had no direct heir, sold his county to King Henry II in 1177. When it did not, accompanying their princes in a joint crusading venture, as the lord of Amboise accompanied Fulk V or Hugh VI de Lusignan William IX, created new personal links. The political spin-offs from crusading are therefore more difficult to calculate than at first glance they might appear.

Nevertheless it is clear that the chief gainer was Louis VII. The irony of this lay in the fact that the Second Crusade was counter-productive in Outremer, embittered relations with Byzantium, and resulted in the deaths of enormous numbers of its participants, particularly those drawn from the non-aristocratic classes. Yet it consolidated the king's position within France, partly through the skilled regency of Suger, but also because, in taking on himself the leadership of the expedition, Louis re-emerged as a credible ruler of men. His noble gesture appeased those churchmen who had been appalled by his early obstinacy over the archbishopric of Bourges. The disasters that befell his army paradoxically heightened his personal charisma: even the barons of Outremer continued to look on him as their one potential saviour.[89] His friendship with Raymond V of Toulouse, a fellow warrior, reversed the trend of history since the middle of the tenth century, in bringing the princes of the far south back into the king's *mouvance*. The crowds of Burgundians who accompanied the king learned to respect him; on their return, they sought the arbitration of the royal court in their disputes, and they welcomed Louis's intervention within the counties that fringed the duchy of Burgundy.[90] As William of St Denis put it,

You could see men from the uttermost limits of the kingdom, from the Limousin, from Bourges, from Poitou and Gascony, commending themselves to his protection . . .; and he so satisfied them, sometimes by his resources, sometimes by his counsel, that they no longer set themselves apart from any of the kings.[91]

Even as early as 1147 it was apparent that the crusading movement had provided a new sense of aristocratic cohesion in the realm. The great joint expeditions, the combined leaderships, although not without friction, had been justified by their outstanding achievement, the conquest and maintenance of Jerusalem. They were the *Gesta Francorum*, the deeds of the Franks, or the *Gesta Dei per Francos*, God's deeds performed through the Franks, as two of their earliest chroniclers entitled them. But what was missing before 1147 was a clear sense of who the Franks were. The Second Crusade, however, was launched with St Bernard's ringing appeal to the count and barons of Brittany:

Therefore most noble knights, let us gird on our swords; and he who has none, let him buy one. Do not forsake your king, the king of the Franks—nay indeed, the King of Heaven, for whose sake he (Louis) undertakes so long and dangerous an expedition.[92]

In taking his place at the head of the Second Crusade, the *Rex Francorum* decisively hastened the transformation of the Franks into the French.

CHAPTER 12

The Principalities 1108–1180

(a) The royal principality

Louis VI and Louis VII were singularly lacking in those personal qualities which contributed to the prestige of their rivals. As military leaders, they were failures—defeated at Brémule, ejected from Flanders, reduced to pathetic impotence at Damascus, ignominiously extruded from Normandy in 1174. Then, though Walter Map was perhaps a little unkind in recording that Louis VII might have been thought an imbecile,[1] even their admirers never claimed for the kings the learning of Henry II or Henry the Liberal. The kings patronized neither troubadours nor romance poets; among the men of culture, only the theologians of Paris met with their liberality. They were unchivalric figures: not for them the heroism of Robert II or the courtly conduct of Philip of Alsace. Even their piety lacked the warmth and appeal of Thibaud IV's.

Yet in the dourness of their court lay their strength, for it inspired no jealousy. Louis VII could sleep almost alone in a wood, fearless of an enemy's sword, since no man sought to kill him.[2] Then there is the famous story of how, when he compared his own small wealth against the treasures of Frederic Barbarossa and Henry II, the king concluded with great satisfaction, 'Here in France we have only bread, wine, and joy.'[3] Walter Map's anecdote has perhaps commanded more scholarly attention than it deserves; it was, after all, by way of being a moral lesson to acquisitive courtiers rather than a statement of historical fact. If by chance it does reflect Louis's cast of mind, then 'joy' meant lightness of heart, absence of care—certainly not pleasure, for the only mildly frivolous thing Louis was ever rebuked for indulging in was a game of chess. And Sir Richard Southern[4] was probably correct in connecting that absence of care with the effortless moral superiority of Louis's dynasty, at once the

most odious and the most admirable characteristic of the
later Capetians. The combination of personal featurelessness
and profound confidence in their own integrity was the
secret of their success; on account of this their subjects could
easily raise their eyes above the personalities of their kings
to the higher abstraction of good kingship.

The one trait of Louis VI to emerge clearly from Suger's
Life was his obesity, which towards the end of his life prevented him from mounting his horse, and therefore put an
end to his peregrinations around the royal demesne. There
had been little to impress the casual observer of these forays
—Louis had had to destroy Hugh du Puiset's castle three
times, to campaign twice against the evil Thomas de Marle.
It might appear that the hard battles of Henry I and Philip I
had been for naught, that the problem of independent
castellans was intractable, that the king, unlike the duke of
Normandy or the count of Flanders, was incapable of
impressing on his own lords the unwisdom of obstinate
rebellion. Yet, as was often the case with the Capetians,
there was more to it than met the eye. For Louis's were
the last such campaigns to be undertaken. In the end he
succeeded in destroying even Montlhéry, that thorn in his
father's flesh, which, in true Carolingian spirit, he declared
illicite constructum,[5] illegally built; the doctrine that all
fortifications needed royal authorization was being put into
effect again. His campaigns against Thomas de Marle were
fought with the full backing of the church, as the punishment of an excommunicate and a violator of the peace.
Despite assistance to the rebels from Thibaud IV and
Henry I, Louis managed to isolate recalcitrant barons, to
deprive them of moral justification, to force them one
by one into paying liege homage and accepting strictly feudal
terms of tenure, to re-establish his lordship over their castles.
Then he and his successor together persuaded them that
the proper course of action when faced with provocation
was to seek justice in the royal court. There was still a long
way to go before private war could be forbidden on the royal
demesne. But a substantial start had been made in that
direction.

Wealth was a necessary constituent of power; and here the

Capetian fortune took an unexpectedly large stride forward. The Île de France became, in the first half of the twelfth century, a major producer of wine. Vines were planted on the slopes around Paris and all the southern area of the royal demesne; the excellent river network allowed the easy transport of wine to Brittany, Artois, Flanders, and Frisia. By the second half of the century the expanding towns in Flanders, with their large populations employed in an industry that robbed them of time or opportunity to grow their own food, had exhausted the corn supplies of the Artois; their demand now stimulated further land-clearance in the Île de France.[6] For the first time in their history, the rich soils of the Seine valley were notably productive. The kings were fortunate in enjoying this general wave of prosperity.

Yet they also exploited their situation. For much of the corn-growing profit would have been lost to them had they not preserved and extended their rights in Picardy, in the rich plains where, if royal pressure or royal oversight relaxed for one minute, the counts of Flanders were waiting in the wings to seize their chance; and where royal rights must in any case be exercised with great discretion if they were not to arouse local hostility. Not until 1191 could the king take his control of Picardy as an established fact; yet well before then it was a highly profitable area. Even in the long-held parts of the demesne, Louis VI and Louis VII were quick to enhance their wealth by making business agreements: they entered into *pariages*; they encouraged land clearances, selling rights to new settlers in return for an annual tribute; they exploited forest rights; they bought from their neighbours pieces of land which would consolidate their own estates (Louis VII even went into the marriage market with this end in mind; his marriage with Adela of Champagne secured his holdings in the northeast of the demesne); and they derived solid incomes from the *consuetudines* of the growing towns. Hence their reputation as bourgeois kings.

Their total income from good fortune and clever exploitation cannot be calculated exactly. But Benton's study[7] concluded that Louis VII's usual annual return from manorial resources was about 20,000 *livres parisis*: his irregular returns

—from profits of justice, 'banal' resources, and regalian rights—were probably about twice this. At 60,000 livres per annum royal revenue compared well with that of the richest territorial princes of the day. And because their landed holdings were fairly compact, the cost of administering them was relatively low. This, combined with a court life on the dowdy side, and the opportunity to enjoy lavish hospitality from monastic houses and bishoprics, made for financial soundness. Even before the staggering expansion of the royal demesne under Philip Augustus and Louis VIII, the kings of France were rich men.

In administration the two Louis followed Philip I's lead. *Prévôts* continued to collect the varied taxes and tolls due to the king across the demesne and to see that his interests were protected. For the first quarter of the century, the household officers played a large part in government; but the dismissal of Stephen Garland from his post as seneschal in 1127 marked the beginning of their decline. In the second half of the century, the old posts were hereditary and becoming honorific. The crucial stage in the evolution of government came with Louis VII's absence on crusade, when Suger as regent relied on chamberlains, men of knightly birth, and cut the old links between *prévôts* and household officers, making the *prévôts* directly dependent on himself. On Louis's return, the king was regularly surrounded by administrators of the new sort. In his ordinary life, he thereafter had less contact with his aristocrats than any other prince of his day. Bournazel[8] has detected a group of counsellors, in almost permanent session, serving the king's interest with all the devotion of men who owed their position to this alone; of these the most important were Thierry Galeran, who became a Templar, Stephen d'Avon, Josbert Briard, and Matthew de Beaumont. The notable speed with which Louis seized his opportunities for self-aggrandizement in the 1160s and 1170s should doubtless be ascribed to the advice he received from them.

In strictly territorial terms, the demesne did not expand very much in this period, the disappointing result of the 1152 divorce between Louis and Eleanor of Aquitaine. Nevertheless the fourteen years that the marriage lasted did lay the base for later expansion. In 1141, for example, Louis intervened to protect the church of Angoulême against the count, the first royal intervention in the area since the tenth century.[9] Then in his capacity as duke of Aquitaine—a title by no means universally conceded to him—he claimed overlordship in Berry over all those who had not yet acknowledged a liege lord.[10] So he moved from Bourges down into the south of Berry, put the house of Blois under pressure, and retained enough influence there to embarrass Henry II after Aquitaine passed from Louis's to Henry's control with Eleanor's marriage to Henry in 1152.

Still, these were relatively small gains. And the only other additions were on the fringes of the demesne, in Bourges and its environs, in Picardy and on the frontier with Champagne. A map of the demesne in 1180 would show only marginal gains on that of 1108. But in this case, as in many others, a map would be misleading. For the real difference was that Louis VII was undisputed master within the demesne, while beyond it he had acquired rights, in Angoulême, the Mâconnais, the Auvergne, Chalon, and Nevers, which constituted important stepping-stones to later expansion.

(b) Duchies and counties

Those lands not under Angevin rule in 1180 are discussed first, from south to north, followed by Angevin lands in descending order of governmental evolution.

(i) Toulouse

When Raymond IV of St Gilles departed on the First Crusade, he put at risk those fragile bonds between and within his scattered lands in Toulouse, Gothia, the Rouergue, and Provence that it had been his achievement to create. Although his successors, Bertrand (1095–1112), Alphonse-Jourdain (1112–47), and Raymond V (1148–95) were able and energetic men, they were frequently distracted from their efforts at consolidation. As a consequence, by 1180 the effectiveness of the administrative system they had built up was checked by the disunity of their realm.

Their chief headache came from rivalry with the house of Barcelona, by which they felt threatened throughout Gothia, the Rouergue, and Provence. In 1112 Raymond

Berengar III of Barcelona married Douce, the heiress to much of Provence, the county of Gévaudan, the viscounty of Millau, half the viscounty of Carlat, and honours in the Rouergue. Her lands formed a reasonably coherent block for the younger son of their marriage, who increased them by marrying the heiress of Melgueil. As soon as he attained his majority, Alphonse-Jourdain went to war to protect his interests against this new power-block and, if possible, to increase his holdings in Provence. As it turned out, this proved an unwise step, for it rekindled Raymond Berengar's interests in the county of Carcassonne, in which his rights had been ignored by the viscount of Béziers (see p. 171); to reassert them, the count of Barcelona entered into a firm alliance with his step-brother, Viscount Amery of Narbonne. Bernard Aton was therefore forced by this combination to accept that he held Carcassonne as a fief of Barcelona. In 1125 peace was restored in Provence by a division of the area: the coastal lands between the Rhône, the Durance, the Alps, and the sea—conventionally called the county of Provence—went to Barcelona, while Toulouse acquired the much smaller marquisate north of the Durance. But Toulousan ambitions were not satisfied; given the opportunity, its counts pressed for more; and Alphonse-Jourdain schemed to bring Bernard Aton back into his *mouvance.*

Something like a state of cold war continued in the south until 1166. By that date the cadet branch of Barcelona that had held Provence, Gévaudan, and Millau was represented only by a young heiress, Douce, whom Raymond V of Toulouse aspired to marry. Because this plan endangered the Barcelona strategy, the counsellors of the young Alfonso II, king of Aragon and count of Barcelona (Raymond Berengar III's grandson) intervened decisively. From the county of Provence, Barcelonese armies pressed into the marquisate, threatening Raymond V's Provençal inheritance. By way of retaliation, Raymond stirred up trouble in Béziers and Nîmes against their Trencavel viscounts: in Béziers Raymond Roger was killed. Raymond V then tried to prevent Roger II, his son, from succeeding to his father's inheritance. These manœuvres delayed, but did not prevent, Barcelona's victory in Provence. In 1176 Raymond was forced to accept the division of 1125 and to renounce by treaty his hopes for further expansion beyond the Rhône. In return, however, the count of Barcelona seems tacitly to have recognized Toulousan overlordship over the Trencavel viscounts, which Raymond had brought about by an alliance with his erstwhile enemy Roger II in 1171; Roger married his daughter. It appeared that the way had thus been prepared for permanent peace in the south. But in 1179 Roger II again sought the aid of Aragon against Raymond V, because his Toulousan overlord had called on the Pope for assistance in eliminating the Catharist heresy in Béziers. Alfonso's decision to aid his former vassal, to accept him back into his *mouvance*, and to defend him against his enemies, was the signal for war within Toulouse.

In the meantime, Catalan ambitions had been complicated by Poitevin aggression. Duke William IX of Aquitaine's claims to Toulouse, deriving from his wife Phillippa's rights, were not forgotten by his successors. In 1159 they were revived by Henry II of England, married to William's granddaughter Eleanor. Though he was foiled in his first attempt, in 1159, to incorporate Toulouse within his already huge empire, by 1173 Henry's constant pressure had forced Raymond V into some recognition of Angevin overlordship. The real danger for Raymond in attempting to renounce this enforced allegiance lay in an Angevin–Barcelonese alliance against him; by 1179 it was clear that this was happening. As a consequence, Raymond entered into a dangerous agreement with Henry II's dissatisfied son, the Young King, whose death in 1183 irretrievably weakened Raymond's position.

Defence against Barcelona and Poitiers compelled the counts of Toulouse to reverse their traditional southward alignment by seeking again the lordship of the king of France. In accompanying Louis VII on the Second Crusade, Alphonse-Jourdain had prepared the way; in 1154 Raymond V took the decisive step of marrying Louis's sister Constance. This marriage was far from happy—in 1165 Constance withdrew from Raymond's court, complaining to her brother that the count neglected her completely;[11] it nevertheless produced two sons who were, for some time, the only male children of the Capetian line. Louis's need to protect them explained in part his rapid answer to Raymond's appeal for help against Henry II in 1159; his action was the decisive step in reintegrating Toulouse within the French kingdom. In the long term, royal intervention was not in Raymond's interests: in 1155 Louis crossed the county on his way to Compostela, using the opportunity to offer his protection to the bishops of the Narbonne province; and after the failure of Constance's marriage, the king moved in to form ties with secular lords as well; Roger II of Béziers, on marrying Louis's niece, did homage for a castle on his land hitherto held allodially, so entering the royal *mouvance*.[12] More importantly, Louis encouraged the viscountess of Narbonne to seek his protection in 1164 (see p. 375). The count of Toulouse could not withstand royal competition in the scramble for Occitan allegiances.

Raymond's other potential ally was the Papacy, by tradition well-disposed towards the counts, on account of Raymond of St Gilles's and Alphonse-Jourdain's distinction as crusaders. In 1161 Eudes, legate of the Holy See, was assisted by Raymond when Louis VII refused to help him; and in 1163 Raymond was the chief figure in the welcoming party that met Alexander III when he disembarked at Maguelonne to begin his exile within France. Though Raymond's alliance with Frederick Barbarossa, along with his son's treatment of the archbishop of Grenoble, later soured relations with the Papacy, he still felt sufficiently confident of Alexander's goodwill to plead for his assistance against the heretics of Languedoc in 1179. Exactly what lay behind this appeal is still in doubt. But whatever the roots of the Catharist movement in Languedoc—and here is not the place to discuss the complex and controversial phenomenon[13]—it clearly received a powerful injection of lay support in the 1160s and 1170s. The counts of Foix and the Trencavels, whose anti-clericalism was noted, were willing protectors of the heretics, either through self-interest or through genuine respect for their austere way of life. Raymond V may have been shocked by their attitude; but he may also have anticipated that widespread sympathy for tough comital discipline would be generated by publicizing the faults of his unruly and independent vassals. So he appealed to the

Cistercians and to the Pope to assist him. His letter to the abbot of Cîteaux ran:

> I am impotent to put an end to the general desertion of the faith. The task is beyond my feeble resources. The greatest vassals of my dominion are themselves infected with heresy and with them a great number of their subjects. I neither can nor dare impose my will upon them.[14]

The resulting expedition of 1181 persecuted mercenaries at least as much as heretics. But it did cause Alfonso of Aragon to distance himself, at least temporarily, from Roger II of Béziers, and elicited a promise from the Trencavels to suppress heretics. Its true significance, however, lay in the precedent it set: the weapon Raymond V had helped to design, the crusade against heretics, was ultimately to prove fatal to his house.

In this complex world of alliance and counter-alliance, Alphonse-Jourdain and Raymond V made headway—though often only temporarily—in increasing their *mouvance*. Alphonse-Jourdain earned prestige by mediating in 1131 between the count of Melgueil, the bishop of Béziers, and Roger and Raymond Trencavel; later he won the fidelity of the count of Comminges, a blow both to Aragonese and to Angevin pretensions in Gascony. Raymond V became one of William of Montpellier's many overlords in 1164, though he derived little advantage from the connection; more successful in the short term was his marriage alliance with Roger II of Béziers in 1171. But his most solid and lasting *coup* proved to be in persuading Beatrice of Melgueil to cede her county to him in 1171, in expectation of the marriage of her daughter with Raymond's son. The benefit here lay not only in detaching Melgueil from Barcelonese and Montpellieran overlordship, but also in providing Raymond with at least partial control over the Melgueil currency, the commonest coinage circulating with Toulouse. So there was some substance behind Gervase of Tilbury's contention that, although Raymond was always attacked and defeated by Henry of England and Berengar of Barcelona, he cheated them out of their victories by his astuteness.[15] His other success was gained in pursuit of his Provencal ambitions: here, by entering into the lordship of the Emperor Frederick Barbarossa, he won the county of Albon as a fief for his younger son Alberic, the offspring of his second marriage with Richilda of Provence. So his defeat in Provence in 1176 was somewhat sweetened.

By contrast with the fluidity of their control over peripheral areas, within their demesne lands Alphonse-Jourdain and Raymond V chalked up solid achievements. Their most frequent residence, St Gilles, had both wealth and strategic value as a jumping-off point for Provençal campaigns. The Spanish Jew, Benjamin of Tudela, commented that it was a place of pilgrimage for the Gentiles, who came thither from the ends of the earth;[16] its renowned patron saint beckoned those bound for Compostela to call there on their way. But it also had one of the best harbours in the western Mediterranean, from which imported luxury goods could easily be re-exported northwards up the Rhône. Its merchants therefore trafficked with the recently established crusader ports of Outremer, and the Military Orders used the town as a storage centre for goods to be transported to · Palestine. All this was beneficial to the comital treasury. Toulouse, too, continued to provide wealth for its count, at least until 1147, from its well-organized judicial procedures, and from the trade that flowed down the Garonne, linking the Mediterranean with the Atlantic. Even after 1147, when the town's privileges limited the count's right to collect tallages and forced loans at will,[17] he still received an annual tax from its increasingly independent citizen body. In Beaucaire, the Jewish community lay under the count's protection,[18] a valuable financial asset which Raymond owed, whether directly or indirectly, to the Roman-law heritage of Gothia.

Some at least of Raymond's wealth was channelled into the patronage of troubadours, particularly Jaufre Rudel, who sent him one of his songs, and Bertrand de Born, whom he hired to write propaganda against the Barcelonese attack of 1179.[19] Though he achieved no more by this patronage than many lesser lords within Toulouse, it did provide him with at least some counterweight to the northern orientation of his politics, and it may also have made his court a pleasanter place of resort for those whom he obliged to attend, the Trencavels from time to time, and the lords of Toulouse and Albi far more often. For as time went on, Raymond took an increasingly assertive line on his feudal overlordship; in 1171 he required the lords of Verlogues to pay homage to Giraud Amic, whom he had enfeoffed with Verlogues;[20] in 1174 he held a great assembly of his vassals at Beaucaire; and in 1179, in preparation for the war against Barcelona, he enfeoffed his servants with lands in Trencavels' possession, in order to create bonds of mutual interest in prosecuting the campaign.[21]

There were other signs that Raymond was imitating his northern counterparts: firstly, he enforced the peace by the sword within the Toulousain and the Albigeois. The effectiveness of his justice is suggested by an agreement made with the Trencavels that their vassals resident within his lands should be allowed forty days' grace to make reparations after a breach of the peace, before they became liable to comital punishment.[22] A different indication of assertiveness is to be seen in the emergence of a chancery of St Gilles around 1160,[23] which became the chief centre for his government. Affected by Italian and imperial example, the formulae Raymond's chancellors used were impressive: he was regularly referred to as *dux Narbonne, comes Tolose, marchio Provincie*, traditional titles that he had no intention of abandoning. Yet despite his energy and ambition, Raymond had little chance of making the duchy of Gothia a reality; and his attempt to become count as well as marquis of Provence involved relaxing his hold on Toulouse, the real kernel of his power. In fact, his defeat in 1176 strengthened rather than weakened him, by forcing him to concentrate on the area of his greatest potential; for Gothia, Provence, and the Rouergue could never have been more than ephemerally subjected to the rule of Toulouse.

(ii) Burgundy

The twelfth century brought marked prosperity to Burgundy, with the expansion of the wine trade and an increase in commerce on all the major trade routes that crossed the duchy. New villages were created, towns grew, land was cleared;

even inhospitable ground was turned to profit by the Cistercian monks. The growing wealth was ploughed back into church-building of almost unrivalled splendour, into fortifications, and into huge town walls.

Against this background, the somewhat unadventurous external policies of the Burgundian dukes may be ascribed to a canny instinct for long-term self-enrichment; their abstention from heroic enterprise allowed them regular residence within the duchy and protected the old ways in financial administration. After Eudes I's famous Spanish expedition, they abandoned to Toulouse and Aquitaine the leadership of French armies south of the Pyrenees, and while maintaining their links with Portugal on a family level, they risked little for the connection. It is true that crusading in the Holy Land was more attractive—Eudes I died there in 1101, as Duke Hugh III was to do in 1192—but Burgundian contingents were never important elements in twelfth-century crusades. In contrast with the counts of Flanders or those of Toulouse, the dukes of Burgundy kept a low profile on the international scene. Their one notable success outside France—the creation of new ties with the imperial court under Frederick Barbarossa—was achieved, not by the sword but by marriages; Hugh III's two wives, Alix of Lorraine and Beatrice of Albon, brought him fiefs within imperial territory and imperial friendship. Otherwise, the dukes confined their attention to the lands which fell within what had once been Richard the Justiciar's principality, the duchy proper, Chalon, Auxerre, Mâcon, Troyes, Langres, and the surrounding lands.

Here they were conspicuously successful. Slowly they increased their demesne lands, redefined their rights, created personal links, encouraged attendance at their court, till by the end of Hugh III's reign the duchy proper had emerged as an important and extensive landblock, set within counties and episcopal states in which the duke's moral authority had been reinforced by land-acquisitions. Much of this achievement should be ascribed to their good relations with the leading bishops of the area. At a time when other princes were troubled by hostile reformers or the exigencies of adapting their ways to new canon-law norms, the dukes of

Burgundy were able to keep potential church–state conflict within the bounds of family dispute. The bishoprics of Langres and Autun were usually held by ducal clients: Eudes I's younger brother Robert became bishop of Langres, Eudes II's brothers numbered among them two bishops of Autun and one of Langres. And while it is true that this arrangement did not obviate all conflict—Hugh III struggled with his uncle Walter of Langres, Eudes II was even excommunicated by Henry, bishop of Autun—the odd moments of tension counted for far less than the regular years of co-operation, to which the substantial number of ducal fiefs on ecclesiastical land bore witness. Admittedly these fiefs limited the duke's feudal supremacy, because they involved him in paying homage to his bishops; but this was more than compensated for by the solid gains in wealth and power.

In their relations with the great Burgundian abbeys, Hugh II, Eudes II, and Hugh III showed characteristic opportunism. Although most abbeys on their lands were exempt from their jurisdiction, either through old Carolingian immunity or through new free-alms tenure, those that still recognized ducal guardianship were made to pay dearly for the privilege. The ancient right of hospitality was regularly demanded; aids for the marriage of the duke's daughter or for his expenses on crusade became matters of course; the inhabitants of·abbey lands might find themselves liable for military service in the duke's army, as did those of Notre-Dame-de-Châtillon. And other charges on the temporalities of abbey lands were converted into annual taxes for the ducal purse.

But productive though abbeys became, ducal expansion at the expense of laymen was more conspicuous. Here the dukes showed the same hard-headed business sense as their royal cousins. Whenever they could they bought from their financially embarassed social inferiors: in 1113, Hugh II bought Le Châtelet from Savary de Donsy, so gaining a toehold in the county of Chalon, outside ducal control since the end of the tenth century; Eudes II and Hugh III used exchange as a means of obtaining Guy de Saulx's share of the county of Langres. They were not, however, averse to the use of force if it seemed prudent. In 1174 Hugh III captured the count of Nevers and would not release him until he had paid homage for the estates and fiefs he held within the confines of the duchy. The one fly in the ointment was Louis VII who, in the 1160s and 1170s, was pursuing identical methods to extend his estates and *mouvance* within the frontiers of the old Burgundian duchy. Though the cousins at first pursued their objectives without friction, by 1180 it was clear that a real conflict of interest had arisen. Characteristically, it was to be among Philip Augustus' early achievements to provoke war on the issue.

Though limited by royal intrusion, Burgundian ducal lordship expanded rapidly throughout the twelfth century. One clue to the duke's success in convincing hitherto independent lords that there were benefits to be gained by becoming his vassals lies in the plasticity of his lordship. When in 1143 Thibaud IV and II of Champagne met Eudes II on the frontier between their respective territories and agreed to pay homage, he performed an act of courtesy in deference to Burgundy's ancient claims on Troyes. In accepting that both the county and the town of Troyes were held as fiefs of the duke, Thibaud bound himself neither to military service nor to any other burden. His homage, therefore, involved little more than the oath of fidelity which lay at its heart. Yet from Eudes's point of view there was a solid gain in what Lemarignier called this *homage en marche*: it preserved a claim which might otherwise have been totally forgotten, and it cemented an alliance soon to be of great economic import as the Champagne fairs grew.[24]

Thibaud's homage was quite different in character from the ceremony the duke demanded of his castellans. The ducal army depended to a large extent on the efficacy of vassalage. The case of Gaudry of Touillon (who, while engaged in the siege of Grauncey in 1112-13, sought Duke Hugh's permission to leave and enter a monastery, and, on being refused permission, went into battle unarmed)[25] may suggest that the duke did not always derive full benefit from his castellans' scrupulous recognition of their obligations. Nevertheless their compliance was remarkable, given that most were large allodial landholders, dependent on the duke only for their castles. An agreement drawn up between Hugh III and

Ouri II of Bagé in 1185[26] included the stipulation that the duke would act as *defensor*, guardian, for Ouri's castle of Cuisery and its dependencies; if anyone captured them, it was the duke's obligation to restore them to Ouri. If this was typical of Burgundian agreements, then the castellans will have gained security of tenure by an act of vassalage which in return bound them both to fight for the duke and to render up their castles to him on demand. Their acquiescence in discipline becomes comprehensible.

The varying import of vassalage is indicative of the essential character of the duchy: its conservatism, its reliance on personal ties, its absence of inflexible rules. In keeping with this conservatism, the only significant internal governmental developments were the emergence of a proper chancery around 1174, and of the ducal archive around 1180; these provided greater competence in drawing up and preserving the many different agreements with clerics and laymen into which the duke had entered. Seen in this light, the appearance of the ducal archive, the first princely archive in France, should be interpreted rather as a means of preserving the *status quo* than as a revolutionary move towards better government. In other respects, the dukes had no need of governmental innovation. Their financial needs were modest, their lands both prosperous and expanding. Sophisticated methods of audit and account were unnecessary. For them justice continued to be enshrined in arbitration and in the preservation of agreements made; neither Roman law nor feudal systematization made much impact in a land where schools were rare, ecclesiastical power well developed, and fiefs only adjuncts to allodial lands. In the absence of pressure from without, the incentives for change were few.

In one way, however, there was change: the duchy came to be centred on Dijon, to the extent that the duke was referred to in imperial documents as *dux Divionensis*, the duke of Dijon. The essential step in this development came when, after a serious fire in the town in 1137, Eudes II built a new rampart around it and proclaimed his lordship over all within it, so excluding vicecomital and ecclesiastical interests.[27] It was perhaps characteristic of the dukes that they, alone of all the French princes, should establish their capital in a town which was not an episcopal see (Dijon had grown up around the great monastery of St Bénigne, whose guardian was the duke). So from 1137 ducal vassals flocked to Dijon, as did those counts and bishops who had traditionally frequented the ducal court. The great days of the Burgundian duchy were still well in the future at the accession of Philip Augustus. Yet perceptive men, even then, may have foreseen future grandeur; for the absence of internal conflict, the flexibility of personal relations, the goodwill between church and duke, made Burgundy close to the Carolingian ideal. And its prosperity pointed to a potential for rapid development, should that ever seem desirable.

(iii) Blois

Blois began the twelfth century as the senior partner in the family alliance; between 1125 and 1152, it had the same ruler as Champagne; in 1152 it fell to Thibaud IV's younger son and namesake; by 1180, despite Thibaud V's evident ability, it was clearly less important than Champagne. Indeed, the very far-sighted might almost have detected that its closeness to the royal demesne, both physically and emotionally, was beginning to sap its vitality.

The century began well under the formidable Adela, daughter of William the Conqueror, who as regent imported a Norman slant on government; her palace at Chartres, decorated with paintings of Old Testament and classical themes, became a resort for scholars; she introduced a chancery on the English model; she took a tough line on enforcing justice; and she developed vassalic links.[28] But the most notable policy she pursued, her alliance with her brother Henry I of England, seemed to operate in his interests rather than hers. Orderic said of her son Thibaud IV: 'Descended from the stock of kings and counts, (he) was one of the greatest magnates in Gaul; he was endowed with wealth and power and conspicuously high rank, and had many powerful vassals, who were violently hostile to their fellow countrymen and neighbours.'[29] If Suger is to be believed, on one occasion his vassals deserted the count;[30] normally, however, Thibaud's wars on his uncle's behalf suited their book. But fighting was less popular with the church; after a long legal struggle the monastery of Marmoutier won its case that it was not obliged to send troops to Thibaud's armies when he opposed the king.[31] And in the long term, Blois derived no benefit from its count's endless entanglements in Normandy.

Nevertheless, Thibaud's truculence was not unprovoked. In 1101, King Philip I had acquired by purchase the viscounty of Bourges; his son, Louis VI, developed links with the archbishopric of Bourges; and Louis VII systematically built on his inheritance from both.[32] But Upper Berry provided a vital link between the Blois family lands around Chartres and in Champagne; the Berrichon lords within the Blois *mouvance* were a solid asset to the rulers of Blois and Champagne. (In the course of his reign, Thibaud IV won a notable victory in adding the lords of Bourbon to his list). The count therefore could hardly view the royal intrusion in Berry with equanimity. This clash of interests was sharpened when, in 1137, Louis's marriage with Eleanor of Aquitaine united the Capetian kernel at Bourges with substantial Aquitanian interests in Lower Berry. Fear led Thibaud to exploit to the full Louis's conduct over the disputed election to the archbishopric of Bourges in 1144; and St Bernard's intervention turned the incident wholly to the count's advantage. But the resulting alliance between the king and Thibaud could only be maintained by defusing trouble in the Berry area. A joint expedition against Geoffrey le Bel in the Touraine distracted attention from problems closer to home, and had the advantage for Thibaud of creating a strong, though short-term, link with the lord of Amboise.[33] Then Thibaud's concentration on Champagne in the last decade of his life helped to relax the atmosphere.

Even so, it seems that the division of family lands that occurred on Thibaud's death was greeted with relief by the king; for as early as 1154, young Thibaud V was invited to take up the post of the king's seneschal, which he held till he died; in return for loyal service, he also obtained the traditional title of Count Palatine, which one contemporary regarded as making him 'second-in-command within the kingdom'.[34] An amiable, fairly popular man and noted patron of poets, Thibaud V was highly regarded for his learning in the law; but Louis relied on him as much for his advice on economic matters as for his legal knowledge.[35] Respect was enhanced by affection: Thibaud was married to Louis's daughter, Louis maried Thibaud's sister. All in all, Thibaud was a more important figure at the royal court than he was within Blois-Chartres—one of the first of a long line of French princes of whom that could be said.

On the Loire, Thibaud lost the initiative his father had gained at Chaumont, a strategic centre captured from a cadet of the Amboise house;[36] for in 1160 Henry II proved his military skill in a brilliant siege of the castle. And in Berry, Thibaud allowed his friendship with the king to inhibit him from defending his own interests. Within the kernel of his principality, around Chartres, he did contrive to keep alive the old bonds, to attract to his court the great men of the area on whose friendship his rule depended; yet the kind of rule he exercised—based on gentlemen's agreements and traditional goodwill—demanded for its continuance both regular attention and a modicum of external success. Lacking the spur of massive new wealth that animated his brother Henry the Liberal, Thibaud showed neither the dedication nor the forcefulness necessary to build on what he had inherited. It was not that Blois was irretrievably weakened in his time; rather, nothing special was achieved, at a time when achievement was necessary to fight off the challenge of renewed royal authority. As it turned out, Thibaud's passivity was a luxury Blois could ill afford.

(iv) Champagne

As late as 1125 the emergence of a strong principality in Champagne could not have been predicted with any certainty. Squashed between the royal demesne and the great bishoprics of Rheims, Châlons, and Langres, the count of Troyes's lands were of limited geographical extent and agriculturally backward—though the Cistercian houses being planted there, precisely because the county was undeveloped, were achieving large-scale land clearance. The count's feudal position was complicated; he held Meaux of the king, Troyes of the duke of Burgundy, a castellany in Lorraine of the emperor, lands from the archbishops of Sens and Rheims, others from the bishops of Langres and Châlons and the abbot of St Denis. And within the very fluid frontiers of the county, only a few important families recognized that they were his vassals.

Yet by the death of Henry the Liberal in 1181, Champagne had evolved into a state in which the old public rights of the Carolingian past had been gathered back into the count's hands, and in which recognition of the count's feudal supremacy was fast gaining ground. The *Feoda Campanie* of 1172 (see pp. 250-3) demonstrates both: all lords and knights were obliged to serve Henry in time of war; comital control over all fortifications was taken for granted in the elaborate arrangements for castle-guard; and almost half the aristocracy owned the count as their liege lord. In order to ensure the proper performance of military service, Henry ordered his great vassals to reside on their fiefs;[37] along with the foot-soldiers recruited from the towns, they constituted a solid defence force for the county. Unlike his fellow princes, Henry the Liberal took but little part in wars beyond his frontiers—his personal authority was enhanced in fields other than those of battle—so his military needs were more than satisfied by these measures.

The double exploitation of Carolingian and feudal rights was also evident in his developing jurisdiction. As early as 1161, in a charter for St Loup, he moved to exclude justice of blood from the jurisdiction of an ecclesiastical institution; this became his regular policy when he confirmed privileges.[38] His own court therefore had to step into the breach. But at the same time, the growing circle of his vassals looked to him for judgement in their quarrels and for protection. The resulting increase in the business of his courts led to the emergence of a fully developed chancery. This, along with the highly successful exploitation of the count's exclusive rights over coinage[39] and the innovative bureaucracy evident in *Feoda Campanie*, made Champagne a shining example of adminstrative competence which had a profound impact on Henry's nephew, the young Philip Augustus.

The contrast between 1125 and 1181 demands explanation. By the second half of the twelfth century, there were of course both Flemish and Norman precedents to be followed. Commercial contacts with Flanders were strengthened by personal friendships and by a cultural similarity which made it natural for Chrétien de Troyes to seek patronage at both courts. And it may have been Henry's wife's relationship with the English royal family that facilitated the borrowing of Norman administrative methods in *Feoda Campanie*. Yet the model which inspired Henry's sudden and rapid acquisition of rights could equally well have been German—as a close friend of Frederick Barbarossa, he can hardly have been ignorant of Frederick's claim, set forth at the Diet of Roncaglia, to regalian rights within Italy. This provided a heady example of the uses of law and history to a ruler of a land in which existing custom provided only a frail framework for power.

But the interesting question is rather how Henry was able to make good his claims. And the answer to this lies at least partly in his father's reign. For it was Thibaud IV (1102-52) who, when he inherited Troyes and Meaux in 1125, made the crucial decision to take up residence there rather than in Chartres, his own and his family's traditional home, and on his death, to leave Champagne to his eldest son. Thibaud's choice was perhaps inspired by fear; Louis VI favoured the succession of his uncle's illegitimate son Eudes of Champlites, so Thibaud had to fight for Champagne. Nevertheless the move to Troyes loosened Thibaud's ties with his uncle Henry I of England, provided a counter-attraction to the Anglo-Norman succession in 1135 (which he left to his brother Stephen), and in the long term smoothed the path to good relations with Louis VII, which Henry the Liberal was careful to cultivate.

A second consequence of the move to Champagne was Thibaud's chance to see much of St Bernard, who became an intimate friend, and whose companionship shed on Thibaud the lustre of a secular hero, a twelfth-century version of Gerald of Aurillac. Like Gerald, Thibaud wished to withdraw into the cloister, but was persuaded that he could better perform God's work in the role to which he had been called. So he patronized the Cistercian houses in his county, particularly Clairvaux; he became, in the words of one of his contemporaries, 'the father of orphans, shield of widows, eye of the blind, foot of the lame,'[40] and established a reputation for good rule which, as late as the end of the twelfth century, still made him a natural choice as model prince in Gerald of Wales's *De Instructione Principum*.[41] In narrowly political terms, Bernard's friendship ensured for him moral domination over the young Louis VII. In 1144 Louis attacked Champagne to secure the nomination of his own candidate to the see of Bourges (against the papal nominee whom Thibaud was protecting). St Bernard's appalled reaction to Louis's behaviour had so deep an impact upon the young king that his decision to take the pilgrim route to Jerusalem was probably connected with it, and his attitude towards Thibaud changed over night to one of respectful admiration.

There was, however, a third and much more concrete advantage of the move to Troyes: the time was exactly ripe for the counts to reap advantage from the growing commerce across their eastern territories. The favourable situation was due largely to developments far beyond their control: to the opening of Mediterranean ports through the conquests of Sicily and Outremer; to the Italian cities' response in building up merchant fleets; and to the widespread demand for Flemish cloth in northern and Mediterranean lands. The transport of cloth from Flanders to Italy automatically followed the old river routes, the Seine and Marne across northern France, the Saône and Rhône down to the Alpine crossings. Therefore Champagne lay at the crossroads, forming the natural meeting-place for Flemish cloth-sellers and Italian merchants. But if Thibaud and Henry were lucky, they exploited their luck with great skill. For until the fourth decade of the century, the most important trade route had run through the episcopal cities of Langres, Châlons, and Rheims. By dint of offering merchants efficient protection, properly organized fairs under comital peace, and an abundance of sound local currency in which to conduct their business, Thibaud and Henry diverted much of this traffic through their own lands. The six great Champagne fairs, two each year in Troyes, two in Provins, one at Bar-sur-Aube and one at Lagny (all comital towns), were proof of organizational flair; they also produced, in tolls and customs-dues, a substantial income for the hitherto not outstandingly affluent comital house.[42]

But fairs in Champagne could not flourish unless the princes of the neighbouring areas were sympathetic to their existence. Thibaud took the vital step of cementing friendship with Flanders by a treaty of 1143, which Henry later ratified. In the same year, the long-term good will of the duke of Burgundy was secured when Thibaud paid homage, accepting that Troyes was held as a ducal fief, in a ceremony on the frontiers of the duchy which has been hailed as one of the most important northern illustrations of *hommage en paix*—homage which created no implication of service but established mutual trust.[43] The following year, after Louis VII's burning of Vitry, peace was secured with the royal demesne. So all the major access-routes to the county were then open.

In the next reign, Henry the Liberal complemented alliances with neighbours by clever but strictly limited diplomatic advances further afield. He cultivated courteous exchanges with Henry II of England, married to his mother-in-law, as a sufficient excuse for his amiable determination to remain outside the quarrels between Henry and Louis. He sought the goodwill of Frederick Barbarossa, whom he was proud to acknowledge as his overlord for a Lorraine castellany; yet he did not allow this bond to draw him more than fleetingly into Frederick's ecclesiastical policies or his ambitious campaigns abroad. Beneath his courtly manners, Henry measured out friendship with the spoon of self-interest. And he was as swift to follow his own advantage in family policy as in friendships. Soon after he succeeded his father in 1152, he achieved a major diplomatic *coup* in acquiring Louis VII's two daughters by Eleanor of Aquitaine as brides for himself and his brother. His wife Marie shed lustre on his court as well as bringing his children royal blood. But the death of the king's second wife brought an even better opportunity: Henry urged Louis to take his sister Adela as a bride, sweetening the choice by a dowry of much-desired land to the north-east of the royal demesne. Henry prevailed, though others thought the sister of a mere count unsuitable to be queen of France. Philip Augustus, the fruit of this marriage, was to feel somewhat threatened in the first year of his reign by the intimidating presence of his three uncles, the count of Champagne, the count of Blois, and the formidable William Whitehands, archbishop of Sens, then Rheims. Only Henry the Liberal's death in 1181 eased the tension.

The combination of peace, prestige, and wealth the counts of Champagne enjoyed, at least from 1144 to 1181, had a powerful attractive force for their lords. If the riches accruing from the fairs were shared in some measure by other lords within the county, it would explain their acquiescence in the count's more demanding lordship, as exemplified in *Feoda Campanie*. Straight bribery is another possible explanation; Walter Map declared that Henry's sobriquet, 'the Liberal' was well deserved.[44] In any case as Henry's own career demonstrated, it need not always be assumed that all benefits in a feudal relstionship were derived by the lord, even if lords were more inclined to keep a record of other men's obligations to them than of their own. To be a vassal of a man of Henry's European standing was an honour; for the court of Champagne was a noble and distinguished one. Although recent research has painted it as a more sober and learned place than nineteenth-century historians, lured by the writings of Andreas Capellanus, conceived,[45] nevertheless the knightly arts were encouraged, poets found patronage, and men of influence from across France and Germany were drawn there. Some of the great lords of Champagne may have shared Henry's taste for theology (commended by John of Salisbury)[46] or his interest in monastic discipline. And those who did not might still appreciate the standing they conferred—as Nicholas the Monk wrote to Henry 'Holding the balance between the literate and the knightly orders, you make both magnificent.'[47] For Champagne and Burgundy, alone among the principalities of France, shared with the royal court that old, relaxed relationship between churchmen and the laity which had elsewhere been the victim of reforming zeal. The count guarded the monasteries, appointed the bishops of Troyes, protected Becket, and co-operated with his formidable brother, William of the Whitehands, Archbishop of Rheims. The Cistercians' firm loyalty to his family survived his very brief flirtation with the anti-pope Victor IV and proved a source of real moral support throughout his reign. Nicholas the Monk may not have been alone in seeing in Henry the Platonic ideal of the philosopher-statesman.

(v) Flanders

By the beginning of the twelfth century, the people of Flanders saw themselves as a community, knit together under the rule of their count, distinguished from their neighbours both politically and culturally. Galbert of Bruges spoke of Flanders as *nostra patria* (our country), its count as *naturalis dominus et princeps*, natural lord and prince;[48] the same self-awareness emerged in a more emotional form in a poem *De Laude Flandriae* (In praise of Flanders) written about 1100 by Petrus Pictor, a canon of St Omer.[49] The twelfth-century counts of Flanders, sensitive to this, exploited and fulfilled their people's expectations, by playing a dashing and chivalric role on the European scene.

The backdrop to the century of Flanders' greatness was steadily increasing prosperity. The cloth industry, which had spurted in the last years of the eleventh century, became, by the second half of the twelfth, Europe's most significant money-spinner, supplying the growing markets of the west, penetrating to Scandinavia and Italy, even in increasing quantities to Byzantium and the East. Arras, Douai, Ypres, Lille, St Omer, Ghent, and Bruges spread, grew rich and sophisticated on the profits of their workers' labours. Flanders developed her international links: with England and to a lesser extent Spain, as suppliers of her wool; with Champagne and Italy, as middlemen in her trade; with those areas of France, particularly Picardy and the royal demesne, which could supply the grain her increased population found essential. From being a well-governed but comparatively isolated northern frontier post, Flanders became the hub of the Atlantic seaboard area. Hardly surprisingly, the rapidity of the change created tensions within Flemish society, as expanding urban societies attempted to fit into the conventional political framework. All this brought new challenges for the counts, whose role as peace-keepers grew more arduous in a more complex society. Until the death of Philip of Alsace in 1191, the counts of Flanders contrived brilliantly to control the new situation; but the task was always harder than their brilliance revealed; disruptive forces were never far from the surface.

The chief efforts of Baldwin VII (1111-19) and Charles the Good (1119-27) were devoted to converting the *pax Dei* into the *pax comitis*, to providing security for merchants on the highway and at fairs by establishing long-term and tight control over criminal jurisdiction within the county. Following the precedents of Robert I and Robert II, they undermined the old reliance on episcopal judgements and sanctions for enforcing peace, substituting a harsh, violent, but effective system of secular courts under comital control. From the start of the century, they maintained the right to judge infractions of the criminal law by knights in their own courts. Baldwin VII executed justice ferociously; Herman of Tournai recounts that on one occasion, he ordered a knight who had stolen a poor woman's cows to be boiled alive; on another, he forced ten violators of the peace to hang each other in succession, helping the tenth to his death with his own hands.[50] His successor Charles the Good was noted for his harsh punishment of those who oppressed the poor, and for his refusal to allow the lords of maritime Flanders to carry bows and arrows.[51] Under the princes of the house of Alsace, Thierry (1128-63) and Philip (1163-91), there was a drive to express the *pax comitis* in more legalistic form. As they confirmed charters they reserved to the comital court all cases involving the death penalty or fines of £60 or above; then they ordered substantial increases in the size of fines normally levied. In the charter of Furnes, Thierry elaborated a system for tracking down criminals, and stipulated inquest as the standard means of trying them.[52] These achievements were in every way as remarkable as those of Henry I and Henry II of England in the field of criminal law.

However legal reform was not confined to the sphere of crime. Thierry and Philip moved in the direction of standardizing legal custom across the country, by exerting on the beneficiaries of charters a pressure toward conformity. This was particularly noticeable after 1178, when Philip imposed a new uniformity in urban law, putting an end to the period in which the *boni homines* of Bruges at least had been free to develop their own customs, by his insistence on the count's role as the ultimate controlling force in all law throughout the county.[53] His example was to have a potent effect on his godson, Philip Augustus, who was in many ways his disciple.

If the legal achievements of Thierry and Philip were outstanding, their administrative improvements did not fall far short. They began the century with a competent network of officials—the receivers in each castellany, the chancellor at St Donatian's in Bruges; but as revenues soared from judicial fines, tolls and customs, and new demesne lands, the old machinery began to seem inadequate. By the second half of the century, Philip was experimenting with *baillis*, salaried officials appointed by the count and dismissible at will; their chief function was to collect occasional comital revenues within the castellany, but they could also be relied on to implement comital mandates, to undertake a whole host of petty administrative tasks, to ensure that the judicial tribunals operated according to law and that their judgements were enforced. In the thirteenth century, *baillis* were to achieve a more clearly defined role in Flemish administration; but even in their experimental days, they substantially increased the count's executive arm. Their employment was probably a factor in the appearance of the *Grote Bref*, the first comital account, of 1187[54] (see p. 285).

The *Grote Bref* illustrates the competence of the chancery at Bruges, which produced the roll and added up the sums. This was also manifested in the large number of charters produced—over 600 survive for the reigns of Thierry and Philip—and in the professionalism that came to characterize their form. The priest Philip of Harvengt commented on the number of learned laymen to be found at Philip of Alsace's court;[55] there were plenty of tasks for them to perform. Among these was the provision of an adequate and stable coinage for the great fairs of the county. By the second half of the century, the treasuries at Bruges and Veurne had developed a system of assaying money by weight, to check the purity of the silver, so that neither the count nor others should suffer the effects of unintentional debasement. Comital officials could function effectively in all these spheres in the princes' frequent absences on crusade or on wars; yet when they were present, Thierry and Philip controlled their incipient bureaucracies in a highly personal way.

As bureaucracy increased, the castellans withdrew from administration, and concentrated on the military role. At the same time, their ranks were permeated by greater families, sometimes even by men of distinction from outside the county—the lords of Nesle and Soissons, for example, became hereditary castellans of Bruges.[56] But their political influence was limited by the prohibition of private war throughout the county, which left the count as the only man entitled to summon troops to battle. The potential size of the Flemish army was increased substantially by the urban militias, supplying vitally needed foot-soldiers. Although after 1127 any Flemish knight who wished to buy himself out of military service could do so, the count was still able to attract up to one thousand five hundred knights to his array. The problem of keeping all these troops occupied explained the proliferation of tournaments within the county, and perhaps had some connection with the frequent expeditions to Jerusalem; Philip's reputation as a warrior may not have been entirely unforced.

When the story is told like this, it achieves a certain inevitability: wealth leading to administrative and legal development, ensuring military power. Yet a brief consideration of the events of 1127-8, the only period of breakdown in the century, soon reveals that ruling Flanders in a period of social change was far from easy. The implications of these events for the growing independence of Flemish towns have already been discussed (see p. 271). It also seems that the Erembalds' murder of Charles the Good came as a relief to at least one section of the old Flemish aristocracy, which had resented Charles's tough enforcement of the peace.[57] For these men, Clito's initial success in reasserting comital control provided the spur to seek other claimants. Had their interests been identical with those of the towns, chaos might have reigned for longer; in fact the cloth towns' determination to have Thierry, and Thierry's own adroit handling of them, brought the anarchy to an end relatively soon. But the count still faced a long uphill battle against discontented lords. For while a year's absence of strong government had been enough

to convince most Flemings that comital justice, harsh though
it was, was an improvement on civil war, aristocratic sensibilities remained easily wounded by comital punishment.
Skill in propitiating as well as strength in subduing were
therefore essential to effective lordship in Flanders.

Abroad, diplomacy was as necessary as at home. The
counts walked a tightrope of conflicting loyalties as liegemen
of the French kings, fief-holders of the emperor, and close
friends of the Engish kings. Loyal vassals of Louis VII, they
were embarrassed by his conflict with Henry II, both on
account of the long-standing military agreements which
bound them to lavish aid for English kings in time of war,
and because there were close family ties (Henry II was
Thierry's nephew by marriage). Only the conflict among
Henry's sons let Philip off the hook; he supported the Young
King against his father in 1173—though perhaps because he
did not expect him to win. On the other hand, Philip's own
ambitions in Picardy created a source of potential conflict
with Louis which it needed all his tact to defuse. His determination that the young Philip Augustus should marry his
niece Isabella of Hainault may have been intended as a long-
term solution to this problem; in the event it proved disastrous for Flanders, for on Isabella's death her dowry, the
Artois, remained in the king's hands as an apanage for their
son, the future Louis VIII. So on the international scene
the only relaxed relationship Philip enjoyed was with the
emperor; Frederick Barbarossa's policy of conciliating all his
great princes allowed the counts of Flanders to sit as
imperial dignitaries at the great diets, while slowly pushing
back the frontiers of their imperial fief at the emperor's
expense.

Closer to home, the house of Alsace enjoyed a long run of
good luck in the south of the county. Boulogne, so independent and powerful in the early years of the twelfth century,
was successfully claimed on William's death for Philip's
younger brother and heir presumptive Matthew (though to
obtain it he had to drag Matilda, daughter of King Stephen
of England and the last surviving member of the Boulonnais
comital family, out of her abbey at Romsey and force her
into marriage); on Matthew's death, Philip acted as guardian

for his daughter Ida.[58] Then around 1151, Hesdin and the lordship of Lillers escheated to Thierry; in 1160 Lens too came into comital hands. So, with the exception of the formidable counts of St Pol—who nibbled away at Flemish lands from the edges of their county—and the lesser counts of Guînes, all the other great independent fiefs of southern Flanders were at least temporarily resumed. The path to further expansion in Picardy was now invitingly open; and Philip's marriage to the heiress of Vermandois had ensured that he would take it.

Walter Map said of Philip: 'Of all the princes of these days, except our own king, he is the mightiest in arms and in the art of ruling.'[59] *Flandria generosa* held him worthy of comparison with one of the Maccabees in what he achieved for Flanders.[60] Though not a crowned head and careful never to exceed his comital title, Philip was a major political force in Europe. John of Salisbury pressed him into service as an arbiter between Henry II and Becket; William of Tyre saw him as a potential regent for Jerusalem. Drawing on the wealth of his principality, Philip made his court a centre for chivalry and the knightly arts, in virtue of which he received the dedication of Chrétien de Troyes's *Perceval*. His was a remarkably secular lordship, owing little to papal friendship, monastic protection, or episcopal co-operation. Like Henry II, he was remembered for his wealth, his military prowess, his good adminstration, and his harsh judicial innovation. For most of his life he overshadowed Louis VII of France; as a consequence, he earned Philip Augustus' dislike; and Flanders never quite recovered from the blows the new king was to inflict on it.

(vi) Normandy

The link with England framed the political and institutional history of Normandy in the first four decades of the twelfth century, conferring on the duchy a distinctive character that survived and outlasted even Philip Augustus' conquest of 1203-4. The strong exploitative lordship to which it was subjected caused a rapid evolution of government and bureaucracy, an unusually sharp development of feudal obligations, and a marked subjection of the church's temporalities to ducal control. Normandy's integrity was, by twelfth-century standards, impressive. Yet between 1089 and 1144 it was a prey to succession-disputes which had no parallel elsewhere in France; for the duchy was worth fighting for; and its neighbours had incentives to encourage strife.

On Henry I's accession to the English throne in 1099, his first task was to secure stability in England by conquering Normandy; because only when Robert Curthose's and his son William Clito's claims to the duchy were extinguished could those English barons who held lands on both sides of the channel rest easily in their loyalty to Henry. The battle of Tinchebrai in 1106, a brilliant victory for Henry, should therefore have put an end to rival claims. That it did not, despite the overwhelming support Henry now enjoyed within Normandy itself, was due to the self-interested backing Clito received from neighbouring prices. Prince Louis had cashed in on the English succession crisis of 1099 to ensure his hold on the Vexin français, which Rufus had attacked, and also to drive into the Vexin normand, which he hoped to annex. The count of Maine—a local lord whose title to the office was through marriage and unacceptable to Rufus—had benefited by the breathing-space to re-establish himself in the county and reassert links with Anjou. Fulk had greeted this development with enthusiasm. Even Baldwin VII of Flanders, though protective of the English wool-trade, had found relief in 1099; for he worried about Norman interests in Ponthieu (whose count William the Conqueror appears to have secured a vassal) and also in Boulogne, a Flemish fief but an English ally. The coalition therefore upheld Clito's claims by force of arms. In battle Henry, ably backed by Thibaud of Blois, usually had the advantage. But he had more to lose than his opponents. Then bad luck, in the shape of the death of his only legitimate son William in 1120, deprived him of the benefits that had thus far accrued to him, and kept alive Clito's chances of succession.

Prince William's death necessitated a complete reframing of alliances for Henry, especially when, in 1127, Clito became count of Flanders. At this moment, when his enemies appeared to hold all the trump cards, he sought to secure the succession of his daughter Matilda, widow of the Emperor

Henry V, to the throne of England and the duchy of Normandy, by marrying her to Geoffrey le Bel of Anjou. It was
a step of desperation. Its immediate consequence was the
expected one of detaching the Angevins from the pro-Clito
alliance; yet that alliance itself foundered with Clito's death
at the battle of Aalst in 1128. In the medium term, the
results of the marriage were disastrous, because it proved the
biggest factor in making Matilda unacceptable as ruler to
the Norman barons; for whatever Henry might think of
Geoffrey, to the Normans he was an old enemy whose
dominance in Maine filled them with resentment. So they
supported Stephen of Blois's candidature, and faced Geoffrey's wrath. The marriage therefore plunged Normandy
ino a war that did not end before Geoffrey's total conquest of the duchy in 1144; and it also brought anarchy
to England. But in the long term, the son of that marriage,
Henry II, as ruler over both Normandy and Anjou, brought
peace to Maine and, until 1173, concord both with Flanders
and with Louis VII.

1144 was therefore a turning-point in the duchy's history.
The old Norman dynasty was gone—it was noticeable that
Geoffrey, who had no love for his wife, encouraged her
absence in England—and the duchy was now part of a larger
French unit. Although Geoffrey was scrupulous in observing
Normandy's administrative independence, and largely relied
on its existing household for his operations, there were
innovations. The appearance of baillages in his reign—
districts over which a salaried official maintained control of
the *prévôts* and performed unspecified administrative,
financial, and judicial tasks,[61]—suggests that the heavy
outside commitments of the Angevin duke-count stimulated
internal administrative reform (it perhaps also explains the
difference between Norman *baillis* and English sheriffs, which
used to puzzle those who took it for granted that the latter
were models for the former). More importantly, the succession-
disputes were over; and the elimination of Maine as a trouble-
spot altered the politics of north-west France. Then Geoffrey
moved to propitiate Louis VII, who, in any case, had favoured
the Angevin advance because he had feared that Stephen
would swing the whole might of England behind Thibaud IV,

still his enemy. So, as soon as the fighting was over, Geoffrey did homage in person to Louis for Normandy; and in 1151, when he handed over the duchy to his young son Henry, he made the prince go to Paris and pay liege homage at the very start of his career.[62] This symbolized an important change for Normandy: it was no longer ruled by a family at odds with the French king that regarded obeisance as demeaning; its new rulers were bred of a dynasty conspicuous for its loyalty, the oldest and staunchest royal allies in the kingdom. The omens for a quieter life were good.

And indeed Normandy did benefit until 1173. Admittedly there were tensions elsewhere, particularly in Aquitaine after Eleanor's marriage with Henry in 1152, and in Anjou, where Louis backed his one-time enemy Thibaud IV in an attack on the Touraine. But these were localized affairs. It was only with the Young King's revolt against his father in 1173, and Louis's rather cynical exploitation of the situation, that war broke out once more on the Norman frontier. Then Philip of Flanders entered the duchy from the north-east, Louis from the south-east, and the Breton rebels from the south-west. But the strength of Henry's position within Normandy was swiftly attested in the humiliating defeats he imposed on his enemies; in 1174 Louis's siege of Rouen was raised with almost contemptuous ease. The great rebellion was over. Henry's reputation as a giant among his contemporaries had been vindicated. Yet, in the relief which followed, his embittered sons were driven into closer relations with the court at Paris, an alliance which threatened Henry for the rest of his reign, and to which, as an old man, he finally succumbed.

The decisive factor in Norman military history was the loyalty of the barons to Henry I and to Henry II. In many ways, it was an unexpected phenomenon- since, though both kings spent much of their working lives in Normandy, they had other commitments that inhibited the growth of friendship with their barons, and the justiciars who represented them in their absence might either alienate baronial sympathies or centre loyalties on themselves. Besides, the kings made heavy demands on their lords, yet denied them the compensation of local independence. On the other hand,

Le Patourel has pointed out that, for those who possessed cross-Channel estates—the Bigod earls of Norfolk, the Mohun family, the lords of Aumale, Boulogne, Eu, Chester, Mortimer, and Wigmore, the Mowbray and Lacy families—the relief of obeying only one ruler in both their territorial blocks was sufficient to account for the large measure of support they gave Henry I and Henry II.[63] The overall number of families that found themselves under this constraint cannot be established; and it does seem clear that, by the reign of Henry II, cross-Channel estates were becoming rarer. However, the argument points to a wider truth: all Norman barons knew they could rely on Henry I and Henry II to protect their possessions, against external enemies by the sword, against internal ones by the law. They initially favoured Stephen's succession because they thought he would do likewise; his failure and Geoffrey le Bel's good sense in not disinheriting his erstwhile opponents convinced them of their error. It was not to be until 1203-4, in the face of an army backed by huge resources and led by a king of iron will, that the Norman barons, pragmatists as they were, yielded and abandoned their loyalty to the house of Anjou. And it was illustrative of Normandy's unusual homogeneity that then the whole duchy (except the Channel Islands) went over to Philip in a matter of months.

Therefore the internal government of Normandy, for all its harshness and exploitative character, was in itself an inspiration to loyalty in that it provided a guarantee of security; in a sense, it was part of the 'customs' of the duchy, to which all Normans were fiercely attached. By posing as his grandfather's true successor, Henry II showed understanding of this, and also deprived his critics of the only allegation—innovation—that might, in a highly conservative society, carry weight against him. According to Robert of Torigny, in 1171 Henry

caused an investigation to be made throughout Normandy as to the lands which King Henry his grandfather had held on the day of his death; and inquiry was also made into what lands, woods, and other property had been occupied by barons and other men since the death of King Henry his grandfather; and by this means he doubled his income.[64]

The principle here was the same as that which lay behind the inquest into knights' fees also described by Robert of Torigny (see p. 252): time did not run against the duke; what he had once enjoyed should continue to be his, unless of his grace he chose to grant it away. When this was formulated clearly, in the late thirteenth century, its deleterious results for aristocratic privilege could be plainly detected. In the twelfth century, however, it sounded a reassuringly conservative note, even if the results were always to the duke's advantage. The procedure employed to ascertain the duke's rights was that of sworn inquest, used occasionally under Henry I, and made part of the normal machinery under Geoffrey le Bel[65]—to the eye of the historian, a notable innovation; to Geoffrey's contemporaries a revived Carolingian form.

The duke's position as defender of the law and keeper of the peace lay at the heart of the loyalty he evoked. Again, there was a substantial increase in ducal jurisdictional competence during the century: by the end of Henry II's reign it was accepted that the duke might declare the law, particularly in cases where there was confusion in custom, and that he might claim as monopolies for his own court the 'pleas of the sword'—declared in a list drawn up before 1174 to include murder and manslaughter, mayhem, robbery, arson, rape, and premediated assault, along with offences against the peace of the house, the plough, the duke's highway, his court or his coinage.[66] Then, so that the duke's rights could be translated into action, he might appoint justices, whether local or itinerant, to hold courts across the duchy; and he might be represented in court in his absence by his justiciar. Although all these developments owed something to English practice, they were direct growths from the Norman past; English and Norman laws were kept distinct. To the Norman lords, Henry's extensions were simply a reassertion of the traditional authority that Dudo of St Quentin had ascribed to Rollo and William Longsword.

Peace-keeping and inquests touched everyone.[67] Henry's lords were in all probability only dimly aware of the administrative developments that facilitated efficiency in these fields, which historians have hailed as major triumphs. Of these, the most important was the exchequer. Its evolution was stimulated by Henry I's repeated absences from the duchy and by his urgent need for money to finance the wars in which he ceaselessly wore himself out until 1128. Because no Pipe Roll (statement of account) survived for Normandy before 1180 (though in the eighteenth century a roll for 1136 was said to be extant), the exchequer's procedure in its early years is a matter for conjecture. But there is a strong probability that it bore a marked resemblance to its twin in England, both in the methods of account used and in the efficiency with which it policed the activities of local officials. The roll of 1198 showed receipts for Normandy as 98,000 pounds Angevin—£24,500,[68] (a sum surprisingly much larger than that for Flanders in the *Grote Bref* of 1187, around £10,000. The difference is probably to be explained by omissions in the *Grote Bref*; nevertheless it attests the Norman exchequer's competence).

The exchequer clerks were only part of a growing bureaucracy in the duchy. When Henry II became king, he preferred the advice and help of 'new men' rather than those he had inherited from this father.[69] His reign was a period of experimentation, in which many officials simply carried out *ad hoc* commissions, and few had precise names or duties. Nevertheless they formed a solid corpus devoted to fulfilling the duke's will; from the lowest *prévôt* up through the *baillis*, the viscounts, the justices, to the justiciar himself, they expected to receive writs, to carry out orders, and to answer before the duke's court for their conduct of their duties. As his secretary, Peter of Blois, recorded of Henry:

He does not linger in his palaces like other kings, but hunts through the provinces enquiring into everyone's doings and especially judges those whom he has made judge of others.[70]

The furious energy of the Angevins made Henry a dominant force to be reckoned with; it would therefore have needed extraordinary perception to see that the age of personal government was slowly giving way to that of bureaucracy. In fact norms were being established which would, in the future, restrain the duke himself; in the long term, the guarantee of Norman customs was to be found rather in its civil service than in the person of its duke. But

this was something the Norman barons only discovered after
1203-4.

(vii) Brittany

The most distinguished son of Brittany, Peter Abelard, dismissed it as 'a barbarous land with an unknown language
and a brutal and savage population',[71] and Baudry of Dol
bemoaned his exile from Angevin territory, saying that in
Brittany 'I dwell among scorpions, surrounded by a double
wall of bestiality and perfidy'.[72] But for its natives, the
beginning of the twelfth century was a time of unaccus-
tomed peace, prosperity, and cultural flowering. There were
at last friendly relations with Normandy; Alan Fergent IV
recognized Norman suzerainty without a struggle, and
rendered invaluable assistance to Henry I at the battle of
Tinchebrai in 1106; he was presumably a party to the agreement at Gisors in 1113, when Louis VI was forced to accept
that Brittany was a Norman fief; he married a daughter of
William the Conqueror, and his son's wife was Maud, illegitimate daughter of Henry I. At the same time, Alan cultivated
cordiality with Anjou: his second wife was a daughter of
Fulk, and Breton soldiers were sent to assist the count of
Anjou in attacking the brigands who infested his lands. So
Breton scholars were welcomed at the schools of Angers,
while Angevin churchmen took up appointments in Brittany.
The high wall behind which Breton culture had hidden was
in the process of being lowered, with effects on either side
of the barrier: this was the time at which the great Breton
hero, King Arthur, took his place in the French *chansons
de geste*.

External threats were small. The real problem lay within
the duchy: the extensive ducal demesne, the product of
successful marriage alliances, was difficult to keep intact;
local officials tended to usurp revenues, castellans asserted
rights of lordship. And beyond the demesne, the duke's
relations with other lords within the duchy were ill-defined
—so ill-defined as to make his lordship often nominal.
Homage may have been done but, if so, the obligations
which accompanied it were of the slightest, and there are
only very rare indications of ducal courts. In the reign of

Alan's successor Conan III (1112-48), there was a serious internal rebellion led by Robert de Vitré, with some Angevin complicity, which inflicted grave humiliation on Conan before he eventually suppressed it; the rebels' support came from the small lordships on the borders between Brittany, Maine, and Normandy, a particulary vulnerable point.

Ducal administration has left very few records, which would suggest that it was of a primitive and highly personal kind. Yet it cannot have been ineffectual, for both Alan and Conan were able to mobilize armies for the defence of their Norman overlords and even, on occasion, to assist the king of France. In 1127 Conan attempted to deprive local lords of their right to wrecks washed up on their shores; since they had often been responsible for the destruction, it is unlikely that he met with cooperation in this matter.[73] Rather more subtle and persuasive was his use of a church council, convened to plan ecclesiastical reform, to produce a decree abolishing the vestiges of slavery within the duchy, an act later fortified by a papal letter.[74] Both these measures point to a strengthening of ducal initiative, which was perhaps only to be expected at a time when the Norman overlords were distracted by their own problems.

On Conan's death, a succession-crisis occurred: Conan had one son, Hoël, whom he chose to dispossess in favour of his daughter Berthe and her husband Alan the Black; but before Conan's own death, Alan died (1146); Berthe then married Eudes of Porhoët—by far the most important lord in the duchy—who was generally recognized as duke. Inevitably, though, his position was challenged by Hoël, Berthe's bother, who seized Nantes by force. In 1156 the people of Nantes rose up against Hoël, expelled him, and appealed for protection to Henry II of England, presumably in his capacity as duke of Normandy, therefore overlord of Brittany. Henry was happy to intervene, especially because he already had living at his court Conan, son of Berthe and Alan the Black, whom he had recognized as the legitimate holder of the English honour of Richmond. In September 1156, Conan IV crossed into Brittany and claimed the duchy, excluding Nantes, which was given to Henry II's brother Geoffrey (thus extricating Henry from

an embarrassing position, for he had recently disinherited
Geoffrey in Anjou, contrary to the terms of his father's
will). Henry had every reason to feel pleased. A duke of
Brittany who was both vassal of the duke of Normandy
for the duchy, and vassal of the king of England for the
honour of Richmond, was tightly bound to his lord. This
was demonstrated when, on Geoffrey's death in 1158, Conan
tried to seize Nantes. In no time, Henry secured his own
possession of the city, humiliated Conan, and demonstrated his impotence. Using Nantes as a centre, Henry's
troops subdued the troublesome marcher barons; in 1166
they levelled the castle of Fougères, a long-time haven for
rebels. The ease with which this was achieved convinced
Henry that Conan was either unable or unwilling to control
his vassals and force his lordship upon them. (In fact, Conan
may simply have been rather more sensitive to Breton custom
than his formidable overlord.) So in the autumn of 1166,
Henry betrothed Conan's daughter Constance to his own
son Geoffrey, persuaded Conan to retire, and formally took
possession of the duchy in his son's name.

From 1166 to 1181, while Brittany was ruled by Henry
as regent, its whole internal organization was overhauled.
The extensive demesne was fully exploited for the first
time, and added to by the annexation of Penthièvre (on the
death of its count in 1170) and by a considerable slice of
Porhoët after Eudes's unsuccessful rebellion of 1173. The
wealth and manpower of this large land-block supplied what
was needed for an effective administration, now committed
to the seneschal of Brittany, the king's trusted servant,
who issued writs and carried out the day-to-day business
of government. It may hve been in this period that the duchy
was divided into eight *baillages*, each with its own seneschal
to control the *prévôts* and to ensure the operation of
justice.[75] There are signs, too, that royal ordinance was
used to modify existing legal customs, at least in relation
to surety for debt. And Henry obtained election of his
clients to the sees of Rennes, Nantes, and Dol, a necessary
preliminary to enjoying better relations with the church
than his predecessor had achieved.

What the Breton lords thought of Angevin government is

not clear. Eudes of Porhoët's rebellion was followed in 1179 by a rising led by the viscount of Léon; but the ease with which this was crushed does not suggest widespread support The others may, however, have been restrained more by fear than by contentment. But if quiescence was all that could be expected from the aristocracy, Angevin rule brought solid advantage to lesser men. Breton independence had, in the past, cut her off from the enjoyment of her strategic commercial position at the mouth of the Loire; now traffic could flow as easily as the currents of that treacherous river would allow. Then fears of Angevin or Norman attack were finally stilled; and Brittany participated in the twelfth-century renaissance. It is true that this development meant the surrender of its distinctive cultural tradition—no small loss, but inevitable as the tide of ecclesiastical reform swept the duchy, and irreversible well before 1166. Besides, the choice of Arthur as the name for Geoffrey's son suggested that the new dynasty was prepared to absorb at least something of old Breton tradition into the new chivalry it encouraged. And in the long term, Brittany was to gain from her incorporation into France; Angevin rule provided the necessary governmental structure on which the Breton duke was to raise himself in the thirteenth and fourteenth centuries, to pre-eminence among the peers of France.

(viii) Anjou

The author of the *Gesta Consulum Andegavorum* greeted with relief the death of Fulk le Réchin in 1109.[76] Better times were sure to come. And indeed they did. The first half of the twelfth century was a period of reconstruction under Fulk V of Jerusalem (1109–29; died 1142) and Geoffrey le Bel (1129–51). Strong overlordship returned to the county, the vineyards flourished, trade down the Loire revived, Angers and Tours attracted scholars in their thousands, returning stability was celebrated in fine new castles and great abbey churches.

To their own monks, Fulk and Geoffrey were heroes. At the priory of St Sauveur in Langeais, it was recorded that 'Fulk the Younger, count of Anjou, since he built churches, raised the needy and the poor, helped the oppressed and wretched, set down the proud and haughty, preserving the mean in all things, proved superior to Cato in the rigour of his justice, and to Job in his generosity and patience'.[77] John of Marmoutier, reflecting on Geoffrey's policies, declared they could best be summed up in the splendid line in which Vergil epitomized Rome's aims: *parcere subiectis et debellare superbos*—to be merciful to the submissive and to crush the arrogant.[78] While it is true that the motive for penning these praises was to set standards for their successors rather than to tell the literal truth, they should not be dismissed as mere flattery. There were solid grounds for contentment.

The situation which faced Fulk in 1109 called for caution. For Angevin barons were now securely holding castles which had once been comital, regarding lands of which they had once been merely custodians as their hereditary property, and prizing new feudal ties with the counts of Blois and Poitou. These developments could neither be reversed nor condoned. What was required was a reassertion of the doctrine that all fortifications were comital property —a reassertion to be secured by pulling castles down around the ears of those barons would not otherwise submit to it—and the acceptance of hereditary right for castellans and fiefholders in return for clearly defined feudal services: in other words, an extension to the whole of the county and to Touraine of the terms on which fiefs were held within the narrow kernel of the demesne. Fulk and Geoffrey have sometimes been accused by historians of inconsistency and lack of purpose, in that they stormed the castles of recalcitrant barons—Geoffrey attacked (among others) those of Lisiard de Sable, Thibaud de Blaison, Supplicius of Amboise, and Gerald of Montreuil-Bellay[79]—reduced the rebels to their mercy, and then left them in the enjoyment of their patrimony. Yet it was precisely this that John of Marmoutier regarded as proof of their wisdom. The aim was to put overwhelming force behind the princes' interpretation of law, not to violate justice in their own interest. In negotiating with barons whose resistance had been crushed, they made clear demands for *ost* and *chevauchée*, which assisted them in similar ventures. And if, a few years later, those same barons rose again in revolt, and had to be crushed again, this was no argument for the theory that harsher policies should have been pursued. For harshness might have united the opposition, making revolt harder to suppress; it might also have alienated ecclesiastical support. In the end Fulk's and Geoffrey's patience paid off. By 1151, the lesson was being preached to the lords of Amboise that they could not with impunity harbour robbers or harass merchants, and that they must fulfil their obligations to the count of Anjou, who alone could shield them from the fury of Thibaud of Blois.

There was another side to Fulk's and Geoffrey's lordship: they were neighbours and friends of their lords as well as rulers. Hugh of Amboise, related to Fulk V's bride the countess of Maine, was invited to Fulk's wedding and greeted with warmth as a newly-acquired relative.[80] On his death he commended his son Supplicius into Geoffrey le Bel's care. Barons from Anjou accompanied the young Geoffrey when he went to Normandy to be knighted, and again when he set out for his wedding to the empress Matilda; and many Angevin lords made the Jerusalem journey with Fulk V in 1129 to see him received in the new kingdom he was to rule. In participating in their princes' exploits the lords took pride and pleasure. If churchmen chose to emphasize the counts' iron hand, Angevin lords may have been just as conscious of the velvet glove. It was this that they would miss when the chief locus of comital power moved to England.

With internal consolidation went the steady expansion of areas under Angevin lordship. Admittedly, external circumstances were favourable: William IX and William X of Aquitaine were chiefly preoccupied in the south; the count of Blois spent the early part of the century in wars on the Norman frontier, the second quarter largely in establishing peace in Champagne. So the neighbours who had hampered Fulk le Réchin were not threatening. Even so, the scale of Angevin achievement in the first half of the twelfth century was remarkable. Fulk V's marriage with the countess of Maine bore fruit in his reign, consolidating Angevin pre-eminence at the expense of Norman in Le Mans. Henry I of England, a potentially formidable foe, was forced by the

exigencies of his succession problems into an Angevin marriage alliance from which all the advantages were derived by
the Angevins. Chance had much to do with Geoffrey le Bel's
brilliant advancement. Yet he fought with skill and determination to overcome Norman resistance to his domination,
and by 1144 there was no opposition to him as duke of
Normandy. Perhaps just as remarkably, he knew where
to stop. He made no attempt at all to claim England
for himself—refusing all assistance to Matilda. Arguably his greatest mistake was in permitting his young
son Henry to visit England in 1148-9 as the first step in
securing the succession to the English throne; for, in the
long term, it was England that was to prove harmful to
Anjou.

So between them Fulk and Geoffrey united (under their
rule) western France from the Loire to the Canche. They
showed some sensitivity to the sensibilities of their new
subjects; Fulk kept the county of Maine separate from his
Angevin realms, preserving its old ways, and favouring the
title 'count of Anjou and count of Maine'. Under Geoffrey,
these units were brought into closer contact—perhaps
because Geoffrey feared his brother Helias's designs on
Maine; but Normandy, once his, was kept entirely distinct, with a separate administration, based on the old
capital at Rouen. On his deathbed, Geoffrey warned the
young Henry never to rule one province by the customs
of another,[81] a principle to which Henry usually adhered.
Still, some cross-fertilization of ideas can be detected in
Geoffrey's reign. The use of inquest, which he standardized
and extended in Normandy, was also found in Anjou; an
early example showed the count accepting a verdict against
his own interests.[82] And he failed to keep the chanceries
of Anjou and Normandy as distinct as he had no doubt
intended.[83]

The annexation of Maine and Normandy necessarily promoted administrative expansion within Anjou. In the first
half of the century, there were *prévôts* at Angers, Tours,
Loches, Montbazon, Beaufort, Thouars, Loudun, Saumur,
Le Flèche, and Baugé, to collect domanial and comital dues
and to carry out comital orders. By contrast in Maine,

where the comital demesne was small, the counts relied chiefly on goodwill. In Normandy, Geoffrey inherited a well-developed administration, largely in the hands of men who had been initially hostile to him but who, once forced into submission, proved reasonably trustworthy. The Norman chancery thereafter occasionally drew up charters for his other possessions. In financial terms, the Norman exchequer was more efficient than the Angevin treasury; on the other hand, the Angevin currency slowly began to push out other coinages throughout Geoffrey's domains.

All this took organization. The men attracted to comital service rose in social status; one of Geoffrey's *prévôts* was a knight. And though the Angevin administrators continued to be unpopular with the people as a whole, the career offered solid material advantages. Some at least of the count's clerks were affected by the intellectual ferment in the Loire valley; Bernard Sylvester's *Book of Forms* may have been used as the model for some comital letters;[84] Thomas of Loches, Fulk's chancellor, was no mean performer with the pen.[85] And Geoffrey's own standard of learning makes it probable that there were other literate laymen at his court. The famous Platonic scholar William of Conches, who fell under the suspicion of heresy, dedicated to Geoffrey his *Dragmaticon Philosophiae*, in which the count featured as one of the questioners in the dialogue.[86] Geoffrey was sufficiently *au fait* with classical military terminology to benefit from Vegetius' advice when the monks of Marmoutier provided it; and both Fulk and Geoffrey were scholars enough to feel flattered by the strongly classical flavour of the *Gesta Consulum Andegavorum*.

All in all, the first half of the twelfth century was a time of peace, prosperity, and brilliant cultural achievement. Yet the whole system rested on the personality of the prince, on his skill in sieges, his diplomacy, his friendships, his personal magnetism. The drawback to Fulk's and Geoffrey's achievement was that it led to expansion on a scale that weakened the very bonds on which they had built. Though Maine and Normandy could be absorbed without overstraining the system, when Geoffrey's heir Henry (1151-89) added Aquitaine through his marriage with Eleanor in 1152, and then England by inheritance in 1154, the intimacy that had been a feature of Angevin government was severely strained. Despite his enormous energy, Henry was not often in his patrimony. It says much both for the loyalty of the Angevin barons and for Henry's ability that the fabric of social relations survived at all.

Henry's reign began badly, with a dispute reminiscent of that between Geoffrey the Bearded and Fulk le Réchin, over Geoffrey le Bel's arrangements for his second son Geoffrey. Exactly what had been intended was not clear: perhaps Geoffrey was to inherit Anjou when Henry became king of England; he was certainly to enjoy immediately four important Angevin castles, including Chinon, in which was situated the count's treasury and his arsenal. This stipulation seriously inconvenienced Henry. (Geoffrey le Bel has been much blamed for this; but its unwisdom cannot have been completely obvious, for Henry himself once proposed that his youngest son John might be given the same inheritance, though he later changed his mind). Henry's solution to the problem was to drive his brother to revolt, and then to use his rebellion as justification for disinheriting him. Angevin opinion was split on this manœuvre; Thibaud of Blois hastened to fish in troubled waters; Geoffrey's chief supporter proved to be the viscount of Thouars, whose lordship in northern Poitou was so large that he came near to enjoying princely rank himself, although he was the vassal of the counts of both Anjou and Poitou. In the end, Geoffrey was defeated, handed over his castles, and left for Nantes, which Henry secured for him, and where he died in 1158. The viscount of Thouars suffered a rare display of Angevin ruthlessness: he was totally disinherited. Then the other Angevin barons settled down again to enjoy strong rule. Without much more justification than Fulk le Réchin, Henry had shown a force of character and ability that his great-grandfather had completely lacked.[87] So he avoided the consequences of what might have been a dangerous quarrel.

After that, Anjou was quiet. In Henry's absence, it was ruled by a seneschal, at first operating on *ad hoc* commissions, after 1173-4 by permanently delegated authority.

Goslin de Tours and Étienne de Marcay, who exercised this office, were exemplary in their loyalty. Before 1175, they had the backing of constables in charge of the army, the most famous of whom was Maurice de Craon; after 1175, the seneschal took over the army as well. As a system, the administration worked quite well. The treasury at Chinon was filled, and could act as a reserve for large parts of the Angevin empire in time of emergency. The seneschal strengthened comital jurisdiction; Angevin currency achieved widespread circulation. An occasional visit from the king and his great retinue, usually bound for Aquitaine, meant a flurry of charters from the royal chancery which travelled with him. There were few signs of discontent. Even in the great revolt of 1173, only a few nobles from Anjou and the Touraine took part (though there was more support for the rebels in Maine).[88]

Yet Henry's acquisitions had brought the barons of his own land no advantage. It would obviously have been unwise to encourage colonization by Angevins in the rest of his empire, for Normandy, England, and Aquitaine all had entrenched aristocracies which could not be dispossessed; Henry II's position was quite different from that of William the Conquerer. On the other hand, the indifference of the Angevin barons had its own latent danger for his line, especially in view of his prolonged absences from the county. After 1174, the seneschal tended to provide the only focal point in Angevin social life; beyond this, the lords devoted themselves to purely local affairs, with rather little regard for the person of their count. Though not disloyal they seemed apathetic; in 1203 they were to demonstrate this by acquiescing without a murmur in the decision of their seneschal William des Roches to switch loyalties from John to Philip Augustus.

But whatever the Angevins felt about Henry, in his own eyes he remained an Angevin to the last. When it came time for him to die in wretchedness and humiliation, it was to Fontevrault that he was carried, to the abbey dear to his father's and grandfather's hearts, where his aunt had been abbess, where his wife and son were also to be buried. For like the Capetians, the Angevins had a family mausoleum;

but unlike St Denis, Fontevrault was an Angevin foundation, and one which, by making lavish provision for women in a world largely heedless of their needs, epitomized the Angevin originality of approach.

(ix) Aquitaine and Gascony

The Pilgrims' Book of Compostela is not a source that inspires even minimal confidence.[89] Yet its description of the peoples of south-west France is perhaps worth repeating, on account of its vividness. The author admired the Poitevins, who were heroes, swift on horseback, elegant in their dress, handsome, witty, and hospitable. But their neighbours were less attractive: 'The Saintonge people already speak in a rather uncouth way, but those of Bordeaux are even rougher.' And the Gascons fascinated by their strangeness: 'The Gascons are frivolous, talkative, and full of mockery, debauched, drunken, greedy, dressed in rags, and they have no money; nevertheless they have been well taught how to fight and are remarkable in their hospitality towards the poor.'[90] Whatever the value of these impressions, they do at least point to contemporaries' awareness that there was little cultural homogeneity within the realms under the sway of the counts of Poitou.

The defeat of William IX in 1120 had effectively limited Poitevin control in Gascony to the area north of Fézensac and Lomagne. Further south, the intervention of the kings of Aragon in Béarn and Bigorre increased substantially in the early years of the century, strengthened not only by geographical proximity but also by the ambitions of the viscounts of Béarn and Bigorre in the Spanish *reconquista*.[91] Local experiments in representative government in these areas testified to the depth of Spanish political influence.[92] Then Armagnac, whose count had disputed Guy Geoffrey's claim to the duchy, always afterwards leant towards Aragon. In 1131, Alfonso I of Aragon launched an attack in the Bayonne region that indicated the potential for Spanish expansion in the area. Only the penetration of Poitevin coinage into southern Gascony went some way to counteracting Aragonese influence. Further north, Poitevin power was more effectively displayed; but the Bordelais alone remained completely under the duke's administration.

Within the frontiers of Aquitaine, the duke's regular passages from Poitiers to Saintes and Bordeaux continued to create resentment in the counts of Angoulême and La Marche. That their bitterness could be dangerous was demonstrated by their opposition to William X's plan to marry the heiress of the Limoges viscounty; in the face of their protests, the duke had to concede defeat and watch with chagrin her marriage to Vulgrin, count of Angoulême, with its consequent threat to ducal control in Limoges.[93] Without skilful diplomacy to soften the blows, incidents of this kind could threaten the break-up of the duchy.

There was even trouble within Poitou. In 1111 a war between William IX and Hugh VII de Lusignan, backed by the lord of Parthenay, provoked an Angevin incursion. The same quarrel flared up again in 1118, only to be dampened by William X's destruction of Parthenay. The temporary peace thus secured was expensive, both in the resources needed to secure it, and in its long-term consequences; for after this, the lords of Parthenay, though much weakened, could be relied on as allies for any rebels in northern Poitou;[94] and the lords of Lusignan had gained confidence in their potential as trouble-makers. This unfortunate legacy was compounded by William X's ecclesiastical policy. His blunder in adhering to the Roman Anacletus in the papal schism of 1130 brought him up against the bishops of Limoges, Saintes, Périgueux, and Poitiers, the last of whom was exiled for five years between 1130 and 1135. Until he finally gave in to St Bernard's pressure in 1134, William's obstinacy provided his political opponents with plenty of propagandistic ammunition; and, unlike his father's anti-clericalism, William's Anacletan sympathies provoked no special sympathy among his lay subjects, to compensate for the animosity they stirred up in the church.

So despite his less adventurous external policies, William X did little to solve the problems his predecessor had left him; while in the matter of the succession, he failed miserably. His only brother Raymond had quit his homeland to become prince of Antioch many years before. His own marriage to the daughter of the viscount of Châtellerault—undertaken to strengthen his political position in Poitou—had resulted only in two daughters. So before departing on the pilgrimage to Compostela on which he died in 1137, William married the elder of the two, Eleanor, to the young prince Louis Capet, in the hope that, as king, Louis would show himself a good overlord and husband in protecting Eleanor's rights. But immediately after the wedding, Louis set off on a progress of Aquitaine, arranged an inauguration ceremony at Bordeaux, granted and signed charters as duke of Aquitaine, and treated his wife's lands as his new possessions. His assertiveness provoked dislike among the traditional friends of the ducal house, though not among its enemies. After this foray, he withdrew to the north; then neither he nor Eleanor visited the duchy for any length of time for the rest of their marrige, though he passed through in 1141; Orderic recorded that 'Louis, king of France, leading an expedition against the Goths and Gascons, is haunted by unremitting cares.'[95] The rarity of his visits pleased the count of Angoulême and Geoffrey, lord of Rançon, his lieutenant in the area; but for the lesser of the Aquitaine lords, the poor first impression he had created was compounded by his later indifference.

Louis's unpopularity explained the ease with which Henry II established himself after his marriage with Eleanor in 1152. Unlike Louis, he had the advantage of some acquaintance with the area, as count of Anjou and the lord of Loudun. The Poitevin lords who accepted him as duke of Aquitaine may have realized that, for the first time since the late tenth century, Angevin interests could no longer be called into play against the ducal; if this was a loss for potential troublemakers, it was a gain for everybody else. Unlike Louis, Henry appreciated the need for personal government within the duchy: before the Peace of Montmirail in 1169 he visited often; after it, until 1174, Eleanor with their second son Richard was in constant residence; with Eleanor's disgrace and imprisonment in 1174, Richard took over. To reinforce this personal focus for loyalty, Henry was represented in the duchy by a seneschal, in whose hands new vigour crept into the conduct of business.

But neither the initial goodwill nor Henry's sensible ways

of government could provide more than temporary peace in a land which unsympathetic English chroniclers regarded as plagued by turbulent barons, but which might more charitably be seen as a federation held together only by weak and conservative bonds of loyalty, regularly strained by the competing interests of duke and lords. In Poitou itself, Henry took the unusually tough step of disinheriting the powerful viscount of Thouars, who had supported his brother. For a while, this act of overweening lordship intimidated potential opposition. But the lords of Lusignan soon moved into alliance with the Rançon family, natural opponents of the new ruler, and in 1168 they, ably seconded by the count of Angoulême, led a rebellion which caught Henry at an extremely inconvenient moment; in the course of it his lieutenant, Patrick earl of Salisbury, was slain. Only the seriousness of his other problems caused the king to make generous terms with the defeated rebels at Montmirail in 1169; and he paid for it in 1173, when Geoffrey de Lusignan joined the king's sons in the great rebellion. Yet even now, harsh measures were avoided; Geoffrey suffered little—in fact, his self-confidence grew with every unsuccessful *coup* in which he engaged. In 1177, when Henry bought the county of La Marche from its last count (who was setting out for Jerusalem and needed money) Geoffrey de Lusignan put in an impudent counter-claim, to which he and his family adhered with obstinacy until 1199, when John was weak enough to concede it.[96] Angevin unwillingness to crush the Lusignans—Richard was to protect their interests on the Third Crusade—has excited surprise. Henry in fact consistently followed Geoffrey le Bel's line in seeking conciliation, no matter how often he was disappointed; the contrast with his treatment of the viscount of Thouars was sharp.

If the Lusignans were the most troublesome of the Poitevin vassals, the counts of Angoulême were the least loyal of the major lords in the duchy. Their participation in the revolts of 1168 and 1173 added weight to the rebels' cause; and when, in 1176, they rose against Richard's rule, they were joined for the first time by most of the duchy's chief families, the viscounts of Limoges, Ventadour, and Turenne, the lords of Chabanais and Mastac. The ensuing campaign provided Richard with his first opportunity to demonstrate that military prowess for which he was soon to be famed throughout Christendom. On this occasion, the defeated rebels did suffer some confiscation of property; but they were dispossessed neither of their titles nor of their chief estates. William of Angoulême led one last armed protest before he departed on crusade in 1179, and his heirs remained to bother the Angevins for many years to come.

So Henry and Richard were faced with regular and open defiance. Preserving the duchy intact was a full-time operation that not only absorbed the superabundant Angevin energy but also imposed a heavy burden on resources. The great castles erected across the land and the bands of mercenaries paid to fight the duke's cause were far from cheap. Yet it may be that the costs involved were considerably less than the profits from tolls and customs in the duchy: for the foundation of La Rochelle in 1130 had both assisted and further stimulated the flow of Atlantic trade, which Henry's marriage with Eleanor safeguarded. England was the perfect market for Gascon wine, in that she produced rather little of her own, and was accessible by sea (land transport of heavy wine-barrels was still an uneconomic proposition); in addition, she needed the dyes produced within Aquitaine for her cloth-manufacture. In return, English grain, cloth, and silver entered the duchy in sizeable amounts. By 1180 this exchange was vital to the economies of both regions; and the profits it engendered ensured that, with Bordeaux and La Rochelle in his grasp, the duke of Aquitaine was a wealthy man.[97]

A trading surplus is suggested by the fact that Angevin resources were sufficient not just to maintain but also to extend ducal control. Though the Aragonese could not be ejected from the south of Gascony, their influence was limited by a campaign of Richard's in 1178; as a consequence the count of Bigorre swore fealty to the duke and surrendered two castles as surety. This small incident in fact proved to be a turning-point in the area. Even more importantly, Henry II's aggressive campaign against Toulouse brought him lordship over Quercy in 1159 and the homage of Raymond V in 1173.

In the Auvergne, he rebutted Louis VII's claims in 1167; and in 1177 he obtained a judgement from the Auvergnat barons that the suzerainty of the county belonged to the duke, the king's rights being limited to patronage of the bishopric of Clermont. This diplomatic triumph was, however, spoiled by Louis's refusal to accept the verdict, the consequence of pique at Henry's growing influence in Berry. For in 1177 Henry had demonstrated the reality of his control among the southern barons in Berry by successfully enforcing his claim as overlord to the wardship of the heiress of Déols, whom he married to his trusted servant Baldwin de Redvers.[98] The acquisition of Quercy and Déols were trifles for a king whose lands already stretched from the Pyrenees to the Tweed. But they were clear signs that his government in the south was dynamic, that its competence went beyond mere self-preservation.

By 1180 then, though Henry's and Richard's lordship relied more blatantly on force than their predecessors', the periodic rebellions they faced were always crushed; indeed, they almost seem like tournaments, occasions for display rather than for the resolution of conflicts. Richard was admired as well as feared within Aquitaine; his courts at Poitiers and Limoges attracted the duchy's lords as well as its troubadours. And Henry had taken care that his son should exploit the ancient traditions of the land that he ruled, for if the inauguration ceremony that Richard underwent in 1170 was the same as the one described in a surviving early thirteenth-century account,[99] then his coronation was deliberately reminiscent of the past: Richard was the direct heir of the Carolingian sub-kings of Aquitaine.

So Aquitaine could set the benefits of personal rule against the more exploitative feudal relationship—the claim of wardship and aids—and the determined reassertion of ducal control over fortifications which marked the Angevin dominance. For Poitou, the incorporation within the Angevin empire strengthened and extended the grip of northern culture, as Angevin legal custom and Angevin coins spread widely across the county. Gascony on the other hand remained culturally distinct; but the containment of Aragonese political influence, along with the new commercial ties across the Bay of Biscay, ensured that the trans-Pyrenean drift was irrevocably halted. With hindsight, it can be seen that the years 1152-80 were crucial in moulding the duchy's future; the scene was being set for the later medieval division between French Poitou and English Gascony.

(c) The Angevin Empire

'These lands were simply cobbled together. They were founded, and continued to survive, on unholy combination of princely greed and genealogical accident' (J. C. Holt).[100] With the elimination of the adjectives 'princely' and 'genealogical', this verdict might apply equally to many other great empires. What distinguished the Angevin empire from others was simply that it did not last long enough to acquire a justifying ideology; nor did it feel the want, for it was solidly based on custom. Whether this makes it 'unholy' is disputable. And to infer a connection between the absence of such an ideology and the disintegration of the empire in 1204 is anachronistic. Philip Augustus' move against Normandy was preceded by a judgement of his court depriving John of his lands as a recalcitrant vassal. Not all those who acquiesced in French conquest necessarily thought that Philip was in the right. But Angevin rule had taught them to take seriously the implications of feudal overlordship; and John did not dispute that Philip had been his overlord for Normandy. The proceedings created just enough doubt in the minds of John's supporters for them to hang back and await the judgement of God; his large armies and determined campaigning ensured this for Philip. Once the decision was clear, there were no grounds for reopening the matter. Normandy and Anjou were lost because the barons respected the interpretation of feudalism the Angevins had encouraged; and because they lacked those close personal relations with John—who had concentrated on England before his accession—that might have caused them to overrule feudal scruple in the name of fidelity.

While the empire lasted, its inhabitants gained. Because almost the whole of the Atlantic coast was under one ruler, trade quickened, merchants met with fewer obstructions;

the English market encouraged wine-production in Gascony, particularly in the Bordelais; Gascon wine-flagons became everyday household goods in England. Then old feuds were buried: at last the struggle between Normandy and Anjou over Maine and Brittany became meaningless, and Angevin influence ceased to undermine the duke of Aquitaine's control in northern Poitou. The price to be paid however, turned out to be a sharpening of conflicts between Angevin and Capetian interests, in Berry, in the Auvergne, and above all in the Vexin. And although by 1180, Henry II had had the best of the battles, Louis's alliance with his sons suggested that in the end the king of France might win the war. Open conflict would favour the Capetians, whose lands were compact, against the defenders of the long, vulnerable frontier of the Angevin empire. Nevertheless Philip Augustus' determined aggression against Richard and John could not have been predicted; and in its absence, the undoubted internal strains of Angevin rule were insufficient to bring about the empire's disintegration.

Ties between the member-states of the empire remained fairly loose. As in the case of the British empire, policy was to build up connections with the centre, rather than to eliminate frontiers. So the chief cohesive force was supplied by Henry and his household, with his chamber and chancery, travelling across the lands he governed.[101] The king's long-term solution to the exhausting inefficiency of this procedure was to groom his younger sons as rulers of the various provinces, leaving for his eldest son Henry the Young King the succession to Anjou, Normandy, and England, the family patrimony. This admirably conceived plan—very similar to that later produced by Louis VIII of France for the succession to his huge estates—foundered on the rock of family quarrels. Yet for a short time it provided that element of continuity and personal contact so badly needed in Aquitaine; and for six years till Geoffrey's death in 1186, it was beneficial in Brittany. It has been criticized as feudal rather than imperial[102]—and certainly it was entirely within the medieval tradition. But perhaps it should be thought of as post-imperial: Aquitaine, Brittany, and Ireland were intended to attain dominion status. This was symbolized in the splendid inauguration ceremony for Richard at Limoges and Poitiers in 1170 (see p. 345), and by the if anything grander ceremony which marked Geoffrey's accession to the county of Brittany in 1180—for which Chrétien de Troyes wrote *Erec*.[103]

The real problem lay not so much with the apanages—if one may employ the term used for Louis VIII's subdivisions—as with the core of the empire, with England, Normandy, and Anjou. Henry could hardly alienate his inheritance; nor could he justly designate it to any but his elder son. Had his heir been less extravagant, more patient, or perhaps simply more tactfully handled, rebellion might have been averted. But it was hard for the eldest son to see his brothers provided for while he was expected to wait until his father's death. And his discontent divided loyalties among the magnates more effectively than any other issue, much to Louis VII's evident satisfaction.

Day-to-day government was supplied throughout the empire by the king's seneschals or justiciars, normally—except in Normandy—working on *ad hoc* commissions in the early years of the reign, and gaining viceregal powers in the 1170s. Normally these men were locals; it was rather exceptional for Henry to send a servant across frontiers. There was therefore little corporate sense of identity among the king's administrators, no equivalent of the British colonial service. And the lower ranks of officials were quite unaffected by belonging to a larger grouping of territories. Therefore it is surprising that there was any impact of a specifically imperial kind at all. Yet there was a little. The ordinance on surety for debt in 1177 was applied in Normandy, Anjou, Aquitaine, and Brittany. The same measures were adopted everywhere for the collection of the Saladin tithe. The appointment in Brittany and Anjou of officials whose function was supervisory, and who had clearly defined districts within which to operate, owed something to Norman experience. The inquest into knight service and other military obligation, perfected in the English Assize of Arms in 1181, had continental precedents.[104] None of this was significant. Taken together, however, the measures do suggest that, if it had had longer to mature, the Angevin empire would have become more of a community.

For its subjects, the drawback of Angevin government lay in its combination of strength and unpredictability. Without its, for the period, highly effective bureaucracy, the inherent contradiction in its procedures would have been hidden; as it was, the switches between old-style personal government and new bureaucratic methods caused distress. Henry pushed his French possessions down the road to impersonal government faster than either he or they wanted, because it was the only way to maintain his huge realms. At least by the 1170s his viceregal officials in Normandy and Anjou were establishing rules of feudal obligation, judical procedure, and financial organization, to serve the king's interests and to provide a clear framework of convention within which his subjects must live. This, the product of Henry's administrative genius, was no doubt unwelcome at first to his subjects, because it was a systematization of strong exploitative lordship; but it brought at least the compensating advantages of security and certainty. On the other hand, the king still expected, when he visited Normandy, to profit from the warmth of fidelity, the flexibility of old-style judicial processes, and the hugeness of his personality. At Christmas 1182, the king established his court at Caen, with his son Henry the Younger, his son-in-law Henry the Lion, Richard the Lionheart, and Geoffrey of Brittany, along with many bishops, 'together with the province-ful of counts and barons'.[105] The seneschal of Normandy used the occasion to bring serious accusations against William de Tankerville, hereditary chamberlain of Normandy. (Unfortunately Walter Map, who was present and recounted the story, did not explain what these accusations were, because it did not suit the moral of his tale that any substance should be attributed to them.) Although Henry had been inclined towards suspicion of William, he was moved to pardon him completely, when he saw William's ostentatious and rather unmannerly insistence on performing in person his traditional role as water-bearer to the king. Walter regarded this as evidence of Henry's mercy even to those whom he did not like. It might, however, equally well be seen as proof that the old personal rules of justice still obtained in the king's presence, that political considerations, respect for rank, and the need for support remained vital factors in determining Henry's verdicts. But in the king's absence, these could not be so regarded by his subordinates.

It is possible that the chief advantage Angevin and Norman barons ultimately reaped by Philip Augustus' conquest was that of a king who remained in Paris, thereby relieving them of the exhausting and unsatisfying mixture of bureaucratic and personal government to which they had been subjected. Nevertheless it is unlikely that before 1204 they could have imagined the potential advantage in such a situation. For while the contradictory principles behind Angevin justice did create bitter grievances—particularly in the reign of John, when they were exploited to the full[106]—they also created hope: the seneschal's judgement could be tempered by the king's mercy, the king's wrath bought off by application of the sensechal's rules. It was only when king and seneschal were fully in accord that life was not worth living. 'Our lord the king has long been moved against me, and himself and through his justiciars he harasses me at every turn',[107] Arnulf of Lisieux moaned in 1179. But the real burden of his complaint was that the wrath of Ralph fitzWilliam, seneschal of Normandy, whom he described as *princeps omnium et magister,*[108] prince and master of all things, was aimed relentlessly at him, unrestrained by the command of his overlord the king, to whom Arnulf had sworn allegiance, and from whom he had hoped for kindness. 'Pity me therefore; pity me; for the time for pity has come; so that, having put aside all the labour of temporal affairs, I may devote myself to the divine recreation of contemplation, where sedulous devotion may produce prayers effective for my own salvation and that of your majesty and your issue.'[109] For a plausible pleader of Arnulf's stamp, the prospect of living according to fixed rules of conduct, impartially imposed, would not have been an alluring one; for Angevin justice, though always unpredictable, was as likely to prove accommodating as inflexible. In fact, the aged bishop of Lisieux, though strongly suspected of treachery, was permitted by Henry to resign his see and left to die in peace. He would have suffered a worse fate under many other regimes.

(d) The rest of France

If the eleventh century had seen few major changes in those areas of France outside the principalities, the twelfth witnessed their disintegration. For the most part, they became a prey to their better-organized neighbours; where they did not, they lost identity.

(i) The bishopric of Langres

The most distinguished bishop of Langres in the century was Godfrey de la Roche, ex-prior of Clairvaux and close friend of St Bernard, who rose to prominence in the Second Crusade. He preached the need for a crusade to the crowds who assembled at Bourges for the Christmas court of 1145; he attempted, unsuccessfully but not unpersuasively, to induce Louis to attack Constantinople in 1147 when suspicions of Manuel Comnenus' intentions had arisen among the crusading host;[110] and on the return voyage after the total débâcle, he introduced Louis to Roger of Sicily as a prelude to a new alliance.[111] His career illustrates the powerful political influence a bishop of the post-reform era could wield. But that influence was based on his spiritual leadership, not on his position as the governor of an episcopal principality. And though on occasion the bishop's spiritual authority might strengthen his territorial lordship—St Bernard in 1128 persuaded Thibaud of Champagne to do homage to the bishop of Langres with the words: 'Receive as is fitting, with more abundant honour, him who is both our bishop and yours; and pay him reverently and humbly due homage for the fief which you hold of him'[112]—on other occasions it might weaken it: Godfrey made both monetary and political concessions to the inhabitants of Langres, in order to finance his crusade.[113]

For the bishop's government of Langres, the real problem lay where it always had: because he could not protect himself, he needed a lay protector. The obvious candidate was the duke of Burgundy, to whom several of the twelfth-century bishops were in any case related. But in return for their assistance, the dukes showed true Capetian skill in reclaiming ancient rights of hospitality, in acquiring fiefs within the bishopric, and in persuading the bishop's castellans into their *mouvance*. In 1168 Duke Hugh III was permitted to fortify Châtillon-sur-Seine; in 1170 he bought the de Saulx family office of *vidame*, in a move that seriously threatened episcopal independence, despite the fact that he immediately enfeoffed it to the count of Bar (which somewhat soothed the bishop).

At the same time, the duke's only potential competitor, the king, was equally active in the field. In fact, Louis VII had been preparing for dominance over Langres since the very early years of his reign: in 1138 he had ridden there from Auxerre, taking homage of barons on the way; in 1147 he had crossed the bishop's territory on his way to Vézelay; in 1153, he had encouraged Bishop Godfrey to present in the royal court complaints against Duke Eudes II for failure to fulfil his vassalic duty to the bishop; and in 1163 he heard Bishop Walter's petition against Henry the Liberal.[114] So, in 1179, when Walter appealed to him after a fight with his nephew, Duke Hugh III, Louis gladly issued a charter taking the city of Langres and the whole episcopal fief firmly and irrevocably under crown protection.[115] The royal victory, which much injured ducal interests, was a perfect example of Louis exploiting the crown's relative remoteness and weakness to entice into surrender lords under pressure from more powerful neighbours. As a consequence the bishop's position returned to approximately what it had been in the days of Louis IV.

(ii) The Rouergue

The twelfth century saw the break-up of the Rouergue into three separate, weak units. The central part, around Rodez itself, had been leased to the viscount of Millau by Raymond of St Gilles on his departure for Jerusalem in 1095. In 1113 Alphonse-Jourdain sold it outright to the viscount, who took the title Count of Rodez, a name soon to be made famous by the family's exploits in the crusades and the Spanish reconquest. Millau itself went as dowry with Douce, heiress to much of Provence and the Gévaudan, when she married the count of Provence in 1112; and it subsequently passed into the hands of Raymond Berengar III of Barcelona (see

p. 300). The rest of the Rouergue remained loosely under the hegemony of Toulouse, as a frontier region, until in the late twelfth century it began to crystallize around Villefranche. The sense of identity which had lent coherence to the county's aristocratic society disappeared; outsiders penetrated, but did not absorb, the county; the great castellans survived untamed in their formidable eyries. Protected by the Massif Central, too distant for Capetian or Angevin tentacles to spread into it, the Rouergue remained suspended in a vacuum, outside those pressures to conformity which were felt elsewhere. So its lords joined with the bishop of Rodez in enforcing the Peace of God, as their grandfathers and great-grandfathers had done.[116] Yet despite its social conservatism, the Carolingian structure of the county had gone; sooner or later, reshaping would become inevitable. In fact the county's rude awakening was postponed till the aftermath of the Albigensian crusade.

(iii) Hardly surprisingly, the twelfth century produced no ephemeral states.

(iv) Picardy

The mosaic of small but well-organized lordships in Picardy benefited in the twelfth century from a more distinctively feudal social organization—the spread of fief, vassalage, defined military service, feudal incidents—which strengthened lordship everywhere. But the other side of this coin was that rivalry between the crown and the count of Flanders, dormant in the eleventh century, revived and intensified.

In the north-west, the early years of the century saw the county of Boulogne achieve international fame as the cradle of the kings of Jerusalem. When Stephen of Blois married its heiress, Matilda, it was linked with the English royal family. But the last of Stephen and Matilda's male children died in 1162, and at once Thierry of Alsace swiftly moved in to obtain the county for his second son Matthew. The abbess of Romsey, Stephen's daughter, was dragged forth from her convent, forced into matrimony for a few years, then divorced for a younger woman. From Matthew's

death in 1173 until 1180, Philip held the county in wardship for its infant heiress Ida, taking it firmly into the
Flemish orbit for the first time since the end of the tenth
century.

The count of Flanders' power in the lands surrounding
Boulogne was equally striking. Around 1151, the lordships
of Hesdin and Lillers had escheated to Thierry; in 1160
he obtained Lens. Though Guînes maintained its independence, its count was often at Philip's court, his heir was
educated in Philip's household. Only the count of St Pol,
who had rebelled against and been crushed by Count Charles
the Good, escaped Philip's discipline, reasserted his independence, and put pressure on the frontiers of the county.
With this one exception, Flanders looked set to reassert
forceful lordship over at least half of Picardy. But in 1180
Philip took the fatal step of granting away much of his
richest territory in the area—Artois, St Omer, Aire, and
Hesdin—as a marriage-portion for his niece Isabella of
Hainault on her wedding to Philip Augustus. In a bid for
immediate political influence—from which he derived only
marginal profit—Philip had bartered away the core of his
Picard hegemony. For the young Philip Augustus, once
granted a foothold, was not the man to let it slip.

From the king's point of view, Artois and its surroundings were less strategically significant than Vermandois,
which had been since the reign of Philip I closely linked with
the Capetians (see p. 218). Philip of Alsace's marriage to
Elizabeth, elder daughter of count Raoul II, was a serious
threat to the crown's interests; on Raoul's death in 1168
it brought Vermandois into the Flemish orbit; with it went
a goodly part of what had once been Raoul of Crépy's territory. Only the king's guardianship of the bishopric of
Amiens remained as a foundation for royal power in
southern Picardy. So Elizabeth of Vermandois's death in
1183, without issue, was to provide an opportunity which
could not be missed. Philip Augustus challenged Philip of
Alsace's rights in the county, prepared war, and, when
the count of Flanders gave in to moral pressure, deprived
him of his claims to Vermandois. Therefore the events of

1180 and 1183 totally altered the balance of power in southern Picardy, preparing the way for the eventual royal dominance of the whole area.

(v) Upper Berry

Upper Berry and the Auvergne, similar for much of their history, shared the same fate in the twelfth century: that of becoming a battleground for powers beyond their frontiers. In both cases, internal disputes led to appeals for external aid, and hence to the kindling of acquisitive ambitions.

For Upper Berry, Philip I's purchase of the viscounty of Bourges in 1101 had proved a turning-point; for though Louis VI showed only moderate interest, Louis VII often resided in Bourges, where, in addition to vicecomital rights, he enjoyed the prestige conferred by his guardianship over the archbishopric. From this central position he claimed lordship over all aristocrats who were not vassals either of the counts of Blois or of the counts of Anjou; he created close links with certain catellan houses, for example that of Sully; and he entered into *pariage* agreements to increase his demesne land. Hardly surprisingly, his extending influence was opposed first by Thibaud of Blois and then by Henry II. Had the aims of Blois and Anjou been compatible, the opposition might have enjoyed success; but Thibaud and Henry could not commit themselves whole-heartedly to alliance, since the elimination of the king was for each of them only a preliminary to the removal of the other. For Blois, Berry was crucial in providing access to Champagne, while Angevin interests in Lower Berry had been strengthened by Henry's marriage with Eleanor. By 1180, it was becoming clear that the house of Blois was the loser in the three-cornered contest. The lords of Berry therefore eagerly applied themselves to playing off Henry II against Louis VII, to appealing from the courts of one to the other. Upper Berry was naturally drawn more into the Capetian orbit, while Lower seemed dominated by Anjou. But the trial of strength between them was postponed until 1187.[117]

(vi) The Auvergne

There is a famous letter of Peter the Venerable, in which he declared that the Auvergne was without either king or count, and therefore was protected by the church.[118] But the distinguished abbot of Cluny's elegant phrase seems to be somewhat at odds with the facts. The first half of the twelfth century saw Louis VI intervening in 1122 and 1126, to protect the bishop of Clermont from the count, and his son answering similar appeals from the canons of Brioude in 1138 and 1139; by the second half of the century, royal protection over the church in the Auvergne was evolving from episodic intervention to a permanent obligation. On the other hand, the lay lords of the Auvergne were increasingly likely to turn to their traditional overlord, the duke of Aquitaine, whose once minimal influence in the area was consolidated in the first half of the twelfth century. In his protest of 1126 against Louis VI's intrusion, William X argued that Louis's proper course would have been to appeal to him, as the count of Auvergne's overlord, to prevent the count from harassing the bishop;[119] here, then, was a clear claim to ducal feudal suzerainty. When that claim was inherited by Henry II, on his marriage with Eleanor, it was natural enough that king and duke should find themselves on a collision course in the Auvergne. In 1170 Henry wrote to Becket that 'Friends of mine in France have warned me that the king of France is preparing to take action against my vassals in Auvergne, to harm them and my lands; and the men of Auvergne have also notified me of it and begged my help.'[120] In 1177 an inquest was held into the respective rights of king and duke within the county, in which the Auvergnat lords declared themselves unequivocally the *fideles* of Henry II; Louis's unwillingness to accept this verdict meant that the battle-lines were drawn up. It was to take two decades of fighting before the Capetian victory in the Auvergne was finally assured.

This brief résumé suggests that by 1180, virtually nowhere in France had escaped entirely from the advancing tide of princely ambition—even part of the Rouergue fell under Aragon; while most places which had traditionally been beyond the frontiers of principalities were now torn apart by rival interests. Of these rival interests, the crown was by far the most conspicuous, seeking to extend its sway in every corner of the realm. Princes were faced with the dilemma of either yielding to royal claims they regarded as illegitimate, or facing the dangers of war against a monarch who would invoke a full range of propaganda weapons in his own defence.[121] It was not a happy choice.

CHAPTER 13

Aristocratic life 1108–1180

(a) Feudalism

Twelfth-century feudalism was a paradox. On the one hand, feudalism's *raison d'être*, warfare, evolved in a way which rendered feudal military service purely ancillary; incipient bureaucracies began to perform functions once the prerogative of castellans; privileged ⟨towns and rural franchises cut into the judicial rights of aristocrats. The characteristics that had made France notably feudal in Maitland's or in Marc Bloch's senses of the word (see p. 12 and 42) were becoming blurred, if not disappearing. On the other hand, fiefs and vassalage spread fast into areas where they had hitherto been rather exotic oddities, liege homage became normal, even the great princes were finally drawn without equivocation into the network. So, as France grew less feudal, she became more feudalized; or, to put it another way, as the military aristocracy's monopoly of political and legal influence was challenged, it chose to organize itself systematically on the social and legal framework long familiar to its lower ranks, the knights; a framework which many lords had hitherto evaded completely, and which the others had treated as a loose guide, not a restrictive code.

The process of systematizing feudal arrangements was complicated by two different and not wholly compatible approaches. The simpler was that of recording individual agreements in writing, as the southerners had long been accustomed to do. A documentary record required the terms of an agreement to be clearly framed, so that they could easily be enforced in the lord's court; it could not, however, ensure similarities between agreements. *Convenientiae* could be like that between Raymond V of Toulouse and Roger, viscount of Albi, Carcassone, and Razès, in which Raymond undertook to defend Roger against all his enemies except Raymond's own vassals, who would be subjected to comital justice;[1] or the oath—recorded both in Latin and in Romance —sworn by William VI of Montpellier's vassals, which bound them not to harm the persons or possessions of their lord and his heir, not to poison them, nor to deprive them of their city;[2] or Geoffrey le Bel's gift of various lands and dues to his faithful servant Fulk de la Roussière, in exchange for liege homage and military service;[3] or the treaty between Louis VII and the count of Melun, regulating the obligations of the inhabitants of Gournai.[4] There was no common denominator.

The second approach took as its starting-point not people but principle. Thibaud IV, for example, proceeded on the assumption that all those who paid him homage owed him suit of court when he demanded it. Therefore when the count of Nevers, who held a fief of him, failed to respond to his summons in 1113, Thibaud had him captured and kept him in gaol for three years. The drawback to this approach lay in the fact that, while any lord might enunciate any principle he cared to, he was unlikely to get it accepted if it ran counter to another lord's view of his rights. In this case, Louis VI rebutted Thibaud's claim, on the grounds that the count of Nevers was a royal liegeman, whose service to the king overrode any demands other lords might make. The moral, that introducing feudal principles was more likely to benefit kings than lesser men, was not lost on Louis VII, who capitalized in Berry and southern Burgundy on the ingenious invention that the king was the natural lord of all aristocrats who hitherto had not acknowledged one.

Exactly how individual bargains were to be integrated into the broad canvas of feudal principles was not clear. Exceptions and dispensations were the inevitable concomitant. Yet there was a way of diminishing the confusion: to systematize according to the results of inquest. When Henry II enquired of his Norman tenants-in-chief how many knights' services they owed him (see p. 252), he had no intention of revoking the (unwritten) agreements his predecessors had reached with their barons—though he was certainly not averse from using moral pressure to obtain an increase in emergency. What he did intend was that the information obtained in 1172 should create a royal right in the future: barons would automatically be required either to produce the service or to pay scutage or to pay a fine for failure of service. In pursuing this policy, Henry was simply a little in advance of his time. The rule-making mentality did ultimately prevail; in the later thirteenth century, it was codified in important works like Beaumanoir's *Coutumes de Beauvaisis*; but it prevailed upon the foundation of existing vested interests.

However they proposed to enforce it, all princes expected more of their vassals in the twelfth century. It is true that one or two great men—the count of Nevers, the count of Angoulême—might still on occasion play off two competing princes against each other, and so retain an element of bargaining power. But by 1180 it was clear that only the greatest of feudatories could hope to play this game for long. The viscounts of Thouars, whose position had been based on their skill in pitting Poitou against Anjou, came to grief when Henry II dominated both. Further down the social scale, the castellan of Amboise was reduced to dependence on Anjou after Supplicius II had ruined the family fortunes by alienating both his overlords at once. Clearly defined liege homage had eaten away at independence.

This trend was accentuated as the other princes of France followed the Norman example in confounding their justice with the maintenance of peace. It came to be expected that overlords would punish their recalcitrant vassals, no matter how socially elevated, if they engaged in violence. Thibaud took strong measures in 1111-12 against the viscount of Châteaudun, who had seized land from Marmoutier;[5] during the regency, he demanded of Suger that the viscount of Sens's son, the king's man, be disciplined for attacking merchants.[6] It was no longer regarded as an act of grace on a vassal's part to submit himself to the judgement of his lord's court; it was his bounden duty, and force could legitimately be used against him if he failed. Admittedly, the political consequences of harsh punishment had to be considered. Henry II only resorted to banishment for those allies of the Lusignan family who murdered Patrick, Earl of Salisbury in 1186.[7] And where accident played a part, arbitration might still be regarded as appropriate. But expectations had changed. Princes could find support in inflicting severe punishment on disturbers of the peace.

The distinction between the violent and the merely disobedient remained fine. The ultimate sanction of a feudal lord against a recalcitrant vassal was disinheritance—thirteenth-century customary law permitted it to the lords of Western France, including Poitou.[8] But if the vassal were sufficiently exalted, this course might be politically most unwise; for a man who also held allodial lands or fiefs of other lords would not be ruined by it but he would be embittered. In Normandy, where the majority of all landholdings were fiefs, disinheritance was not too dangerous. Henry I resorted to it against Robert of Bellême in 1102 and against William of Mortain after the battle of Tinchebrai in 1106. In Flanders the murder of Charles the Good caused such widespread revulsion that Thierry of Alsace, once safely in control, was able to disinherit some castellan families thought guilty of supporting the Erembalds.[9] But it was more usual for a prudent prince to content himself by pulling the castle down about the ears of a rebellious castellan, and refusing him permission to build another. The monk William, Suger's biographer, declared that when the abbot was regent, he never disinherited for a first offence, only resorting to it in cases where it was obviously a lesser evil than allowing the vassal to remain.[10] St Bernard chided Thibaud for disinheriting; he pleaded that even if the lord himself suffered, his wife and family should keep his lands intact. Henry II bound himself by the treaty of Amboise in 1174 not to disinherit those who had rebelled against him;[11] although there were some later complaints that the treaty had been violated, for the most part its terms were kept.

In fact, it was rarely necessary for princes to go as far as the actual disinheritance of their important vassals, simply because they had many other ways of showing their illwill against the recalcitrant. Of these, the most effective depended on luck. Though a prince was bound by feudal convention to respect the hereditary rights of his lords, those rights were only in the process of becoming defined. Therefore the death of a fiefholder without a son to succeed him might result in the lord claiming the honour as an escheat, as did Thierry of Alsace with the honour of Lens. There was, however, no need to await propitious circumstances in order to show goodwill towards the favoured or malevolence towards defeated rebels; intervention in their vassals' family affairs was not confined to the succession. As the century went by, other princes imitated the Normal dukes in claiming wardship of the infant heirs and the right to marry female heiresses, in compensation for the protection they afforded these otherwise weak and defenceless parties. In parts of the south there was strong resistance to this new practice. William X of Aquitaine was forced by the protest of Limousin barons to yield up his claim to marry the viscountess of Limoges; Henry II had to override similar vigorous protest in marrying the heiress of Déols to Baldwin de Redvers.[12] But elsewhere and in other circumstances, princes were earnestly begged to intervene in family affairs. Mary, duchess of Burgundy, begged Louis VII's assistance in extorting her dowry from her son Hugh III;[13] Ida of Nevers expected Suger, as her lord, to stand in for her husband, absent on crusade, in exacting what was due from her debtors;[14] Conan IV of Brittany fled to Henry II of England for support against his uncle; William X sought Louis VI's protection of his heiress Eleanor.

These examples also illustrate the more general proposition that, though documentary evidence usually stresses the advantages to lords in the feudal relationship, those of vassals were also important. Because it was the prince's function to keep the peace, it became his responsibility to preserve his vassals' fiefs from the incursions of others. Shortly after the count of Forez had commended himself to Louis VII, he wrote a letter warning the king that he anticipated an attack on his lands by the counts of Mâcon and Lyons, which would constitute a gesture of contempt against Louis, who was now his overlord.[15] In 1179 Alfonso II of Aragon regarded the incursion on Roger II of Bézier's lands as an insult to his lordship. In effect, princes were now obliged to extend to their vassals the sort of protection they had long exercised over those abbeys and monasteries within their *garde*. The development explains the rapid spread of feudal commendation among those families in France which had deliberately avoided it up till now; for the lordless man would find himself at a disadvantage. This was especially true in regions of hitherto weak government, in Berry, the Auvergne, and in Picardy; but the phenomenon was found everywhere. Occasionally other inducements may have been added—bribes for example; or even force. Whatever the immediate cause, one way or another feudal contracts became the norm, land hitherto held allodially was commended to the duke of Burgundy, or the count of Champagne, or the count of Toulouse.

Remaining outside a *mouvance* was no longer a distinction. In the Old French poetry of the period, the word 'vassal' was a term of praise; as Charlemagne said in the *Song of Roland*, 'Barons franceis, vos estes bons vassals.'[16] The *chansons de geste* were largely preoccupied with extolling chivalric virtue exercised in the interests of a lord. Wace's versification of Geoffrey of Monmouth's *History of the Kings of Britain*, along with the different Arthurian tradition contained in Chrétien de Troyes's poems, ensured the appeal of Arthur's knights as exemplars of chivalric conduct. To miss out on this relationship was to be seriously deprived. The mighty Henry II authorized his administrator, Hugh Cleer, to write a treatise claiming for him the hereditary right to the seneschalship at King Louis's court, which would confer on him—in addition to judicial rights—the privilege of cutting the king's bread, of carrying his plate.[17] The emotional appeal of service, even in a domestic capacity, had been rekindled.

From the princes' point of view, there was one fly in the ointment: good vassals required good lordship. If they did not, in their opinion, receive it, they felt justifiably aggrieved. If their lord refused to hear their case in court or, having heard it, refused to pronounce judgement against the proven offender; or if he sought to disinherit a vassal without proper trial, there were grounds for seeking a remedy against him. But the only possible source of remedy against a prince was the king himself. Here again, the vernacular poetry played a part in creating expectations, for the good lord of the *chansons* and the courtly poems was almost invariably a king. When William of Ypres heard a rumour that Thierry of Flanders intended to disinherit his son Robert on his death, he wrote to Louis asking him to enfeoff his heir with the county.[18] Though Louis did not in fact move, William's action was a straw in the wind. It was a small leap from the course he recommended to the one actually taken by Philip Augustus in proclaiming John disinherited for failing to do justice to Hugh X de Lusignan.

But Louis VII's temperament was not that of Philip Augustus. Rejoicing in having reclaimed his princes' homage, he was prepared to be flexible. As a consequence, it is sometimes difficult to gauge the warmth of his princes' sentiments towards him. In 1163, for example, Thierry of Alsace renewed with Henry II the treaty originally drawn up for Robert II of Flanders and King Henry I (see p. 212). It might be deduced from this that the count was niggardly in the performance of his obligations to King Louis, to whom he undertook to give only the minumum assistance compatible with his status of vassal, should Louis choose to invade Henry's lands. Yet on a different occasion, when Louis's younger brother had threatened the royal demesne during the king's absence on crusade, Thierry had written to Suger:

When it pleases you that I should come to you and treat of the affairs concerning the land committed to you, call me confidently and let me know whether I should come with few or many men. For I am ready in all things to defend the land to the honour of my lord the king, and to shirk no dangers or labours so that I may faithfully serve him.[19]

A more dutiful vassal could hardly have been hoped for.

Inconsistency was apparently written into the French princes' view of their feudal obligations. Thibaud of Blois supported his uncle Henry I in campaigns against Louis VI; yet in 1124 he served in person under the royal standard against the emperor Henry V; then by 1137 he was maintaining that he need not participate in the royal expedition to Aquitaine that followed on Louis's marriage with Eleanor. Louis might be forgiven for thinking that Thibaud interpreted his homage in accordance with his own convenience. Yet on occasion there were displays of punctilious deference, as when in 1159 Henry II withdrew from the siege of Toulouse, or in 1184 Philip of Alsace abandoned his campaign in Vermandois, although both lost heavily by their actions. These apparently quixotic gestures point to the dilemma in which late twelfth-century princes found themselves: if they defended their interests, they set a bad example to their own vassals. So defiance could only be justified by their overlord's naked aggression. In this way also, then, the development of feudalism became a prop of masterful kingship.

(b) The princes and the church

The Anacletan schism of 1130 marked a new phase in ecclesiastical history. The church emerged from the turmoil of struggle with new self-confidence, to concentrate now on administrative and canon-law reform, on the spawning of new monastic orders in keeping with the reformed spirit, and on the defence of orthodoxy. The change afforded a breathing space for the laity, in which to take stock of their new position.

There was no time for nostalgia. The Norman Anonymous' treatise[20] reasserting the Carolingian model of church government was a last cry in the wilderness. It was now accepted on all sides that the distinction between spiritual and temporal spheres of control was proper; the concern was with working out its practical implications. But because the reformers had been respecters of persons, the problems waiting to be solved varied across the length and breadth of France; there could be no single 'princely' solution to them. And this was to prove a fatal weakness. Up till now, the strength of princely rule had lain in its adaptability, its capacity to respond to challenge on a local scale. But the Papacy of the post-reform era set itself against purely local solutions in the search for rules which could be widely enforced. It viewed French society from a distance, as a kingdom like any other, whose princes were only great nobles. To this rule, the pontificate of Calixtus II—a Burgundian aristocrat—had proved a welcome exception; but there were to be no Calixtuses among the popes of the post-1130 era. Popes dealt with kings, and encouraged their bishops to do likewise. One count was like another in the eyes of Rome.

Because Normandy had survived the reform movement with less structural alteration than any other principality,[21] throughout the twelfth century her dukes retained their control over the bishoprics, and the laity enjoyed patronage in many if not most of her parish churches. The duke remained without question the secular sword of the church. The price he paid for this privilege was the superficially small one of abandoning pretensions to theocratic rule; Henry I agreed that the staff and ring, spiritual symbols of the bishop's office, should be bestowed by the churchmen, while the king confined himself to demanding homage. The practical consequences of the 1107 agreement were, however, wider than this: on the one hand, it stimulated judicial activity within the duchy, because the duke's court now carried a heavy responsibility for the church's temporalities; on the other, it confined the duke to a wholly secular role. And the more successfully he performed this, the more firmly he imposed his peace over the duchy as a whole, the less reason there was for the church to feel any particular sense of obligation towards him. Clerics were beneficiaries of his administrative competence to the same degree and in the same way as everyone else. The archbishop of Rouen reacted to the political crises of the period like any other Norman baron; his contribution to Henry II's triumph in 1174 was as great as any of theirs; Walter de Coutances at least was one of Henry's chosen clerks. The incisive distinction between spiritual and temporal authority in the 1107 agreement bore fruit in that the church's temporal government became little more than a support to that of the state.

Nowhere else in France were Norman conditions replicated; yet the Norman example had some effect on the counts of Flanders, despite their much weaker hold on the church. Baldwin VII took upon himself the office of supreme advocate for all Flemish monastries, and wielded the sword with vigour in the interests of ecclesiastical peace. Charles the Good went so far as to rebuke a critical abbot with the words: 'Your role is to pray for me; mine to protect and defend the churches'[22]—a fine Norman note. The loss of Arras to Louis VI in 1128 deprived their successors of the last remaining Flemish episcopal guardianship, which may explain their less forceful approach; but Thierry's and Philip's justice continued to satisfy the monastic communities of Flanders, and so denied Louis the prospect of intervention.

In the second half of the century, Henry II and the counts of Flanders pursued similar religious policies: they displayed conventional piety, exercised a certain amount of patronage, defended the church with care; yet there was something almost impersonal in their attitudes. They did not prepare their younger sons for ecclesiastical careers (the exception was Thierry's third son Peter, who began his career as a clerk, but happily abandoned it to marry the heiress of Nevers); Henry II took the true Carolingian line that bishoprics were only suitable for bastard sons. They did not associate themselves strongly with any of the new monastic orders; they formed no link of special friendship with Rome. Churchmen inside their lands had reason to be grateful to them, bar the occasional friction caused by their domineering ways; but those outside saw no reason to praise them. Their only concession to the prevailing religious susceptibilities of their age was their passionate interest in crusading, which William of Tyre at least attributed rather to acquisitive instincts— they both had claims to the throne of Jerusalem—than to piety.[23] And if William was too harsh, what stuck in the popular imagination was the number of Turks Thierry and Philip had slain, rather than their devotion to the Holy Places; while men correctly attributed the huge treasure Henry II bestowed on the Temple at Jerusalem to penance for Becket's death, not to zeal for the cause of Christendom. Here, as everywhere else, their lordship was regarded as essentially secular.

In Aquitaine, Henry and Richard set themselves the same goals as in Normandy. This came as a relief to ecclesiastics there, grateful for new and more forceful protection, and for the new rulers' adherence to the correct candidate in the papal schism, and to orthodoxy against Catharism. So only the conflict with Becket generated a temporary sharpness. But in Anjou, Henry was heir to a rather different religious tradition, to which he was not insensitive. His grandfather, Fulk V, had been a friend of the wandering preacher Robert of Arbrissel and his hermits in the forest of Craon; when Robert was persuaded, by episcopal disapproval of his rootlessness, to establish himself at Fontevrault, Fulk had offered his protection to the new mixed community Robert attracted to himself. After the preacher, called by God, had abandoned his abbey for his former career, Fulk continued to guard and patronize it, encouraging its modest expansion, its fine new buildings. His daughter Mahaut later became its abbess; his other daughter Sybilla exacted munificence for it from her husband Thierry of Alsace, and both Geoffrey and Henry II were devoted to it. Fontevrault did have a few daughter houses, though it never developed as a major religious order, perhaps because, outside Anjou, the ancient idea of a mixed monastery was frowned upon. Nevertheless, it was the one place that elicited more than merely the conventional pious response from the ruling house of Anjou.

The contrasting style of Burgundy and Champagne is marked. Here the princes' options were narrowed by the royal *garde* over all bishoprics in the area, except Troyes, and by the protection Louis VI extended to the Cluniacs in 1119 and to Cîteaux rather later. The dukes of Burgundy were notably successful in exploiting what was left to them, by guaranteeing the peace of the ancient Benedictine abbeys within the duchy; and their proximity to Langres, Mâcon, Autun, Auxerre, and Chalon meant in practice that their military support was often more useful to the bishops than that of the king. The counts of Champagne retained control over Troyes, along with influence in Meaux. But both families took a notably low-profile approach to the abbots and bishops with whom they dealt, preferring to a blanket statement of rights the personal link, the individual agreement, and treating with deference such royal interventions as blocked their path. That this was not ineffectual was a consequence of their intimacy with the bishops of their area, and with reforming abbots. Unlike the Angevins, for the whole of the twelfth century the dukes of Burgundy successfully placed their younger sons in the surrounding bishoprics, or occasionally in monasteries, a policy which had the double advantage of preserving the ducal demesne from division (although Hugh II did have to make some arrangement for his fifth and sixth sons), and of ensuring that, whatever their constitutional links with the king, the bishops would in fact be frequent visitors to the ducal court. Though the counts of Champagne could not begin to rival the dukes, Thibaud launched his third son, William of the White Hands, on an ecclesiastical career of striking success, culminating in his election to the archbishopric of Rheims.

Because they were on close terms with ecclesiastics, they were quick to appreciate new expressions of the monastic spirit. Champagne was one of the earliest European bases for the Order of the Temple;[24] Count Hugh so favoured it that in 1125 he abdicated and joined its ranks, a gesture that brought the struggling soldier-monks much-needed publicity. This was a curtain-raiser to Thibaud IV's legendary generosity towards Clairvaux, which in the end provoked St Bernard to fear that the monks' asceticism might be undermined. Thibaud himself was only dissuaded from putting on the Premonstratensian habit by St Norbert's assurance that he could do more for God's cause by continuing to shoulder his earthly burden. His friendship with Bernard made so deep an impression on the popular imagination that in future generations he was remembered, not as the obstreperous aggressor described by Suger in his *Life*, but as a model prince. Bernard was also a friend of Hugh II of Burgundy—his father had been a ducal vassal—and of his wife; he reaped the value of this relationship when he needed a powerful prince to admonish Duke William X of Aquitaine for his adherence to Anacletus; Hugh willingly sent a letter urging him to support Innocent.[25] But Hugh had a closer connection with Cîteaux, on Burgundian territory, than with Clairvaux, on that of Champagne. An early gift from the duke to Cîteaux had helped the struggling house to survive;[26] it was a prudent investment, for by 1152, Cîteaux was the chief abbey of an order which had spread across the whole of Europe. As its patron, Duke Hugh III was present at the order's general chapter in 1170, where he exempted all Cistercian houses from any tolls or dues they might face anywhere on his lands.[27] It was a grand gesture performed in a very public way.

So if the counts of Champagne and the dukes of Burgundy were hesitant in projecting themselves as the sword for the defence of the church, they were happy to publish abroad their devoted adherence to its spiritual well-being. Neither of these stances could be easily adopted by Raymond V of Toulouse. The only bishopric within his control, Toulouse, did benefit on occasion from his assistance; but his long absences in St Gilles and Provence limited his effectiveness. And although a few Templar and Cistercian houses had been established on his lands in the enthusiasm of the 1130s, they were too small and insignificant for his protection to earn him much honour. By the 1160s and 1170s, what religious enthusiasm there was in the Toulousan area was being channelled into the spread of Catharism, the one new movement that it was inexpedient for princes to patronize. Thus Raymond's sole means of attracting ecclesiastical support lay in exploiting the traditionally close links of his house with the Papacy. He was among the throng of southern lords who flocked to greet Alexander III when he landed at Maguelonne in 1163; and he later maintained his contact with the Curia. In the south, however, a contact of this kind was unremarkable—the lord of Montpellier, who recognized the pope as his feudal overlord, preserved just such a link. Besides, Alexander was somewhat suspicious of Raymond's alliance with his enemy, the emperor Frederick Barbarossa, and less than happy with his son's treatment of the archbishop of Grenoble. So Raymond got rather less out of his devotion to papal primacy than he may have hoped—and besides, it exasperated Roger II of Béziers.

The king's relations with the church triumphantly co-ordinated all the methods pursued by his princes. More than half of the bishoprics of France benefited from Louis VII's protection, as did both the Cluniacs and the Cistercians; and if his sword was less sharp than the Duke of Normandy's, his enemies were far more inclined to flee the field before his approach. His brother Henry, a Cistercian monk, as bishop of Beauvais and later archbishop of Rheims, symbolized in his person the junction of the new monasticism with ancient ecclesiastical dignity. Louis himself was a devoted friend of Bernard after his conversion by the saint in 1144. His return from the crusade brought encouragement for the Temple in Paris, and also the recruitment of some Templars into the royal household. The climax of Louis's career came in 1164 when he sheltered Alexander III at Sens against the indignation of Frederick Barbarossa, and Becket at Pontigny in the face of Henry II's wrath, so acting, in the eyes of his admirers, as a shield of the faithful. Thus he had given substance to his father's proud boast that the French kings were friends of popes in their tribulations and that their loyalty could never be prised from the Roman church.[28]

(c) The princes' dilemma

1180 marks a natural break in the history of France. Until that date, the king and his princes ruled together. With the accession of Philip Augustus, the monarchy set out to establish its authority as different in kind from that of any subordinate power within the kingdom. Those princes who survived the assault Philip launched against them did so by accepting the monarchy's framework and adapting their own practices to suit; those who refused were either humbled or ejected. There were no compromises. By the late twelfth century it was clear that there was no room for the nonconformist.

The ease with which Philip Augustus and Louis VIII won their victories, as compared, for example, with the defeat of John by much lesser men, inevitably provokes speculation as to the inherent weakness of the French princes' position. Searching for weaknesses as early as 1180 may seem somewhat absurd, for this date could be taken as the obvious climax of princely power, the year in which the venerable and mighty Henry II showed paternal concern for the young Philip while Richard chalked up successes in Aquitaine and Geoffrey assumed rule in Brittany; in which Henry the Liberal and Philip of Alsace peacefully counted the benefits of their long and successful rule before troubles hit their respective counties; in which even Raymond V of Toulouse scored a point in the fight against Aragon. There was nothing to suggest that the days of power and prominence of men like these were numbered.

Yet despite their huge achievements, the twelfth century had not been easy for the princes in France; in the course of it, the more successful of their number had had to adapt their image to a greater extent than might on the surface appear. For their traditional strength had lain in what those ancient Roman senators they had been taught to admire referred to as *auctoritas*, the reputation for leadership, authority of utterance or appearance, the personal ascendancy over their fellows by which princes had attracted men to their *mouvance* and cases to their arbitration. By *auctoritas* they had defended churches, made themselves feared in battle and respected among their equals. Although this was a personal characteristic, it could be developed by education or by experience in most men; in fact, the few who failed to develop it—Eudes III of Troyes, Hoël of Brittany, perhaps Fulk le Réchin—were insignificant. Those who possessed it in abundance—Richard the Justiciar, Arnoul I, William V, Fulk Nerra, Geoffrey Martel, Baldwin V, Guy Geoffrey, William the Conqueror, Henry the Liberal, Philip of Alsace, and Henry II—had been the most remarkable figures of their ages.

The last three however, represented the Indian summer of *auctoritas* as a cohesive force in principalities. For when the ecclesiastical reformers had struck down one of its sturdiest pillars by insisting that rulers were only men like other men, the sole substitute for divine appointment to guide the church—and a very poor substitute it was—was the right of ecclesiastical patronage; and though this did enhance princes' prestige, it was widely shared by those below them in the social scale. The Cistercians, the orders of canons, the military orders, were supported by, and shared their lustre with, the meanest knights as well as the greatest lords. The quick-witted among the princes had therefore responded to the challenge by creating around themselves an alternative secular, chivalrous *ambiance* in which poets and historians played the role once filled by hagiographers; in which *auctoritas* was upheld by the reputation for learning or for discrimination; in which princely courts became the arbiters of taste. Their contribution to the more creative and the more romantic aspects of the twelfth-century renaissance was crucial. Yet by 1180, their inspiration had been absorbed by the whole military class: troubadours found patrons

among castellans as well as counts; the lords of Guînes and
Amboise were the subjects of *Gesta*; William of Montpellier
hired Alan of Lille as tutor for his son;[29] Baldwin of Guînes
was famed for his knowledge of theology;[30] William Marshal
was regarded as the ideal of knighthood.[31] Far from enhancing the princes' uniqueness, princely culture had polished and
refined the whole French aristocracy. Chrétien de Troyes
could boast that *chevalerie* had flown from Greece and Rome
to take up its home in France;[32] there was, however, only
marginal profit in the move for those who had been its chief
instigators. Indeed, it was ironical that one of their favourite
themes, 'the matter of Britain', should contribute to bathe
in romantic glow the one prince who made little effort on
his own behalf, the king of France.

So all that remained of *auctoritas* was personal magnetism,
a fickle and undisciplinable attribute. The obvious remedy
was to back it by *potestas*, the classical office, jurisdiction,
magistracy. Much of this part of the book has been devoted
to the way in which princely government emerged to put
muscle behind princely command. It was a very solid and
remarkable achievement. Yet in the long term it proved
counter-productive to the princes' retention of untrammelled
control over their own provinces. For *potestas* either operates
according to rules, in which case the faceless bureaucrat on
the spot becomes as important locally as his master; or it acts
arbitrarily, thereby provoking opposition against its source.
But either way, it automatically moulds a whole series of
juridical concepts—rights, obligations, privileges—which
sap the strength of personal rule. Having created government,
the princes had no option but to accept it when it was
imposed on them from above. For the future the only chance
of preserving their old ways lay in humbly subscribing to
the theory of Capetian supremacy while in practice capitalizing on royal weakness and inefficiency—a game at which the
dukes of Burgundy and Brittany were to exhibit consummate
skill. The alternative, open resistance, permitted the king
to exploit provincial government against the princes, as
the Angevins and the counts of Flanders were to find to
their cost.

Conclusion

THE inhibitions a historian may have about referring to 'France' before 1100 disappear very rapidly thereafter. Yet the solid juridical grounds that justify the change belong to the reign of Louis VII and not before. For since France was seen as a political confederation, the homages of Geoffrey le Bel (1144) and his son Henry (1151), Henry's treaty of 1158 and Raymond of Toulouse's in 1154, were vital in establishing Louis as liege lord of the princes who governed the country. Of these acts of submission, Raymond's was perhaps the most important, in that it altered the southward drift of an area which, without it, might well have become part of Spain.[1] There was less serious chance of Normandy becoming completely detached; although Henry I had refused homage in person, he had agreed that his son and heir, William, should perform it in 1120. Nevertheless, the acquiescence of its Angevin rulers in Louis's feudal overlordship was a victory for Louis. And though in immediate political terms the 1158 treaty was bitter, in that Louis had to set aside his chagrin at Eleanor's swift remarriage with Henry, it did ensure the feudal status of Aquitaine and Gascony. So by 1158, France existed as a kingdom in the sense that all its great princes acknowledged they held their honours in fief of Louis.

This was not unprecedented. Indeed, it might be viewed as a return to late ninth- and early tenth-century practice. Yet there was a clear difference in the practical meaning of the princes' fidelity to Louis IV and that accorded to Louis VII: though twelfth-century princes were far from consistent in carrying out their feudal obligations, they did recognize that they had some; their homage implied more than simple goodwill (see p. 262); and because their principalities had territorial definition, as their tenth-century predecessors' had not, Louis's feudal overlordship also had territorial expression. In 1163, when Raymond of Toulouse wrote to the king, asking approval for the marriage he had arranged between his son and the heiress to Albon (the Dauphiné), he remarked that the union would assist in extending Louis's lordship over new lands.[2] For him therefore, Louis was suzerain over all his vassals' possessions. If this conclusion was not accepted without qualification elsewhere, its appearance was still a significant development for royal power.

Louis's title remained the ancient *rex Francorum*, king of the Franks; but Suger frequently referred to the area over which he ruled as *regnum Franciae*, the kingdom of France. (Territory had therefore replaced race in the description, following the example already set in the great principalities.) Often Suger's *regnum Franciae* meant nothing more than the equivalent of *regnum Normanniae* or *regnum Flandriae*;[3] it referred only to the royal principality. But on occasion it was certainly used to cover the whole country over which Louis was recognized as suzerain. In 1164 the viscountess of Narbonne wrote to Louis, appealing for help in a struggle with a knight who asserted, on the strength of Roman Law, that since women could not be judges, she had no authority over him. Louis's reply ran thus:

In your country things are decided according to the laws of the emperors, in which it is laid down that power of judging is not permitted to women. Much kinder is the custom of our kingdom where, if the stronger sex fails, it is allowed to women to succeed and to administer the inheritance. Remember therefore that, because you are of our kingdom, we wish you to preserve the custom of our kingdom.[4]

Here *regnum* was used in both senses: in the narrow one when referring to the custom of the Île de France, in the broad one when asserting that Ermengarde was part of the kingdom. In fact, Louis was claiming the viscountess as in some sense his subject; her status permitted him to dispense her from the operation of what both parties agreed to be the law of her land. It was a precedent pregnant with consequence for the future development of the French monarchy.

Louis and his ministers had much to gain from the new concept of the wider French kingdom. Yet abstract juridical notions need to fall on receptive ground if they are to flourish. As it happened, ordinary people were already searching for a means of describing the land from Flanders to the Pyrenees: in 1149 William of Auvergne, departing for the Holy Land, left special instructions in the eventuality that he should die in Outremer or on the journey to Jerusalem; he described these places as *extra regnum Franciae et ducatus ipsius*[5]—outside the kingdom of France and its duchies. Here he was using *regnum Franciae* narrowly as the Île de France; but he was also assuming that the independent duchies belonged to the kingdom, that the whole was in some sense a confederation. His was as neat a way of explaining political realities in territorial terms as could be devised.

Perception of France's territorial integrity was, of course, hindered by the lack of clarity on her frontiers. The south was particularly obscure, for Catalan and Aragonese lordship in Gothia and Gascony was not subject to homage to the king of France; the defeat of Peter of Aragon at the hands of Simon de Montfort at Muret in 1213 was a necessary preliminary to the definition of the Pyrenean frontier. In the east, the Provençal–Burgundian–Imperial frontier was still fluid, largely as a consequence of French opportunism. Though an assize was held in 1288 to determine its northern edge,[6] it was not until the early fourteenth century, in the reign of Philip the Fair, that French expansion reached frontiers which satisfied its rulers for the rest of the middle ages. Only in the west, the Atlantic continued to provide certainty; for after 1158, there was a clear distinction between the Angevin lands in France, acknowledged as fiefs of the French crown, and the lands in Britain held allodially by the king of England.

In compensation for its haziness of outline, France was fortified by a dawning sense that those who dwelled within its confines constituted one people. Here, as has already been said,[7] the Second Crusade played a decisive part by bringing together lords from all over the kingdom, Flemish, Toulousan, Burgundian, Norman, in a common enterprise behind their king. Furthermore, it provided an opportunity to meet Germans in large numbers; Odo of Deuil's contempt for Conrad's men, the *Teutonici*, was symptomatic of French awareness that they were a race apart from the only other people historically entitled to call themselves *Franci*. The French had become for the crusaders the sole descendants of Charlemagne's warriors. Besides, their name had a second connotation: Pseudo-Turpin declared:

The land which used to be known as Gaul is now called France, that is, free from all servitude of other nations. A Frenchman is called free because the honour and mastery over all other peoples is properly his.[8]

For *Franci* were by definition *franci*, free men; and a free man might still be equated with a lord. Pseudo-Turpin's arrogant claim was justified by verbal associations. Bretons, Poitevins, Burgundians, who had in the past thought of the Franks as a distinct people, could now take pride in being counted among them. For to be French was to be a member of a master race.

This sense of community was fostered by the developing similarities among vernacular dialects in the course of the century. The author of the *Pilgrims' Guide to Compostela* found the tongue of the Saintonge and Bordeaux strangely rough; he did not think of it as a completely different language. Now that Breton, Basque, and Flemish had all been pushed to peripheries, a man could make himself understood, albeit with difficulty, across the country. The Angevin and Capetian courts, with their wide range of visitors, encouraged linguistic adaptability. Richard the Lionheart spoke Anglo-Norman in England, yet wrote Provençal verse like any other troubadour; Raymond V of Toulouse travelled to Jerusalem with Louis VII, brought Eleanor and her ladies back to France, married Louis's sister, and had his younger son brought up at Louis's court; his can hardly have been an exclusively Provençal environment. Then court cultures themselves encouraged linguistic uniformity. Though the Romance charters of the south were produced in a variety of dialects, the troubadours wrote for their aristocratic patrons in a common tongue;[9] so it is likely that the norms they established affected the speech of southern courts. If in the north court poets did not achieve so high a degree of agreement, the poetry of Chrétien de Troyes could nevertheless be enjoyed in Champagne, Flanders, and Brittany. And the scribes who wrote down the poems, by the mere act of recording, played their part in ending the infinite fluidity which had distinguished vernacular speech since the fall of the Roman Empire. Though there were two literary vernaculars in twelfth-century France, the *langue d'oc* and the *langue d'oïl*, their mere appearance was proof that some common ground had been attained in the speech of its people.

It follows from what has been said that French language bolstered the French sense of unity more obviously against Germans than against Catalans or Englishmen. Though Suger was clear on it,[10] it was in the main to be left to the thirteenth century to distinguish Englishmen from Frenchmen;[11] arguably there never has been a clear distinction between French and Catalans. But Louis VI and Louis VII were glad of any help they could get in asserting the distinctiveness of their kingdom and people from those of the German emperors, especially during the reign of Frederick Barbarossa, when imperial claims were flaunted most vigorously. For the kings recognized that the origin of their rule lay in the division of the Carolingian empire; therefore any projected reunification of that empire was a real threat to their position. Their defence lay in three centuries of custom, in their annexation of the Frankish inheritance, and in the will of their people. Suger was correct in perceiving Louis VI's great army of 1124, mustered to rebut Henry V, as the climax of his reign;[12] a historian might also see in it the real birth of the *regnum Franciae* in its wider sense.

The reigns from Philip Augustus to Philip IV were taken up in creating the monarchical structure, expressed in public law, by which France was welded into a true state. The king's feudal suzerainty over his princes came to include rights of wardship, marriage, and escheats; his court heard appeals from lesser courts throughout the country; he acquired limited legislative rights; he began to tax beyond the frontiers of the demesne. Then suzerainty slid into sovereignty: his judgement was final in temporal matters; time could not run against him; what had once been his could not be alienated. It was a far cry from the kingship of Philip I, or even from that of Louis VII, which had rested above all on moral rather than legal superiority. Crucial to the creation of this new kingship was the subjugation of the princes. Where

CONCLUSION 379

Louis VII had attained his ends by diplomacy, Philip Augustus used force. The destruction of the Angevin empire was followed by attacks on Flanders, and on Toulouse. Under Philip Augustus' successors, the task was pushed further: Poitou joined Normandy, Anjou, Maine, and the Touraine within the royal demesne by treaty in 1259; Toulouse was finally annexed in 1274; control of Blois fell into the king's hands in 1234; and marriage brought Champagne to the crown in 1284. The only principalities to survive, Gascony, Brittany, Flanders, and Burgundy, later revived, and together they came close to destroying the kingdom of France in the Hundred Years' War. But between 1180 and 1328 all except Burgundy faced threats to their very existence. For a century and a half the momentum of the monarchy seemed unstoppable.

Nevertheless the rise of the French monarchy was in a real sense superstructural. For its public law never fully integrated with the private law which continued beside it; so, though some princes might disappear, the provinces they had created, with their customary laws and their feudal hierarchies, lived on. The politics of Paris were not and could not be the politics of the country as a whole; nor could the cultural fashions of Paris obliterate the powerful provincial sentiments born in the tenth and eleventh centuries. 'La France se nomme diversité; said Michelet. 'How can anyone govern a nation that has two hundred and forty-six different kinds of cheese?', asked de Gaulle. Capetian kings from Philip Augustus to Charles IV had reason to experience for themselves the mixture of pride and frustration that was to prompt both these statements.

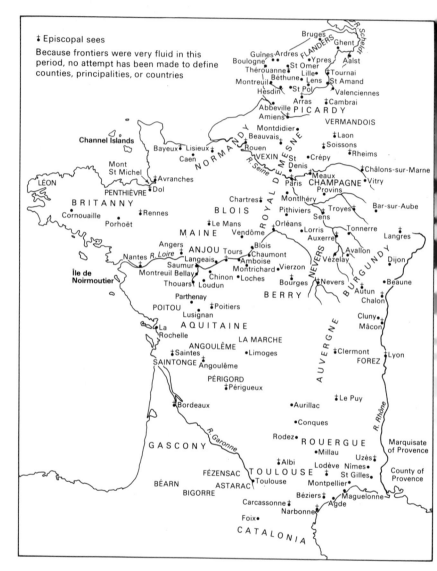

Map 3. France in the Twelfth Century

Genealogical Tables

NB. These tables make no claim at all to be comprehensive. It is very hard to trace those who died young, insignificant younger sons, or unmarried daughters, far more so illegitimate children; and the task has not been attempted. The tables are intended simply to assist in understanding the text.

CAPETIAN KINGS OF FRANCE

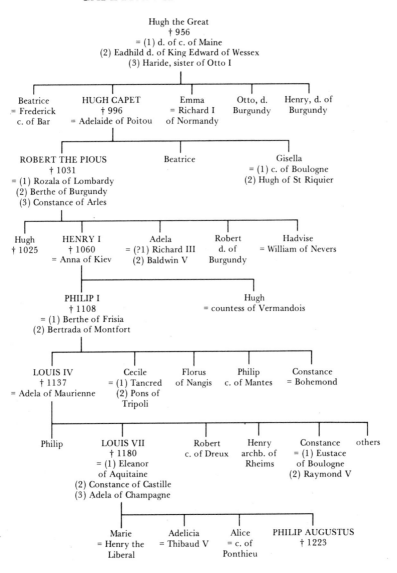

DUKES OF AQUITAINE

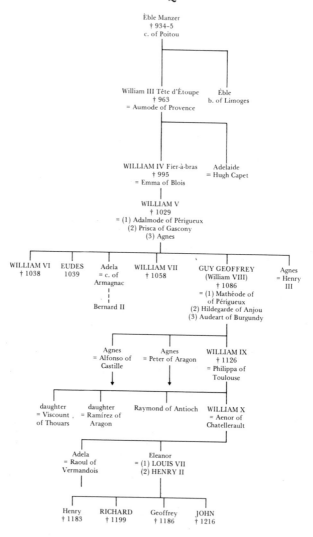

Èble Manzer
† 934–5
c. of Poitou

William III Tête d'Étoupe   Èble
† 963   b. of Limoges
= Aumode of Provence

WILLIAM IV Fier-à-bras   Adelaide
† 995   = Hugh Capet
= Emma of Blois

WILLIAM V
† 1029
= (1) Adalmode of Périgueux
  (2) Prisca of Gascony
  (3) Agnes

WILLIAM VI   EUDES   Adela   WILLIAM VII   GUY GEOFFREY   Agnes
† 1038   1039   = c. of   † 1058   (William VIII)   = Henry
                           Armagnac   † 1086   III
                                                           = (1) Mathéode of
                           Bernard II   of Périgueux
                                                             (2) Hildegarde of Anjou
                                                             (3) Audeart of Burgundy

                Agnes   Agnes   WILLIAM IX
                = Alfonso of   = Peter of Aragon   † 1126
                Castille   = Philippa of
                                                     Toulouse

daughter   daughter   Raymond of Antioch   WILLIAM X
= Viscount   = Ramírez of   = Aenor of
of Thouars   Aragon   Chatellerault

        Adela   Eleanor
        = Raoul of   = (1) LOUIS VII
        Vermandois   (2) HENRY II

Henry   RICHARD   Geoffrey   JOHN
† 1183   † 1199   † 1186   † 1216

DUKES OF BURGUNDY

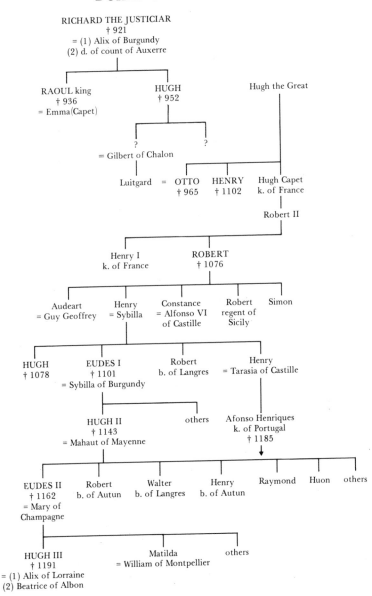

DUKES OF GASCONY

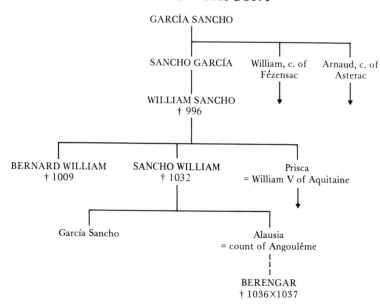

DUKES OR COUNTS OF BRITTANY

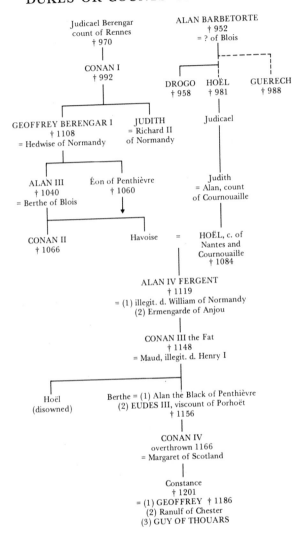

Judicael Berengar
count of Rennes
† 970

ALAN BARBETORTE
† 952
= ? of Blois

CONAN I
† 992

DROGO
† 958

HOËL
† 981

GUERECH
† 988

GEOFFREY BERENGAR I
† 1108
= Hedwise of Normandy

JUDITH
= Richard II
of Normandy

Judicael

ALAN III
† 1040
= Berthe of Blois

Éon of Penthièvre
† 1060

Judith
= Alan, count
of Cournouaille

CONAN II
† 1066

Havoise   =   HOËL, c. of
Nantes and
Cournouaille
† 1084

ALAN IV FERGENT
† 1119
= (1) illegit. d. William of Normandy
(2) Ermengarde of Anjou

CONAN III the Fat
† 1148
= Maud, illegit. d. Henry I

Hoël
(disowned)

Berthe = (1) Alan the Black of Penthièvre
(2) EUDES III, viscount of Porhoët
† 1156

CONAN IV
overthrown 1166
= Margaret of Scotland

Constance
† 1201
= (1) GEOFFREY † 1186
(2) Ranulf of Chester
(3) GUY OF THOUARS

COUNTS OF ROUEN, DUKES OF NORMANDY

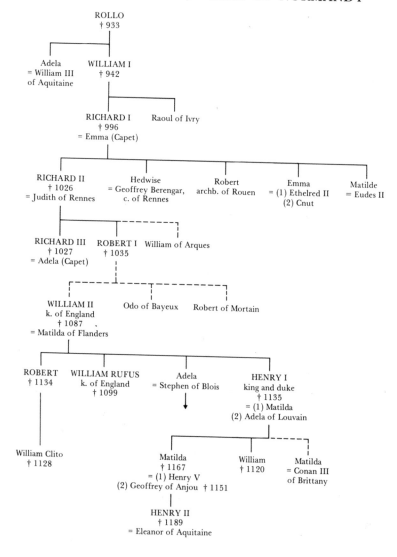

COUNTS OF ANJOU

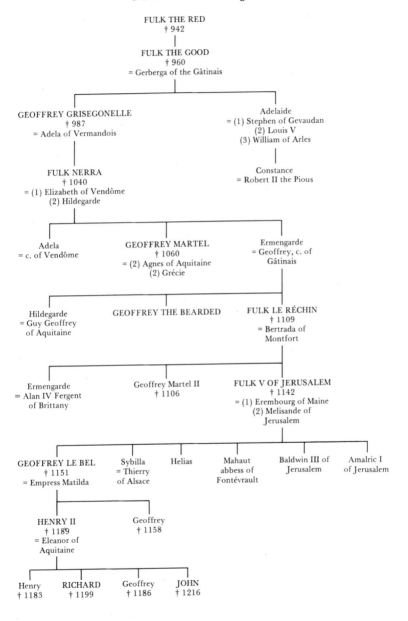

FULK THE RED
† 942

FULK THE GOOD
† 960
= Gerberga of the Gâtinais

GEOFFREY GRISEGONELLE
† 987
= Adela of Vermandois

Adelaide
= (1) Stephen of Gevaudan
(2) Louis V
(3) William of Arles

FULK NERRA
† 1040
= (1) Elizabeth of Vendôme
(2) Hildegarde

Constance
= Robert II the Pious

Adela
= c. of Vendôme

GEOFFREY MARTEL
† 1060
= (2) Agnes of Aquitaine
(2) Grécie

Ermengarde
= Geoffrey, c. of
Gâtinais

Hildegarde
= Guy Geoffrey
of Aquitaine

GEOFFREY THE BEARDED

FULK LE RÉCHIN
† 1109
= Bertrada of
Montfort

Ermengarde
= Alan IV Fergent
of Brittany

Geoffrey Martel II
† 1106

FULK V OF JERUSALEM
† 1142
= (1) Erembourg of Maine
(2) Melisande of
Jerusalem

GEOFFREY LE BEL
† 1151
= Empress Matilda

Sybilla
= Thierry
of Alsace

Helias

Mahaut
abbess of
Fontévrault

Baldwin III of
Jerusalem

Amalric I
of Jerusalem

HENRY II
† 1189
= Eleanor of
Aquitaine

Geoffrey
† 1158

Henry
† 1183

RICHARD
† 1199

Geoffrey
† 1186

JOHN
† 1216

COUNTS OF BLOIS AND CHAMPAGNE

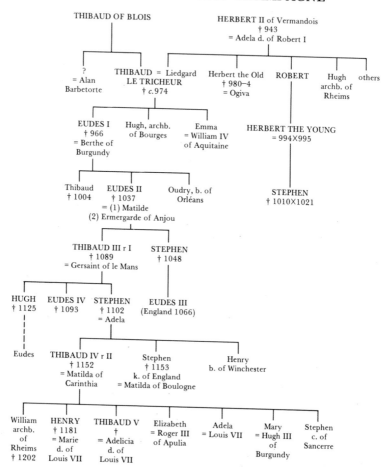

COUNTS OF FLANDERS

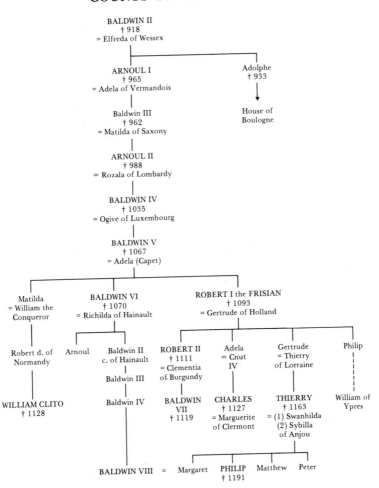

COUNTS OF TOULOUSE

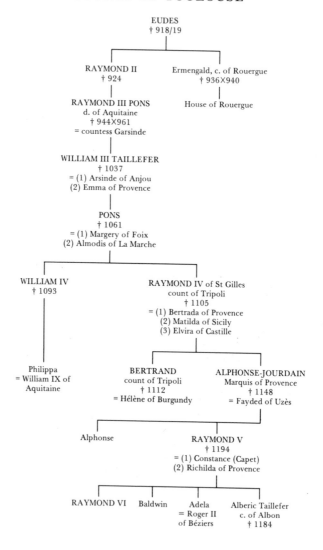

EUDES
† 918/19

RAYMOND II
† 924

Ermengald, c. of Rouergue
† 936×940

RAYMOND III PONS
d. of Aquitaine
† 944×961
= countess Garsinde

House of Rouergue

WILLIAM III TAILLEFER
† 1037
= (1) Arsinde of Anjou
(2) Emma of Provence

PONS
† 1061
= (1) Margery of Foix
(2) Almodis of La Marche

WILLIAM IV
† 1093

RAYMOND IV of St Gilles
count of Tripoli
† 1105
= (1) Bertrada of Provence
(2) Matilda of Sicily
(3) Elvira of Castille

Philippa
= William IX of
Aquitaine

BERTRAND
count of Tripoli
† 1112
= Hélène of Burgundy

ALPHONSE-JOURDAIN
Marquis of Provence
† 1148
= Fayded of Uzès

Alphonse

RAYMOND V
† 1194
= (1) Constance (Capet)
(2) Richilda of Provence

RAYMOND VI

Baldwin

Adela
= Roger II
of Béziers

Alberic Taillefer
c. of Albon
† 1184

Notes

Chapter 1

1. Nithard, *Histories in Carolingian Chronicles*, tr. B. W. Scholz with B. Rogers (Ann Arbor paperbacks, 1972), 174.
2. E. Magnou-Nortier, *La Société laïque et l'Église dans la province ecclésiastique de Narbonne de la fin du VIIIe à la fin du XIe siècle* (Toulouse, 1974), 239.
3. *Recueil des actes de Robert Ier et de Raoul*, ed. J. Dufour (Paris, 1978), 95.
4. Richer, *Histoire de France*, ed. R. Latouche (2 vols., Paris, 1937), ii. 162.
5. Largely collected in B. and M. Lyon (eds.), *Frankish Institutions under Charlemagne* (Providence, RI, 1968), and in *The Carolingians and the Frankish Monarchy: Studies in Carolingian History*, tr. J. Sondheimer (London, 1971).
6. See p. 58 and *Vita Sancti Geraldi*, PL cxxxiii, col. 654.
7. Ibid., col. 664.
8. Richer, loc. cit.
9. H. A. L. Fisher (ed.), *The Constitutional History of England* (London, 1931), 23-4.
10. J. Dhondt, *Études sur la naissance des principautés territoriales en France (IXe-Xe siècles)* (Bruges, 1948).
11. PL cxxv, col. 1085: *Ad regem ut bonos diligat consiliarios.*
12. e.g. W. Ullmann, *The Carolingian Renaissance and the Idea of Kingship* (London, 1969), 96-8.
13. Ed. and tr. T. Gross and R. Schieffer (Hanover, 1980).

Chapter 2

1. *Les Annales de Flodoard*, ed. P. Lauer (Paris, 1905).
2. See Ch. I n. 4 above.
3. B. Smalley, *The Historians of the Middle Ages* (London, 1974), 113.
4. *Chronique*, ed. J. Chavanon (Paris, 1897).
5. P. Grierson (ed.), *Les Annales de Saint-Pierre de Gand et de Saint-Amand* (Brussels, 1937), 1-73, esp. 17 n. 7, 21.
6. PL cxli, col. 879.
7. *Cartulaire de Saint-Bertin*, ed. B. Guérard (Paris, 1840), 15-168.
8. PL cxxxiii, cols. 639-704.
9. Ed. O. Holder-Egger, MGH SS xv. 298-303.
10. *Les Miracles de saint Benoît*, ed. E. de Certain (Paris, 1858).
11. *Le Livre des miracles de sainte Foy*, ed. A. Bouillet and E. Servières in *Sainte Foy, vierge et martyre* (Rodez, 1900).

12. The *Actes* of Eudes by R. H. Bautier (Paris, 1967); of Charles the Simple by P. Lauer (Paris, 1940-9); of Robert I and Raoul by J. Dufour (Paris, 1978); of Louis IV by P. Lauer (Paris, 1914); and of Lothaire and Louis V by L. Halphen and F. Lot (Paris, 1908).

13. *Actes*, ed. Lauer, 35-7.

14. G. Tessier, *Diplomatique royale française* (Paris, 1962), 88.

15. J.-F. Lemarignier, *Le Gouvernement royal aux premiers temps capétiens (978-1108)* (Paris, 1965), 30.

16. *Actes*, ed. Dufour, p. xi.

17. *Actes*, ed. Lauer, 89.

18. K. F. Werner, 'Kingdom and principality in twelfth-century France', in T. Reuter (ed.), *The Medieval Nobility* (Oxford, 1979), 252-6.

19. W. Kienast, 'Der Wirkungsbereich des französischen Königtums von Odo bis Ludwig VI. (888-1137) in Südfrankreich', *Historische Zeitschrift* 209 (1969), 529-65, esp. 529-30.

20. J.-F. Lemarignier and his disciples. See discussion below, p. 130.

Chapter 3

1. Tr. R. Poupardin, *Cambridge Medieval History*, iii (Cambridge, 1922), 62-3.

2. *Raoul Glaber, les cinq livres de ses histoires (900-1044)*, ed. M. Prou (Paris, 1886), 8.

3. Ed. de Certain, 104.

4. I rely on J.-F. Lemarignier, *Institutions*, iii. 54; W. M. Newman, *Le Domaine royale sous les premiers Capétiens (987-1108)* (Paris, 1937), 67-95; P. R. Gaussin, *L'Abbaye de la Chaise-Dieu 1043-1518* (Paris, 1962), 67, 68.

5. J. W. Thompson, *The Dissolution of the Carolingian Fisc in the Ninth Century* (Berkeley, 1935).

6. *Actes*, ed. Bautier, 65-7. no. 14; id. 'Le règne d'Eudes', 419.

7. *Histoire de France*, i. 16.

8. *Gerbert of Rheims, Letters, with his Papal Privileges as Silvester II*, ed. and tr. H. P. Lattin (New York, 1961), nos. 55 and 53.

9. The legend originated in Hincmar's *Vita Sanctii Remigii, MGH SSRM* iii. 297, and was popularized by Aimon of Fleury in his *Historia Francorum, PL* cxxxix. col. 538.

10. See B. Schneidmüller, *Karolingische Tradition und frühes französisches Königtum: Untersuchungen zur Herrschaftslegitimation der westfränkisch-französischen Monarchie im 10. Jahrhundert* (Wiesbaden, 1979), 170-85.

11. P. H. Sawyer, *The Age of the Vikings* (London, 1962), 12-47. On this whole question see J. M. Wallace-Hadrill, 'The Vikings in Francia', *Early Medieval History* (Oxford, 1975) 217-36.

12. *MGH SS* xv. 302.

13. *Chronique*, 166-7.

14. *Miracles de saint Benoît*, 96-8.
15. *Historia Ecclesiae Remensis*, ed. J. Heller and G. Waitz, *MGH SS* xiii (Hanover, 1881), 573.
16. *PL* cxxxi, cols. 11-12.
17. C. L. H. Coulson, 'Fortresses and Social Responsibility in Late Carolingian France', *Zeitschrift für Archäologie des Mittelalters* 4 (1976), 36, quoting Borell's confirmation of 986; and see n. 22 below.
18. *Actes*, ed. Bautier, 41-5.
19. *Actes*, ed. Prou, 315-17.
20. *La Société aux XIe et XIIe siècles dans la région mâconnaise* (2nd edn., Paris, 1971), 100-2.
21. *La Terre et les hommes en Picardie jusqu'à la fin du XIIIe siècle* (2 vols., Paris, 1968), ii, 490-6.
22. *Chartres et ses campagnes, XIe-XIIIe siècles* (Paris, 1973), 271.
23. *Le Berry du Xe siècle au milieu du XIIe. Étude politique, religieuse, sociale et économique* (Paris, 1973), 123-35.
24. L. A. Manyon (tr.), *Feudal Society* (London, 1961), 1. On castles in general, see M. P. Héliot, 'Remarques sur les châteaux-forts bâtis en France du Xe au XIIe siècle', *Comptes rendus de l'Académie des inscriptions et belles-lettres* 1965, 169-74; and G. Fournier, *Le Château dans la France médiévale: essai de sociologie monumentale* (Paris, 1978).

Chapter 4

1. e.g. Ademar of Chabannes, *Chronique*, 166, 168.
2. *Historia Pontificum et Comitum Engolismensium*, ed. J. Boussard (Paris, 1957), 32.
3. *Actes*, ed. Bautier, 180.
4. See particularly K. F. Werner, 'Quelques observations au sujet des débuts du "duché" de Normandie', *Études Yver*, 691-709; W. Kienast, *Der Herzogstitel in Frankreich und Deutschland* (9. bis 12. Jahrhundert) (Munich, 1968); K. Brunner, 'Der fränkische Fürstentitel im neunten und zehnten Jahrhundert', *MIÖG* 24 (1973) 179-340.
5. *Actes*, ed. Halphen-Lot, 47.
6. *Cartulaire de Saint-Bertin*, 134.
7. *Actes*, ed. Lauer, 10: 'qui est in omnibus regnis nostris secundus a nobis'.
8. *Annales*, 205.
9. *Diplomata Belgica ante annum millesimum centesimum scripta*, ed. M. Gysseling and A. C. F. Koch (Brussels, 1950), 144.
10. Schneidmüller, 179.
11. *Histoire de France*, i. 12.
12. A. C. F. Koch (ed.), in *Révue bénédictine* 70 (1960), 126.
13. *Diplomata Belgica*, 143-6.
14. *PL* cxxxiii, cols. 671-2.

15. R. C. Watson, 'The Counts of Angoulême from the Ninth Century to the Mid-Thirteenth Century' (unpublished Ph.D. thesis, Univ. of East Anglia, 1979), cites a sales tax within Angoulême.

16. F. Dumas-Dubourg, *Le Trésor de Fécamp et le monnayage en Francie occidentale pendant la seconde moitié du Xe siècle* (Paris, 1971), 23, 48-55, 197-9.

17. M. de Bony de Lavergne, *Une descendance des seconds rois d'Austrasie: les vicomtes de Limoges* ([Clairvivre], 1965), 118, 205.

18. *PL* cxxxiii, col. 661.

19. J. P. Poly and E. Bournazel, *La Mutation Féodale, X^e-XIIe siècles* (Paris, 1980), 129-31.

20. G. Fournier, *Le Peuplement rural en Basse-Auvergne durant le Haut Moyen Âge* (Paris, 1962), 366; J. Boussard, 'Services féodaux, milices et mercenaires dans les armées, en France, aux Xe et XIe siècles', *Settimane Spoleto* 15 (1968), 131-68.

21. J. Boussard, 'L'Origine des familles seigneuriales dans la région de la Loire moyenne', *Cahiers de civ. méd.* 5 (1962), 321.

22. *Chartes de Cluny*, ed. A. Bernard and A. Bruel (6 vols., Paris, 1876-1903), no. 656; O. Guillot, *Le Comte d'Anjou et son entourage au XIe siècle* (2 vols., Paris, 1972), ii. 14.

23. Guillot, *Le Comte d'Anjou*, ii. 21-3.

24. *PL* cxxxiii, cols. 646, 656.

25. Ibid. 654, 656.

26. *Actes*, ed. Bautier, 38-40; E. Warlop, *The Flemish Nobility before 1300*, tr. J. B. Ross and H. Vandermoere (Kortrijk, 1975), i. 30 nn. 59, 59a.

27. *PL* cxxxiii, col. 647.

28. *Annales Vedastini*, ed. B. von Simson, *MGH SSRG* (Hanover and Leipzig, 1905), 67.

29. *PL* cxxxiii, col. 661.

30. *Cartulaire de Brioude*, ed. H. Doniol (Clermont-Ferrand, 1863), no. 309.

31. J. Lafaurie, 'Numismatique. Des Carolingiens aux Capétiens', *Cahiers de civ. méd.* 13 (1970), 117-37.

32. *Chronique*, 152; see Guillot, *Le Comte d'Anjou*, i. 6-8.

33. *PL* cxxxiii, cols. 663, 664.

34. This account makes use of J. Martindale, 'The Origins of the Duchy of Aquitaine and the Government of the Counts of Poitou, 902-1137' (unpublished D.Phil. thesis, Oxford, 1965), hereafter referred to as Martindale, 'The Counts of Poitou'.

35. *Gesta Pontificum Autissiodorensium*, ed. L. M. Duru, *Bibliothèque historique de l'Yonne ou collection de légendes, chroniques et documents* (Auxerre, 1850), i. 367.

36. Quoted in M. Chaume, *Les Origines du duché de Bourgogne* (Dijon, 1925), 351.

37. *Historia Ecclesiae Remensis, MGH SS* xiii. 576.

38. *PL* cxli, col. 379.

39. *Annales*, ed. Lauer, 65.

40. This account makes use of J. Richard, *Les Ducs de Bourgogne et la formation du duché du XIe au XIVe siècle* (Paris, 1954) and of Y. Sassier, *Recherches sur le pouvoir comtal en Auxerrois du Xe au début du XIIIe siècle* (Paris, 1980).

41. J. Boussard, 'Les destinées de la Neustrie du IXe au XIe siècle', *Cahiers de civ. méd.* 11 (1968), 15-28; K. F. Werner, *Études Yver*, 691-709.

42. K. F. Werner, 'L'acquisition par la maison de Blois des comtés de Chartres et de Châteaudun', in *Mélanges de numismatique, d'archéologie et d'histoire offerts à Jean Lafaurie* (Paris, 1980), 265-72.

43. *Actes*, ed. Lauer 10.

44. Kienast, *Der Herzogstitel*, 53-9; Ganshof, 'A propos de ducs et de duchés du haut moyen âge', *Journal des savants* (1972-3), 16; K. Brunner, 'Der fränkische Fürstentitel', 262, 279-82.

45. *Genealogiae Comitum Flandraie*, ed. L. C. Bethmann, *MGH SS* ix, 303.

46. J. Gardelles, 'Le palais dans l'Europe occidentale chrétienne du Xe au XIe siècle', *Cahiers de civ. méd.* 19 (1976), 125.

47. H. Pirenne, *Histoire de Belgique*, i (3rd edn., Brussels, 1909), 99-100.

48. Quoted in C. Brühl, *Fodrum, Gistum, Servitium Regis* (Cologne, 1968), 276-7.

49. H. Platelle, *La Justice seigneuriale de l'abbaye de Saint-Amand* (Louvain, 1965), 57-8.

50. This account makes use of F. L. Ganshof, *La Flandre sous les premiers comtes* (Brussels, 1949) and of J. Dhondt, *Les Origines de la Flandre et de l'Artois* (Arras, 1944).

51. R. d'Abadal de Vinyals, *Els primers comtes catalans* (Barcelona, 1958), 13-17; quoted in P. Bonnassie, *La Catalogne du milieu du Xe à la fin du XIe siècle: croissance et mutations d'une société* (Toulouse, 1975, 1976), 164.

52. R. H. J. Collins, 'Charles the Bald and Wifred the Hairy', in M. Gibson and J. Nelson (eds.), *Charles the Bald: Court and Kingdom* (BAR International series 101, 1981), 178-9; Bonnassie, 171, 177-80.

53. See R. W. Southern, *The Making of the Middle Ages* (London, 1959), 124.

54. Bonnassie, 165.

55. Ibid. 137.

56. Ibid. 138.

57. E. James, *The Origins of France from Clovis to the Capetians, 500-1000* (London, 1982), 187.

58. I owe this point to T. N. Bisson.

59. See R. H. C. Davis, *The Normans and their Myth* (London, 1976).

60. *Annales*, 72, 74, 75.

61. *Chronicon Hugonis Monachi Virdunensis et Divionensis, Abbatis Flaviniacensis*, ed. G. H. Pertz, *MGH SS* viii, 360.

62. *Histoire de France*, ii. 328.
63. See F. Dumas-Dubourg, 11.
64. See the discussion in D. Bates, *Normandy before 1066* (London, 1982), 34-6.
65. This account makes use of D. Bates, and of J. Le Patourel, *The Norman Empire* (Oxford, 1976).
66. *Annales*, 55.
67. *Chronique de Nantes, 570 environ—1049*, ed. R. Merlet (Paris, 1896), 91-2.
68. *Histoires*, 30.
69. A. R. Lewis, *The Development of Southern French and Catalan Society 718-1058* (Texas, 1965); Magnou-Nortier, *La Société laïque*.
70. *Annales*, 90.
71. Quoted by Magnou-Nortier, 255.
72. F. Cheyette, 'The castles of the Trencavels: a Preliminary Aerial Survey', in *Order and Innovation*, 255-72.
73. B. Cursente, *Les Castelnaux de la Gascogne médiévale* (Bordeaux, 1980), 30-1.
74. Aimon of Fleury, *Vita Abbonis*, PL cxxxix, col. 499.
75. C. Higounet, *Histoire de Bordeaux*, ii. *Bordeaux pendant le Haut Moyen Âge* (Bordeaux, 1963), 47.
76. Dhondt, *Étude*; J.-F. Lemarignier, 'Political and monastic structures in France at the end of the tenth and the beginning of the eleventh century', in F. Cheyette (ed.), *Lordship and Community in Medieval Europe* (New York, 1968), 102-11; K. F. Werner, 'Kingdom and principality in twelfth-century France', in *The Medieval Nobility*, 243-90.
77. 'Kingdom and Principality', 248.
78. *Actes*, ed. Halphen-Lot, xxix, 71-3.
79. I rely on Sassier, 29 n. 127.
80. E. Magnou-Nortier, *La Société laïque* 237.
81. Ed. G. Waitz, *MGH SS* xiii (Hanover, 1881), 251.
82. See M. Bur, *La Formation du comté de Champagne v. 950-v. 1150* (Nancy, 1977), 472.
83. 'La dislocation du *pagus* et le problème des *consuetudines*'. *Mélanges . . . L. Halphen* (Paris, 1951), 401-10.
84. Fossier, *Picardie*, i. 174-7; ii. 486-8.
85. Devailly *Le Berry*, 109-35.
86. P. R. Gaussin, *L'Abbaye de la Chaise-Dieu*, 63-91; G. Fournier, *Le Peuplement*, 365-99.

Chapter 5

1. Adalbéron de Laon, *Poème au roi Robert* ed. C. Carozzi (Paris, 1979), 2, l. 22.
2. K. Schmid, 'The Structure of the Nobility in the Earlier Middle Ages', in *The Medieval Nobility; Liber Memorialis Romaricenis*,

ed. Hlawitschka, Tellenbach, and Schmid, *MGH Libri Memoriales* i (1970).

3. *Chroniques des comtes d'Anjou et des seigneurs d'Amboise*, ed. L. Halphen and R. Poupardin (Paris, 1913), 25.

4. *Miracles of St Foy*, 478-9.

5. *Chronique de Saint-Maixent, 751-1140*, ed. J. Verdon (Paris, 1979), 78.

6. A. W. Lewis, 'Anticipatory Association of the Heir in Early Capetian France', *American Historical Review* 83 (1978), 906-27.

7. *PL* cxxxiii, col. 642.

8. K. F. Werner, 'Important Noble Families in the Kingdom of Charlemagne—a Prosopographical Study of the Relationship between King and Nobility in the Early Middle Ages', in *The Medieval Nobility*, 149-73.

9. K. F. Werner, 'Untersuchungen zur Frühzeit des französischen Fürstentums: Zu den Anfängen des Hauses Anjou', *Die Welt als Geschichte* 18 (1958), 264-89. But see the more flexible approach adopted by the same author in 'Liens de parenté et noms de personne. Un problème historique et méthodologique', in G. Duby and J. Le Goff (eds), *Famille et parenté dans l'Occident médiévale* (Rome, 1977), 13-18, 25-34. And C. Bouchard, 'The origins of the French nobility. A reassessment', *AHR* 86 (1981), 501-32.

10. J. Martindale, 'The French Aristocracy in the Early Middle Ages: a Reappraisal', *Past and Present* 75 (1977), 32-3 and n. 111.

11. B. Guenée, 'Les généalogies entre l'histoire et la politique: la fierté d'être capetien, en France, au moyen âge', *Annales* 33 (1978), 450-77. Cf. Bur, 99-113.

12. *Feudal Society*, 77-8, 166, 214-15.

13. *Société*, 125 n. 57.

14. Ademar, *Chronique*, 145.

15. Ibid. 152; Guillot, *Le Comte d'Anjou*, i. 6-8.

16. *Histoire de France*, i. 120-2, 188-90.

17. Flodoard, *Annales*, 31; J. Boussard, 'Services féodaux', 140.

18. E. Magnou, 'Note sur le sens du mot *fevum* en Septimanie et dans la Marche d'Espagne à la fin du Xe et au début du XIe siècle', *Annales du Midi* 76 (1964), 141; P. Bonnassie, *La Catalogne . . .* 146; and 'Les conventions féodales dans la Catalogne du XIe siècle', *Les Structures sociales de l'Aquitaine, du Languedoc, et de l'Espagne au premier âge féodal* (Paris, 1969).

19. Ed. Guérard, 135.

20. 'L'aristocratie normande au XIe siècle', 78, in P. Contamine (ed.), *La Noblesse au Moyen Âge* (Paris, 1976).

21. *Société*, 125-7.

22. *PL* cxxxiii, col. 654.

23. O. Guillot, *Le Comte d'Anjou*, i. 137, 138.

24. *MGH SS* ii (Hanover, 1829), 255.

25. Hariulf, *Chronique de l'abbaye de Saint-Riquier*, ed. F. Lot (Paris, 1894), 230.

26. Ed. de Certain, 159.
27. Hariulf, *Chronique*, 206-7.
28. Ibid. 229; see also 205.
29. See J. Lemarignier, *Institutions*, iii. 18.
30. M. de la Motte-Callas, 'Les possessions territoriales de Saint-Germain-des-Prés . . .', *Memorial du XIVe centenaire de l'abbaye de Saint-Germain-des-Prés* (Paris, 1957), 49-80.
31. *Histoires*, 62.
32. Ed. Merlet, 113-16.
33. *Annales*, 78.

Chapter 6

1. Ed. G. Waitz, *MGH SS* ix (Hanover, 1851), 364-9.
2. See p. 399 n. 25.
3. *Epitoma Vitae Regis Rotberti Pii*, ed. R. H. Bautier (Paris, 1965).
4. Ed. J. A. Lair (Paris, 1865).
5. *Histoire de Guillaume le Conquérant*, ed. and tr. R. Foreville (Paris, 1952).
6. *Gesta Normannorum Ducum*, ed. J. Marx (Rouen, 1914).
7. *Ecclesiastical History*, ed. and tr. M. Chibnall (6 vols, Oxford, 1969-80).
8. *Chroniques des comtes d'Anjou*, 232-8.
9. Ibid. 25-73.
10. *Recueil d'annales angevines et vendômoises*, ed. L. Halphen (Paris, 1903), 80-90; *Chroniques des églises d'Anjou*, ed. P. Marchegay and E. Mabille (Paris, 1869), 217-328.
11. *MGH SS* ix, 305-8. See L. Genicot, *Les Généalogies*, Typologie des sources du moyen âge occidental, 15 (Turnhout, 1975), 19.
12. *MGH SS* ix, 305.
13. See p. 399 n. 5.
14. See p. 394 n. 2.
15. See p. 398 n. 67; G. Devailly, *Histoire religieuse de Bretagne*, 47.
16. *PL* clxxiv, 1368-438.
17. See p. 394 n. 8.
18. *The Letters and Poems of Fulbert of Chartres*, ed. and tr. F. Behrends (Oxford, 1976).
19. *Correspondance d'Yves de Chartres*, ed. and tr. J. Leclerq (Paris, 1949).
20. G. Tessier, *Diplomatique royale française* (Paris, 1962), 129-30.
21. *Le Gouvernement royal*, 121-3.
22. O. Guillot, *Le Comte d'Anjou* ii; i. 419-21.
23. *Actes des comtes de Flandre 1070-1128*, ed. F. Vercauteren (Brussels, 1938), particularly pp. xlix-cxii.
24. *Recueil des actes des ducs de Normandie de 911 à 1060*, ed. M. Fauroux (Caen, 1961); *Regesta Regum Anglo-Normannorum, 1066-1154*, ed. H. W. C. Davis, i (Oxford, 1913).

25. J. Martindale, 'The Counts of Poitou', 50-6.
26. See K. F. Werner, 'Kingdom and Principality', 282 n. 38.
27. M. Rouche, 'Les survivances antiques dans trois cartulaires du Sud-Ouest de la France au Xe et XIe siècles', *Cahiers de civ. méd.* 23 (1980), 97 n. 45, quoting cartulary of St Jean d'Angély, 130.

Chapter 7

1. *Annales angevines,* 57-8.
2. Ed. Carozzi, 30, l. 390.
3. *PL,* cxxxix, col. 478. For other means of achieving the same end, see B. Guenée, 'La fierté d'être capétien', 452-3; G. Spiegel, 'The *Reditus Regni ad Stirpem Karoli Magni:* A New Look', *French Historical Studies* 7 (1971), 151-2.
4. See p. 400 n. 3.
5. Ibid. 77, 128. See F. Barlow, 'The King's Evil', *EHR* 95 (1980), 3-27, especially 17.
6. *Liber de edificatione Fiscannensis monasterii, PL* li, col. 720. I am grateful to Dr P. Morison for this information.
7. B. de Gaiffier, *L'hagiographie dans le marquisat de Flandre et le duché de Basse-Lotharingie au XIe siècle,* Subsidia Hagiographica 43 (Brussels, 1967).
8. A. W. Lewis, *Royal Succession in Capetian France* (Cambridge, Mass., 1981), 47.
9. W. Kienast, 'Der Wirkungsbereich', 552.
10. *Letters and Poems,* 26.
11. Gerbert, *Letters,* no. 114.
12. *Actes,* ed. Prou nos. 86, 87; Lemarignier, *Le Gouvernement royal,* 116.
13. J.-F. Lemarignier, 'Les fidèles du roi de France (936-987)', *Recueil Brunel,* ii. 161. See F. L. Ganshof, *Revue historique de droit français et étranger* (1968), 268-9.
14. G. Duby, *The Early Growth of the European Economy: Warriors and Peasants from the Seventh to the Twelfth centuries,* tr. H. B. Clarke (London, 1974), 123-39; cf. F. Dumas-Dubourg, *Le Trésor de Fécamp,* 59-60.
15. *Miracles of St Foy,* 469.
16. *Chronique de Saint-Maixent,* 175; P. Wolff, 'The Significance of the "Feudal Period" in the Monetary History of Europe', in *Order and Innovation,* 75-85; D. Bates, *Normandy,* 96-7; F. Dumas-Dubourg, *Le Trésor de Fecamp,* 64.
17. G. Duby, *Rural Economy and Country Life in the Medieval West,* tr. C. Postan (London, 1968), 61-231.
18. *Miracles of St Foy,* 513.
19. Ibid. 495.
20. Hariulf, *Chronique,* 229.
21. See p. 210.

22. C. Coulson, 'Rendability and Castellation in medieval France', *Château Gaillard* 6 (1972), 59-61.
23. Suger, *Vie de Louis le Gros*, ed. and tr. H. Waquet (Paris, 1964), 38.
24. G. Duby, 'French Genealogical Literature' in *The Chivalrous Society*, tr. C. Postan (London, 1977), 149-57. Also ibid. 102-3.
25. J. Boussard, 'L'origine des familles seigneuriales dans la région du Loire moyen', *Cahiers de civ. méd.* 5 (1962), 302-22.
26. J. Baumel, *Histoire d'une seigneurie du Midi de la France: naissance de Montpellier (985-1213)* (Montpellier, 1969), 33-5; L. Musset, 'L'aristocratie normande', 75.
27. Hariulf, *Chronique*, 230.
28. G. Duby, *Société*, 266 n. 13.
29. G. Duby, *Rural Economy*, 187-90;
30. Ed. I. Heller, *MGH SS* xxiv (Hanover, 1879), 624-5.
31. G. Fournier, *Le Château dans la France médiévale: essai de sociologie monumentale* (Paris, 1978), 311.
32. G. Ourliac, 'L'esprit du droit méridional', *Études Yver*, 588. See too the argument by F. Cheyette, 'The castles of the Trencavels: A Preliminary Aerial Survey', in *Order and Innovation*, 256-72, which suggests that the castellans of that part of the world were not primarily, if at all, 'banal' seigneurs (that is, lords who exercised the *ban*, the public right of command).
33. J.-F. Lemarignier, 'La dislocation du "pagus" et le problème des "consuetudines" (X-XIᵉ siècles)', *Mélanges Halphen*, 401-10.
34. *MGH SS* xxiv, 613-14, 616-17.
35. Fournier, *Le Château* 311.
36. *MGH Capitularia Regum Francorum*, ed. A. Boretius and V. Krause (Hanover, 1890) ii, i. 291-2.
37. Ed. C. Pfister, *Études sur le règne de Robert le Pieux* (Paris, 1885), pp. lx-lxi, no. 12.
38. See H. E. J. Cowdrey, 'The Peace and Truce of God in the Eleventh Century', *Past and Present* 46 (1970), 42-67 *Correspondance d'Yves de Chartres*, 178-84.
39. *Miracles of St Benedict*, 191-8.
40. *Chronicon Hugonis Monachi Virdunensis et Divionensis, Abbatis Flaviniacensis*, ed. G. H. Pertz, *MGH SS* viii (Hanover, 1848), 477.
41. E. Magnou-Nortier, *La Société laïque*, 292-309; G. Duby, 'The Evolution of Judicial Institutions: Burgundy in the Tenth and Eleventh centuries' in *The Chivalrous Society*, tr. C. Postan (London, 1977), 25.
42. G. Duby, 'The Laity and the Peace of God', and 'The Origins of Knighthood', op. cit., 123-33, 169.
43. H. E. J. Cowdrey, *The Cluniacs and the Gregorian Reform* (Oxford 1970), 19-22, 29-36.
44. *Chronique*, 182.
45. *The Epistolae Vagantes of Pope Gregory VII*, ed. H. E. J. Cowdrey (Oxford, 1972), 151, no. 67.

46. R. Foreville, 'The Synod of the Province of Rouen in the Eleventh and Twelfth Centuries', in C. N. L. Brooke, D. Luscombe, G. Martin, and D. Owen (eds.), *Church and Government in the Middle Ages* (Cambridge, 1976), 19–30.

47. *Chronique de Saint-Maixent*, 149; *Chartes et documents pour servir à l'historie de l'abbaye de Saint-Maixent*, ed. A. Richard, no. 172.

48. Tr. H. Waddell, *More Latin Lyrics from Vergil to Milton*, ed. F. Corrigan (London, 1976), 279–80.

49. O. Guillot, *Le Comte d'Anjou*, i. 252–62.

50. *Actes*, ed. Prou, no. 152.

51. J. C. A. Verlinden, *Robert Ier le Frison, comte de Flandre* (Antwerp, 1935), 127–9.

52. G. Cholvy (ed.), *Histoire des diocèses de France*, iv: *Montpellier* (Paris, 1976), 69–74.

53. G. Devailly, *Histoire religieuse de la Bretagne*, ed. G. M. Oury, (Chambray, 1980), 50–8.

54. Sassier, 26–30.

55. Ed. G. Waitz, *MGH SS* ix (Hanover, 1851), 345.

Chapter 8

1. G. Fourquin, *Les Campagnes de la région parisienne à la fin du Moyen Âge* (Paris, 1964), 99.

2. The best survey remains W. M. Newman, *Le Domaine royal sous les premiers capétiens (987–1180)*, (Paris, 1937).

3. *Actes*, ed. Prou, no. 125.

4. J. Lemarignier, *Le Gouvernement royal*, 61–2 and n. 93.

5. Suger, *Vie de Louis le Gros*, 36–8.

6. Lemarignier, *Le Gouvernement royal*, 123, and tables at the end of the book.

7. See p. 140.

8. Ed. Carozzi, 6, ll. 68–76; 8, ll. 112–14.

9. See p. 402 n. 37; see R. Bonnaud-Delamare, 'Les institutions de paix dans la province écclesiastique de Reims au XIe siècle', *Bulletin historique et philologique du Comité des Travaux historiques et scientifiques, années 1955 et 1956* (Paris, 1957), 143–200.

10. Lemarignier, *Le Gouvernement royal*, 165–6.

11. R. d'Abadal de Vinyals, 'A propos de la "domination" de la maison comtale de Barcelone sur le Midi français', *Annales du Midi* 76 (1964), 315–45.

12. E. Magnou-Nortier, *La Société laïque*, 239–40; Baumel, 60–83.

13. Magnou-Nortier, op. cit., 521–4.

14. A. Fliche in *Institutions* i. 82–3; Baumel, 75.

15. Magnou-Nortier, op. cit., 309.

16. J. Mundy, *Liberty and Political Power in Toulouse, 1050–1230* (New York, 1954), 23–5; 30–1; 104.

17. *Chronique*, 163.

18. Ibid. 165.

19. Ibid. 156-7, 205; Richer, *Histoire de France*, ii. 330.

20. J. Martindale, 'The Counts of Poitou', 50-8.

21. Fulbert, *Letters*, 194.

22. *Conventum inter Guillelmum Aquitanorum comitem et Hugonem Chiliarchum*, ed. J. Martindale, *EHR* 84 (1969), 528-48. See also G. Beech, 'A Feudal Document of Early Eleventh-century Poitou', *Mélanges Crozet*, i. 203-13.

23. On Angevin interests in general, see G. Beech, *A Rural Society in Medieval France: The Gâtine of Poitou in the Eleventh and Twelfth Centuries* (Baltimore, 1964), 42-70; appendix, 139-42; and B. S. Bachrach, 'Toward a Reappraisal of William the Great, Duke of Aquitaine', *Journal of Medieval History* 5 (1979), 11-21.

24. *Chronique*, 163.

25. R. Bonnaud-Delamare, 'La paix en Aquitaine au XIe siècle', *Recueils de la Société Jean Bodin* 14, (1961), 415-57; H. E. J. Cowdrey, 'The Peace and Truce', 59.

26. *Vita Abbonis*, *PL*, cxxxix, col. 410.

27. J. Martindale, 'The Counts of Poitou', 126.

28. M. Garaud, *Les Châtelains de Poitou et l'avènement du régime féodale, XIe et XIIe siècles* (Poitiers, 1967), 35-8.

29. G. B. Ladner, 'Terms and ideas of renewal', in R. L. Benson and G. Constable (eds), *Renaissance and Renewal in the Twelfth Century* (Oxford, 1982), 5; also P. Dronke, 'Profane elements in literature', ibid. 580-1.

30. 'Lubricus', *Gesta Regum* ii, ed. W. Stubbs (London, 1889), 510.

31. *Histoire de France*, ii. 330.

32. *Actes*, ed. Prou, no. 83.

33. Richard, *Les Ducs*, 4 n. 1.

34. Sassier, 29.

35. Sassier, 30-62. This reflects the antipathy between Henry I and his brother, who rebelled against him.

36. *Société*, 137-65; cf. id., 'The Evolution of Judicial Institutions in Burgundy in the Tenth and Eleventh Centuries', *The Chivalrous Society* 15-58.

37. J. Richard, *Les Ducs*, 50-110; J. Richard, 'Aux origines du Charolais', *Annales de Bourgogne* 35 (1963), 81-114.

38. *Ecclesiastical History*, vi. 430.

39. M. Chaume, 'Les premières croisades bourguignonnes au-delà des Pyrénées', *Annales de Bourgogne* 18 (1946), 161-5; M. Defourneaux, *Les Français en Espagne aux XIe et XIIe siècles* (Paris, 1949).

40. O. Guillot, *Le Comte d'Anjou*, i. 18.

41. Richer, *Histoire de France*, ii. 292.

42. G. Beech, *A Rural Society in Medieval France: the Gâtine of Poitou in the Eleventh and Twelfth Centuries* (Baltimore, 1964), 45 and appendix, pp. 139-42.

43. *Chroniques des églises d'Anjou*, 260.
44. *Annales angevines,* 86. See the unforgettable description of Fulk in R. W. Southern, *The Making of the Middle Ages* (London, 1959), 87-92.
45. O. Guillot, 'Administration et gouvernement dans les États du comte d'Anjou au milieu du XIe siècle', *Histoire comparée de l'administration (IVe -XVIIe siècles)*; W. Paravicini and K. F. Werner (eds.), *Actes du XIVe colloque historique franco-allemand 1977* (Zurich, 1980).
46. *Histoire de Guillaume le Conquérant*, 38.
47. See Guillot, *Le Comte d'Anjou*, i. 49 n. 237, 372-5; 382-3.
48. *Histoires*, 129-30.
49. See Fulk's own account in *Chroniques des comtes d'Anjou*, 237.
50. Guillot, *Le Comte d'Anjou*, i. 193, 256-60.
51. Ibid. 285.
52. *Chroniques des comtes d'Anjou*, 232.
53. R. Poupardin, 'Généalogies angevines du XIe siècle', *Mélanges de l'École française de Rome*, 20 (1900) 199-208; G. Duby, 'French Genealogical Literature', 152.
54. B. Guenée, 'La fierté d'être Capétien', 452.
55. *Histoires*, 86.
56. See M. Bur, *La Formation du comté de Champagne, v..950-v. 1150* (Nancy, 1977), 114-16.
57. See G. Duby, *Medieval Marriage. Two Models from Twelfth-century France* (Baltimore and London, 1978), 46-9.
58. Richer, *Histoire de France*, ii. 330.
59. Bur, 153-73.
60. Lemarignier, *Le Gouvernement royal*, 61-2 and n. 93.
61. Fulbert, *Letters*, 152-5; and see p. 236 above.
62. Bur, 195-6.
63. Ibid. 461-99.
64. A. Chédeville, *Chartres et ses campagnes, XIe -XIIe siècles*, 40.
65. Devailly, *Le Berry*, 129-35, 166-7, 351-2.
66. Ed. Merlet, 108.
67. Chédeville, 271.
68. Ibid. 288.
69. S. D. White, '*Pactum . . . legem vincet et amor judicium.* The Settlement of Disputes by Compromise in Eleventh-century Western France', *American Journal of Legal History* 22 (1978), 288.
70. Bur, 211 and n. 57.
71. Werner, 'Kingdom and Principality', 257.
72. H. D. Clout, *Themes in the Historical Geography of France* (London, 1977), 192.
73. H. Poisson, *Les Ducs de Bretagne de la maison de Cornouaille: Hoël, Alain Fergent, Conan III* (Lorient, 1968), 7.
74. See Merlet, introduction to *Chronique de Nantes*, p. xxxi nn. 1 and 2.

75. Merlet, pp. xxv-xl—though the date he suggests is unacceptable.
76. *Histoires*, 31.
77. H. Hoffmann, 'Französiche Fürstenweihen des Hochmittelalters', *DA* 18 (1962), 110.
78. W. Kienast, *Der Herzogstitel*, 146-51.
79. Ed. Merlet, 99-101.
80. *Histoires*, 20.
81. *Ecclesiastical History*, iv. 82; R. H. C. Davis, *The Normans*, 14-15.
82. C. H. Haskins, *Norman Institutions* (Cambridge, Mass., 1919), 281-4.
83. M. de Bouard, 'Sur les origines de la trêve de Dieu en Normandie', *Annales de Normandie* 9 (1959), 179-89.
84. D. Bates, *Normandy before 1066* (London, 1982), 151.
85. D. C. Douglas, 'The Earliest Norman Counts', *EHR* 61 (1946), 129-54; L. Musset, 'L'aristocratie normande au XIe siècle', in P. Contamine (ed.), *La Noblesse au Moyen Âge* (Paris, 1976), 71-96.
86. See most recently, Bates, 122-8.
87. L. Musset, 'A-t-il existé en Normandie au XIe siècle une aristocratie d'argent?', *Annales de Normandie* 9 (1959), 285-8.
88. *Ecclesiastical History*, iii. 94; see R. Foreville, 'The Synod'.
89. C. W. Hollister, 'Normandy, France and the Anglo-Norman regnum', *Speculum* 51 (1976), 202-42.
90. *Histoires*, 20.
91. *Histoire de France*, ii. 328.
92. Ed. Lair, 171, 182-3.
93. Ibid. 261-2.
94. Ed. F. Barlow, Camden 3rd series (London, 1949), 46 (translation slightly altered).
95. See the letter from Archbishop Gervaise of Rheims, *De Vita S. Donatiani, MGH SS* xv. 85.
96. *Histoire de Guillaume le Conquérant*, 48.
97. See their genealogy, ed. L. C. Bethmann, *MGH SS* ix. 299-301.
98. Warlop, *Flemish Nobility* i. 86 and n. 280.
99. *Chronicon, MGH SS* viii. 403.
100. H. Platelle, 'La violence et ses remèdes en Flandre au XIe siècle', *Sacris Erudiri* 20 (1971), 101-73; *Vita Arnulfi*, cols. 1412, 1414.
101. Verlinden, *Robert le Frison*, 127-9.
102. J.-F. Lemarignier, 'Paix et reforme monastique en Flandre et en Normandie autour de l'année 1023', *Études Yver*, 456-7; R. Bonnaud-Delamare, 'La paix en Flandre pendant la première croisade', *Revue du Nord* 39 (1957), 151.
103. Warlop, *Flemish Nobility*, i. 136-55.
104. *Actes* ed. Vercauteren, 30 no. 9, given in the name of his son Robert.
105. *Diplomatic Documents Preserved in the Public Record Office*, ed. P. Chaplais (Oxford, 1964), i. 1-4.
106. J. Richard, *Les Ducs de Bourgogne*, 52.

107. Ibid. 10; J. Dhondt, 'Quelques aspects du règne de Henri I, roi de France', *Mélanges Halphen*, 207.
108. See F. Claudon, *Histoire de Langres et de ses institutions municipales jusqu'au commencement du XVIe siècle* (Dijon, 1955), 32-3.
109. *Cartulaire de Conques*, ed. G. Desjardins (Paris, 1879), nos. 20, 25.
110. Cf. e.g. 530, 538-9, 539-40.
111. Ibid. 545-6.
112. P. Feuchère, 'Une tentative manquée de concentration territoriale entre Somme et Seine: la principauté d'Amiens-Valois au XIe siècle', *Le Moyen Âge* 60 (1954), 1-77.
113. Hariulf, *Chronique*, 206-7, 230.
114. See Fossier, ii. 480-8.
115. *Miracles of St Foy*, 541-2.
116. *Miracles of St Benedict*, 192-8.
117. *Chronique*, 205.
118. *Histoire de Guillaume le Conquérant*, 74, 76, 82, 84, 88.
119. *Flandria Generosa*, ed. L. C. Bethmann, *MGH SS* ix (Hanover, 1851), 321-2.

Chapter 9

1. See p. 406 n. 95 above.
2. Bates, 164-5; *Chronique de Saint-Maixent*, 175, 183; but see also T. N. Bisson, *The Conservation of Coinage: Monetary Exploitation and its Restraint in France, Catalonia and Aragon, c.1000-1225 AD* (Oxford, 1979) for attempts to limit this.
3. See H. Platelle, *Le Temporel de l'abbaye de Saint-Amand des origines à 1340* (Paris, 1962), 159-61.
4. *Chronique*, 182.
5. Ed. Bouillet-Servières, 469-72.
6. Ibid. 549. See also the rather different account that emerges from *Cartulaire de Conques*, nos. 18, 20.
7. Guillot, *Le Comte d'Anjou* ii. no. 150.
8. Ibid. ii. no. 126.
9. Ibid. ii. no. 384.
10. *PL* clvii, cols. 203-4.
11. P. Ourliac, 'L'esprit du droit', 588. See also Ademar, *Chronique*, 161, for Duke Bernard William of Gascony's execution of Abbo of Fleury's murderers.
12. C. H. Haskins, *Norman Institutions*, 281-4.
13. See p. 168.
14. O. Guillot, *Le Comte d'Anjou*, i. 373-4; ii. no. 80.
15. J.-F. Lemarignier, *Recherches sur l'hommage en marche et les frontières féodales* (Lille, 1945), 19-22; J. Le Patourel, *The Norman Empire* (Oxford, 1976), 265-7.
16. Guillot, i. 49, n. 237.

17. See Eudes of St Maur, *Vie de Bouchard le Vénérable, comte de Vendôme, de Corbeil, de Melun et de Paris (X^e et XIe siècles)*, ed. C. Bourel de la Roncière (Paris, 1892), appendix.
18. J. Martindale, *EHR* 84 (1969), 541.
19. *Gesta Consulum*, in *Chroniques des comtes d'Anjou*, 65.
20. Poly–Bournazel, 280–3.
21. *Gesta Ambaziensium Dominorum*, in *Chroniques des Comtes d'Anjou*, 93.
22. See p. 406 n. 105.
23. See in general J. Boussard, 'Services féodaux'.
24. Fulbert, *Letters*, 90–2.
25. Carozzi, introd. to Adalbéron, *Poème au roi Robert*, pp. lxiv–lxviii
26. Martindale, '*Conventum*', 547.
27. Duby, *Société*, 163.
28. See above, p. 230.
29. William of Poitiers, *Histoire de Guillaume le Conquérant*, 88.
30. Guillot, i. 343.
31. Lemarignier, *Le Gouvernement royal*, 61–2 and n. 93.
32. Beech, *The Gâtine of Poitou*, 43–9.
33. Baumel, 80.
34. *Epitoma*, 76.
35. *De moribus et actis primorum Normanniae ducum*, 247.
36. Fulbert, *Letters*, 152–4.
37. *Histoire de Guillaume le Conquérant*, 66.
38. *Ecclesiastical History*, vi, 76; Guillot, i. 123, 124.
39. *Vita Sancti Roberti*, RHF xiv. 69.
40. *RHF* xii. 268.
41. Compare B. Guenée, 'La fierté d'être capetien', 457.
42. C. B. Bouchard, 'Consanguinity and Noble Marriages in the Tenth and Eleventh Centuries', *Speculum* 56 (1981), 268–87.
43. Adam of Eynsham, *Life of St Hugh of Lincoln*, ed. D. L. Douie and H. Farmer (2 vols., London, 1961), i. 115–18.
44. *Histoire de Guillaume le Conquérant*, 64, 46.
45. Brühl, *Fodrum, Gistum*, 264.
46. F. Sœhnée, *Catalogue des actes d'Henri I, roi de France (1031–1060)*, Bibliothèque de l'École des hautes études, 161 (Paris, 1907), no. 56.
47. Guillot, ii. 238, charter 384.
48. Bates, 152.
49. *RHF* xiv. 177.
50. H. E. J. Cowdrey, 'The Anglo-Norman *Laudes Regiae*', *Viator* 12 (1981), 44.
51. *RHF* xiv, 141.
52. J. O. Prestwich, 'The Military Household of the Norman Kings', *EHR* 96 (1981), 1–35.
53. Anna Comnena, *Alexiad*, ed. and tr. E. A. S. Dawes (London, 1967), 179–80.
54. *Cartulaire de Conques*, 341–2, no. 470.

55. Bates, 211.
56. Ibid. 155.
57. *Chroniques des comtes d'Anjou*, 94.

Chapter 10

1. *Chroniques des comtes d'Anjou*, 25–73.
2. Ibid. 73–132.
3. Ibid., pp. xxxii–xxxiii.
4. See p. 396 n. 35. See R. H. Bautier, 'L'historiographie en France au Xe et XIe siècles (France du nord et de l'est)', *Settimane Spoleto* 17 (1970), 809–12.
5. *Gesta Normannorum Ducum*, 8.
6. *MGH SS* ix, 299–301.
7. *MGH SS* ix, 308.
8. *Chroniques des comtes d'Anjou*, 26.
9. 'Untersuchungen', *Die Welt als Geschichte* 18 (1958), 264–89.
10. *Chroniques des comtes d'Anjou*, 232; Duby, 'French Genealogical Literature', 154.
11. *MGH SS* ix. 335.
12. *Chroniques des comtes d'Anjou*, 37–46.
13. Ibid., pp. xxxiv–xxxv.
14. *La Chanson de Roland publiée d'après le manuscrit d'Oxford*, ed. J. Bédier (Paris, 1927), e.g. l. 3039.
15. *Chronique des comtes de Anjou*, 65, 67.
16. Ibid. 163.
17. Ibid. 140.
18. Ibid. 74.
19. *Documents relatifs au comté de Champagne et de Brie 1172–1363*, ed. A. Longnon, i (Paris, 1901); id., *Les Fiefs*, 1–172. I rely on T. Evergates, *Feudal Society in the baillage of Troyes under the Counts of Champagne 1152–1284* (London, 1975), 9–10, 60–2, 91–5.
20. Op. cit. 90–6.
21. See C. Seignobos, *Le Régime féodal en Bourgogne jusqu'en 1360* (repr. Geneva, 1975), 96, for the suggestion in relation to the dukes of Burgundy.
22. *Chronicles of the Reigns of Stephen, Henry II and Richard I*, ed. R. Howlett, iv (London, 1889), appendix, p. 349.
23. *Regesta Regum Anglo-Normannorum*, iii: *1135–1154*, ed. H. A. Cronne and R. H. C. Davis (Oxford, 1969), 372, no. 1007.
24. A. de Bouard, *Manuel de diplomatique française et pontificale* (Paris, 1929), 144 n. 2.

Chapter 11

1. *PL* clxxxvi, col. 1436.
2. See p. 402 n. 23.

3. Ibid. 240.
4. L. Halphen, 'La place de la royauté dans le système féodal', *A travers l'histoire du moyen âge* (Paris, 1950), 266-74.
5. E. Panofsky, *Abbot Suger on the Abbey Church of St Denis and its Art Treasures* (2nd edn., Princeton, 1969), 36-7.
6. *Historia Calamitatum*, ed. J. Monfrin (Paris, 1967), 89-91.
7. Halphen, 'La place', 268.
8. Poly-Bournazel, 283-310.
9. Odo of Deuil, *De Profectione Ludovici VII in orientem*, ed. and tr. V. G. Berry (New York, 1948).
10. R. W. Southern, *Medieval Humanism and Other Studies* (Oxford, 1970), 148-9.
11. Barlow, 'The King's Evil', 17.
12. W. Kienast, 'Der Wirkungsbereich', 552.
13. Lemarignier, *Le Gouvernement royal*, 166-9.
14. *Gesta Pontificum*, 458.
15. H. Hoffmann, 'Französische Fürstenweihen', 102-3.
16. T. N. Bisson,'The Organized Peace in Southern France and Catalonia (*c.*1140-*c.*1238)', *American Historical Review* 82 (1977), 295-6.
17. Duby, *Société*, 404-15.
18. M. Pacaut, *Louis VII et les élections épiscopales dans le royaume de France* (Paris, 1957), 73-82.
19. *RHF* xii. 281.
20. See above, p. 189.
21. *RHF* xvi. 16; J.-F. Lemarignier, *Hommage en marche*, 99-100.
22. Cf. K. F. Werner, 'Kingdom and Principality', 274, on the absence of an 'estate of princes'.
23. A. Grabois, 'De la trêve de Dieu à la paix du roi', *Mélanges Crozet* (Poitiers, 1966), 594-6.
24. Suger, *Vie*, 218-30.
25. See G. Spiegel, ' "Defence of the Realm": Evolution of a Capetian Propaganda Slogan', *Journal of Medieval History* 3 (1977), 115-25.
26. For other aspects of royal coinage, see *Institutions*, ii. 210-12.
27. Grabois, op. cit., 593; A. Luchaire, *Études sur les actes de Louis VII* (Paris, 1885), 195, no. 296.
28. *RHF* xvi. 16-17.
29. *RHF* xii. 339-42.
30. *RHF* xvi. 4.
31. Duby, *Société*, 412-15.
32. Luchaire, *Études*, 154-5, no. 173.
33. Cf. Chédeville, *Chartres*, 304; Thibaud IV reserved justice over murder, rape, and arson at Bonneval, *quia durum erat monachis de talibus judicare*.
34. E. Kantorowicz, *The King's Two Bodies: a Study in Medieval Political Theology* (repr. Princeton, 1981), 340-1.
35. Walter Map, *De nugis curialium*, ed. and tr. M. R. James, rev. C. N. L. Brooke and R. A. B. Mynors (Oxford, 1983), 442.

36. A. Luchaire, *Les Communes françaises* (Paris, 1911); criticized by C. Petit-Dutaillis, *Les Communes françaises* (repr. Paris, 1970), who was in turn criticized by J. Dhondt, 'Petit-Dutaillis et les communes françaises', *Annales* 7 (1952), 378-85.

37. Chédeville in G. Duby (ed.), *Histoire de la France urbaine: la ville médiévale* (Paris, 1980), 81-3, 126-31; C. Verlinden, 'Marchands ou tisserands?A propos des origines urbaines', *Annales* 27 (1972), 396-406.

38. *Self and Society in Medieval France. The Memoirs of Guibert of Nogent 1064-1125*, ed. J. F. Benton (New York, 1970), 174.

39. Petit-Dutaillis, 78.

40. *The Murder of Charles the Good*, ed. and tr. J. B. Ross (repr. Toronto, 1982).

41. *Actes*, ed. Vercauteren nos. 127, 293-9.

42. Chédeville, *La Ville*, 164.

43. Mundy, *Liberty*, 23-33, 43-60.

44. *De Oorkonden der Graven van Vlaanderen, 1191-1206*, ed. W. Prevenier (Brussels, 1966), ii. 14, no. 1.

45. *PL*, clxxxvi, col. 1405; cf. Devailly, *Le Berry*, 386 n. 3, 388.

46. M. Prou, 'Les coutumes de Lorris et leur propagation aux XIIe et XIIe siècles', *Nouvelle Revue historique de droit français et étranger* 8 (1884), 139-209, 267-320, 441-457, 523-556.

47. A. Giry, *Les Établissements de Rouen. Études sur l'histoire des institutions municipales de Rouen, Falaise, Port-Audemar, etc.* (Paris, 1883-5).

48. A recent survey by G. Fourquin is in G. Duby and A. Wallon (eds)., *Histoire de la France rurale*, i (Paris, 1975), 476-521.

49. Baumel, 134.

50. Mundy, *Liberty*, 46-7.

51. *Monumenta Vezeliacensia. Textes relatifs à l'histoire de l'abbaye de Vézelay*, ed. R. B. C. Huygens (1976), 99-100, 111-28, 189.

52. See above, p. 252.

53. M. S. Amos and F. P. Walton, *Introduction to French Law*, 3rd edn. (Oxford, 1967), 27; for grouping of *coutumes*, see J. Yver, *Égalité entre héritiers et exclusion des enfants dotés: essai de geographie coutumière* (Paris, 1966).

54. P. Ourliac, 'L'esprit de droit', 577-94; for a local study, Baumel, 142-3, 175-81.

55. *Actes*, ed. Vercauteren, nos. 66, 156.

56. Quoted by J. Chartrou, *L'Anjou de 1109 à 1151. Foulque de Jérusalem et Geoffroi Plantagenêt* (Paris, 1928), 88.

57. Y. Bongert, *Recherches sur les cours laïques du Xe au XIIIe siècle* (Paris, 1948), 219-21.

58. *Letters of John of Salisbury*, i, ed. and tr. W. J. Millor and H. P. Butler (Oxford, 1955), 233.

59. *Regesta Regum*, iii. 373, no. 1008.

60. *Vita Gaufredi*, in *Chroniques des comtes d'Anjou*, 194.

61. *Actes*, ed. Vercauteren, nos. 106, 241.

62. *Praedicatio Goliae ad terrorem omnium*, ed. T. Wright, Camden Society, 16 (London 1841), ll. 53-6.
63. *Policraticus*, ed. C. J. Webb, iv, ch. 2.
64. Herbert of Torres, *PL*, clxxxv, 1324-5.
65. *Recueil des actes de Henri II*, ed. L. V. Delisle (Paris, 1906-27), nos. 162, 291-2.
66. *Chroniques des comtes d'Anjou*, 222-3.
67. Book V, ch. 2.
68. E. Bournazel, *Le Gouvernement capétien au XIIe siècle. 1108-1180. Structures sociales et mutations institutionnelles* (Limoges, 1975), 23-7, 74-82.
69. *Regesta Regum*, iii, p. xxxv; Southern, *Medieval Humanism,* 211-18.
70. Bournazel, *Le Gouvernement*, 170, 171.
71. *PL*, ccvii, 198.
72. Le Patourel, *Norman Empire*, 222-9; *Dialogus de Scaccario*, ed. C. Johnson, rev. F. E. L. Carter and W. E. Greenway (Oxford, 1983), pp. xxii, xxvii, xxviii, 14.
73. A. Verhulst and M. Gysseling, *Le Compte général de 1187 connu sous le nom de 'gros Bref' et les institutions financières du comté de Flandre au XIIe siècle* (Brussels, 1962); B. Lyon and A. E. Verhulst, *Medieval Finance. A Comparison of Financial Institutions in Northwestern Europe* (Providence, RI, 1967).
74. *Actes*, ed. Delisle, i. pp. ccxxix, 370.
75. *Chroniques des comtes d'Anjou*, 185-191.
76. Tr. H. Waddell, *More Latin Lyrics*, 249.
77. *Chroniques des comtes d'Anjou*, 218-19.
78. *Policraticus*, vi. ch. 18.
79. See above, p. 212.
80. Suger, *Vie*, 222.
81. G. Duby, *Le Dimanche de Bouvines, 27 juillet 1214* (Paris, 1973), 103-10.
82. See most recently F. H. Russell, *The Just War in the Middle Ages* (Cambridge, 1975), 45-6, 60-71.
83. *RHF*, xiv. 240.
84. *Chroniques des comtes d'Anjou*, 178-80.
85. Lambert of Ardres, *MGH SS* xxiv. 604-5.
86. H. E. J. Cowdrey, 'Pope Urban II's preaching of the First Crusade', *History* 55 (1970), 177-88; H. E. Mayer, *A History of the Crusades*, tr. J. Gillingham (Oxford, 1972), 290-1.
87. *Actes*, ed. Vercauteren, nos. 87, 195.
88. *Vita Sugeri, PL*, clxxxvi, col. 1201.
89. e.g. *RHF* xvi. 27-8, Bohemond to Louis VI; ibid. 36-8, Amalric to Louis.
90. Duby, *Société*, 404.
91. *Vita Sugeri*, col. 1202. The same point is made on other grounds in W. Kienast, *Deutschland und Frankreich in der Kaiserzeit 900-1272* (Stuttgart, 1974-5), 193-8.

92. *RHF* xv. 607.

Chapter 12

1. *De nugis curialium*, 442.
2. Ibid. 452.
3. Ibid. 450. I translate *gaudium* as 'joy', not 'gaiety'.
4. *Medieval Humanism*, 147-8.
5. Suger, *Vie*, 42; F. Olivier-Martin, *Histoire du droit français* (Paris, 1948), 131.
6. D. Nicholas, 'Structures de peuplement, fonctions urbaines et formation du capital dans la Flandre médiévale', *Annales* 33 (1978), 406-7.
7. 'The Revenue of Louis VII', *Speculum*, 42 (1967), 84-91.
8. *Le Gouvernement*, 161-8.
9. Pacaut, 70-1.
10. Devailly, *Le Berry*, 402.
11. *RHF* xvi. 126.
12. Luchaire, *Études*, nos. 613, 293. See Bisson, 'The Organized Peace'.
13. For a full study, see C. Thouzellier, *Catharisme et valdéisme en Languedoc à la fin du XIIᵉ et au début du XIIIᵉ siècle* (Paris, 1966). In English, see W. L. Wakefield, *Heresy, Crusade and Inquisition in Southern France, 1100-1250* (London, 1974).
14. J. Sumption, *The Albigensian Crusade* (London, 1978), 23-4.
15. *Otia Imperialia*, MGH SS xxvii, 392, quoted in E. G. Léonard, *Catalogue des actes des comtes de Toulouse* iii (Paris, 1932), p. vi.
16. *The Itinerary of Benjamin of Tudela*, ed. and tr. N. M. Adler (London, 1907), 4.
17. J. Mundy, *Liberty and Political Power*, 30.
18. *Itinerary*, 4 n. 2.
19. *Actes*, ed. Léonard, xiv, xvii; see R. R. Bezzola, *Les Origines et la formation de la littérature courtoise en Occident 500-1200* iii (Paris, 1963) pp. ii, 330-1.
20. *Actes*, no. 56.
21. Ibid. no. 87.
22. Ibid. no. 30.
23. Ibid. pp. xviii-xlix; Mundy, *Liberty and Political Power*, 115.
24. *Recherches sur l'hommage en marche et les frontières féodales* (Lille, 1945), 157-60.
25. Richard, *Les Ducs*, 130.
26. Ibid. 134 n. 3.
27. Ibid. 156.
28. Bur, 481 and n. 53, 400; Chédeville, *Chartres*, 297.
29. *Ecclesiastical History*, vi. 160.
30. *Vie*, 134.
31. See above, p. 288.
32. Devailly, *Le Berry*, 382-413.

33. *Chroniques des comtes d'Anjou*, 122.
34. W. Kienast, 'Comes Francorum und Pfalzgraf von Frankreich', *Festgabe für Paul Kern zum 70. Geburtstag* (Berlin, 1961), 80-92.
35. Bezzola, 400-1, 446; John of Salisbury, *Letters*, i. 233; Bournazel, *Le Gouvernement*, 22; Bisson, *Conservation*, 162-3.
36. Suger, *Vie*, 152-68.
37. Bur, 402.
38. Y. Bongert, *Recherches sur les cours laïques du Xe au XIIIe siècle* (Paris, 1948), 125-6.
39. T. N. Bisson, *Conservation*, 130-3.
40. Robert of St Mary of Autun, *RHF* xii, 293.
41. Ed. Brewer (London, 1946), i. 198-9; see also *Map, De nugis curialium*, 462.
42. R. H. Bautier, 'Les foires de Champagne', *Recueil de la Société Jean Bodin*, 5 (1953) 97-147.
43. Lemarignier, *Hommage en marche*, 157-60.
44. *De nugis curialium*, 450.
45. J. F. Benton, 'The Court of Champagne as a Literary Center', *Speculum* 36 (1961), 551-91; see also J. H. M. McCash, 'Marié de Champagne and Eleanor of Aquitaine: A Relationship Re-examined', ibid. 51 (1979), 698-711.
46. *Letters*, ii, ed. W. J. Millor and C. N. L. Brooke (Oxford, 1979), no. 209.
47. *RHF* xvi. 700.
48. Tr. Ross, 7; J. Dhondt, 'Les solidarités médiévales', *Annales* 12 (1957), 529-60.
49. In M. Manitius, *Geschichte der lateinischen Literatur des Mittelalters* (3 vols., Munich, 1911-31), iii. 880-1.
50. *RHF* xiii. 394-5. See H. Platelle, 'La violence', 120.
51. Walter of Thérouanne, *Vita Karoli*, ed. R. Kopke, *MHG SS* xii. (Hanover, 1856), 544.
52. F. L. Ganshof, *Recherches sur les tribunaux de châtellenie en Flandre avant le milieu du XIIIe siècle* (Antwerp, 1932), 18-21.
53. Chédeville, *La Ville*, 164; F. L. Ganshof, 'Les transformations de l'organisation judiciaire dans la comté de Flandre jusqu'à l'avènement de Bourgogne', *RBPH* 18 (1939), 56.
54. L. M. de Gryse, 'Some Observations on the Origin of the Flemish Bailiff (Bailli): the Reign of Philip of Alsace', *Viator* 7 (1976), 243-94.
55. *PL* cciii, col. 816.
56. Warlop, 210.
57. Ibid. 209-46; Herman of Tournai, *RHF* xiii. 400.
58. Robert of Torigny in *Chronicles*, ed. Howlett, 207.
59. *De nugis curialium*, 278.
60. *RHF* xviii. 562.
61. *Regesta Regum*, iii, pp. xxxviii-xxxix.
62. Lemarignier, *Hommage en marche*, 94; Chartrou, 65. Cf. W. L. Warren, *Henry II* (London, 1973), 225-6.

63. *The Norman Empire*, 191--201.
64. *Chronicles*, ed. Howlett, 261.
65. C. H. Haskins, *Norman Institutions*, 196-212.
66. Ibid. 187.
67. For the beneficent effects of Henry II's legislation in Normandy, see J. Yver, 'Le "très ancien coutumier" de Normandie, miroir de la législation ducale?', *Tijdschrift voor Rechtsgeschiedenis*, 39 (1971), 367-74.
68. F. Lot and R. Fawtier, *Le Premier Budget de la monarchie française: le compte général de 1202-1203* (Paris, 1932), 138.
69. *Regesta Regum*, iii, p. xxxv.
70. *PL* ccvii, col. 198.
71. *Historia Calamitatum*, 98.
72. Quoted by Devailly, *Histoire religieuse*, 58.
73. J. L. Montigny, *Essai sur les institutions du duché de Bretagne à l'époque de Pierre Mauclerc et sur la politique de ce prince (1213-1237)* (Paris, 1961), 24-5.
74. B. Pocquet du Haut-Jussé, *Institutions*, i. 271.
75. A. Oheix, *Étude juridique sur les sénéchaux de Bretagne des origines au XIVe siècle* (Paris, 1913), 232-3.
76. *Chroniques des comtes d'Anjou*, 67.
77. J. Chartrou, *L'Anjou*, 347.
78. *Chroniques des comtes d'Anjou*, 194.
79. Ibid. 199-223.
80. Ibid. 74, 209.
81. Ibid. 224.
82. Chartrou, 151-5 and *pièce justificative* no. 42.
83. *Regesta Regum* iii, pp. xxxiii-xxxiv.
84. A. de Bouard, *Manuel de diplomatique*, i. 145-6.
85. *Chroniques des comtes d'Anjou*, pp. xxiv-xxx.
86. R. L. Poole, *Illustrations of the History of Medieval Thought* (London, 1884), 346.
87. W. L. Warren, *Henry II*, 45-8 takes a rather less cynical view of Henry's behaviour.
88. Ibid. 122.
89. C. Hohler, 'A Note on *Jacobus*', *Journal of the Warburg and Courtauld Institutes* 35 (1972), 31-80.
90. *Liber sancti Jacobi: Codex Calixtinus*, ed. W. M. Whitehill (Santiago de Compostela, 1944), 355.
91. Defourneaux, 154-65.
92. P. Tucoo-Chala, *Institutions*, i. 323-5.
93. Geoffrey of Vigeois, *RHF* xii. 435.
94. Beech, 59-64; see the different assessment in M. Garaud, *Les Châtelains* 37-8.
95. *Ecclesiastical History*, vi. 550.
96. S. Painter, 'The Lords of Lusignan in the Eleventh and Twelfth Centuries', *Speculum* 23 (1957), 27-47.
97. J. Gillingham, *Richard the Lionheart* (London, 1978), 46-7.

98. Devailly, *Le Berry*, 410-11.
99. *RHF* xii. 451-3.
100. J. C. Holt, 'The End of the Anglo-Norman Realm', *Proceedings of the British Academy* 61 (1975), 239-40.
101. J. Le Patourel, 'The Plantagenet Dominions', *History* 50 (1965), 289-308.
102. Ibid. 299; Holt, 20-2.
103. Hoffman, 'Französische Fürstenweihen', 107-9, 111; J. Leclerq, *Monks and Love in Twelfth-century France* (Oxford, 1979), 130.
104. Holt, 7-8; and see p. 252.
105. Walter Map, *De nugis curialium*, 488.
106. J. E. A. Joliffe, *Angevin Kingship* (2nd edn., London, 1963), particularly 131-6.
107. Arnulf of Lisieux, *Letters*, ed. F. Barlow, Camden 3rd ser., 61 (London, 1939), letters 127, 194.
108. Ibid., letters 191, 182.
109. Ibid., letters 121, 186.
110. Odo of Deuil, *De Profectione Ludovici VII*, 7, 69-71.
111. *PL* clxxxvi, cols. 1394-5.
112. *PL* clxxxii, col. 147; B. Scott James, *The Letters of St Bernard of Clairvaux, Newly Translated* (London, 1953), no. 41.
113. Claudon, 41.
114. Richard, *Les Ducs*, 154-6; *RHF* xvi. 119.
115. A. Luchaire, *Études*, no. 765, 338.
116. Bisson, 'The Organized Peace', 296 n. 31; 299.
117. Devailly, *Le Berry*, 381-413.
118. *Letters*, ed. G. Constable (2 vols., Cambridge, Mass. 1967), no. 171 and nn.
119. *Vie*, 240; cf. *Actes*, ed. Delisle, 387-8, nos. 240-1.
120. *Materials for the History of Archbishop Thomas Becket*, ed. J. C. Robertson and J. Brigstocke Sheppard (London, 1885), vii. 400.
121. 'It was standard Capetian practice to clothe even the most transparent of aggression under the cloak of legality supplied by the obligation to protect the church as a royal defender', G. Spiegel, ' "Defence" ', 117.

Chapter 13

1. *Actes*, ed. Léonard, 43, no. 61.
2. Baumel, 118.
3. *Regesta Regum*, iii. 372-3, no. 1007.
4. Luchaire, *Études* 223, no. 385.
5. Chédeville, *Chartres*, 287.
6. *RHF* xv. 503.
7. They pleaded that his death was an accident; John of Salisbury, *Letters*, ii. 56, no. 272.
8. J. Yver, 'Les caractères originaux du groupe de coutumes de

l'Ouest de la France', *Revue historique de droit français et étranger* 30 (1952), 32-4.

9. Warlop, i. 209-24.
10. *PL* clxxxvi, col. 1196.
11. *Letters of St Bernard*, tr. Scott James, nos. 39-41, *Actes*, ed. Delisle, ii. 19-21.
12. *RHF* xii. 435; Devailly, *Le Berry*, 410-11.
13. *RHF* xvi. 68.
14. *PL* clxxxvi, cols. 1355-6.
15. *RHF* xvi. 49.
16. Ed. Bédier, l. 3335. I am grateful to Dr E. Kennedy for help on this point.
17. *Chroniques des comtes d'Anjou*, 244-5; Poly-Bournazel, 297.
18. *RHF* xvi. 63-4.
19. *PL* clxxxvi, col. 1383.
20. K. Pellens, *Das Kirchendenken des Normannischen Anonymus* (Wiesbaden, 1973).
21. R. Foreville, 'The Synod', 35-7.
22. *RHF* xiii, 396, quoted in H. Platelle, 'La violence', 123.
23. *A History of Deeds Done beyond the Sea*, ed. and tr. E. A. Babcock and A. C. Krey (repr. New York, 1976) ii. 193 and n. 11, 268, 417-35.
24. V. Carrière, *Histoire et cartulaire des templiers de Provins* (Paris, 1919).
25. *Letters of St Bernard*, tr. Scott James, 199; letter in *RHF* xv. 557.
26. *Chartes et documents concernant l'abbaye de Cîteaux*, ed. J. Marilier (Rome, 1961), no. 67.
27. Ibid. no. 192.
28. *RHF* xv. 339-40, Louis VI to Calixtus II.
29. Baumel, 182.
30. Lambert of Ardres, *MGH SS* xxiv. 598.
31. S. Painter, *William Marshal, Knight-errant, Baron and Regent of England* (Baltimore, 1933).
32. *Cligés* ed. W. Foerster (Halle, 1901), ll. 30-5.

Conclusion

1. See pp. 301-2.
2. *RHF* xvi. 70.
3. Kienast, *Deutschland und Frankreich*, 499-502; C. T. Wood, '*Regnum Francie*: a Problem in Capetian Administrative Usage', *Traditio* 23 (1967), 117-18.
4. *RHF* xvi. 91.
5. C.-L. Hugo, *Annales Praemonstratenses*, i. 1 (Nancy, 1734), p. cxliv, William of Auvergne to St. Andrew's, Clermont. I am most grateful to Professor Giles Constable for this reference. See also the use of the motif by Bertrand de Born, in M. T. Clanchy, *England and its Rulers 1066-1272* (Glasgow, 1983) 114-15.

6. R. Dion, *Les Frontières de la France* (Paris, 1947), 27.
7. See p. 293.
8. *Liber Sancti Jacobi*, 339.
9. P. Wolff, *Western Languages. A.D. 100-1500*, tr. F. Partridge (London, 1971), 147, 151.
10. *Vie*, 10.
11. See M. T. Clanchy, 241-4.
12. *Vie*, 230.

Further Reading
(excluding source material)

Political surveys

It has been conventional for political surveys to be divided according to royal dynasty. But one old work, J. Flach, *Les Origines de l'ancienne France* (4 vols., Paris, 1886-1917) crosses the boundary; though its chief preoccupations seem very dated, it remains a mine of useful source material. For the Carolingians, two classics remain essential reading: L. Halphen, *Charlemagne and the Carolingian Empire*, tr. G. de Nie (Amsterdam, 1977) and F. Lot, *La Naissance de la France* (Paris, 1948, 2nd edn. 1970). To these should now be added E. James, *The Origins of France from Clovis to the Capetians, 500-1000* (London, 1982) and R. McKitterick, *The Frankish Kingdoms under the Carolingians 751-987* (London, 1983). For the Capetians, R. Fawtier, *The Capetian Kings of France*, tr. L. Butler and R. J. Adam (London, 1960) is the clearest survey, though there is much new material in E. M. Hallam, *Capetian France 987-1328* (London, 1980).

On royal government, F. Lot and R. Fawtier, *Institutions*, ii (Paris, 1958) is valuable, if somewhat dated. C. Brühl, *Fodrum, Gistum, Servitium Regis* (Cologne, 1968) has added a rich harvest of insights into royal itineraries and royal rights of hospitality. On the demesne there is no general study that fills the gap between J. W. Thompson, *The Dissolution of the Carolingian Fisc in the Ninth Century* (Berkeley, 1935) and W. M. Newman, *Le Domaine Royal sous les premiers Capétiens 987-1180* (Paris, 1937); on the ecclesiastical demesne, J.-F. Lemarignier in *Institutions*, iii (Paris, 1962) is important, but has not completely eclipsed E. Lesne, *Histoire de la propriété écclésiastique* ii (Paris, 1928). G. Tessier, *Diplomatique royale française* (Paris, 1962) and A. de Bouard, *Manuel de diplomatique française et pontificale* (3 vols., Paris, 1929) are valuable guides to the use of diplomatic evidence. R. H. Bautier, 'Le règne d'Eudes (888-98) à la lumière des diplômes expédiées par sa chancellerie', *Comptes rendus de l'Académie des inscriptions et belles-lettres* (1961) is a model for its use in a political study, and W. Kienast, 'Der Wirkungsbereich des französischen Königtums von Odo bis Ludwig VI. (888-1137) in Südfrankreich', *Historische Zeitschrift* 209 (1969), 529-65 puts the same techniques to different application. But the most sustained and original use of charter evidence is to be found in J.-F. Lemarignier, *Le Gouvernement royal aux premiers temps capétiens (987-1108)* (Paris, 1965), which is essential reading for all students of the period. A slightly narrower but nonetheless fruitful approach is taken by E. Bournazel in *Le Governement capétien au XIIe siècle 1108-1180* (Paris, 1975). Against these M. Paucaut, *Louis*

VII et son Royaume (Paris, 1964) is a conventional summary. J. F. Benton, 'The Revenue of Louis VII', *Speculum* 42 (1967), 84–91 is a notable contribution.

The weight of recent research has shifted from the 'constitutional' aspects of royal power to the charismatic, in the wake of two brilliant studies, E. Kantorowicz, *The King's Two Bodies: A Study in Medieval Political Theology* (Princeton, 1957) and M. Bloch, *The Royal Touch*, tr. J. E. Anderson (London, 1973). Bloch's work has been somewhat modified by F. Barlow, 'The King's Evil', *English Historical Review* 95 (1980), 3–27. B. Schneidmüller, *Karolingische Tradition und frühes französisches Königtum: Untersuchungen zur Herrschaftslegitimation der westfränkisch-französischen Monarchie im 10. Jahrhundert* (Wiesbaden, 1979) is a thought-provoking illustration of this new trend. One aspect of charismatic kingship is fully covered in E. Kantorowicz, *Laudes Regiae. A Study in Liturgical Acclamation and Medieval Ruler-worship* (Berkeley, 1946); also interesting are G. Spiegel, 'The Cult of St. Denis and Capetian Kingship,' *Journal of Medieval History* 1 (1975), 43–69; and 'The *Reditus Regni ad Stirpem Karoli Magni*: A New Look', *French Historical Studies* 7 (1971), 145–74. For an imaginative and reflective treatment of an important issue, see A. W. Lewis, *Royal Succession in Capetian France* (Cambridge, Mass., 1981).

The Principalities

Here the fundamental work is J. Dhondt, *Études sur la naissance des principautés territoriales en France (IXe-Xe siècles)* (Bruges, 1948). The only other work that rivals Dhondt in breadth of vision is W. Kienast, *Der Herzogstitel in Frankreich und Deutschland (9. bis 12. Jahrhundert* (Munich, 1968), which retains it value despite the justified criticism levelled at it for excessive emphasis on racial factors in the evolution of French principalities. For the English reader a convenient summary of the juridical view of principalities can be found in K. F. Werner, 'Kingdom and Principality in Twelfth-century France' in, *The Medieval Nobility*, 243–90. On princely titles see the well-nuanced approach of K. Brunner, 'Der fränkische Fürstentitel im neunten und zehnten Jahrhundert', *MIÖG* 24 (1973), 179–340. H. Wolfram, 'The Shaping of the Early Medieval Principality as a Type of Non-royal Rulership', *Viator* 2 (1971), 33–51; E. Hallam, 'The King and the Princes in Eleventh-century France', *Bulletin of the Institute of Historical Research* 53 (1980), 143–56, and G. Duby, 'L'image du prince en France au debut du XIe siècle', *Cahiers d'histoire* 17 (1972), 211–16, are all worthy of note. And on twelfth-century accession-ceremonies there is an important contribution by H. Hoffman, 'Französische Fürstenweihen des Hochmittelalters', *DA* 18 (1962), 92–119. The relation between princes and king in the tenth century is explored by J.-F. Lemarignier, 'Les fidèles du roi de France (936–987), *Recueil des travaux offert à M. Clovis Brunel* (Paris, 1955); and for the later period there is C. W. Hollister, 'Normandy, France and the Anglo-Norman *regnum*', *Speculum* 51 (1976), 202–42.

Finally, *Institutions*, i. (Paris, 1957) contains brief histories of all the principalities, of which those of Ganshof on Flanders, and B. Pocquet du Haut-Jussé on Brittany, remain valuable; but the volume as a whole is spoilt by weak editorial policy.

Political power: regional studies

Anjou

The major work for the earlier period is now O. Guillot, *Le Comte d'Anjou et son entourage au XIe siècle* (2 vols., Paris, 1972); see also the same author's study of Angevin administration in W. Paravicini and K. F. Werner (eds.), *Histoire comparée de l'administration (IVe-XVIIe siècles): actes du XIVe Colloque historique franco-allemand, 1977* (Munich, 1980). But L. Halphen, *Le Comte d'Anjou au XIe siècle* (Paris, 1906) remains a clear summary of events. The early twelfth century is less well served in J. Chartrou, *L'Anjou de 1109 à 1151— Foulque de Jérusalem et Geoffroi Plantagenêt* (Paris, 1928). W. L. Warren in his magnificent biography of Henry II (London, 1973) shed some light on Angevin affairs; and J. Boussard, *Le Gouvernement d'Henry II* also contributes. On government, there are the important remarks of R. H. C. Davis and H. Cronne in *Regesta Regum Anglo-Normannorum*, iii (Oxford, 1969), pp. xxxii–xxxix, which apply to Normandy and Anjou. On culture and religious life, see F. Lebrun (ed.), *Histoire des diocèses de France*, xiii, *Angers* (Paris, 1981).

Aquitaine

There is an overall view of the duchy, as well as some still unpublished material, in J. Martindale, 'The Origins of the Duchy of Aquitaine and the Government of the Counts of Poitou, 902–1137' (unpublished D.Phil. thesis, Oxford, 1965). M. Garaud, *Les Châtelains de Poitou et l'avènement du régime féodal, XIe et XIIe siècles* (Poitiers, 1967) is interesting, though too legalistic to convince, P. Villard, *Les Justices seigneuriales dans la Marche* (Paris, 1969), R. C. Watson, 'The counts of Angoulême from the Ninth Century to the Mid-thirteenth Century' (unpublished Ph.D. thesis, Univ. of East Anglia, 1979) and G. Beech, *A Rural Society in Medieval France: The Gâtine of Poitou in the Eleventh and Twelfth Centuries* (Baltimore, 1964) all contribute to the mosaic. S. Painter on the castellans of Poitou in *Speculum* 1956, and on the lords of Lusignan, ibid. 1957, deserves attention. There is a thought-provoking picture of Aquitaine in the twelfth century in J. Gillingham, *Richard the Lionheart* (London, 1978). R. Bonnaud-Delamare, 'Les institutions de paix en Aquitaine au XIe siècle', *Société Jean Bodin* 14 (1962) is the fullest study of the peace movement. B. S. Bachrach, 'Towards a Reappraisal of William the Great, Duke of Aquitaine', *Journal of Medieval History* 5 (1979) 11–21 has a point, but overstates it.

Auvergne

G. Fournier, *Le Peuplement rural en Basse-Auvergne durant le Haut Moyen Âge* (Paris, 1962) covers the tenth century. There is a surprising amount of political information in P. R. Gaussin, *L'Abbaye de la Chaise-Dieu, 1043-1518* (Paris, 1962), and his *Le Rayonnement de la Chaise-Dieu* (Brioude, 1981).

Berry

The fundamental work is G. Devailly, *Le Berry du Xe siècle au milieu du XIIIe. Étude politique, religieuse, sociale et économique* (Paris, 1973).

Blois

K. F. Werner, 'L'acquisition par la maison de Blois des comtés de Chartres et de Châteaudun', in *Mélanges de numismatique, d'archéologie et d'histoire offerts à Jean Lafaurie* (Paris, 1980) 265-74 is important. There is much information in M. Bur, *La Formation du comte de Champagne v. 950-v. 1150* (Nancy, 1977). The major work on the area is A. Chédeville, *Chartres et ses campagnes, XIe-XIIIe siècles* (Paris, 1973).

Brittany

I have found reliable secondary literature on Brittany hard to come by. Note B. Pocquet du Haut-Jussé, in *Institutions* i. cited above. For the tenth century the summary in R. McKitterick, op. cit., 241-8 is useful. H. Poisson, *Les Ducs de Bretagne de la maison de Cornouaille: Hoël, Alain Fergent, Conan III* (Lorient, 1968) fills a gap; and there is much about the earlier period in J. L. Montigny, *Essai sur les institutions du duché de Bretagne à l'époque de Pierre Mauclerc, et sur la politique de ce prince (1213-37)* (Paris, 1963). See also J. Boussard, *Le Gouvernement d'Henry II Plantagenêt* (Paris, 1955) 103-12. On the Church and culture, see the valuable remarks of G. Devailly in G. M. Oury (ed.), *Histoire religieuse de la Bretagne* (Paris, 1980); on administration A. Oheix, *Étude juridique sur les sénéchaux de Bretagne des origines au XIVe siècle* (Paris, 1913).

Burgundy

M. Chaume's pioneering work *Les Origines du duché de Bourgogne* (Dijon, 1925) makes sensitive use of the literary sources. J. Richard's excellent *Les Ducs de Bourgogne et la formation du duché du XIe au XIVe siècle* (Paris, 1954) is more juridical in tone. These have been supplemented by G. Duby's seminal *La Société aux XIe et XIIe siècles dans la région mâconnaise* (2nd edn., Paris, 1971) and more recently by Y. Sassier, *Recherches sur le pouvoir comtal en Auxerrois du Xe au début du XIIIe siècle* (Auxerre, 1980). On Langres there is F. Claudon, *Histoire de Langres et de ses institutions municipales jusqu'au commencement du XVIe siècle.* J. Richard, 'Aux origines du Charolais', *Annales de Bourgogne* 24 (1963), 81-114 should be noted. On the

Spanish crusades see M. Defourneaux, *Les Français en Espagne au XIe et XIIe siècles* (Paris, 1949) and M. Chaume, 'Les premières croisades bourguignonnes au-delà des Pyrénées', *Annales de Bourgogne* 18 (1946), 161-5. There is much of interest to be found in G. Duby, *The Chivalrous Society*, tr. C. Postan (London, 1977), especially the essay on Burgundian juridical institutions. And on Burgundian feudalism there is an important section in J.-F. Lemarignier, *Recherches sur l'hommage en marche et les frontières féodales* (Lille, 1945).

Catalonia

For the early period see R. d'Abadal de Vinyals, *Els primers comtes catalans* (Barcelona, 1958). There is a convenient treatment in English by R. Collins in *Early Medieval Spain 400-1000* (London, 1983). The major study for the period is that of P. Bonnassie, *La Catalogne du milieu du Xe à la fin du XIe siècle: croissance et mutations d'une société* (Toulouse, 1975, 1976).

Champagne

M. Bur, op. cit., is a major contribution to the study of the area, though not all the author's views are uncontroversial. T. Evergates, *Feudal Society in the Baillage of Troyes under the Counts of Champagne 1152-1284* (London, 1975) is a rich source for social history. There is also much to be gained from J. Leclercq, *Monks and Love in Twelfth-century France: Psycho-historical Essays* (Oxford, 1979). On the fairs, R. H. Bautier, 'Les foires de Champagne', *Recueil de la Société Jean Bodin*, 5, 1953 97-147. On court life, J. F. Benton, 'The Court of Champagne is a Literary Center', *Speculum* 36 (1961), 551-91; J. H. M. McCash, 'Marie de Champagne and Eleanor of Aquitaine: a Relationship Re-examined', *Speculum* 54 (1979), 698-711.

Flanders

Secondary literature is more accessible for tenth- and eleventh- than for twelfth-century Flemish history. The best introduction is F. L. Ganshof, *La Flandre sous les premiers comtes* (Brussels, 1949); see also J. Dhondt, *Les Origines de la Flandre et de l'Artois* (Arras, 1944). There is a brief summary of the whole period in H. Pirenne, *Histoire de Belgique* i (3rd ed., Brussels, 1909). J. C. A. Verlinden. *Robert 1er le Frison, comte de Flandre* (Antwerp, 1935) retains its value despite its nationalistic flavour. On the 1127 crisis there is an important article by J. Dhondt, 'Medieval "solidarities:" Flemish society in transition, 1127-1127-8', in F. Cheyette (ed.), *Lordship and Community in Medieval Europe* (New York, 1968), 268-290. The emergence of Flemish government has been covered in two works by R. Monier, *Les Institutions centrales du comté de Flandre du XIe siècle à 1384* (Paris, 1943) and *Les Institutions financières du comté de Flandre du XIe siècle à 1384* (Paris, 1948); and in A. Verhulst and M. Gysseling, *Le Compte général de 1187 connu sous le nom de 'Gros Bref' et les institutions financières du comté de Flandre au XIIe siècle* (Brussels, 1962). On the peace-movement see J.-F. Lemarignier, 'Paix et réforme monastique en Flandre et en Normandie autour de l'année 1023', *Études Yver*, 443–68; and R. Bonnaud-Delamare, 'La paix en Flandre pendant la première croisade', *Revue du Nord* 39 (1957), 147–52. On the theme of justice, there are the brilliant contributions of H. Platelle, 'La violence et ses remèdes en Flandre au XIe siècle', *Sacris Erudiri* 20 (1971), 101–73 and *La Justice seigneuriale de l'abbaye de Saint-Amand du XIe au XVIe siècle* (Louvain, 1965). See also F. L. Ganshof, *Recherches sur les tribunaux de châtellenie en Flandre avant le milieu du XIIIe siècle* (Antwerp, 1932) and 'Les transformations de l'organisation judicaire dans le comté de Flandre jusqu'à l'avènement de Bourgogne', *RBPH* 18 (1939), L. M. de Gryse, 'Some Observations on the Origin of the Flemish Bailiff (Bailli): the Reign of Philip of Alsace', *Viator* 7 (1976), 243–94, draws on much material published in Flemish. On towns the classic study of H. Pirenne, *Les Villes du Moyen Âge* (Brussels, 1927) should be supplemented by C. Verlinden, 'Marchands ou tisserands? A propos des origines urbaines', *Annales* 27 (1972), 396–406; A. Verhulst, 'An Aspect of the Question of Continuity between Antiquity and the Middle Ages: the Origin of the Flemish Cities between the North Sea and the Scheldt', *Journal of Medieval History* 3 (1977), 175–205; and D. Nicholas, 'Structures du peuplement, fonctions urbaines et formation du capital dans la Flandre médiévale', *Annales* 33 (1978), E. Warlop, *The Flemish Nobility before 1300*, tr. J. B. Ross and H. Vandermoere (4 vols., Kortrijk, 1975) is a rich source of information on many important topics, though its generalizations need critical handling.

Gascony

B. Cursente, *Les Castelnaux de la Gascogne médiévale* (Bordeaux, 1980) should be set against the somewhat different picture offered in J. Gardelles, *Les Châteaux du Moyen Âge dans la France du Sud-Ouest. La Gascogne anglaise de 1216 à 1327* (Paris, 1972). C. Higounet, *Histoire de Bordeaux*, ii: *Bordeaux pendant le Haut Moyen Âge* (Bordeaux, 1963) is useful for the city, but the generalizations it offers on Gascony should be treated with caution. Note the same author's intriguing study of commerce on the Garonne in *Annales du Midi* 88 (1976).

Gothia

E. Magnou-Nortier, *La Société laïque et l'Église dans la province ecclésiastique de Narbonne de la fin du VIIIe à la fin du XIe siècle* (Toulouse, 1974) is a mine of information on an area wider than that in her title; but not all will agree with her assessment of the area's political stability. J. Baumel, *Histoire d'une seigneurie du Midi de la France: naissance de Montpellier (985–1213)* (Montpellier, 1969) uses a very early lay archive to excellent effect. Then there is A. R. Lewis, *The Development of Southern French and Catalan Society, 118–1058* (Texas, 1965). In *Order and Innovation*, F. Cheyette uses aerial photography to shed light on the castles of the Trencavels. R. d'Abadal de Vinyals, 'A propos de la "domination" de Barcelone sur le Midi français', *Annales du Midi* 76 (1964), 315-45 offers far more than the title promises. E. Le Roy Ladurie, *Histoire du Languedoc*, in the Que-sais-je? series (Paris, 1967) squeezes much information, especially on the economy, into very little space. See also T. N. Bisson, 'The organized peace in southern France and Catalonia (*c.*1140-*c.*1233)', *American Historical Review* 82 (1977), 290-311.

Île de France

J. Boussard, 'Les destinées de la Neustrie du IXe au XIe siècle', *Cahiers de civ. méd.* 11 (1968), 15-28; and the same author's volume in the Nouvelle Histoire de Paris series, covering the period from the Viking attack of 885-6 to the reign of Philip Augustus (Paris, 1976) are helpful. All the works on royal government cited above are relevant here. G. Fourquin, *Les Campagnes de la région parisienne à la fin du moyen âge* (Paris, 1964) has much to offer the historian of the earlier period. On peace, see R. Bonnaud-Delamare, 'Les Institutions de paix dans la province ecclésiastique de Reims au XIe siècle', *Bulletin historique et philologique du Comité des travaux historiques et scientifiques, années 1955 et 1956* (Paris, 1957), 143-200 and A. Grabois, 'De la trêve de Dieu à la paix du Roi', *Mélanges Crozet* (Poitiers, 1966). Note also M. de la Motte-Collas, 'Les possessions territoriales de Saint-Germain-des-Prés du début du IXe au début du XIIe siècle', *Memorial de XIVe centenaire de l'abbaye de Saint-Germain-des-Prés* (Paris, 1949), 49-80.

Normandy

Because English scholars have stressed the importance of the Norman inheritance in England, the literature in English is extensive. The two most recent surveys, D. Bates, *Normandy before 1066* (London, 1982) and J. Le Patourel, *The Norman Empire* (Oxford, 1976) both combine reviews of recent scholarly literature with a number of original and stimulating interpretations. They often cast doubt on the conclusions of C. H. Haskins, *Norman Institutions* (Cambridge, Mass., 1918); yet the value of this work's analysis of documents still survives. D. C. Douglas's biography of William the Conqueror (London, 1964) has now been joined by F. Barlow's of William Rufus (London, 1983). In addition to these, on the Norman aristocracy see D. C. Douglas, 'The Earliest Norman Counts', *English Historical Review* 61 (1946), 526-45, and L. Musset, 'L'aristocratie normande au XIe siècle' in *La Noblesse au Moyen Âge*, ed. P. Contamine (Paris, 1976), 71-96. On the Carolingian foundation of Norman government, J. Yver, 'Les premières institutions du duché de Normandie', *Settimane Spoleto* 16 (1969), 299-366; M. de Bouard, 'De la Neustrie carolingienne à la Normandie féodale: continuité ou discontinuité?', *Bulletin of the Institute of Historical Research* 28 (1955), 1-14. On the Truce of God, M. de Bouard, 'Sur les origines de la trêve de Dieu en Normandie', *Annales de Normandie*

9 (1959), 179–89, and his amplification in *Annales de Normandie* 13 (1963); and on its effects, J. Yver, 'Contribution à l'étude du developpe-ment de la compétence ducale en Normandie', *Annales de Normandie* (1958), 139–83. There is an interesting comment on Norman castles by M. de Bouard in *Les Structures sociales de l'Aquitaine, du Langue-doc et de l'Espagne au premier âge féodale* (Centre national de la recherche scientifique, Paris, 1969). J. O. Prestwich, 'The Military Household of the Norman Kings', *English Historical Review* 96 (1981), 1–35 deserves to be appreciated for its contribution to Norman as well as to English history. C. W. Hollister, 'Normandy, France and the Anglo-Norman *regnum*', *Speculum* 51 (1976), 202–42 casts light on relations with the kings of France. On coins see F. Dumas-Dubourg, *Le Trésor de Fécamp et le monnayage en Francie occidentale pendant la seconde motié du Xe siècle* (Paris, 1971); and on the effects of a money economy on the duchy, L. Musset, 'A-t-il existé en Normandie au XIe siècle une aristocratie d'argent?', *Annales de Normandie* 9 (1959), 285–8.

Picardy

For political events, see the works of Ganshof, Dhondt, and Platelle cited under Flanders; see also M. Bur on Champagne. For Picardy as a whole, R. Fossier, *La Terre et les hommes en Picardie jusqu'à la fin du XIIIe siècle* (2 vols., Paris, 1968).

Toulouse

The early history of Toulouse has received surprisingly little attention. Those parts of A. R. Lewis, op. cit., that relate to Toulouse should be used with caution. J. H. and L. Hill, *Raymond IV de Saint-Gilles* (Toulouse, 1959) includes a careful study of the exiguous sources for Raymond's life before the First Crusade. J. Mundy, *Liberty and Political Power in Toulouse, 1050–1230* (New York, 1954) is essential reading, particularly on the organization of justice. P. Wolff, *Histoire du Languedoc* (Toulouse, 1965) is strong on cultural aspects.

The Angevin Empire

In addition to Warren's biography of Henry II and Gillingham's of Richard I, there is much of value in J. Boussard, *Le Gouvernement d'Henry II Plantagenêt*, despite its tendency to exaggerate the integrity of the empire. For a different, and convincing, reinterpre-tation, see J. Le Patourel, 'The Plantagenet dominions', *History* 50 (1965), 289–308. For an explanation of the empire's disintegration see J. C. Holt, 'The End of the Anglo-Norman realm', *Proceedings of the British Academy* 61 (1975), 223–65. Raleigh Lecture.

Other topics

Economy

The best material is to be found in the regional surveys, particularly perhaps those of Fossier on Picardy, Chédeville on Chartres, Devailly on Berry, Bates on Normandy, and Bonnassie on Catalonia; the articles of Nicholas and Verlinden on Flemish towns are important, as is Bautier on the Champagne fairs. There are, however, some recent and convenient general surveys: G. Duby, *The Early Growth of the European Economy: Warriors and Peasants from the Seventh to the Twelfth centuries*, tr. H. B. Clarke (London, 1974); id., *Rural Economy and Country Life in the Medieval West*, tr. C. Postan (London, 1968); G. Fourquin in G. Duby (ed.) *Histoire de la France rurale*, i (Paris, 1975); G. Duby (ed.), *Histoire de la France urbaine* ii; A. Chédeville, *La Ville médiévale* (Paris, 1980). On coinage, J. Lafaurie, 'Numismatique. Des Carolingiens aux Capétiens', *Cahiers de civ. méd.* 13 (1970), 117-37; F. Dumas-Dubourg, op. cit.; P. Wolff, 'The significance of the "Feudal Period" in the monetary history of Europe', *Order and Innovation*, 75-85; T. N. Bisson, *Conservation of Coinage: monetary exploitation and its restraint in France, Catalonia and Aragon (c. 1000-c. 1125)* (Oxford, 1979). On finance, B. Lyon and A. Verhulst, *Medieval Finance: a comparison of financial institutions in North-Western Europe* (Bruges, 1967), somewhat modified by T. N. Bisson's study *Fiscal Accounts of Catalonia under the Early Count-kings (1151-1213)* (Berkeley–Los Angeles, 1984).

Law

In this subject, the text books have not yet incorporated much recent work. Nevertheless M. S. Amos and F. P. Walton, *Introduction to French Law*, 3rd edn. by F. H. Lawson, A. E. Anton and L. Neville Brown, (Oxford, 1967), Y. Bongert, *Recherches sur les cours laïques du Xe au XIIIe siècle* (Paris, 1949), R. Aubenas, *Cours d'histoire du droit privé* (Aix-en-Provence, 1956-62) and F. Olivier-Martin, *Histoire du droit français* (Paris, 1948) have all proved useful. The articles of Ganshof and Platelle on Flanders and of Duby on Burgundy cited above should be read with L. Halphen's classic 'Les institutions judiciaires en France au XIe siècle', *Revue Historique* 77 (1901), 279-307, and with Ganshof, 'Les transformations de l'organisation judiciaire dans le comté de Flandre jusqu'à l'avènement de Bourgogne', *RBPH* 18 (1939).

Of the regional studies, Chédeville on Chartres and E. Magnou-Nortier on Narbonne are particularly helpful. Stimulating recent literature in English includes R. C. Van Caenegem, 'Law in the Medieval World', *Tijdschrift voor Rechtsgeschiedenis* 49 (1981), 13-46; F. L. Cheyette, '*Suum cuique tribuere*', *French Historical Studies* 6 (1970), 287-99; G. I. Langmuir, 'Community and legal change in Capetian France', ibid. 275-86; and S. D. White, '*Pactum . . . legem vincit et amor judicium*. The Settlement of Disputes by compromise in Eleventh-century Western France', *American Journal of Legal History* 22 (1978).

On the development of *consuetudines* see also J.-F. Lemarignier, 'La dislocation du "pagus" et le problème des *"consuetudines"* ', *Mélanges Halphen* (Paris, 1951), 401-10; J. Boussard, 'Le droit de *vicaria*, à la lumière de quelques documents angevins et tourangeaux', *Mélanges E. R. Labande* (Poitiers, 1974), 39-54. New vistas have been opened by J. Yver, *Égalité entre héritiers et exclusion des enfants dotés: essai de géographie coutumière* (Paris, 1966); his earlier essay into customary geography in *Revue historique de droit français et étranger* (1952), 18-79 is also valuable, as are the collected essays dedicated to him by his pupils in *Droit privé et institutions régionales* (1976). On the development of Roman law in the South, while Baumel's history of the Montpellier lordship is valuable for academic study, there seems still to be little other literature than Aubenas, op. cit., and G. Ourliac in *Études Yver*.

Social Structures

All the regional surveys, and all the legal literature, concern themselves in some measure with castles, castellans, and castellanies. G. Fournier, *Le Château dans la France médiévale: essai de sociologie monumentale* (Paris, 1978) has brought much recent scholarship together with documentary evidence to produce an excellent summary. It may profitably be supplemented by the thought-provoking piece of J. Gardelles, 'Le palais dans l'Europe occidentale chrétienne du Xᵉ au XIIᵉ siècle', *Cahiers de civ. méd.* 19 (1976), 115-34. See also *Les structures sociales de l'Aquitaine, du Languedoc, et de l'Espagne au premier âge féodale* (Centre national de la recherche scientifique, Paris, 1969). On the physical remains, C. Laurent, *L'Atlas des châteaux-forts en France* (Strasburg, 1977).

On feudalism, F. L. Ganshof, *Feudalism*, tr. P. Grierson (3rd English ed., London, 1964) remains a useful starting-point for the north. It should be read with the radically different E. Magnou-Nortier, *Foi et fidelité. Recherches sur l'évolution des liens personnels chez les Francs du VIIIᵉ au IXᵉ siècle* (Toulouse, 1976) and P. Bonnassie in *Les structures sociales*. Both on the legal and on the psychological aspects of feudalism, see now the extremely stimulating study of J.-P. Poly and E. Bournazel, *La Mutation féodale. Xᵉ-XIIᵉ siècles* (Paris, 1980).

On aristocratic life, M. Bloch, *Feudal Society*, ed. and tr. L. Manyon (London, 1961) and R. W. Southern, *The Making of the Middle Ages* (London, 1953) continue to fascinate. There is much of interest in G. Duby, *The Chivalrous Society*, tr. C. Postan (London, 1977). For the life of one particular tenth-century aristocrat, see the intriguing piece of J. Schneider, 'Aspects de la société dans l'Aquitaine carolingienne d'après la *Vita Geraldi Auriliacensis'. Comptes rendus de l'Académie des inscriptions et belles-lettres* (1973). J. Leclerq, *Monks and Love* (see above) and Benton on the court of Champagne have their ecclesiastical as well as their secular interest. On the education of the aristocracy, see now M. Rouche, *Histoire générale de l'enseignment et de l'éducation en France*, (Paris, 1981). On lay culture in general, R. R. Bezzola, *Les Origines et la formation de la littérature courtoise en Occident 500-1200*, iii (Paris, 1963) is a convenient summary. On courts, L. Paterson, 'Great court festivals in the south of France and Catalonia in the twelfth and thirteenth centuries', *Medium Aevum* 51 (1982), 213-24.

On nobility, the essays in *The Medieval Nobility* provide the broad European background. Account should be taken of the essays by Musset, Higounet, and Duby in P. Contamine (ed.), *La Noblesse au Moyen Âge* (Paris, 1976). L. Genicot, 'La noblesse au Moyen Âge dans l'ancienne "Francie"', *Annales* 17 (1962), 1-22 remains valuable. On particular aristocratic families, seminal work is to be found in F. Werner's contributions to W. Braunfels (ed.), *Karl der Grosse* (4 vols., Düsseldorf, 1965-8), tr. in T. Reuter (ed.), and in *Die Welt als Geschichte*, 18 (1958), 256-89; 19 (1959), 146-93; 20 (1960), 87-119. See also his 'Liens de parenté et noms de personne. Un problème historique et méthodologique', in G. Duby and J. Le Goff (eds), *Famille et parenté dans l'Occident médiéval* (Rome, 1977). See also J. Boussard, 'L'origine des familles seigneuriales dans la région de la Loire moyenne', *Cahiers de civ. méd.* 5 (1962), 303-22. For the problems inherent in constructing genealogies, see the thoughtful remarks of M. Heizelmann in *Le Moyen Âge* 83 (1977) 131-44 and C. B. Bouchard, *American Historical Review* 86 (1981), 501-32. On genealogies in general, see L. Genicot in the series *Typologie des sources du Moyen Age occidental*; also B. Guenée, 'Les Généalogies entre l'histoire et la politique: la fierté d'être capétien, en France, au Moyen Âge', *Annales* 33 (1978), 450-77. For an interesting contribution in English see J. Martindale, 'The French aristocracy in the Early Middle Ages: a Reappraisal', *Past and present* 75 (1977), 5-45. On marriage see G. Duby, *Medieval Marriage: two models from twelfth-century France*, tr. E. Forster (Baltimore, 1978).

On warfare there are general introductions in J. F. Verbruggen, *The Art of Warfare in Western Europe during the Middle Ages*, tr. S. Willard and S. C. M. Southern (Amsterdam, 1977) and P. Contamine, *War in the Middle Ages*, tr. M. Jones (Oxford, 1984). J. Boussard, 'Services féodaux, milices et mercenaires dans les armées, en France, aux Xe et XIe siècles', *Settimane Spoleto* 15 (1968), 131-68 is an original, if controversial, study. On crusading, the seminal work remains C. Erdmann, *The Origin of the Idea of the Crusade*, tr. M. W. Baldwin and W. Goffart (Princeton, 1977) despite the fact that it has been the subject of much revision. On the Peace and Truce of God, see, in addition to the works of Bonnaud-Delamare, de Bouard, Duby, Bisson, and Ganshof cited in the regional section, H. E. J. Cowdrey, 'The Peace and Truce of God in the eleventh century', *Past and Present* 46 (1970), 42-76. There is also much relevant discussion in G. Duby, *Le Dimanche de Bouvines, 27 juillet 1214* (Paris, 1973).

The Aristocracy and the Church

Despite the relatively abundant source material and the extended treatment the topic receives in regional studies—most constructively in Guillot and Devailly—there are few general works, with the exception of J.-F. Lemarignier in *Institutions* iii, and his 'Political and monastic structures in France at the end of the tenth and the beginning of the eleventh century' in F. Cheyette (ed.), *Lordship and Community in Medieval Europe* (New York, 1968), 100–27. M. Pacaut, *Louis VII et les élections épiscopales* (Paris, 1957) is useful. For the early period, see the contributions of Koch and Platelle to *Révue bénédictine* 70 (1960), a volume dedicated to Gerard of Brogne. For many perceptive comments on aristocratic attitudes, see now P. Morison, 'The Miraculous and French Society circa 950–1100' (unpublished D.Phil. thesis, Oxford, 1983).

France as a Concept

Kienast, *Der Herzogstitel* and Brunner, 'Der frankische Fürstentitel', cited above, have much to say on the subject, as has E. Kantorowicz, *The King's Two Bodies*, whose approach is totally different. W. Kienast, *Deutschland und Frankreich in der Kaiserzeit, 900–1270* (2 vols., Stuttgart, 1974) bubbles over with ideas and apposite quotations. Also useful on different aspects are C. T. Wood, '*Regnum Francie*: a problem in Capetian administrative usage', *Traditio* 23 (1976), 117–18; P. Wolff, *Western Languages. AD 100–1500*, tr. F. Partridge (London, 1971); and R. Dion, *Les Frontières de la France* (Paris, 1947).

Index